MULTICULTURAL AND DIVERSITY ISSUES IN STUDENT AFFAIRS PRACTICE

Publication Number 3

AMERICAN SERIES IN STUDENT AFFAIRS
PRACTICE AND PROFESSIONAL IDENTITY

Edited by

NAIJIAN ZHANG, Ph.D.

West Chester University
Department of Counselor Education
West Chester, Pennsylvania

MULTICULTURAL AND DIVERSITY ISSUES IN STUDENT AFFAIRS PRACTICE

A Professional Competency-Based Approach

Edited by

NAIJIAN ZHANG

and

MARY F. HOWARD-HAMILTON

(With 26 Other Contributors)

CHARLES C THOMAS · PUBLISHER, LTD.
Springfield · Illinois · U.S.A.

Published and Distributed Throughout the World by

CHARLES C THOMAS • PUBLISHER, LTD.
2600 South First Street
Springfield, Illinois 62704

ISBN 978-0-398-09292-4 (paper)
ISBN 978-0-398-09293-1 (ebook)

Library of Congress Catalog Card Number: 2019020910 (print)
2019980992 (ebook)

With THOMAS BOOKS *careful attention is given to all details of manufacturing
and design. It is the Publisher's desire to present books that are satisfactory as to their
physical qualities and artistic possibilities and appropriate for their particular use.*
THOMAS BOOKS *will be true to those laws of quality that assure a good name
and good will.*

Printed in the United States of America
MM-C-1

Library of Congress Cataloging-in-Publication Data

Names: Zhang, Naijian, editor. I Howard-Hamilton, Mary F., editor.
Title: Multicultural and diversity issues in student affairs practice:
  a professional competency-based approach/ Edited by Naijian Zhang and
  Mary F. Howard-Hamilton; (With 26 Other Contributors).
Description: Springfield, Illinois, U.S.A. : Charles C Thomas, Publisher,
  LTD., [2019] I Series: American series in student affairs practice and
  professional identity; Publication Number 3 I Includes bibliographical
  references and index.
Identifiers: LCCN 2019020910 (print) I LCCN 2019980992 (ebook) | ISBN
  9780398092924 (paperback) | ISBN 9780398092931 (ebook)
Subjects: LCSH: Student affairs services--Administration--United States.
  Student affairs administrators--Training of--United States.
  Multicultural education--United States.
Classification: LCC LB2342.9 .H69 2019 (print) I LCC LB2342.9 (ebook)
  DDC 371.4--dc23
LC record available at https://lccn.loc.gov/2019020910
LC ebook record available at https://lccn.loc.gov/2019980992

ABOUT THE EDITORS AND CONTRIBUTORS

Editors

Dr. Naijian Zhang is a full professor of Higher Education Counseling/ Student Affairs in the Department of Counselor Education at West Chester University of Pennsylvania. He received a B.A. in English from Xi'an Foreign Languages University, an M.A. in College Student Personnel and an M.A. in Counseling and Guidance from Bowling Green State University, and a Ph.D. in Counseling Psychology and Student Personnel Services from Ball State University. He has held positions of Acting Chair and Graduate Program Coordinator in the Department of Counselor Education at West Chester University of Pennsylvania. Previous administrative positions were held in the Division of Student Affairs at Ball State University (Indiana). He has had more than 20 years experiences of teaching in higher education counseling /student affairs and authored, coauthored, and edited over 40 articles, book chapters, and books. He is a recipient of the Travel Award from the American Psychological Association (APA), Outstanding Research Award, and Outstanding Service Award from the American College Personnel Association (ACPA). He is also a licensed psychologist in Pennsylvania, and frequently gives presentations and conducts professional training workshops internationally.

Dr. Mary F. Howard-Hamilton is the Dreiser Distinguished Research Professor and Chair of the Department of Educational Leadership in the Bayh College of Education at Indiana State University. She is a recipient of the Presidential Medal from the Association for the Study of Higher Education in 2018, the Contribution to Knowledge Award from the American College Personnel Association in 2017, as well as the Indiana State University Presidential Medal for Exemplary Teaching and Scholarship and the Theodore Dreiser Distinguished Research and Creativity Award in 2015. She also received the Bayh College of Education, Holmstedt Distinguished Professorship Award for 2012-2013. Dr. Howard-Hamilton received her Bachelor of Arts and Master of Arts degrees from The University of Iowa and a Doctorate of Education, Ed.D., from North Carolina State University.

She has published over 90 articles and book chapters. The most recent co-authored books are, "Diverse Millennial Students in College," "Multiculturalism on Campus: Theories, Models, and Practices for Understanding Diversity and Creating Inclusion," "Unleashing Suppressed Voices on College Campuses: Diversity Issues in Higher Education" and "Standing on the Outside Looking In: Underrepresented Students' Experiences in Advanced Degree Programs."

Contributors

Evette L. Allen, Ph.D., is the Director of Multicultural Affairs at Arkansas State University. During her time in student affairs she has worked in various areas on college campuses such as new student orientation, academic advising, and multicultural affairs. Allen has a research agenda that focuses on the experiences of Students of Color in Higher Education and social justice education. Her research can be found in Higher Education journals such as the International Journal of Qualitative Studies in Education, Equity and Excellence in Education, and NASPA Journal about Women in Higher Education.

Mindy Suzanne Andino, Ed.D., is an Assistant Professor in the Educational Leadership-College Student Affairs program at Bloomsburg University of PA. Prior to teaching, Dr. Andino was employed in various positions in Student Affairs departments. Her 15-year career spanning a large research one public land-grant institution, a mid-size state university, an Ivy League university, and a private liberal arts university provide her with a unique lens and collection of diverse experiences from which to draw. Her research interests include community organization in the higher education setting, drunkorexia and alcohol use, and multicultural competency in student affairs practitioners.

Samantha Babb, M.Ed., is a Residence Coordinator at Duke University. In her work with first-year students in residential communities, she focuses on issues of justice and equity particularly as they relate to race, gender, systems of power, and college access. She earned her bachelor's degree in Learning Behavior Specialist I & Elementary Education from Bradley University and her M.Ed. in Counselor Education (Student Affairs) from Clemson University.

Stephanie Bambrick, M.S. is a recent graduate of West Chester University's Higher Education Counseling/Student Affairs program. During her time at West Chester University she served as a graduate assistant for the Office of

Fraternity and Sorority Life and the Athletic Mentoring Program. In both of her roles she focused on student development through a leadership and academic lens. Through her work with college students, Stephanie has developed an interest in the infusion of multiculturalism on college campuses, as well as exploring technology and the role it plays in identity development.

V. Barbara Bush, Ph.D., is an Associate Professor and Master's Degree Coordinator in the Higher Education Program at the University of North Texas. She teaches classes in student development theory, higher education administration, and cultural pluralism. She worked for several years as a student affairs professional, including the role of senior student affairs officer, in public and private colleges and universities. Her student affairs publications have been in the areas of community college student affairs, and student services such as financial aid and learning support. Other publications have addressed collaboration efforts involving K-12, community colleges and universities.

Michelle L. Boettcher, Ph.D., is an Assistant Professor at Clemson University. She teaches research, law, and ethics in the student affairs M.Ed. program. Prior to her work as a faculty member, she worked in residence life and student conduct. Her research interests include senses of belonging in higher education with a particular focus on first generation college students.

Tony W. Cawthon, Ph.D. is an Alumni Distinguished Professor of Higher Education and Student Affairs at Clemson University. His career spans over 25 years, working as faculty and as an educator in University Housing. His research focuses on career and professional development, inclusion and diversity, marginalized student populations, particularly LGBT students, and student affairs partnering with academic affairs.

Mary Kay Schneider Carodine, Ph.D. is the Assistant Vice President for Student Affairs at the University of Florida. She works with student success initiatives including the career center, first-generation/low income student success, and the disability resource center. She leads the diversity, equity, and inclusion efforts for student affairs. She has prior experience with student involvement, multicultural affairs, leadership, community service, orientation, and dean of students office. Her student affairs-related publications are in the domains of supporting students of color and other marginalized identities as well as leadership and service learning.

Zak Foste, Ph.D., is an Assistant Professor of Higher Education Administration at the University of Kansas. Prior to joining the faculty at

KU Zak was a Postdoctoral Research Associate for the Interfaith Diversity Experiences and Attitudes Longitudinal Survey (IDEALS) at The Ohio State University. His research explores the ways in which whiteness functions to underwrite and support racism on college campuses, how college students with dominant social identities make meaning of their social locations, and interfaith engagement and cooperation in higher education. Zak received his Ph.D. in Higher Education and Student Affairs from The Ohio State University.

Amy French, Ph.D. is an Assistant Professor in the Department of Educational Leadership and Coordinator for the Student Affairs and Higher Education graduate program at Indiana State University. Amy has assessment experience consulting for student affairs divisions and other nonacademic units on college campuses in the Midwest. Equipped with a social justice lens, she prioritizes student learning, identity, positionality, and development. As a Freirean scholar, she encourages utilization of both qualitative and quantitative approaches in multicultural assessment to emphasize the emancipatory potential this work has to promote justice.

Nichole Margarita Garcia, Ph.D., is an Assistant Professor of Higher Education and College Student Affairs at Rutgers University, New Brunswick. As a Chicana/Puerto Rican her research focuses on the intersections race, feminism, and Latinx/a/o communities in higher education. Dr. Garcia has worked as a college preparation consultant for eight years and has dedicated research efforts to examine Latinx/a/o student college access and success. She is a regular contributor to *Diverse Issues in Higher Education Magazine and Motivos: Bilingual Magazine.* She received her PhD in Education from the University of California, Los Angeles.

Chayla Haynes is an assistant professor of higher education administration in the Educational Administration and Human Resource Development Department at Texas A&M University, College Station. She is a critical qualitative researcher with research interests and expertise in critical and inclusive pedagogies, Black women in higher education, and critical race and intersectionality scholarship. Haynes is co-editor of *Interrogating Whiteness and Relinquishing Power: White Faculty's Commitment to Racial Consciousness in STEM Classrooms* (Peter Lang Publishing) and *Race, Equity and the Learning Environment: The Global Relevance of Critical and Inclusive Pedagogies in Higher Education* (Stylus Publishing).

Ebelia Hernández, Ph.D. is an Associate Professor in the Graduate School of Education at Rutgers University. She teaches in the College Student

Affairs and Higher Education programs, specializing in courses focusing on diversity and student development. Her publications and presentations are centered on the Latinx college student experience: Activism, identity development, and membership in Latinx organizations.

Jacqueline S. Hodes, Ed.D., currently serves West Chester University as an associate professor and graduate coordinator in Higher Education Policy and Student Affairs in the Department of Educational Foundations and Policy Studies. Before this role, Dr. Hodes served in a variety of student affairs administrative roles at the same institution. Her scholarship focuses on understanding the professional identity development of student affairs educators, graduate student success and creating change in higher education and student affairs that leads to student success.

Jimmy L. Howard, Ph.D., is the Assistant Dean of Students for Prevention and Response in the Office of the Dean of Students at the University of Oregon and adjunct faculty at Oregon State University. Jimmy oversees prevention education, sexual violence response, and crisis intervention at the University of Oregon. His student affairs experiences include residence life, multicultural affairs, evaluation and assessment. His publications are focused on social justice, critical assessment practices, and issues facing Black women in higher education.

Dena R. Kniess, Ph.D., is an Assistant Professor and Program Coordinator for the M.Ed. in College Student Affairs at the University of West Georgia. She received her doctorate in Educational Leadership—Higher Education from Clemson University in 2013. Prior to moving into a faculty position, Dena spent 11 years as a student affairs practitioner in the areas of residence life and student transition programs. Her research foci are college access and student success, multiculturalism and social justice in student affairs, assessment, and faculty development.

Shani Barrax Moore, MBA, CCDP/AP, is a strategic diversity and inclusion practitioner with 20 years of experience in training and development, strategic planning and change leadership, and inclusive programming and recruitment initiatives. She has served in administrative, faculty, and academic advisor roles in both K-12 and higher education. She serves currently as Director of Diversity and Inclusion at the University of North Texas (UNT) where she delivers learning and development programs, works closely with the Multicultural Center and Pride Alliance, and leads community engagement and programming through events such as UNT's Equity and Diversity Conference.

David Hòa Khoa Nguyễn, J.D., Ph.D., is an assistant professor of urban educational leadership & policy studies at the Indiana University School of Education at IUPUI and adjunct professor of law at the IU Robert H. McKinney School of Law both on the Indiana University – Purdue University Indianapolis campus. Dr. Nguyễn teaches and researches the intersectional implications of law and policy in education among marginalized populations. Prior to academia, he was a practicing attorney representing immigrant communities in a variety of areas, including family, immigration, administrative, and business law. He is licensed to practice in Indiana.

Rebeca Mireles-Rios, Ph.D., is an Assistant Professor in the Department of Education. She received her K-8 Multiple Subject Teaching Credential and her MA from UC Berkeley. Prior to receiving her PhD, she was a middle school teacher in Berkeley Unified School District and worked as a community college outreach coordinator. She examines Latinx student trajectories into higher education. Her focus is on the inequalities in educational outcomes to understand the processes that can potentially increase Latinx high school student college enrollment and retention rates.

Martin Patwell, Ed.D., is Director of Office of Services for Students with Disabilities at West Chester University. Dr. Patwell has been in the field of disabilities since 1974, and has been directing services at the college level for 30 years. He is currently the PI of a TRIO grant for students with disabilities which is in its 24th year. In addition, he has received over 30 grants for research and applied programs in the field and lectured world-wide.

Cristina Perez, M.Ed., is the Curriculum Design Coordinator at Alpha Delta Pi Sorority. In her role, she develops and designs curriculum for member experience and educational programming. She graduated from California State University, Fullerton with a B.A. in Political Science and from earned an M.Ed. in Counselor Education – Student Affairs from Clemson University. Professionally, she has worked in various capacities leading and planning training, development, and educational experiences for college students and staff.

Paul Porter, Ph.D., is Director of Diversity and Inclusion at the University of Saint Francis, where he oversees coordination, and assessment of programs and activities related to diversity, equity, access and inclusion across the University of Saint Francis campus. As an experienced educator, diversity officer and speaker, Dr. Porter has engaged his work on the intersection of higher education and cultural studies with an emphasis on intercultural communication competence, unconscious bias, racial identity and campus experiences for men of color and other historically underrepresented student populations.

Matthew R. Shupp, Ed.D, NCC, BC-TMH, is an associate professor in the Department of Counseling and College Student Personnel at Shippensburg University. He currently coordinates the College Counseling and College Student Personnel specializations within the department. Before this role, Dr. Shupp was a student affairs administrator for 12 years in a variety of institutional settings including the community college, for-profit, private, and public higher education sectors. His research areas of interest focus on multicultural competence and inclusive supervision, student leadership, and holistic college experiences for students.

Saundra M. Tomlinson-Clarke, Ph.D., is Professor and Chair of the Department of Educational Psychology in the Graduate School of Education at Rutgers University. Dr. Tomlinson-Clarke teaches in the School Counseling and Counseling Psychology Programs. She is a licensed psychologist and began her career in higher education working in university counseling centers. Her publications focus on multicultural training models, transformative learning and the influence of socio-cultural and contextual factors on identity.

Rachel Wagner, Ed.D., is an Assistant Professor in Educational and Organizational Leadership Development at Clemson University. Prior to her appointment at Clemson, she spent sixteen years working in various roles in Residence Life. Her research centers human flourishing through two lines of inquiry: gender expansive practices in higher education and social justice approaches to student affairs.

LaWanda W. M. Ward, J.D., Ph.D., is an Assistant Professor of Higher Education and Research Associate in the Center for the Study of Higher Education at The Pennsylvania State University. She is committed to social justice, equity, and inclusion in higher education as evidenced by her research agenda centering on critically analyzing legal issues including race-conscious admissions, free speech, and academic freedom. For over 20 years prior to joining the professoriate, Dr. Ward served as a student affairs educator in various roles including residence hall director and director of Indiana University Robert H. McKinney School of Law's Pro Pono & Public Interest programs.

FOREWORD

When unity is evolved out of diversity, then there is a real and abiding national progress.

Manhur-ul-Haque

Professionals of almost all fields in the United States have become cognizant of the issue of multiculturalism, diversity, social justice, and inclusion and made effort to level the playing field and change the environment to be healthy for minoritized individuals with the aim of becoming competent in practice. Student affairs educators in higher education are no exceptional. Developing awareness, knowledge, and skills in multiculturalism, diversity, social justice, and inclusion has become one of the essential training aspects for every student affairs educator. To achieve this training goal the Task Force of the College Student Educators International (ACPA) and the National Association of Student Personnel Administrators (NASPA) in 2015 established ten professional competency areas for student affairs educators, one of which is about multiculturalism and diversity or social justice and inclusion.

The book *Multicultural and Diversity Issues in Student Affairs Practice: A Professional Competency-Based Approach* is written to assist those who plan to work as student affairs educators soon and those who are new student affairs educators to become competent in social justice and inclusion. This book provides trainees and new student affairs educators not only content knowledge and skills but also strategies and ways to develop competency in social justice and inclusion. As the above being said, the book facilitates the reader on how to transition from students to professionals. The purpose of this book is to enlighten the reader as to how to apply the knowledge and skills on social justice and inclusion in the book to their practical world. In another word, the readers will be able to use the knowledge and skills from years of research and publications plus their life experiences and personal traits to change the world. This book is a matter of building bridges between student affairs educators and the diverse populations they serve.

The book *Multicultural and Diversity Issues in Student Affairs Practice: A Professional Competency-Based Approach* is another essential volume in the American Series in Student Affairs and Professional Identity. As its title indicates, the most valuable aspect of this book is that it targets one of the professional competency areas, social justice and inclusion, set by ACPA and NASPA. The entire book has reflected this competency area comprehensively and meticulously. To be consistent with the revised version of professional competency areas by ACPA/NASPA this book has specifically echoed the "shift from awareness of diversity to a more active orientation." Besides, the book has been aligned with two other themes of the series, building professional identity for student affairs educators and application of knowledge and skills identified by research and literature in practice, the latter is simply action oriented.

Like other volumes in the series, *Multicultural and Diversity Issues in Student Affairs Practice: A Professional Competency-Based Approach* was written by a group of knowledgeable and experienced scholars and practitioners in the field of student affairs in higher education. The book editors, Doctor Mary Howard-Hamilton and I, have published extensively and had years of hands-on experience in student affairs practice. Doctor Mary Howard-Hamilton is, in particular, a leader and one of the major contributors who have made significant impact on the development of student affairs practice in higher education. Moreover, twenty-six additional individuals consist of both scholars/researchers and practitioners who have authored the book chapters. Their years of knowledge, skills, and experiences in the professional competency areas in student affairs practice of higher education have enriched the content of this book. Through their writing these experts have offered you the reader their first-hand experiences and wisdom for being a competent student affairs educator in higher education—the global enterprise.

Specifically, the book *Multicultural and Diversity Issues in Student Affairs Practice: A Professional Competency-Based Approach* will provide you the reader with an understanding of multicultural competency and professional identity in student affairs practice, an opportunity to develop a professional identity that centers on social justice, a comprehension of historical development of multiculturalism and diversity in student affairs practice, knowledge of multicultural theory and its application, an understanding of ethical and legal issues from a multiculturalism, diversity, and social justice perspective, knowledge of culturally appropriate intervention strategies in practice, and understanding of evidence-based practice in student affairs. Moreover, this book will offer the reader knowledge and skills in utilizing theory, research, and assessment to enhance practice, forming professional identity through social justice and inclusion, and on how to create a social justice and inclusive environment for minoritized students and students with special needs.

Finally, the book teaches you the reader on how to work with minoritized students and students with special needs.

The American Series in Student Affairs and Professional Identity is a unique book series that creates an integration of all ten professional competency areas for student affairs educators outlined by ACPA and NASPA in 2015. The series reflects three major themes: professional competencies development, professional identity construction, and case illustrations for theory translation into application. All volumes in the series are targeting graduate students in student affairs programs and new student affairs educators. The series blends contemporary theory with current research and empirical support and uses case illustrations to facilitate the readers' ability to translate what they have learned into application and decision making. Each volume focuses on one area of professional competency and at the same time addresses some major aspects of the Interaction of Competencies. Given what has been said, the series helps graduate students in student affairs programs and new student affairs educators develop their professional competencies (ACPA/NASPA) by: (1) constructing their personal and ethical foundations; (2) understanding the values, philosophy, and history of student affairs; (3) strengthening their ability in assessment, evaluation, and research; (4) gaining knowledge, skills, and dispositions relating to law, policy, and governance; (5) familiarizing with and learning how to effectively utilize organizational and human resources; (6) learning leadership knowledge and developing leadership skills; (7) understanding oppression, privilege, power, and then learning how to understand social justice and apply it in practice; (8) acquiring student development theories and learning how to use them to inform their practice; (9) familiarizing themselves with technologies and implementing digital means and resources into practice; and (10) gaining advising and supporting knowledge, skills and dispositions. As a result, the series helps graduate students in student affairs programs and new student affairs educators foster their professional identity and ultimately achieve their goal of the whole-person education.

Naijian Zhang, Ph.D.
West Chester University of Pennsylvania

PREFACE

This book *Multiculturalism and Diversity: An Evidence-Based Approach* is a part of the American Series in Student Affairs Practice and Professional Identity which exposes graduate students and new professionals in student affairs of higher education to the ten professional competency areas as articulated in the ACPA and NASPA *Professional Competency Areas for Student Affairs Educators* (American College Personnel Association & National Association of Student Personnel Administrators, 2015). Social Justice and Inclusion is one of the competency areas and action oriented, which was renamed from Multiculturalism and Diversity in the previous version of the Professional Competency Areas to emphasize action. To align with the theme of the series this book focuses on professional competency, professional identity, and application.

This book facilitates graduate students and new professionals in student affairs of higher education to develop the essential knowledge, skills, and dispositions outlined for all student affairs educators by ACPA/NASPA. The materials in the book are structured with an emphasis of the development of professional identity based on the values, philosophy, and history of the profession through practice. This text has been written with empirical data, case studies, theoretical concepts, practical application and in some instances the authors' personal experiences to explain how injustice is endemic in this country. Furthermore, the book addresses that higher education must be the catalyst to move this society closer to understanding the innate differences of all humankind. In addition, it provides the readers with the opportunity to develop their awareness, knowledge, skills, and take action to foster a multicultural learning environment for college students. In each chapter, the reader will sense the compassion of every writer's narrative to move college campuses toward community and not chaos.

Book Overview

Chapter 1, "Understanding Multicultural Competency and Professional Identity in Student Affairs Practice" opens the book with the framework for multicultural competence and the importance of understanding how intersectionality presents the opportunity to value all aspects of a person's identity and not from a mono-cultural lens. Additional theoretical frameworks are shared so that the readers will have a multicultural or diversity roadmap to easily navigate the concepts written in this book.

Chapter 2, "Competent Practitioners: Developing A Professional Identity That Centers Social Justice," answers the questions, what is social justice and who are social justice advocates? The authors explain how the term has a negative connotation today because of the contentious social and political environment. However, social justice competencies can be developed and used as a powerful tool for dismantling systemic oppression.

Chapter 3, "Historical Development of Multiculturalism and Diversity in Student Affairs Practice," presents the reader an overall picture of the multiculturalism, diversity, social justice, and inclusion in American colleges and universities from a historical perspective. It reveals how acquiring an education in the United States has historically been a privilege granted to White men who were from affluent families, the difficulty and struggle for minoritized students to be recognized, and the birth of student affairs through diversity.

Chapter 4, "Multicultural and Diversity Competence: Theory and Its Application," highlights germinal diversity and multicultural theories in student affairs. The authors have carefully selected concepts that can be applied from a practitioner's lens. Additionally, a case that provides the application for clarity and practical purposes is detailed.

Chapter 5, "Working with Racially and Ethnically Diverse Students," connects with the previous chapter from a practical perspective. Given the theory, cultural understanding and capacity, and practice linkages this chapter challenges student affairs educators on how to work with diverse students. The authors have compiled a detailed explanation of the opportunities and challenges facing minoritized and marginalized students on college campuses. Moreover, a conversation about the complexities of Whiteness is presented that clearly connects to the need for an open dialogue across identities so that everyone can experience enhanced educational opportunities. Lastly, a discussion of proactive steps that should be implemented on college campuses are shared.

Chapter 6, "Support Students with Various Needs," provides a view of student affairs from the perspective of the marginalized student combined with the complexities of 21st century challenges. Specifically, how technology has emboldened individuals to engage in unfiltered hate speech comfortably through social media. A review of the policies and laws that have been created or enacted to protect the rights of students with various needs is presented with theory to practice implications.

Chapter 7, "Ethical and Legal Issues from A Multiculturalism, Diversity, and Social Justice Perspective," presents legal and ethical considerations from a social justice perspective. The authors cogently narrate the key components of Critical Race Theory as well as legal and ethical issues in higher education. They also note the characteristics of a social justice oriented and multiculturally competent college administrator. Policies, practices, and people intersect in ways that can be toxic or empowering.

Chapter 8, "Toward A Model of Inclusivity for Racially and Culturally Diverse Students on College Campuses: Implications for Research and Practice," shares numerous ways in which the environment has a direct impact on the social, political, cultural, and overall human aggregate on college campuses. The authors elaborate how environmental diversity and inclusion models can be translated to practice on college campuses.

Chapter 9, "Using Culturally Appropriate Intervention Strategies in Practice," raises the question on poorly attended events, programs, and activities on campus and offers the likely reason as inappropriate intervention strategies that were designed by the practitioners who used a monocultural lens when creating the program. The authors then provide suggestions to assist in the development of culturally sensitive programming and intervention strategies. They also believe it is imperative that administrators evaluate and assess the programs and activities facilitated on campus.

Chapter 10, "Multiculturalism, Diversity, Social Justice, and Inclusion: Evidence-Based Practice in Student Affairs," notes that due to the decrease in institutional and operational funding, departments must justify or provide evidence on the need for programs they hope to implement or continue. Evidence based practices in student affairs apply evaluative principles so that inclusivity and excellence are the primary goals.

Chapter 11, "Utilization of Theory, Research, and Assessment to Enhance Multiculturalism, Diversity, Social Justice, and Inclusion," shares the importance of using assessment tools with historical evidence as well as current successes in the field. The author argues on how assessment can illuminate the need for diversity initiatives, programming, and funding to ensure the success of minoritized students on campus.

Chapter 12, "Implementing Social Justice: Forming a Professional Identity," provides a philosophical perspective of developing a professional identity that is grounded in social justice. Specific strategies on how to develop a social justice orientation for student affairs educators are offered.

Chapter 13, "The Profession's Norm: Becoming a Multicultural Competent Student Affairs Educator," presents the author's notations on how to become a multiculturally and interculturally competent student affairs educator. The author suggests that to build professional competency in social justice and inclusion student affairs educators must first build their intercultural communication competence in student affairs practice. Specific strategies on how to build intercultural communication competence are offered.

Overall, this book not only challenges but also provides the reader with a unique approach to learning and understanding social justice and inclusion. It is designed in a format that describes/defines this competency at the foundational, intermediate, and advanced outcomes levels, suggests ways to apply this competency in practice through case studies from student affairs, and provides tools for assessment of competency understanding.

N.Z.
M.F.H-H.

CONTENTS

MULTICULTURAL AND DIVERSITY ISSUES IN STUDENT AFFAIRS PRACTICE

Chapter 1

UNDERSTANDING MULTICULTURAL COMPETENCY AND PROFESSIONAL IDENTITY IN STUDENT AFFAIRS PRACTICE

Dena Kniess & Zak Foste

College and university campuses have witnessed increases in the number of students from different race/ethnicities, gender identities, sexual orientations, abilities, and socioeconomic classes in higher education. Since 1976, the percentage of undergraduate students of color increased by 26.2% and the percentage of women increased by 8%, (Integrated Postsecondary Education System, 2017). Though there is some debate on the total number, approximately two to four percent of the U.S. adult population identified as lesbian, gay, bisexual or transgender (LGBT) (American College Health Association, 2012). Additionally, 11% of college students have a disability (Gose, 2016) and 52% of students enrolled in two-year and four-year colleges are from low income families (Kena et al., 2016). While the compositional diversity on college campuses has increased, students of color, women, LGBTQ+ students, and students with disabilities experience unwelcome, and at times, hostile campus climates. One only needs to view news headlines from 2017:

- "A White supremacist rally in Charlottesville, VA to protest the removal of a Confederate monument erupts in violence killing a 32-year-old woman and injuring 34 others" (Stolberg & Rosenthal, 2017).
- "Baylor University served with a Title IX lawsuit for the sexual assault of college women by members of the university's football team" (Suy, 2017).
- "In February 2017, the Trump administration rolled back guidance that mandated equal accommodations for transgender students under Title IX" (Gardner, 2017).

Students attending college expect administrators and student affairs educators to engage in discussions on current events and move toward creating inclusive campus environments. It is crucial that all employees within higher education and specifically student affairs educators appreciate difference and engage in the work of creating campus climates that are not only multiculturally responsive, but also critically conscious (Linder & Cooper, 2016). Over the past 30 years, the need for multicultural competence in student affairs practice has been well-documented (McEwen & Roper, 1994; Mueller & Broido, 2012; Pope, Mueller, & Reynolds, 2009; Pope & Reynolds, 1997). Most student affairs educators have had a diversity course in their graduate program or engaged in activities through the course of their graduate assistantships to develop multicultural competence (Flowers, 2003; Gayles & Kelly, 2007); however, developing multicultural competence takes continual effort and cannot be confined to a single course or experience (Linder & Cooper, 2016). Expanding upon the call for professional competence in student affairs practice, the American College Personnel Association (ACPA) with the National Association for Student Personnel Administrators (NASPA) jointly developed a set of 10 competencies for student affairs educators including a competency for social justice and inclusion. In order to understand how multicultural competence and professional identity converge, student affairs educators must not only understand multicultural competence, social justice and inclusion but also critically unpack their own social identities. Student affairs educators must be cognizant of how their social identities influence their professional role on campus and how it affects their decisions related to campus policies, practices, and programs.

This chapter provides an overview of multicultural competence, social justice, and inclusion, and a brief history of each in student affairs practice. Abes, Jones, and McEwen's (2007) Reconceptualized Model of Multiple Dimensions of Identity (RMMDI), Watt's (2015b) Privileged Identity Exploration (PIE) Model, and additional critical theories will be used as models for student affairs practitioners to engage in their own self work, which is a critical step toward the development of multicultural competence and professional identity. To help student affairs educators engage in their own self work we will provide a case study and resources for further exploration.

MULTICULTURAL COMPETENCE IN STUDENT AFFAIRS PRACTICE

Diversity, inclusion, and multicultural competence have always been central to student affairs practice; however, the terminology and implementation have changed based on time and context (Winston, Creamer, Miller,

& Associates, 2001). Young (1997) described seven values that are essential to the field: service, truth, freedom, individuation, equality, justice, and community. Though our field holds values synonymous with diversity and inclusion, the concept of multicultural competence first appeared in the literature in the field of counseling psychology. Scholars noted an absence in counseling curricula on effective strategies for working with diverse populations and advocated for including courses to enhance counselors' multicultural competence (Ponterotto & Cases, 1987). Later, McEwen and Roper (1994) called upon professionals in student affairs "to respond more effectively and knowledgeably to diverse student groups on college campuses" (p. 49). At the time they were writing, students and professionals in graduate student affairs programs may not have had required coursework focused on engaging with multicultural student populations.

Using the counseling psychology literature as a framework, Pope and Reynolds (1997) proposed a tripartite model of multicultural competence focusing on the awareness, knowledge, and skills to work with multicultural populations. For student affairs practitioners, *multicultural awareness* means believing that differences in individuals are inherently valuable, willingness to examine one's own preconceived bias about others who are culturally different, and committing to social change (Pope & Reynolds, 1997). *Multicultural knowledge* involves knowing about how gender, race, sexual orientation, ability, and other identities affect individuals and how power, privilege, and oppression operate in institutions (Pope & Reynolds, 1997). As student affairs educators develop multicultural awareness and knowledge, they translate their awareness and knowledge into *multicultural skills* by developing individual and group interventions and programs (Pope & Reynolds, 1997).

Pope, Reynolds, and Mueller's (2004) framework for multicultural competence offers a starting point for individuals to assess their multicultural awareness, knowledge, and skills, however there are critiques of this framework. Landreman, Rasmussen, King, and Jiang (2007) argued "efforts to graduate students with 'multicultural competence' have been hampered by inadequate, overly simplistic ideas regarding what constitutes multicultural learning itself" (p. 276). Critiques of multicultural competence have noted inconsistencies in definitions of multicultural competence, assessments limited to particular cultures, and inattention to within group cultural differences (Linder & Cooper, 2016). Additionally, the multicultural competence framework focuses on individual level skills (Iverson, 2012) without significant attention given to the social, historical, and cultural elements operating in various contexts. Scholars instead have advocated for critical consciousness versus developing multicultural competence (Iverson, 2012; Landreman et al., 2007; Linder & Cooper, 2016).

Critical consciousness goes beyond surface-level approaches to multicultural education by focusing on situating oneself within historical and sociocultural-political contexts (Landreman et al., 2007). Critical consciousness is grounded in Paulo Freire's (1970) *conscientizacao* (critical consciousness in Spanish). Individuals develop critical consciousness by identifying the context of the situation, reflecting on their own identities in relation to the context, and engaging in dialogue in small groups and other efforts to promote social justice. Freire (1970) critiqued the banking concept of education, positioning the teacher at the center of learning, content, and knowledge transmission. By passively absorbing knowledge, one is not encouraged to critically think about the context and societal conditions informing one's reality. By developing a critically conscious mentality, individuals can unpack the social, political, and historical elements of their current reality, reflect on these elements, and engage in dialogue and action toward social change. A central characteristic needed in dialogue is authenticity. Watt (2015a) writes about authenticity as the first component of the Authentic, Action-Oriented, Framing for Environmental Shifts (AAFES) methods as "practitioners commit to listen deeply/actively to multiple voices and competing views, to think critically about their own identities, beliefs, values and positionality, to participate authentically and intentionally in difficult dialogues, and to be open to personal development" (p. 32). Individuals within groups balance moving from dialogue to action as they examine "inequity at multiple levels and intentionally reconstruct an environment for inclusion" (Watt, 2015a, p. 33). In fact, the shift from dialogue toward action-oriented elements is reflected in the ACPA and NASPA (2015) professional competencies.

Two of the leading professional associations for student affairs, ACPA and NASPA, collaborated on a set of professional competencies for student affairs educators. In 2010, both associations published a set of 10 professional competencies. Equity, Diversity, and Inclusion was listed as one competency, focusing mainly on individual awareness of social identities, values, and advocacy for minoritized groups (ACPA & NASPA, 2010). The Equity, Diversity, and Inclusion competency was revised and renamed in 2015 to Social Justice and Inclusion. The revision reflected an action-oriented approach to not only recognizing oppression, but actively engaging in dismantling systems of oppression in campus communities (ACPA & NASPA, 2015). The significance of this change is twofold. First, in the revised 2015 competencies, the authors "aimed to frame inclusiveness in a manner that does not norm dominant cultures but that recognizes all groups and populations are diverse as related to all other groups and populations" (ACPA & NASPA, 2015, 4-5). Second, the authors of the ACPA and NASPA competencies overall intent "was to integrate the concepts of equity, diversity, and inclusion within the active framework of social justice" (ACPA & NASPA,

2015, p. 5). Chapter 2 goes into more depth on the Social Justice and Inclusion competency as well as core concepts of power, privilege, and oppression operating on individual and societal levels. The Social Justice and Inclusion competency is a starting point for student affairs educators to assess their own level of competence in multiculturalism. In the following section, we will discuss the need and significance of multicultural competence, social justice and inclusion on American college campuses.

CURRENT SOCIO-POLITICAL CLIMATE ON COLLEGE CAMPUSES

In order to understand the need and significance of social justice and inclusion, one must understand the history of segregation and exclusion in American higher education. Colleges and universities in the Colonial Era were founded to educate the elite, mainly White men, for clergy, medicine, and law (Thelin, 2011). Women, African Americans, and individuals from lower socioeconomic classes were excluded from higher education. When Women and African American students were included in colleges and universities in the 1800s, it was through the creation of separate institutions, such as women's colleges (e.g. Radcliffe College) and Historically Black Colleges and Universities (HBCUs). Gradually, colleges and universities started embracing co-education and admitted women mainly as a way to stay financially afloat as men entered World War I and II. Racial segregation in colleges and universities was prominent at this time in southern institutions.

After World War II, the Serviceman's Readjustment Act of 1944, otherwise known as the GI Bill, expanded higher education to the masses. Veterans returning from the war were able to enroll at colleges and universities and did so in record numbers. While the GI Bill provided access to education, women's enrollment in higher education declined from 40% in 1930–1940 to 32% in 1950. In addition to lower enrollment, women were and still are underrepresented specifically in business and engineering fields (Thelin, 2011). Black veterans were eligible for GI benefits, however there was no requirement on the part of institutions to demonstrate nondiscrimination; many colleges and universities still discriminated against and excluded non-White students from education. It was not until the *Brown vs. the Board of Education of Topeka, Kansas* (1954) that declared "separate but equal" public secondary education was unconstitutional. Colleges and universities started to follow suit, however integration in the South was slow and not without protest (Thelin, 2011).

During the latter half of the 20th century, policies were enacted to promote access to higher education and remedy past incidents of exclusion. In the *Regents of the University of California v. Bakke* (1978), the Supreme Court ruled that the use of racial quotas in admissions was unconstitutional, however affirmative action to admit students from different racial backgrounds was constitutional in specific circumstances. Title IX, enacted in 1972, prohibits sex discrimination in any educational program that receives federal funding. Originally, Title IX was used to provide equity in collegiate athletics. More recently, colleges and universities have faced lawsuits under Title IX for their inadequate handling of sexual assault cases on campuses. Until early 2017, Title IX also provided protections for transgender students at colleges and universities.

Though legislation has been enacted to increase the structural diversity on college campuses and prevent discrimination, college campuses still remain hostile for members of minoritized student populations. According to the Anti-Defamation League, during the 2016-2017 academic year there were 159 incidents of racist flyers and emails along with visits by White supremacists and anti-Semitic faxes and emails on United States Campuses (2017). Researchers studying college and university campus climates have documented incidences of racial, gender, and sexual identity-based harassment (Garvey & Rankin, 2014; Rankin & Reason, 2005; Strayhorn, 2013). While the diversity of the student population on college campuses has increased, institutional policies, programs, and structures remain unchanged. There are also physical reminders of exclusion on college campuses, such as campus monuments and buildings named after those who endorsed racial segregation (e.g. Calhoun College at Yale University, which is in the process of being renamed). The inability to choose one's preferred name on college admissions applications and while in college contributes to unsafe classroom environments for gender non-conforming and transgender students (Pryor, 2015). Colleges and universities are still unwelcoming for women; in 2016 over 300 colleges and universities were under investigation for their mishandling of sexual assault cases (Kingkade, 2016).

Students on college and university campuses have protested the lack of multiculturally responsive and inclusive campuses. African American students at the University of Missouri protested the lack of racial inclusion on the campus due to racist incidents in 2015, which eventually led to the resignation of Tom Wolfe, the University System President. After bananas were placed on a banner commemorating African Americans at Fort Hill on Clemson University's campus in 2016, over 100 students staged a sit-in at Sikes Hall, the main administration building on campus demanding that the university construct a new multicultural center, prosecute online hate speech, and provide incentives for diversity training for faculty and staff (Bowers, 2017). Campus administrators have responded to protesters' demands by issuing statements, hiring Chief Diversity Officers (CDOs), and requiring diversity training for faculty, staff, and students. While these efforts have been made, more transformational work at all levels on campus (faculty, staff, and students) is still needed. An example of an initiative leading to a policy change is the University of Iowa (UI) Inclusive Student Records Initiative (Linley & Kilgo, 2018). Linley and Kilgo (2018) engaged multiple campus constituencies (e.g. academic and student affairs offices, affinity groups, and senior level administrators) to change how the university asked for and reports gender pronouns, sex, and gender identity. The results of their initiative educated faculty, staff, and students on transgender identities while changing policy to improve the campus climate for transgender college students (Linley & Kilgo, 2018). More efforts like these are needed on college campuses to establish inclusive campus policies and practices. As student affairs educators take part in systemic change on college campuses, they must simultaneously engage in developing their own multicultural identities—a foundational aspect of their professional identity.

MULTICULTURAL COMPETENCY–PROFESSIONAL IDENTITY FORMATION IN PRACTICE

Professional identity can be defined as "the relatively stable and enduring constellation of attributes, beliefs, values, motives, and experiences in terms of which people define themselves in a professional role" (Ibarra, 1999, pp. 764–765; Schein, 1978). Developing a professional identity includes committing to the values of student affairs and investing in continued efforts (e.g. training and personal development) to integrate one's personal values with professional values (Hirschy, Wilson, Liddell, Boyle, & Pasquesi, 2015; Wilson, Liddell, Hirschy, & Pasquesi, 2016). The values, beliefs, and styles must fit with the professionals' perception and other's expectations of their identity (Smith & Hatmaker, 2014) and have the potential to show people in the institution, communities, and society in general that these professionals possess unique, skilled, and scarce competencies and abilities (Van Maanen & Barley, 1984). Some major components of a student affairs professional identity include beliefs and values, expertise/knowledge, practice skills, dispositions which are all explicitly illustrated in the Professional Competency Areas for Student Affairs Educators by ACPA and NASPA (2015).

With ACPA and NASPA standards in place, student affairs educators must engage in activities that develop attitudes congruent with the values they uphold and the knowledge and skills they need to assist student growth and advocate for the development of an inclusive and socially conscious learning environment (ACPA & NASPA, 2015). Some specific steps toward the formation of student affairs professional identity may include (1) attending classes or workshops which focus on knowledge and skills development, (2) participating in student affairs professional organizations like Chi Sigma Alpha, ACPA, and NASPA, (3) attending and presenting at regional and national student affairs professional conferences, (4) establishing mentoring relationships and supervisory relationships (Pittman & Foubert, 2016), (5) conducting ongoing reflective self-work (Ortiz & Patton, 2012), and (6) keeping abreast of current issues impacting student affairs (Linder & Cooper, 2016).

In order to become a competent student affairs professional, one must possess multicultural "knowledge, skills, [and] dispositions needed to create learning environments that foster equitable participation of all groups and seeks to address issues of oppression, privilege, and power" (ACPA & NASPA, 2015, p. 30). With this professional identity, they indicate to others what they know, what they do, and who they eventually become. In another word, the overall professional identity of student affairs educators must reflect their multicultural competency and multicultural identity.

To achieve this goal, student affairs educators must first engage in self-work, one of the critical pathways to developing multicultural competency and multicultural identity, which is a constant activity that requires them to know their own social identities, the context in which those identities are situated, and how these identities operate in relationship to others (Ortiz & Patton, 2012). In addition to self-work, there are other components of developing multicultural competency and professional identity that will be covered in the subsequent chapters of this book.

Self-Work: An Outcome-Oriented Approach

Self-work is an ongoing process, beyond any particular skill set or content knowledge. Such self-work, particularly for professionals holding dominant social identities, (e.g. White, cisgender) requires continual engagement with one's relationship to, and complicity in, larger systems of oppression (Applebaum, 2010). That is, engaging in self-work requires student affairs educators to disinvest in a presentation of the self as innocent, good, and well-meaning, and instead consider the ways in which we are implicated in the normalization and perpetuation of racism, sexism, genderism, ableism, and so many other systems that marginalize and dehumanize. Aanerud (2015) writes about White educators and racial justice education; he describes "a conception of the self as accountable, interconnected, and open to cognitive uncertainty and mystery" (p. 105). In this regard, complicity (Applebaum, 2010) and humility (Aanerud, 2015) represent the starting point for critical self-work.

Unfortunately, this type of self-work is often subverted in favor of traditional diversity trainings that promote awareness and inclusivity (Pope,

1993). Indeed, many student affairs educators with dominant identities are tempted to intellectualize privilege without gaining an affective understanding (Watt, 2007). An exclusive focus on awareness and competence can fuel desires for innocence and "feeling good" that do little to challenge systemic injustice on campus (Applebaum, 2010; Pope, 1993). Because matters of oppression and injustice are so frequently reduced to the level of individuals, becoming "one of the good ones" becomes a primary concern among student affairs educators. Locating oneself as good, a cisgender student affairs educator who advocates for transgender students runs the risk of foreclosing additional self-work on how one is influenced by, and implicated in, systemic genderism. Similarly, the White residence hall director who believes he adequately understands the experiences of students of color will fail to attend to the limitations of his own knowledge. Ahmed (2012) cautioned against this type of thinking: "The reduction of racism to the figure of 'the racist' allows structural or institutional forms of racism to recede from view, by projecting racism onto a figure that is easily discarded (not only as someone who is "not me" but also someone who is 'not us' who does not represent a cultural or institutional norm)" (p. 150).

Yancy (2008) has described the process of White ambush, or the moment White people believe themselves to be fully competent, only to undergo a surprise attack that reminds one how Whiteness influences perspectives, perceptions, and attitudes beyond an individual's conscious control. This line of thinking could easily be extended to cisgender professionals in their work with transgender students, heterosexual practitioners' engagement with gay, lesbian, and bisexual students, and so on.

The language of ambush (Yancy, 2008) conveys the reality that being a good critically competent and socially aware professional is never fully in one's control, because one is always implicated in larger systems of power and privilege. For instance, a White student affairs educator may renounce Whiteness and White supremacy, but this White educator still benefits from White privilege when he is taken more seriously than his peers of color by others on campus. The perception of White people as intelligent and competent is only secured in relation to Black and Brown professionals who are framed as unintelligent or the result of race-conscious hiring practices. The privileges associated with dominance are only secured so long as they can be located in relation to the "other." As such, we advocate a type of self-work that is grounded in humility and that consistently interrogates one's own complicity in oppression (Applebaum, 2010). As Yancy (2015) explains, this level of self-interrogation is not about badness, but the ability to "*linger,* to remain, with the truth about one's white self and the truth about how whiteness has structured and continues to structure forms of relationality that are oppressive to people of color" (p. xv). Because White people desire to be seen as morally good, colorblind individuals, they will typically choose to flee such situations rather than remain in a space of uncertainty and discomfort (Yancy). Ortiz and Patton (2012) echo this line of thinking, noting "it is the notion that our self-awareness conflicts with how others perceive us. However, these tensions allow us to make important choices about whom we wish to become" (p. 22). In order to stay in a place of humility and uncertainty, we encourage student affairs educators to return to Yancy's (2015) play on a question originally posed by W.E.B. Du Bois (1903): What does it feel like to be a White problem? Further, what does it feel like to be a cisgender problem? Just as bell hooks (1997) described Whiteness as a form of terror in the Black imagination, we encourage student affairs educators to engage in a level of self-work that continually interrogates the symbolic representations our identities hold to the students with whom we work. This is a kind of self-work that moves beyond checking boxes and obtaining certifications, and engages in deep, critical thought about our relationships with other professionals and students.

Models for Engaging in Self-Work

There are many useful frameworks for engaging in self-work. We've highlighted three models below that are helpful in exploring individual social identities: Watt's (2007, 2015b) Privileged Identity Exploration (PIE) model, the Model of Multiple Dimensions of Identity (Jones & McEwen, 2000), and critical theories.

Watt—Privileged Identity Exploration (PIE) Model

Watt's (2007, 2015b) privileged identity exploration (PIE) model is a tool that can be used by student affairs educators to identify defenses as a result of experiencing cognitive dissonance. Through her research, Watt (2007, 2015b) developed a set of eight defensive reactions to dissonance-provoking stimuli (DPS), which included Recognizing Privileged Identity (denial, deflection, and rationalization), Contemplating Privileged Identity (intellectualization, principium, false envy), and Addressing Privileged Identity (benevolence and minimization). For those with privileged identities (e.g. White, male, heterosexual, cisgender, able-bodied) in the recognizing privileged identity phase, denial and deflection are common defenses. Individuals may deny that there is any dissonance between the new information and their experience, or they may deflect the situation onto another matter or subject (Watt 2007, 2015b). For example, when confronted with facts indicating differences in funding formulas between multicultural student organizations and other student organizations, a White student affairs educator may deny differences exist or default to the statement, "Well, this is the way we have always calculated funding." In the contemplating privileged identity phase, individuals with privileged identities intellectualize cognitive dissonance by searching for scientific evidence to base their information and may use false envy to compliment a person who holds a minoritized identity. Using the same example above, one may point to declining enrollment and subsequent student fees as justification prior to examining the budgets for multicultural organizations compared to other student organizations and without considering the power dynamics inherent in the decision. While declining enrollment and fees may be one reason, the White student affairs educator is closed off to examining other structural inequities in funding. Individuals with benevolent defense reactions use an act of charity to deflect their cognitive dissonance or minimize the emotional impact of the DPS, characteristic of addressing privileged identity (Watt, 2007, 2015b). An act of charity could include finding additional money for multicultural student organizations for a one-time event without examining the funding model for change. As individuals are more conscious of their privileged identities and their bias, they experience cognitive dissonance and their emotional responses become more complex. Student affairs educators can use the PIE model to explore not only their own reactions to DPS, but also in facilitating diversity training with campus constituents.

Model of Multiple Dimensions of Identity (MMDI)

The Model of Multiple Dimensions of Identity (MMDI) (Jones & McEwen, 2000) offers an additional lens that student affairs educators may use for self-work. It is particularly useful in considering the interaction of the self with larger contexts such as racism, sexism, and systemic privilege. The model consists of a core, one's multiple social identities, and contextual influences (Jones & McEwen, 2000). The core represents those personal attributes and characteristics that one defines as important to a sense of self. Social identities, such as gender, social class, and race, rotate around the core. Depicted as an atom, the closer the identities are located to the core, the more salient they are to the individual. The model is located within a number of larger societal contexts, including sociocultural conditions, family background, and current life experiences. The MMDI departs from other identity theories that posit developmental beginning and endpoints. Instead, the model represents a snapshot of identity at a given time. As Jones and McEwen (2000) explains, "the model is a fluid and dynamic one, representing the ongoing construction of identities and the influence of changing contexts on the experience of identity development" (p. 408). As such, how individuals map their identities on to the MMDI may look very different depending on immediate context. Since its conception, the MMDI has been reconceptualized to consider meaning-making capacities (Abes, Jones, & McEwen, 2007) and critical theories such as intersectionality, critical race theory, and queer theory (Jones & Abes, 2013).

Critical Theories

Student affairs educators are also encouraged to draw on a number of critical theories that might serve as an important foundation for engaging in the self-work described in this chapter. Critical theories mark a departure from earlier theoretical work in that they explicitly and unapologetically foreground systems of power and oppression. As Hernandez (2017) explained, such frameworks "consider how power, privilege, and oppression influence and constrain experiences, meaning making, and the ways in which individuals manage these social forces in their day-to-day interactions with others" (p. 205). For instance, critical race theory (CRT) asserts that racism is a systemic, enduring aspect of American life (Ladson-Billings, 1998; Solorzano & Yosso, 2001). CRT is especially useful in challenging race-neutral policies and perspectives in a supposed colorblind era (Bonilla-Silva, 2013). Through the use of counter storytelling, voices of color are elevated in an attempt to challenge ahistorical, meritocratic, and colorblind dominant ideologies. For instance, when rush season approaches, a Greek Life advisor might challenge her sorority members to consider the historical factors that contribute to the overwhelmingly white nature of the social Greek system. critical race theory, with a focus on the centrality and permanence of racism, could challenge any notions of race-neutrality and colorblindness by illuminating processes and practices that have historically contributed to such segregation. That is, CRT, as a framework, would provide the advisor with language to push back against any belief that segregation in Greek organizations is simply a matter of natural preference. Student affairs educators might also utilize CRT in their everyday practice by valuing and elevating the experiential knowledge of students of color. This is particularly important when voices of color are noticeably absent in a given decision-making process. Rather than subscribing to an overly simplistic, harmonious view of the campus racial climate that is useful in marketing the university to prospective students and their families, student affairs educators should draw on the racialized experiences of students of color to challenge dominant, colorblind ideologies.

Similarly, intersectionality (Crenshaw, 1991) can assist student affairs educators in understanding how multiple systems of oppression intersect to produce and secure relationships of domination and subordination. Intersectionality highlights how oppression functions at the intersections of subordinated identities (Linder, 2016). While the MMDI (Jones & McEwen, 2000) illustrates how multiple identities vary in salience in relation to larger contexts, it should not be confused with intersectionality. The promise of intersectionality lies in its ability to foreground systems of oppression and how such systems intersect in a way that then constitutes multiple marginalized identities (Crenshaw, 1991; Wijeyesinghe & Jones, 2014). Although intersectionality is often conflated with identity theories, this was not the intention of the theory. Writing about the applications of intersectionality in higher education research Wijeyesinghe and Jones (2014) noted "intersectional attends to identity by placing it within a macro-level analysis that ties individual experience to a person's membership in social groups, during a particular social and historical period, and within larger, interlocking systems of advantage and access" (p. 11). Historically the theory has illuminated the ways in which White supremacy and patriarchy operate to create a unique experience for Black women, different from Black men or White women. Patricia Hill Collins' (1990) *Black Feminist Thought* offers a useful example of a particular gendered and racialized standpoint for Black women. Intersectionality offers a powerful toolkit for student affairs educators in that it guards against essentializing the experiences of all students as the same, and instead encourages a nuanced and critical analysis of the interlocking systems of oppression that students experience. Both CRT and intersectionality provide frameworks that student affairs educators can utilize to unapologetically critique larger systems of power, oppression, and privilege that work to secure relationships of domination and subordination on campus. One tenet of CRT is storytelling as it allows one to name "one's own reality" (Ladson-Billings & Tate, 1995, p. 56). For example, in the case study below, student affairs educators should center the voices of minoritized students in student groups to understand how current policies and practices impact them individually and as group moving through the institution. Using the information gathered through focus groups and interviews, change can be initiated by reviewing the membership of the campus funding committee and creating a task force to develop more equitable funding procedures. Although CRT and intersectionality are commonly used in higher education scholarship, we encourage individuals to return to some of the foundational and original writings on both theories (e.g. Crenshaw, 1991; Ladson Billings, 1998), in order to fully engage with the nuances of each. Such a discussion is certainly beyond the scope of this chapter.

Case Study

Student affairs practitioners have the responsibility for creating equitable environments for students, so they can ultimately work, learn, and succeed.

As a student affairs practitioner, we encourage you to examine how your social identities influence your decisions at the professional level. In the following case study, use the PIE, MMDI, and critical theories to frame your response to the case.

Inequitable Funding Case Scenario

You're the new director of student life at Midwestern University. Midwestern University is a mid-sized comprehensive institution with a total enrollment of 13,000 students. Fraternity and sororities play a big role on-campus. Approximately, 1,000 students are involved in one of the 26 fraternities or sororities on campus. There are ten fraternities belonging to the National Interfraternity Council (NIC), nine sororities belonging to the National Panhellenic Council (NPC), six belonging to the National Pan-Hellenic Council (NPHC), and one belonging to the National Association of Latino Fraternal Organizations (NALFO). Members of NPHC and NALFO have come to your office requesting increases in funding and have noted the inequities in the funding models between NIC and NPC groups versus NPHC and NALFO when requests have been submitted. The number of Black and Latinx students who have enrolled at Midwestern University have increased by 7%, but funding has remained the same. Both groups have also complained about the space reservation process noting that NIC and NPC requests are granted routinely without further questions about security available at events held on-campus. As you formulate your approach, consider the following guiding questions.

Guiding Questions

1. How do you conceptualize multicultural competence? How do you use this definition to inform your work in the above case scenario?
2. How do you incorporate multicultural competence/critical consciousness into your professional identity?
3. What self-work do you need to engage in to increase your level of multicultural competence?
4. What is your emotional response to this situation?
5. What identities are salient for you in this situation? How do these identities interact?
6. How does your professional role on campus influence your response?

FURTHER READING FOR SELF-WORK

While the list below is not exhaustive, it does provide a start for engaging in self-work, understanding social justice and inclusion, and creating change on college campuses.

Books

Adams, M., Bell, L. A., Goodman, D. J., & Joshi, K.Y. (Eds.). (2013). *Teachings for diversity and social justice*. New York, NY: Routledge.

Adams, M., Blumefield, W. J., Castaneda, C., Hackman, H. W., Peters, M. L., & Zuniga, X. (Eds.). (2013). *Readings for diversity and social justice* (3rd ed.). New York, NY: Routledge.

Ahmed, S. (2012). *On being included: Racism and diversity in institutional life.* Durham, NC: Duke University Press.

Jones, S. R. & Abes, E. S. (2013). *Identity development of college students: Advancing frameworks for multiple dimensions of identity.* San Francisco, CA: Jossey-Bass.

Pope, R. L., Reynolds, A. L., & Mueller, J. A. (2004). *Multicultural competence in student affairs.* San Francisco, CA: Jossey-Bass.

Pope, R. L., Reynolds, A. L., & Mueller, J. A. (2014). *Creating multicultural change on campus.* San Francisco, CA: Jossey-Bass.

Tatum, B. D. (2017). *Why are all the black kids sitting together in the cafeteria?: And other conversations about race.* New York, NY: Hachette Book Group.

Yancy, G. (2015). *White self-criticality beyond anti-racism: How does it feel to be a white problem?* Lanham, MD: Lexington Books.

REFERENCES

Aanerud, R. (2015). Humility and whiteness: "How did I look without seeing, hear without listening?" In G. Yancy (Ed.), *White self-criticality beyond anti-racism: How does it feel to be a white problem?* (pp. 101–114). Lanham, MD: Lexington Books.

Abes, E. A., Jones, S. R., & McEwen, M. K. (2007). Reconceptualizing the model of multiple dimensions of identity: The role of meaning-making capacity in the construction of multiple identities. *Journal of College Student Development, 48*(1), 1–22.

ACPA: College Personnel Educators International & NASPA–Student Affairs Administrators in Higher Education (2010). *ACPA/NASPA professional competency areas for student affairs practitioners.* Washington, DC: Authors.

ACPA: College Personnel Educators International & NASPA–Student Affairs Administrators in Higher Education (2015). *ACPA/NASPA professional competency areas for student affairs practitioners.* Washington, DC: Authors.

American College Health Association. (2012). *National college health assessment II: Reference group executive summary, Spring 2012.* Hanover, MD: Author.

Anti-Defamation League (9 June, 2017). White supremacists on campus: Unprecedented recruitment efforts underway. Retrieved from: https://www.adl.org/blog/white-supremacists-on-campus-unprecedented-recruitment-efforts-underway?_ga=1.3868912.1741098207.1488839158

Applebaum, B. (2010). *Being white, being good: White complicity, white moral responsibility, and social justice pedagogy.* New York, NY: Lexington Books.

Bonilla-Sliva, E. (2013). *Racism without racists: Color-blind racism and the persistence of inequality in America.* Lanham, MD: Rowman & Littlefield.

Bowers, P. (15 April, 2017). One year after an uncharacteristic sit-in, campus activism lives on at Clemson. Retrieved from: http://www.postandcourier.com/news/one-year-after-an-uncharacteristic-sit-in-campus-activism-lives/article_1ec75478-1e1e-11e7-800e-837704a8cbfa.html

Brown v. Board of Education, Topeka, Kansas (1954).

Collins, P. H. (1990). *Black feminist thought: Knowledge, consciousness, and the politics of empowerment.* Boston, MA: Unwin Hyman.

Crenshaw, K. (1991). Mapping the margins: Intersectionality, identity politics, and violence against women of color. *Stanford Law Review, 43,* 1241–1299.

Du Bois, W. E. B. (1903). *The souls of black folk.* New York, NY: Dover Publications.

Flowers, L. A. (2003). National study of diversity requirements in student affairs graduate programs. *NASPA Journal, 40*(4), 72–82.

Freire, P. (1970). *Pedagogy of the oppressed.* (Rev. ed., M.B. Ramos, Trans.). New York, NY: Continuum. (Original work published in 1968).

Gardner, L. (23 February, 2017). Why trans* students matter. *The Chronicle of Higher Education.* Retrieved from: http://www.chronicle.com/article/Why-Trans-Students-Matter/239305.

Garvey, J. C., & Rankin, S. R. (2014). The influence of campus experiences on the level of outness among trans-spectrum and queer-spectrum students. *Journal of Homosexuality, 62*(3), 374–393.

Gayles, J. G., & Kelly, B. T. (2007). Experiences with diversity in the curriculum: Implications for graduate programs and student affairs practice. *NASPA Journal, 44*(1), 193–208.

Gose, B. (18 September, 2016). As standards change, disability officers race to keep up. *The Chronicle of Higher Education.* Retrieved from: http://www.chronicle.com/article/As-Standards-Change/237781

Hernandez, E. (2017). Critical theoretical perspectives. In J. H. Schuch, S. R. Jones, & V. Torres (Eds.), *Student services: A handbook for the profession* (6th ed., pp. 205–219).

Hirschy, A. S., Wilson, M. E., Liddell, D. L., Boyle, K. M., & Pasquesi, K. (2015). Socialization to student affairs: Early career experiences associated with professional identity development. *Journal of College Student Development, 56*(8), 777–793.

hooks, b. (1997). Representing whiteness in the black imagination. In R. Frankenberg (Ed.), *Displacing whiteness: Essays in social and cultural criticism* (pp. 165–179). Durham, NC: Duke University Press.

Ibarra, H. (1999). Provisional selves: Experimenting with image and identity in professional adaptation. *Administrative Science Quarterly, 44*(4), 764–791.

Iverson, S. V. (2012). Multicultural competence for doing social justice: Expanding our awareness, knowledge, and skills. *Journal of Critical Thought and Practice, 1*(1), 1–26.

Kena, G., Hussar, W., McFarland, J., de Brey, C., Rathbun, A., Wilkinson-Flicker, S., Diliberti, M., Barmer, A., Bullock Mann, F., & Dunlop Velez, V. (2016). *The Condition of Education 2016* (NCES 2016-144). U.S. Department of Education, National Center for Education Statistics. Washington, DC. Retrieved from https://nces.ed.gov/pubsearch/pubsinfo.asp?pubid=2016144

Kingkade, T. (2016, June 16). There are far more Title IX investigations of colleges than most people know. *Huffington Post.* Retrieved from: http://www.huffingtonpost .com/entry/title-ix-investigations-sexual-harassment_us_575f4b0ee4b053d 433061b3d

Ladson-Billings, G. (1998). Just what is critical race theory and what's it doing in a nice field like education? *International Journal of Qualitative Studies in Education, 11*(1), 7–24.

Ladson-Billings, G., & Tate, W. F. (1995). Toward a critical race theory of education. *Teacher's College Record, 97,* 47–68.

Landreman, L. M., Rasmussen, C. J., King, P. M., & Jiang, C. X. (2007). A phenomenological study of the development of university educators' critical consciousness. *Journal of College Student Development, 48*(3), 275–296.

Linder, C. (2016). An intersectional approach to supporting students. In M. J. Cuyjet, C. Linder, M. F. Howard-Hamilton, & D. L. Cooper (Eds.), *Multiculturalism on campus: Theory, models, and practices for understanding diversity and creating inclusion* (pp. 66–80). Sterling, VA: Stylus.

Linder, C., & Cooper, D. L. (2016). From cultural competence to critical consciousness. In M. J. Cuyjet, C. Linder, M. F. Howard-Hamilton, & D. L. Cooper (Eds.), *Multiculturalism on campus: Theory, models, and practices for understanding diversity and creating inclusion* (pp. 379–392). Sterling, VA: Stylus.

Linley, J. L., & Kilgo, C. A. (2018). Expanding agency: Centering gender identity in college and university student records systems. *Journal of College Student Development, 59*(3), 359–365.

McEwen, M. K., & Roper, L. D. (1994). Incorporating multiculturalism into student affairs preparation programs: Suggestions from the literature. *Journal of College Student Development, 35,* 46–53.

Mueller, J. A., & Broido, E. M. (2012). Historical context: Who we were is part of who we are. In J. Arminio, V. Torres, & R. L. Pope (Eds.), *Why aren't we there yet? Taking personal responsibility for creating an inclusive campus* (pp. 57–102). Sterling, VA: Stylus.

Ortiz, A. M., & Patton, L. D. (2012). Awareness of self. In J. Arminio, V. Torres, & R. L. Pope (Eds.), *Why aren't we there yet? Taking personal responsibility for creating an inclusive campus* (pp. 9–31). Sterling, VA: Stylus.

Pittman, E. C., & Foubert, J. D. (2016). Predictors of professional identity development for student affairs professionals. *Journal of Student Affairs Research and Practice, 53*(1), 13–25.

Pope, R. L. (1993). *An analysis of multiracial change efforts in student affairs.* Unpublished doctoral dissertation, University of Massachusetts, Amherst.

Ponterotto, J. G., & Cases, J. M. (1987). In search of multicultural competence within counselor education programs. *Journal of Counseling and Development, 65*(8), 430–434.

Pope, R. L., Mueller, J. A., & Reynolds, A. L. (2009). Looking back and moving forward: Future directions for diversity research in student affairs. *Journal of College Student Development, 50*(6), 640–658.

Pope, R. L., & Reynolds, A. L. (1997). Student affairs core competencies: Integrating multicultural awareness, knowledge, and skills. *Journal of College Student Development, 38*(3), 266–277.

Pope, R. L., Reynolds, A. L., & Mueller, J. A. (2004). *Multicultural competence in student affairs.* San Francisco, CA: Jossey-Bass.

Pryor, J. T. (2015). Out in the classroom: Transgender student experiences at a large public university. *Journal of College Student Development, 56*(5), 440–455.

Rankin, S. R., & Reason, R. D. (2005). Differing perceptions: How students of color and white students perceive campus climate for underrepresented groups. *Journal of College Student Development, 46*(1), 43–61.

Regents of the University of California v. Bakke. Washington, D.C.: University Publications of America. (1978).

Schein, E. H. (1978). *Career dynamic: Making individual and organizational needs.* Reading, MA: Addison-Wesley.

Smith, A. E., & Hatmaker, D. M. (2014). Knowing, doing, and becoming: Professional identity construction among public affairs doctoral students. *Journal of Public Affairs Education, 20*(4), 545–564.

Solorzano, D. G., & Yosso, T. J. (2001). Critical race and LatCrit theory and method: counter-storytelling. *Qualitative Studies in Education, 14*(4), 471–495.

Stolberg, S. G., & Rosenthal, B. M. (2017, August 12). Man charged after white nationalist rally in Charlottesville ends in deadly violence. *The New York Times.* Retrieved from: https://www.nytimes.com/2017/08/12/us/charlottesville -protest-white-nationalist.html?mcubz=1

Strayhorn, T. L. (2013). Measuring race and gender differences in measuring undergraduate students' perceptions of campus climate and intentions to leave college: An analysis in black and white. *Journal of Student Affairs Research and Practice, 50*(2), 115–132.

Suy, P. (2017, August 24). Baylor University hit with another Title IX lawsuit. *Baylor Lariat.* Retrieved from: http://baylorlariat.com/2017/08/24/baylor-hit-with -another-title-ix-lawsuit/

Thelin, J. R. (2011). *A history of higher education* (2nd ed.). Baltimore, MD: Johns Hopkins University Press.

U.S. Department of Education, National Center for Education Statistics. (2017). Integrated Postsecondary Education System (IPEDS). *Digest of Education Statistics.* Retrieved from https://nces.ed.gov/programs/digest/d16/tables/dt16 _302.60.asp

Watt, S. K. (2007). Difficult dialogues, privilege and social justice: Uses of the privileged identity exploration (PIE) model in student affairs practice. *College Student Affairs Journal, 26*(2), 114–126.

Watt, S. K. (2015a). Authentic, action-oriented, framing for environmental shifts (AAFES) method. In S. K. Watt (Ed.), *Designing transformative multicultural initiatives: Theoretical foundations, practical applications, and facilitator considerations* (pp. 23–39). Sterling, VA: Stylus.

Watt, S. K. (2015b). Privileged identity exploration (PIE) model revisited: Strengthening skills for engaging difference. In S. K. Watt (Ed.), *Designing transformative multicultural initiatives: Theoretical foundations, practical applications, and facilitator considerations* (pp. 40–57). Sterling, VA: Stylus.

Wijeyesinghe, C. L., & Jones, S. R. (2014). Intersectionality, identity, and systems of power and inequality. In D. Mitchell Jr., C. Y. Simmons, & L. A. Greyerbiehl (Eds.), *Intersectionality and higher education: theory, research, & praxis* (pp. 9–19). New York, NY: Peter Lang Publishing.

Wilson, M. E., Liddell, D. L., Hirschy, A. S., & Pasquesi, K. (2016). Professional identity, career commitment, and career entrenchment of midlevel student affairs professionals. *Journal of College Student Development, 57*(5), 557–572.

Winston, R. B., Creamer, D. G., Miller, T. K., & Associates (2001). *The professional student affairs administrator: Educator, leader, and manager.* New York, NY: Brunner-Routledge.

Yancy, G. (2008). *Black bodies, white gazes: The continuing significance of race.* Lanham, MD: Rowman & Littlefield.

Yancy, G. (2015). Introduction: Un-sutured. In G. Yancy (Ed.), *White self-criticality beyond anti-racism: How does it feel to be a white problem?* (pp. xi–xxvii). Lanham, MD: Lexington Books.

Young, R. B. (1997). Philosophies and values guiding the student affairs profession. In S. R. Komives, & D. B. Woodard, Jr., & Associates (Eds.), *Student services: A handbook for the profession* (4th ed., pp. 89–106). San Francisco, CA: Jossey-Bass.

Chapter 2

COMPETENT PRACTITIONERS: DEVELOPING A PROFESSIONAL IDENTITY THAT CENTERS SOCIAL JUSTICE

Rachel Wagner, Jimmy Howard, & Tony Cawthon

Recent news items about "social justice warriors" have the unfortunate consequence of discouraging professionals from aligning with and endorsing social justice, but a public commitment to social justice should be a badge of honor, not a label inviting derision. A commitment to social justice means a recognition that all life is connected, that we are in this journey together, and that, as humans, we cannot live a life of meaning when others are prevented from flourishing, and certainly not when others are harmed physically and psychologically. As student affairs educators, it is incumbent upon us to support the flourishing of all students, and, to do so, we have to be aware how the current socio-political reality organizes and structures inequities that limit the life chances and thriving of people of color, poor people, folks in the queer community, people with disabilities, transgenders, youth, elderly, and others who have been minoritized by a system of oppression.

The purpose of this chapter is to illuminate what we mean by social justice, how it is a response to a system of oppression that characterizes social life, and what that means for you as a student affairs educator. We describe how social group markers related to race, gender, ability, and other social identities are taken up by a system that confers advantage to some at the expense of others, and explain how socialization processes function to acculturate us into a system of oppression and maintain the status quo of rampant inequity.

Social Justice as a response to a system of oppression has significant ramifications for individual educators, who must reflect on their own positionalities and social locations and understand how they benefit and are harmed by oppressive systems (Linder & Cooper, 2016). Furthermore, we are called upon to reflect on how we might leverage opportunities through the privilege of professional roles to create access and eliminate personal, institutional, cultural, and systemic manifestations of marginalization, cultural imperialism, violence, powerlessness, and exploitation that are promulgated under an interlocking system of oppression (Young, 2013). Developing a professional identity in which one understands one's own social location, considers the investments one makes in a system of oppression, and acts to disrupt oppression on the micro and macro levels is paramount to student affairs practice. Yet the framing of a professional identity itself can be misleading, as those who are disadvantaged by a system of oppression have fewer opportunities to make a distinction between the personal and the professional.

This chapter provides context for our use of the phrase social justice, traces the emergence of multicultural competence in student affairs practice, clarifies terminology useful for furthering social justice and inclusion competencies, and concludes with a discussion of developing a socially-just professional identity.

SOCIAL JUSTICE IS A GOAL AND A PROCESS

The goal of social justice is a fair and equitable society that is mutually shaped to meet everyone's needs. Scholars argue convincingly that social justice includes both a fair and equitable (re)distribution of resources (Chhachhi, 2001; Rawls, 1999) and recognition practices that respect and affirm the dignity of all people (Lynch & Baker, 2005; Young, 1990). The process for attaining the goals of social justice must be situated in democratic and participatory efforts that foster collective change for the common good without compromising the interests of those most vulnerable within the current system. Essentially, achieving social justice goals requires processes that are conscientious, inclusive, and emancipatory. In the section that follows, we briefly explain previous scholarship that informs distributive, representational, and recognition aspects of social justice before turning to discuss elements of social justice and inclusion competency.

Goals of Social Justice

Lee Anne Bell's (2013) vision of social justice prioritizes equal distribution of resources and an environment where everyone experiences physical security and psychological safety. This vision is in part consistent with the distributive justice articulated by philosopher John Rawls, which calls for every individual to have access to material (shelter, food, clothing) and social (employment, access to education, self-respect) goods (Rawls, 1999). Furthermore, Rawls contends that, within a distributive justice framework, opportunities and access to social and material goods should be given to those who are the least well-off. Therefore, distributive justice demands that two separate but related principles govern how opportunities are distributed. His philosophy accounts for a baseline of basic liberties or access to material and social goods for all people *and* rectification for existing economic and social inequalities. Once everyone's basic liberties are addressed, opportunities to improve one's living conditions should be allocated to those who are the least well-off. This approach reframes fairness to consider what every human needs to flourish and how historical inequities have shaped the life chances of individuals disadvantaged by social oppression.

Nancy Fraser's (1997) work builds upon Rawls to account for recognition and representational (Chhachhi, 2011) practices in pursuit of social justice. Under a system of cultural domination, some groups have less opportunity to see their values, norms, histories, and stories articulated within social institutions. For instance, Jews, Muslims, Hindus and other religious minorities in the United States cannot expect to attend public schools or be employed at places that acknowledge and schedule schooling and work breaks around their religious commitments, whereas any Christian in the United States can anticipate having their high holy days accounted for within the calendar. Additionally, Indigenous folks on this continent can expect that the textbooks their children are subjected to in public schools provide limited or problematic explanations of Native American and European contact that downplays or erases imperialist, colonialist, and genocidal actions and outcomes. Social justice demands that failure to problematize dominant and prevailing discourses that obscure, deny, or misrepresent the experiences of minoritized groups be rectified. Recognition practices refers to the ways in which society must be reorganized so that those disadvantaged by a system of oppression do not continue to experience a cultural curriculum that demonizes, disregards, renders invisible or erases their identities and experiences.

The Process of Social Justice

The process of social justice is characterized by representational practices that are democratic, participatory, and collaborative and that ensure all people can contribute to decisions affecting their lives and livelihoods (Chhachhi, 2011). The goal of representational practices is to ensure that individuals get to act *with* others to improve their lives and the society they live in rather than have their lives acted upon *by* others. The former situation offers agency and human dignity, and acting with others ensures that social conditions and structures are derived through participation and collective engagement, whereas the latter offers no such assurances. If decisions are being made in my locality to move a toxic waste facility to my neighborhood, representation means that my community, which is directly affected, should have a significant voice in the decision-making. Representation also speaks to the process of social justice in that it prioritizes providing mechanisms for people to work collaboratively to enact change. The process of social justice, in part, seeks to enact societal change to redress the inequities that already exist.

Bell (2013) offers strategies to redress these inequities. Collaboration and reciprocity are central to the process of social justice. Collaboration entails creating and implementing mutually derived goals that promote the flourishing of all members of the community, particularly those who are less well-off. Reciprocity complements collaboration in that it ensures that each person has a stake in the development of relationships and the outcomes of action taken by the community. Collaborative, participatory processes characterized by mutuality and democratic engagement are particularly important because coercive tactics, which thrive within systems of domination and oppression, contradict the basic principles of social justice. Therefore, we must shape our journey as carefully as we construct our destination.

OVERVIEW OF SOCIAL JUSTICE COMPETENCY AND INCLUSION

A cursory review of recent national events (i.e. bombings of churches and Muslim centers, police killings of people of color, and protest over removal of monuments) and increased incidents at colleges and universities (i.e. posting of blackface photos, hosting of controversial speakers, and assemblies of the alt-right) serve as daily reminders that our country and profession have significant challenges ahead of us in addressing issues of social justice. To fulfill our role as student affairs educators, we must become multiculturally competent to effectively respond to daily microaggressions or full campus unrest, educate ourselves with the dispositions, skills, and knowledge necessary for creating safe and inclusive communities.

Because our profession attracts people from a range of academic backgrounds, both in terms of amount of education as well as types of graduate programs (from counseling to administration), many enter our profession without established and agreed-upon sets of competencies. In particular, they often enter without the necessary social justice knowledge and skills. Numerous researchers have explored competency development in student affairs and higher education (Bresciani, Swen, Hickmott, & Hoffman, 2010; Burkard, Cole, Ott, & Stoflet, 2005; Castellanos, Gloria, Mayorga, & Salas, 2007; Cuyjet, Longwell-Grie, & Molina, 2009; Dickerson et al, 2011; Herdlein, 2004; Herdlein, Riefler, & Mrowka, 2013; Kuh, Cobb & Forrest, 2008; Lovell & Kosten, 2000; Pope & Reynolds, 1997; Renn & Hodges, 2007; Waple, 2006; Young & Janosik, 2007). Also, Cheatham (1991), Howard-Hamilton, Richardson, and Shuford (1998) and Pope, Reynolds, and Muller (2004, 2014) urge student affairs professionals to be competent in responding to social justice issues.

Herdlein, Riefler, and Mrowka (2013) completed a meta-analysis of over twenty years of research related to competencies, concluding "a developing consensus in student affairs toward a more administrative focus to complement human facilitation skills" (p. 250). While each of these studies identified various competencies or gaps in competencies, Herdlein et al. (2013) reported that multicultural competency was at the top of necessary competencies. In addition, Pope and Reynolds (1997) reaffirmed that multicultural competence frames the basis of valuable and ethical practice.

MULTICULTURAL COUNSELING COMPETENCY

Much of our work on multicultural competence in higher education is grounded in counseling. Arredondo et al. (1996), Sue et al. (1982), and Sue, Arrendondo, and McDavis (1992) were early pioneers in identifying multicultural counseling competencies; Constantine and Ladany (2000) and Constantine et al. (2007) have in recent years provided insights into competencies related to social justice and advocacy.

Designed to both better assist people of color and to educate counselors about the influence of culture, Sue et al. (1982) and Sue et al. (1992) composed 31 multicultural competencies. These multicultural counseling competencies (MCC) addressed the attitudes/beliefs, knowledge, and skills that counselors need in three primary areas: (a) awareness of own cultural value and biases, (b) awareness of client's worldview, and (c) culturally appropriate intervention strategies.

As the profession has evolved, counselor competence focused on issues of social justice and advocacy. Constantine and Ladany (2000) and Constantine et al. (2007) built upon the individual multicultural counseling competencies developed by Sue et al. (1982) to address the issue of social justice competencies, identifying nine social justice competencies. Examining these competencies, they address issues of social oppression, social inequities, positions of power; the need for collaborations with community organizations to promote social change and to challenge counseling approaches inappropriate for marginalized groups.

In reaction to the counseling profession's movement toward advocacy and social justice, Ratts et al. (2015) updated the Multicultural Counseling Competency developed by Sue et al. (1992). On behalf of the Association of Multicultural Counseling and Development in 2015, Ratts et al. presented the Multicultural and Social Justice Competencies (MSJCC). Presented as a framework for counselors as they implement theory and strategies to assist clients, MSJCC organizes the competencies around four developmental domains: (a) counselor self-awareness, (b) client worldview, (c) the counseling relationship, and (d) advocacy interventions. For the first three of these domains, the MSJCC provide attitudes/beliefs, knowledge, skills, and action necessary for competency. An example of an attitude/belief is the acknowledgement that people's privilege impacts their own worldview; an example of knowledge is understanding different communication patterns of privileged and marginalized groups; an example of skills is possessing assessment skills for determining how one's privileged perspective influences the counseling relationship; and an example of action is participating in professional development opportunities to educate oneself on how issues such as privilege, oppression, and power impact privilege and marginalized individuals. The final domain offers competencies on how privileged and marginalized individuals advocate for others in the areas of intrapersonal, interpersonal, institutional, community, public policy and international concerns.

MULTICULTURAL COMPETENCE AND HIGHER EDUCATION

A number of researchers have investigated multicultural competencies for student affairs educators. Below is an overview of this research.

Student Affairs Core Competencies and Characteristics of Multiculturally-Competent Student Affairs Practitioners

In 1997, Pope and Reynolds identified seven core competencies for successful student affairs work as well as characteristics of multiculturally competent student affairs practitioners. Attempting to add clarity to what specific multicultural attitudes, knowledge, and skills were needed to implement the competencies in the model above, Pope and Reynolds (1997) identified 33 characteristics for working with diverse populations. These are organized around the tripartite model developed by Sue et al. (1992), which include the following: (a) multicultural awareness, (b) multicultural knowledge, and (c) multicultural skills. Awareness focuses on one's attitudes, values, and beliefs as well as the ability to reflect upon how one's experiences and identities impact one's work; knowledge emphasizes what one knows about marginalized groups and their experiences; and skills identify the behaviors needed for the application of one's awareness and skills. These characteristics can be used for self-assessment, curriculum development, and training.

Attributes of a Culturally Competent Student

Howard-Hamilton, Richardson, and Shuford (1998) recommended multicultural attributes for students. Organized around awareness, understanding, and appreciation/valuing, the authors identified knowledge, skills, and attitudes for each area. Examples include knowledge of one's cultural identity, issues of oppression, the elements of change, appreciation of other perspectives, challenging discrimination, and engaging in cross-cultural interactions.

The Dynamic Model of Student Affairs Competence

In 2004, Pope, Reynolds, and Mueller adapted the work of Pope and Reynolds (1997) to present the Dynamic Model of Student Affairs Competence. In this model, Pope, Reynolds, and Mueller (2004) identified seven core competencies for student affairs professionals. These included: (a) administration and management; (b) assessment and evaluation; (c) helping and interpersonal; (d) teaching and training; (e) theory and translation; (f) ethical and legal; and (g) multicultural awareness, knowledge, and skills. Recognizing that growth in one competence impacts other competencies, they also advocate that multicultural awareness, knowledge. and skills, while a distinctive skill, must be incorporated with the other competencies. To function competently when working with diverse communities of individuals, all student affairs educators must possess multicultural awareness, knowledge, and skills.

ACPA/NASPA Competencies

Prior to the development of these competencies, Janosik, Carpenter, and Creamer (2006) challenged professional association conference planners to adopt a student affairs curriculum matrix of eight competencies to organize conference programs. Soon thereafter, the American College Personnel Association (ACPA) and the National Association of Student Personnel Administrators (NASPA) assembled a joint group to develop competencies for student affairs. In 2010, the Joint Task Force introduced a set of ten competencies (ACPA/NASPA, 2010) at basic, intermediate, and advanced levels. These competencies provided a foundation for what student affairs educators should be able to know and do. Equity, Diversity and Inclusion (EDI) was one competency area identified.

Because these competencies were designed for regular reviewing and updating, in 2014 both associations assembled the Joint Task Force of Professional Competencies to examine and revise as necessary. After significant work, the revised Professional Competency Areas for Student Affairs Educators were introduced (ACPA/NASPA Competencies, 2015). Revisions included use of the word "dispositions" instead of "attitudes," "basic level" competency became "foundational level," and more discussion was presented on how the competencies include one another. Also as a result of these revision, two competence areas were combined into one ("Ethical Profession Practice" and "Personal Foundations" became "Personal and Ethical Foundations"), one new competence was introduced ("Technology"), and two competencies were renamed ("Advising and Helping" became "Advising and Supporting"; "Equity, Diversity and Inclusion" became "Social Justice and Inclusion").

As the committee clearly articulated, the phrasing of "Social Justice and Inclusion" (SJI) was significant, and it reflected the changes in the literature from professionals simply being aware of diverse issues to one of social action and social change (ACPA/NASPA, 2015). The new competency requires us to do more than simply work with diverse groups but to understand how systems of power, privilege, and oppression impact our practice and policies. Social justice is defined as: "both a process and a goal that includes the knowledge, skills, and dispositions needed to create learning environments that foster equitable participation of all groups and seeks to address issues of oppression, privilege and power" (ACPA/NASPA, 2015, p. 14). Competent professionals understand they control their own actions while also maintain a sense of responsibility to others. Examples of outcomes of social justice and inclusion include: advocate on social justice, power, privilege, and oppression; ensure campus policies, practices, facilities, and structures value and embody the needs of all members of the community; and execute programs and services that are inclusive, promote social justice awareness, and disrupt all systems of oppression.

In addition, soon after these competencies were introduced, a separate group began the arduous work of creating rubrics for competency assessment. The ACPA/NASPA Professional Competence Rubrics (ACPA, n.d.) were organized around the levels of foundational, intermediate, and advanced outcomes centered on the skills, knowledge, and disposition expected for each competency. The rubric allows educators to assess their (a) understanding of self and navigation of systems of power, (b) organizational systemic advocacy, (c) engagement in socially-just practice, and (d) self-directed learning (ACPA/NASPA Professional Competencies Rubrics, 2015). Specifically, the rubric includes items such as ability to facilitate social justice conversations, knowledge of how to assess and measure campus climate, and an understanding of how to integrate knowledge of social justice, inclusion, privilege and power into one's practice.

The Valid Assessment of Learning in Undergraduate Education (VALUE)

The VALUE Institute (Association of American Colleges & Universities, 2018a) provides sixteen learning outcomes designed to improve student success. One key learning outcome identified is Intercultural Knowledge and Competence. This competency utilizes Bennett's (2008) definition of: "a set of cognitive, affective, and behavioral skills and characteristics that support effective and appropriate interaction in a variety of cultural contexts," (p. 95). Intercultural knowledge and competence transforms learning by focusing on culture and creating campuses with meaningful engagements. Utilizing Bennett's Developmental Model of Intercultural Sensitivity and Deardorff's intercultural framework, teams of faculty experts representing colleges and universities across the United States (Association of American Colleges & Universities, 2018b) have developed a rubric to measure six components of: (a) cultural self-awareness, (b) knowledge of cultural worldviews frameworks, (c) empathy, (d) verbal and nonverbal communication, (f) curiosity, and (g) openness.

Student affairs can consult a wealth of resources regarding professional competency in the areas of equity, multiculturalism, and social justice. Having traced the emergence of competencies related to social justice and inclusion, we now turn our attention to key terms and concepts that inform socially-just approaches to professional practice.

SYSTEMS OF OPPRESSION

Recognizing that the current system of social life and life chances is historically and structurally inequitable is an important first step in the pursuit of social justice. A system of oppression and domination characterizes our social order. Bell (2016) noted that oppression is a term employed to "embody the interlocking forces that create and sustain injustice . . . manifested through racism, classism, sexism, heterosexism, transgender oppression, religious oppression, ableism, and youth and elder oppression" (p. 5). Leveraging social group markers that categorize individuals based on a variety of social identities such as race, gender, class, and ability, among others, social life is structured hierarchically to advantage some groups at the expense of others. Thus racism, sexism, classism, ableism, and other forms of oppression advantage and disadvantage groups based on social location.

Through an intensive socialization process, individuals are taught to accept and reproduce systems of inequity. Several concepts and terms are useful for describing what oppression and domination are and how they function on micro and macro levels.

Definitions and Terms

Oppression refers to a system of disadvantage (oppression) and advantage (domination/privilege) based on social group membership (Hardiman, Jackson, & Griffin, 2007). For instance, racism is a system of disadvantage based on the social construction of race. Under racism, White people reap unearned advantage that they may have not asked for while people of color experience marginalization, cultural imperialism, and violence because of their group membership.

Oppression operates on individual, institutional, and cultural levels. Individuals can discriminate against those who are disadvantaged by a system of oppression through attitudes and actions. Institutional levels operate through laws, policies, and procedures that are deployed within institutions such as legal systems, education, media, and healthcare systems. Finally, the cultural level manifests through societal norms, rituals, and art.

The Dominant group holds "the power and authority in society relative to the subordinates and determines how that power and authority may be acceptably used. Whether it is reflected in determining who gets the best jobs, whose history will be taught in school, or whose relationships will be validated by society, the dominant group has the greatest influence in determining the structure of society" (Tatum, 2013, p.6). In contrast, *Subordinant groups* are targets of social oppression within society and must cope with and survive the onslaught of discrimination, devaluation, dehumanization, and exploitation.

Socialization is the process through which individuals in a society are educated, both through what is "caught" or observed and "taught" or explained and reinforced by individuals and social institutions in order to assume dominant (advantaged) and subordinant (disadvantaged) roles. Harro (2013) describes a cycle of socialization that characterizes how both our families and mentors as well as institutions such as schooling or the media condition us to enact unequal roles within a dynamic system of oppression. This conditioning is maintained by powerful enforcements that leverage rewards and punishments to ensure we do not thwart or challenge the system.

Ideology reflects how idea systems shape our experience of the social world. Within a system of oppression and domination, hegemonic ideologies are deployed—that is, idea systems are constructed to protect the ruling or dominant interests, delimiting what is considered to be normal, correct, appropriate, and good.

Privilege, as explained by Allan Johnson (2013), "exists when a group of people has something of value that is denied to others simply because of the groups they belong to, rather than because of anything they've done or failed to do" (p. 17). White privilege, therefore, connotes access to assumptions of goodness, credibility, and innocence that is not earned but rather bestowed because of the racial designation of White. *Social Identities* refer to the categories of difference related to race, gender, sexual orientation, religion, class, age, nation, language, and ability. Our membership in these categories exists in a field of power relegating some memberships advantaged (White, men, wealthy, etc.) and others disadvantaged (people of color, women, trans, and gender non-conforming folks, poor and working-class people, etc.) under a system of oppression.

Locating Oneself in a System of Oppression

Even though we may not think about nor reflect upon our identities regularly, each of us has multiple social identities, such as race, class, gender, etc. Educators must take inventory of their social identities and think about which is important to them. Competent educators ask themselves, Which can change? Are there circumstances that might make one or more feel more significant? What advantages or disadvantages are you aware of that accompany each identity?

This system of oppression and domination co-opts the social identity markers of individuals and groups. Is your race privileged by a system of advantage (racism)? Or is it disadvantaged? Which identities do you think about the most often? More than likely, you think about the ones that confer disadvantage within the system. It is rare to think about our privileged identities because most people don't think about themselves as advantaged. We focus on the things that are harming us rather than the ways we are insulated from harm, but social systems act upon us without regard for our preferences. While individuals might not think about it often or even feel very privileged, their U.S. citizenship confers advantages in regard to finding employment, being eligible for social security, and travelling internationally, all of which are not available to their undocumented neighbors.

Our identities also intersect with and influence each other. Gender is raced and race is gendered. The experiences of all women are not identical, nor the experiences of all people of color. Other identity categories influence how race, for instance, is perceived. Heterosexual orientation might mitigate some aspects of racism that are exacerbated for queer people of color. A framework of intersectionality is useful for both acknowledging an individual's multiple social identities and how those identities are connected to historical and structural inequities (Wijeyesinghe, 2016). Intersectionality accounts for the multiplicity and simultaneity of identities as well as their differential impacts when connected to a larger macro system of oppressions that co-constitute and reinforce each other.

No one is outside of the system of oppression. While we did not create it, it is the social world that we have inherited. Regardless of what we may know ourselves, others may fail to perceive our identities or place emphasis on identities that are less important to us. Our identities inform how we see, make sense of, and operate in the world, and will influence how ideologies of white supremacy and heteropatriarchy and other oppressive ideologies shape the world in which we operate. We can take action to apprehend how oppression is operating in our lives, see where we are advantaged and disadvantaged, make conscious and strategic decisions of where we invest in the system, and act to subvert or transform it. We can build relationships and organize with others to realize substantive organizational and social change (Love, 2013).

Two aspects of socialization can inform how people locate themselves in a system of oppression. Given the substantial institutional and cultural mechanisms in place to acculturate us to roles of domination and subordination within social life and the consequences faced in resisting such roles, individuals internalize dominant and subordinant identities. Unexamined cultural constructions that barrage us repeatedly throughout our socialization into oppressive systems serve as the social differences that we experience as natural and inevitable (Harro, 2013; Johnson, 2013). For instance, when a young girl is taught over and over that women are too emotional and not good at mechanical tasks, she may begin to believe such limiting characteristics about herself. In that sense she has internalized subordination; the work of oppressive systems has been so effective that she is now subjecting *herself* to stereotypes and their consequences.

Internalized dominance functions in a similar way. If young men have internalized advantages conferred by society and ascribe resultant accomplishments to their innate abilities, then we can expect findings like those from national datasets that affirm young men overestimate their academic abilities yet achieve lower grades than women counterparts (Sax, 2008).

DEVELOPING A SOCIAL JUSTICE PROFESSIONAL IDENTITY

Developing a professional identity that is invested in fair and equitable access and utilizes democratic and reciprocal processes is core to socially just and inclusive student affairs practice. Objectively, the aim of professional competencies is growth. Yet, if framing social justice as a form of meritocracy, rewarding measurable effort with valued consequences is seductive and can be problematic (Sen, 2000). While important, professional growth and measurable proficiency towards social justice and inclusion should not overshadow personal commitment and action. Social justice and inclusion require messy, difficult, and uncomfortable moments that challenge our current paradigms and worldview (Rusch & Horsford, 2008).

In capitalist patriarchal society (hooks, 2000) where systems of oppression consistently reduce access to higher education, we must also be aware of the neoliberal context in which we operate (Giroux, 2002; Kandiko, 2010). Within the neoliberal context, educators are often required to rationalize and measure their efforts. Social justice and inclusion competencies and efforts require active evaluation and assessment; however, the call to measure and to fully realize inclusion can deter genuine efforts to learn and grow. As explained earlier, the intention of the competencies is to frame expectations and opportunities for student affairs educators to contextualize their movement toward realizing a socially just reality. If left unexamined, these competencies can produce unintended counter realities within neoliberal and postcolonial frameworks.

Blackmore (2010) argued that much of education's focus on professional development, particularly with regard to social justice, heavily relies on an imperialist/colonialist desire to study the ways of the "other" (Archer, 2003). She continues to underscore that issues of social justice work are not done without an impetus. Blackmore (2010) wrote: "Leadership for inclusion is complex, highly situated, and not readily addressed by simplistic models of leadership. Issues of social justice arise out of particular socio-cultural conditions and histories that have to be addressed" (p. 57). Student affairs educators must resist the urge to compress social justice and inclusion into reductive workshops, trainings, and measures. As educators construct their social justice competency path, they must consider both their motivation and unintended implications for progress. As educators advance through the competencies, space must be made for a sophisticated intersection of professional fluency, personal reflection, and the centering of marginalized and minoritized experiences. To support these endeavors, we recommend the following considerations as you cultivate a professional identity that centers social justice and inclusion.

1. *Critical reflection on where my personal identities fall within social identity markers and how they are implicated in a system of oppression is necessary.* The social justice and inclusion competencies provide goals for advancing one's understanding and participation in the active dismantling of systems of oppression. We caution those who aim to gamify and use these competencies for career advancement without fully realizing the enduring and complex emotional journey of social justice

advocates. Social justice leadership requires critical reflexivity and personal reflection to contemplate social location, power, and privilege; and is unique for each educator (Castellanos, Gloria, Mayorga, & Salas, 2007; Karunaratne, Koppel, & Yang, 2016; King & Howard-Hamilton, 2003; Mueller & Pope, 2001). This level of self-reflection can tax motivation, but it is required to produce environments characterized by equity and justice in student affairs and higher education.

2. *Social justice scholars and practitioners must be constantly made aware of the power and privileges they carry with their social identities (Freire, 1970; Pope & Reynolds, 2017).* Some who hold dominant social locations may discover that their privilege is pervasive, and upon self-reflection seems usual or natural (Feagin, 2001). Others, whose social identity markers lie within the margins, are likely to foreground their marginal identities and focus their reflection on negotiating the histories of their communities with the constructed narratives of those who maintain the power and privilege (King & Howard-Hamilton, 2003). The task of the marginalized and minoritized is daunting because they must reconcile distorted dominant realities with their internalized truths (Castellanos, Gloria, Mayorga, & Salas, 2007; Kirmayer, 2012).

3. *Often notions of professionalism are grounded in dominant norms that appear inevitable and reasonable.* Our professional competencies allow for a dynamic range of possibilities and articulate a shared responsibility for dismantling oppressive systems, but dominant cultural norms persist. These dominant norms subjugate the experience of black and brown, queer, trans, and other marginalized professionals, who often find their professional identity elusive (Bell & Nkomo, 2003; Jourian, Simmons, & Devaney, 2015; Rumens & Kerfoot; 2009). This subjugation is particularly clear when student affairs educators are practicing social justice work. Too often those with dominant identities who actively participate in social justice leadership are celebrated; actions they take to undermine systems of oppression are lauded as valuable, nuanced, and special while those on the margins are expected to lead social justice and inclusion efforts instinctively, and often their social justice leadership is seen as inevitable (Blackmore, 2010).

This double standard has implications for cultivating social justice competence. While a social justice professional orientation for folks with multiple privileged identities may be heralded as a preferred or "above and beyond" qualification, marginalized professionals are likely to feel an obligation to serve their local, national, and global communities. For many, their education and "competency" development around social justice has been a lifelong journey and is likely to continue outside the context of student affairs. Developing professional identity around this competency area is nuanced, complex, and emotionally demanding, for some identities more than others.

4. *Professional and personal identities are not and should not be separate.* While all competencies justify our need to measure our professional growth, we should not submit to the temptation to conceptualize personal and professional identities as distinct. Particularly with regard to social justice and inclusion work, we have a responsibility to examine where our professional responsibilities end and personal politics begin. Within the area of social justice, marginalized professionals and educators often experience this work as vital and nonnegotiable, and its implications reach far beyond the limits of a workweek.

CONCLUSION

For nearly forty years, student affairs has been a professional field of practice that recognizes the importance of multiculturalism and social justice. From earlier iterations of professional competencies that emphasized different cultural worldviews and culturally appropriate techniques to current frameworks that connect an analysis of systems of oppression to inequities in access and outcomes, the field has attempted to capture the dispositions, attitudes, skills, and knowledge necessary for ethical and effective practice. Developing competence across such comprehensive domains is a lifelong practice and requires embracing a personal and professional identity that is committed to equity and social transformation.

CASE STUDY

Your colleague Mei, who is a Chinese American woman, meets you for lunch and shares her frustration about her recent conversation with your supervisor about her annual evaluation. Mei was given feedback that she needs to begin volunteering for more projects, because she does not take as much initiative as other returning staff members. This is familiar to you because you have heard other hall directors in your department complain that Mei "doesn't work as hard," as they do. Mei is surprised and saddened at this feedback because she has provided regular updates to her supervisor in her weekly reports and in her one to ones of the many projects she is involved in, including serving as the only departmental representative on the planning and implementation committee for the woman of color leadership retreat for undergraduate students and advising two Asian American, Pacific Islander (AAPI) affinity groups on campus. Mei states, "I know this work is

important. It actually matters! But it doesn't get rewarded in our department."

Guiding Questions

1. What is the primary dilemma or issue here? Are there other variables
   and factors to consider?
2. What does this remind you of? With whom do you identify most easily (the experience of Mei, or the experiences of other hall directors)?
3. How do your identities influence how you view Mei's experience?
4. What dominant group norms are informing how hard work and initiative are defined?
5. What are immediate and long-term actions that you can take to address the issues surfaced by this case?

REFERENCES

ACPA: College Student Educators & NASPA-Student Affairs Administrators in
Higher Education. (2010). *ACPA/NASPA professional competency areas for student
affairs practitioners.* Washington, DC: Authors.

ACPA: College Student Educators & NASPA-Student Affairs Administrators in
Higher Education. (2015). *ACPA/NASPA professional competency areas for student
affairs educators.* Washington, DC: Authors.

Association of American Colleges & Universities. (2018a). *VALUE.* http://www.aacu
.org/value.

Association of American Colleges & Universities. (2018b). *Intercultural knowledge
and competence VALUE rubrics.* http: www.aacu.org/value/rubrics/intercultural
-knowledge.

Archer, L. (2003). *Race, masculinity, and schooling: Muslim boys and education.*
Maidenhead, England: Open University Press.

Arredondo, P., Toporek, R., Brown, S. P., Jones, J., Locke, D., Sanchez, J., & Stadler,
H. (1996). Operationalization of the multicultural counseling competencies.
Journal of Multicultural Counseling and Development, 24, 42–78.

Bell, E. & Nkomo, S. M. (2003). Our separate ways: Black and white women and
the struggle for professional identity. *The Diversity Factor, 11*(1), 11–15.

Bell, L. A. (2013). Theoretical foundations. In M. Adams, W. J. Blumenfeld, C.
Castaneda, H. Hackman, M. Peters, & X. Zuniga (Eds.), *Readings for diversity and
social justice* (3rd ed., pp. 21–26). New York, NY: Routledge.

Bell, L. A. (2016). Theoretical foundations for social justice. In M. Adams & L. A.
Bell (Eds.), *Teaching for diversity and social justice* (3rd ed., pp. 3–26). New York,
NY: Routledge.

Blackmore, J. (2010). 'The other within': Race/gender disruptions to the professional learning of white educational leaders. *International Journal of Leadership in
Education, 13*(1), 45–61.

Bennett, J. M. (2008). Transformative training: Designing programs for culture learning. In M. A. Moodian (Ed.), *Contemporary leadership and intellectual competence: Understanding and utilizing cultural diversity to build successful organizations* (pp. 95–110). Thousand Oaks, CA: Sage.

Bresciani, M. J., Swen, A., Hickmott, J., & Monzon, R. (2010, March). Expectations of SSAOs and Faculty for Entry-level Professionals. A concurrent session conducted at the National Association of Student Personnel Personnel Administrators (NASPA) National Conference, Chicago, IL.

Burkard, A. W., Cole, D. C., Ott, M., & Stoflet, T. (2005). Entry-level competencies of new student affairs professionals: A delphi study. *NASPA Journal, 42*(3), 283–309. doi:10.2022/1949-6605.1509?src=recsys.

Castellanos, J., Gloria, A. M., Mayorga, M., & Salas, C. (2007). Student affairs professionals' self report on multicultural competence: Understanding awareness, knowledge, and skills. *NASPA Journal, 44,* 64–663.

Chhachhi, A. (2011). Interview with Nancy Fraser. *Development and Change, 42*(1), 297–314.

Cheatham, H. E. (1991). *Cultural pluralism on campus.* Alexandria, VA: ACPA Media.

Constantine, M. G., Hage, S. M., Kindaichi, M. M., & Bryant, R. M. (2007). Social justice and multicultural issues: Implications for the practice and training of counselors and counseling psychologists. *Journal of Counseling and Development, 85,* 24–29. doi:10.1022/j.1556-6678.2007.+b00440.x

Constantine, M. G., & Ladany, N. (2000). Self-report multicultural counseling competency scales: Their relation to social desirability attitudes and multicultural case conceptualization abilities. *Journal of Counseling Psychology, 47,* 155–164.

Cuyjet, M. J., Longwell-Grie, R., & Molina, E. (2009). Perceptions of new student affairs professionals and their supervisors regarding the application of competencies learned in preparation programs. *Journal of College Student Development, 50,* 104–119.

Dickerson, A. M., Hoffman, J., Anan, B. P., Brown, K. F., Vong, L. K., Bresciani, M. J. Monzon, R., & Oyler, J. (2011). Comparison of senior student affairs officers and student affairs preparatory program faculty expectations of entry level professionals' competency. *Journal of Student Affairs Research and Practice, 48*(4), 463–479. Doi:10.2202/1949-6605.6270.

Feagin, J. R. (2001). *Racist America: Roots, current realities, and future reparations.* New York: NY: Routledge.

Fraser, N. (1997). *Justice interruptus: Critical reflections on the "postsocialist" condition.* New York, NY: Routledge.

Freire, P. (1970). Cultural action for freedom. *The Harvard Educational Review Monographs, 1,* 1–12.

Giroux, H. (2002). Neoliberalism, corporate culture, and the promise of higher education: The university as a democratic public sphere. *Harvard Educational Review, 72*(4), 425–464.

Hardiman, R., Jackson, B., & Griffin, P. (2007). Conceptual foundations for social justice education. In M. Adams, L.A. Bell, & P. Griffin (Eds.), *Teaching for diversity and social justice* (2nd ed., pp. 35–66). New York: Routledge.

Harro, B. (2013). The cycle of socialization. In M. Adams, W. J. Blumenfeld, C. Castañeda, H. W. Hackman, M. L. Peters, & X. Zúñiga (Eds.), *Readings for diversity and social justice* (3rd ed., pp. 45–52). New York: Routledge.

Herdlein, R. J., III. (2004). Survey of chief student affairs housing officers regarding relevancy of graduate preparation of new professionals. *NASPA Journal, 42*(1), 51–71. doi:10.2202/1949-6605.1414?src=recysys.

Herdlein, R. J., III, Riefler, L., & Mrowka, K. (2013). An integrative literature review of student affairs competencies: A meta-analysis. *Journal of Student Affairs Research and Practice, 50*(3), 250–269. doi:10.1515/jsarp-2013-0019.

Hooks, B. (2000). *Feminist theory: From margin to center.* Cambridge, MA: South End Press.

Howard-Hamilton, M. F., Richardson, B. J., & Shuford, B. (1998). Promoting multicultural education: A holistic approach. *College Student Affairs Journal, 18*(1), 5–17.

Janosik, S. M., Carpenter, S., & Creamer, D. G. (2006). Intentional professional development: Feedback from student affairs professionals. *NASPA Journal, 44*(1), 127–146.

Johnson, A. G. (2013). The social construction of difference. In M. Adams, W. J. Blumenfeld, C. Castañeda, H. W. Hackman, M. L. Peters, & X. Zúñiga (Eds.), *Readings for diversity and social justice* (3rd ed., pp. 15–21). New York: Routledge.

Johnson, J. R. (2013). Cisgender privilege, intersectionality, and the criminalization of CeCe McDonald: Why intercultural communication needs transgender studies. *Journal of International and Intercultural Communication, 6*(2), 135–144.

Jourian, T. J., Simmons, S. L., & Devaney, K. C. (2015). "We are not expected": Trans* educators (re)claiming space and voice in higher education and student affairs. *Transgender Studies Quarterly, 2*(3), 431–446.

Kandiko, C. B. (2010). Neoliberalism in higher education: A comparative approach. *International Journal of Arts and Sciences, 3*(14), 153–175.

Karunaratne, N. D., Koppel, L., & Yang, C. (2016). Navigating a social justice motivation and praxis as student affairs professionals. *Journal of Critical Scholarship on Higher Education and Student Affairs, 3*(1), 1–19.

King, P. M., & Howard-Hamilton, M. (2003) Becoming a multiculturally competent student affairs professional. *NASPA Journal, 40*(2), 26–28.

Kirmayer, L. J. (2012). Rethinking cultural competence. *Transcultural Psychiatry, 49*(2), 149–164.

Kuh, L., Cobb, B., & Forrest, C. S. (2008). Perceptions of competencies of entry-level practitioners in student affairs. *NASPA Journal, 44*(4), 664–691. doi: 10.2202/1949-6605.1863?src=recsys.

Linder, C., & Cooper, D. L. (2016). From cultural competence to critical consciousness: Creating inclusive campus environments. In M. J. Cuyjet, C. Linder, M. F. Howard-Hamilton, & D. L. Cooper (Eds.), *Multiculturalism on campus: Theory, models, and practices for understanding diversity and creating inclusion* (pp. 379–392). Sterling, VA: Stylus Publishing.

Love, B. (2013). Developing a liberatory consciousness. In M. Adams, W. J. Blumenfeld, C. Castañeda, H. Hackman, M. Peters, & X. Zúñiga (Eds.), *Readings for diversity and social justice* (3rd ed., pp. 601–605). New York: Routledge.

Lovell, C. D., & Kosten, L. A., (2000). Skills, knowledge, and personal traits necessary for success as a student affairs administrator: A meta-analysis of thirty years of research. *NASPA Journal, 37*(4), 535–572. doi:10.2202/1949-6605.1118.

Lynch, K., & Baker, J. (2005). Equality in education: An equality of condition perspective. *Theory and Research in Education, 3,* 131–164.

Mueller, J. A., & Pope, R. L. (2001). The relationship between multicultural competence and White racial consciousness among student affairs practitioners. *Journal of College Student Development, 42,* 133–144.

Pope, R. L., & Reynolds, A. L. (1997). Student affairs core competencies: Integrating multicultural awareness, knowledge, and skills. *Journal of College Student Development, 38*(3), 266–277.

Pope, R. L., & Reynolds, A. L. (2017). Multidimensional Identity Model Revisited: Implications for Student Affairs. *New Directions for Student Services, 157,* 15–24.

Pope, R. L., Reynolds, A. L., & Muller, J. A. (2004). *Multicultural competency in student affairs.* San Francisco, CA: Jossey-Bass.

Pope, R. L., Reynolds, A. L., & Muller, J. A. (2014). *Creating multicultural changes on campus.* San Francisco, CA: Jossey-Bass.

Ratts, M. J., Singh, A. A., Nassar-McMillian, D., Bulter, S. K., & McCullough, J. R. (2015). *Multicultural and Social Justice Counseling Competencies.* Retrieved from http://www.counseling.org/knowledge-center/competences

Rawls, J. (1999). A theory of justice. Cambridge, MA: Harvard University Press.

Renn, K. A., & Hodges, J. (2007). The first year in the job: Experiences of new professionals in student affairs. *NASPA Journal, 44*(2), 367–391. doi:10.2022/1949-66025.1800

Rumens, N., & Kerfoot, D. (2009). Gay men at work: (Re)constructing the self as professional. *Human Relations, 62*(5), 763–786.

Rusch, E. A., & Horsford, S. D. (2008). Unifying messy communities: Learning social justice in educational leadership classrooms. *Teacher Development, 12*(4), 353–367.

Sax, L. (2008). Her college experience is not his. *The Chronicle of Higher Education, 55*(5), A32–33.

Sen, A. (2000). Merit and justice. In K. Arrow, S. Bowles, & S. Durlauf (Eds.), *Meritocracy and economic inequality* (pp. 5–16). Princeton, NJ: Princeton University Press.

Sue, D. W., Arredondo, P., & McDavis, R. J. (1992). Multicultural counseling competencies and standards: A call to the profession. *Journal of Counseling and Development, 70,* 477–486.

Sue, D. W., Bernier, J. E., Durran, A., Feinberg, L., Pedersen, P., & Smith, E. J. (1982). Position paper: Cross cultural counseling competencies. *The Counseling Psychologists, 10,* 545–552.

Tatum, B. D. (2013). The complexity of identity: "Who am I?". In M. Adams, W. J. Blumenfeld, C. Castañeda, H. W. Hackman, M. L. Peters, & X. Zúñiga (Eds.), *Readings for diversity and social justice* (3rd ed., pp. 6–9). New York, NY: Routledge.

Waple, J. N. (2006). An assessment of skills and competency necessary for entry level student affairs work. *NASPA Journal, 43*(1), 1–8. doi:10.2022/1949-6605 .1568

Wijeyesinghe, C. (2016). Editor's notes. Student Services, 2017: 5–13. doi:10.1002 /ss.20204

Young, D. G., & Janosik, S. M. (2007). Using CAS standards to measure learning outcomes of student affairs preparation programs. *NASPA Journal, 44*(2), 341–366. doi:10.2202/1949-6605.1799

Young, I. M. (1990). *Justice and the politics of difference.* Princeton, NJ: Princeton University Press.

Young, I. M. (2013). Five faces of oppression. In M. Adams, W. J. Blumenfeld, C. Castañeda, H. W. Hackman, M. L. Peters, & X. Zúñiga (Eds.), *Readings for diversity and social justice* (3rd ed., pp. 35–45). New York: Routledge.

Chapter 3

HISTORICAL DEVELOPMENT OF MULTICULTURALISM AND DIVERSITY IN STUDENT AFFAIRS PRACTICE

Nichole Margarita Garcia & Rebeca Mireles-Rios

INTRODUCTION

Our story does not begin with ourselves, but rather our Chicano fathers. Our first exposure and entryway into higher education was through their lens as student affairs educators. Garcia's father was the Director of the Center for Multicultural Student Affairs at a four-year, research-intensive predominately white institution. Mireles-Rios's father was a counselor, instructor, and the Director of the Transfer Center at a two-year Hispanic-Serving Institution. As Chicano administrators, our fathers had different experiences, but one commonality is that they served first-generation, underrepresented, and/or low-income students and were routinely tasked with issues of multiculturalism and diversity on their respective campuses.

As Chicanas, we are aware that we would not be here were it not for student activism and equity initiatives that catalyzed change for our fathers and ourselves. An example is the 1960s Chicana/o Student Movement which opened the doors to many Mexican Americans to attend and work in higher education. As junior faculty who examine race and equity at four-year, research-intensive institutions, our professional and personal lives are tasked with how to respond to "diversity" and "multiculturalism" with the changing demographics of the United States. Yet when we refer to "diversity" or "multiculturalism," what do we mean in the higher education context?

Thelin and Gasman (2003) identify the "The Dilemma of Diversity" as emerging in the 20th century after the end of the Civil War and the passage of the Morrill Acts (1862 & 1890) "to serve the statewide public, with enrollment at typical large campuses reaching fifteen thousand to twenty-five thousand" (p. 10). With the expansion of higher education, institutions were met with a variety of student populations and lacked resources to meet these student needs. Thelin and Gasman (2003) explain, "American higher education's capacity to provide access ran ahead of its ability to foster assimilation and parity within the campus. The result was a complex dilemma for campus officials and policy analysts: how best to serve minority groups and new participants in higher education" (p. 10). To date, we are still concerned with how to serve new participants in higher education. In this chapter, we argue that "diversity" and "multiculturalism" are not ahistorical. In fact, "diversity" and "multiculturalism" are ever-evolving.

For this chapter, we are most concerned with this evolution of inclusive and exclusive practices of specific groups and cultures across different institutional types from the 19th to 21st century. The *Merriam-Webster Dictionary* defines diversity and multiculturalism as the following:

- *Diversity: the condition of having or being composed of different elements: the inclusion of different types of people (such as a people of different races or cultures) in a group or organization.*
- *Multiculturalism: of, relating to, reflecting, or adapted to diverse cultures.*

Aligned with the definition of diversity as it pertains to organizations, we will equate our "organizations" to institutions of higher education and "groups" to those individuals that organize to serve, work, or attend institutions of higher education. From this framing, we view multiculturalism as how institutions are adapting to "diverse cultures" rather than assuming that diversity and multiculturalism are one in the same. Current notions of diversity and multiculturalism are strongly associated with racial and ethnic groups while being devoid of historical context. In this chapter, we turn to Geiger's (2011) eras in U.S. higher education history and adapt them to be inclusive of major turns of diversity, multiculturalism, and student affairs: Colonial Colleges (1600–1850), New Departures (1850–1945), and the Academic Revolution (1945–1975). As Geiger (2011) argues, "the character of American higher education has perceptibly shifted in each generation, or approximately every thirty years. The exploration of these successive generations is intended to illuminate these historical dynamics, as well as the underlying processes of which they are composed" (p. 37). Within these historical shifts, diversity and multiculturalism have had and continue to hold various meanings and implications.

We argue that the era of Colonial Colleges (1600-1850) posed historical challenges in diversifying institutions by restricting access to higher education to only white, male Christians. However, that does not mean diversity and multiculturalism were absent from these establishments. In fact, these institutions would ultimately set the stage—as they were some of the first to respond—for approaching diversity and multiculturalism in the wake of inclusionary or exclusionary practices based on gender, race, ethnicity, religion and class. The era of New Departures (1850–1945) shifted college access to include women, which would create change and set the stage for diversity, multiculturalism, and the development of student affairs. The era of the Academic Revolution (1945-2000s) would involve the Civil Rights Movement, which would change institutions of higher education across the nation.

Centuries later in 2010, College Student Educators International (ACPA) and Student Affairs Administrators in Higher Education (NASPA) collaborated to develop the *Professional Competency Areas for Student Affairs Educators* to assist practitioners with the knowledge, skills, and abilities to develop into holistic professionals. Two of the 10 key competency areas identified were: "history, philosophy, and values" and "equity, diversity, and inclusion."[1] The goal of the "history, philosophy, and values" area is to "[ensure] that our present and future practices are informed by an understanding of the profession's history, philosophy, and values" (p. 12). The goal of "equity, diversity, and inclusion" is "to create learning environments that foster equitable participation of all groups while seeking to address and acknowledge issues of oppression, privilege, and power" (p. 14). Considering these two competency areas, we provide a case study of the 1960s Chicana/o Student Movement to pose questions regarding diversity and multiculturalism.

The 1960s Chicana/o Student Movement is seldom examined in student affairs. As a movement occurring mainly in the Southwest, it elucidates the spectrum of "history, philosophy, and values" and "equity, diversity, and inclusion" on college campuses to analyze campus climate, institutional response, and culturally sustaining practices for student affairs educators. As an example, the movement demonstrates how student-led movements can diversify campuses for students and student affairs educators. We conclude with recommendations by looking to minority-serving institutions, which are often overlooked in meeting multicultural and diversity initiatives and which allow student affairs educators to view laws, policies, and programs that work towards social justice aims.

COLONIAL COLLEGES (1600–1850): DIVERSITY IN UNKNOWN PLACES

Thelin (2004) argues that colleges and universities are actually historical institutions. We could not agree more with this sentiment. As institutions of

---

1. This is now called, "Social Justice and Inclusion."

higher education are sites of history, it is important to understand how the creation of student affairs came to be and which professionals were the first to serve and answer the call of inclusionary or exclusionary acts in student affairs practices. The connection between the colonial colleges, diversity, and multiculturalism is a point of exploration because it is the origin of how student affairs came to be. Long (2012) argues, "the roots of the student affairs profession reach all the way back to the colonial era and the earliest years of American higher education" (p. 3). The colonial colleges, the start of American higher education, were established in the Thirteen Colonies before the American Revolution. Modeled after Oxford and Cambridge, colonial colleges—Harvard College, College of William and Mary, Yale University, and Princeton (The College of New Jersey)—set the context of American higher education. Later followed in various colonies by Columbia, Brown, Dartmouth, Rutgers, and the University of Pennsylvania, these institutions would establish the colonial elite. We examine the era of colonial colleges in the 19th century with a lens attuned to diversity and multiculturalism in the wake of the New World. Specifically, in what ways did diversity and multiculturalism exist in the face of colonial revivalism during the creation of American higher education?

Religion, Social Class, Diversity and Colonial Colleges

For the colonial colleges and the shaping of American higher education, one of the first indicators of documented diversity was based on exclusionary acts regarding religious affiliation and social class. For example, New World Puritans, specifically Congregationalists and Presbyterians, strategically created the colonial Harvard, Yale, and Princeton because these men were at odds with the Church of England. To ensure their sons would not have to pledge an oath to the monarch and Church of England like their Oxford predecessors, Puritans quickly established institutions to fit their family backgrounds (Thelin, 2004). Thelin (2004) states, "the early collegians were sons of privilege who at the same time were expected to inherit grave responsibilities as leaders and men of influence in a new world where their religion was central and not subject to government or ecclesiastical constraints" (p. 24). This would model the ideal student who gained access into colonial colleges as white, male, and Christian. In other colonial areas such as Virginia, similar sentiments would be fostered to expand what would become known as the colonial elite. All interests centered on social reproduction and religious affiliations tied to the future male leaders of respective colonies.

Therefore, social class mattered, as attending a colonial college was a marker of class. Within the colonial college, markers of class were evident, even among homogenous populations. For example, students were listed by last name and family rank rather than by alphabetical order, as we know today. Clothing also served as a marker by having academic robes signifying social class. Thelin (2004) points to "commoners" versus "servitors" in student populations. Commoners dined in the common areas and were identified by long robes, whereas, servitors were on scholarship, wore short robes, and served the commoners. The intersections of colonial colleges and those who attended them created the crux of American higher education: privileged white Christian males.

While this is not the diversity we may know today, we can see that during the formation of colonial colleges, religious and social class diversity were important. Yet a lack of multiculturalism existed. It seems that due to the era and ability to create new institutions, when religion and social class became points of contention, marginalized groups created new spaces. What is clear is that eligible students attending colonial colleges were not poor, women, or people of color, thus creating indefinite historical challenges to implement diversity and have institutions of higher education respond to multiculturalism.

Race and Ethnic Diversity and Colonial Colleges

Race and ethnicity ran rampant during colonial revivalism as social constructions were employed to create a hierarchy of inferior versus superior human beings. We do not conflate race and ethnicity as Garcia and Mayorga (2018) have argued, "race is an objective condition that falsely generalizes and stereotypes skin color, or any other biological marker that society understands as race to explain phenotypic differences (Zamudio, Russell, Rios, & Ridgeman, 2011). Ethnicity is used to categorize individuals that share a common cultural heritage, such as language, rituals, nationality, and geographic units" (p. 13). At the time, slavery was still a legal practice, treating Africans as property rather than contributing laborers or knowledge holders of society. Due in larger part to their societal positioning, Black individuals we ultimately denied access into the colonial colleges. However, there was keen interest in "civilizing" American Indian populations thorough educational programs.

The intersection of colonial colleges, religion, and philanthropy created a perfect storm for white Christians who wished to save what they had deemed as "savages," also known as American Indian students. Philanthropists were concerned with "civilizing" and converting American Indians to Christianity through "programs designed to provide a Christian education to those they considered to be savages. Colonial colleges were available, appropriate vehicle to administer such funds to carry out these charitable programs" (Thelin,

2004, p. 15). Colonial colleges served as the perfect medium to create such "Americanization" programs as they were keen on religion, which supported the beliefs of philanthropists who would allocate funds to conduct such practices. Students attending colonial colleges were also given scholarships and professional opportunities if they conducted missionary work to assist in the development and implementation of American Indian student programs.

In this vein, diversifying was not in the interest of American Indian students because it was not inclusive of their culture or group identity. Wright (1991) quotes Robert Gray, an American explorer, "[I]t is not the nature of men, but the education of men which makes them barbarous and uncivil, and therefore change the education of men, and you shall see their nature will be greatly rectified and corrected" (p. 430). Colonial colleges were not demonstrating multiculturalism because they were not adapting culture of American Indian students, rather they were forcibly assimilating them. This is an example of how "diversity" can be used as tool to allocate funds at the expense of a population of color for the interest of an institution, its donors, and its leaders. Wright (1991) makes this connection abundant as he describes:

> Indeed, enterprising colonists and their English benefactors advanced a loftier design to bring higher learning—the 'benefits' of the class liberal arts education to illiterate 'savages.' The 'pious' plan was to educate selected Indians as schoolmasters and preachers, who would then assist the work of conversion among their people. In fact, within a decade of Jamestown 1607 founding, the English had already unfolded plans for an Indian college. (p. 431)

The point of diversity and multiculturalism as it related to race and ethnicity in this era was to assimilate populations to the standards and views of white, male Christians. Other notions outside of the colonial elite were not accepted and considered a threat.

Student Resistance, Diversity and Colonial Colleges

The colonial colleges did not lack student resistance. When students felt dissatisfied and institutions failed to meet their needs, they made it a point to resist since they were not romanticizing the "collegiate way." Long (2012) argues that at the time, student affairs educators or services were not necessarily as established as they are today. Faculty served within these roles, as there was no separation of academic or social roles to serve students. Faculty were tasked with training students academically and socially. Faculty's duty was to focus on the moral development of students to ensure they were equipped with the skills to become future leaders. Long (2012) states:

> The doctrine of in *loco parentis* (literally 'in place of the parent') . . . faculty serve[d] as live-in teachers who supervised the students in the dormitories and dining halls as well as in the classrooms. The faculty developed rules and regulations that governed students' behavior, conduct, and dress, and they enforced college rules and expectations even when students were not on college premises. (p. 3)

Displeasure among students manifested, ranging from complaints of food to not having the ability to exercise personal autonomy. In the 1700s, student, faculty, and administration conflict were at an all-time high due the American Revolution (Peckham, 1967). Student resistance also was enacted as political views shifted between older and younger generations.

During the 19th century in the colonial colleges, diversity and multiculturalism meant religious and class diversity rather than race and ethnic diversity. Diversity and multiculturalism as they are commonly referenced today really began once access was granted to those that did not fit the normalized student profile in the colonial era. In fact, Thelin (2004) found that there is no record of women graduating from the colonial colleges; it would not be until the 1800s that student affairs would emerge with the expansion of higher education institutions and the creation of deanships and student personnel.

NEW DEPARTURES (1850–1945): THE BIRTH OF STUDENT AFFAIRS THROUGH DIVERSITY

As higher education expanded, institutions were met with diversity and the obligation of multiculturalism. When women gained access to higher education, positions were created to help them assist students. As a field of practice, student affairs would emerge to answer student demands and relieve faculty of the social obligations related to students at the institutional level. In this era, women deanships would be diversity and multiculturalism's first step toward inclusion of other groups and coeducation. Diversity and multiculturalism in this era of student affairs meant gender and limited instances of race and ethnicity.

Deanships, Diversity, and Multiculturalism

The Civil War and Morrill Acts (1862 & 1890) would expand higher education to be inclusive of more than just white Christian males. Geiger (2017) states, "More than forty women's institutions were chartered to offer collegiate degrees before Matthew Vassar presumed to give women 'a college in the proper sense of the word' Ashmun Institute (Lincoln University, 1854) in

Pennsylvania and Wilberforce University (1856) in Ohio provided college education for free African Americans" (p. 50).

What we know today as student affairs dates to the 1800s as deanships were created to assist the development of students in the interest of the institutions. Much of the history of student affairs in the 19th and 20th centuries focuses on autobiographies of individuals in leadership positions (Hevel, 2016; Schwartz, 1997, 1998, 2010). These leadership positions also assisted in creating diversity for institutions at a national level.

Hevel (2016) categorizes the history of student affairs into positions and practice, professionalizing, and problems. "Positions and practice" refer to the first established administrative positions that held esteem and the roles of these individuals in higher education settings. "Professionalizing" refers to how individual leaders who held administrative positions established and pushed for the field of student affairs. Finally, "Problems" refers to the ways in which individuals within early administrative positions experienced sexism, racism and homophobia (Hevel, 2016, p. 845). These categories are helpful in examining diversity and multiculturalism because they provide insight into how institutions were becoming more diverse and adapting to multiculturalism through student affairs practices when challenges arose.

"Positions and practice" assisted in initiating gender diversity and the creation of student affairs administrators in the form of deanships. Deanships were to assume responsibility over the disciplining of students. Hevel (2016) explains, "these positions originated as college presidents and faculty members became less interested in monitoring students at the same time that coeducation spread, generating public concern that such monitoring was never more important" (p. 847). Nidiffer (2001) argues that it was Dean of Women positions that helped the Dean of Men to experience success. Practices assigned to the positions included monitoring student housing, maintaining health records of the students, leading student government, and providing resources to assist with financial aid or campus jobs. It is important to note that not all Dean of Men and Women enacted these practices as it depended on the college and the amount of power they were given in their positions. For these reasons, the Deans of Men and Women were often viewed as disciplinarians.

Professionalism would pave the way for membership organization, research, and graduate preparation programs. In 1882, Freeman and Talbot founded the Association of Collegiate Alumnae (ACA), which would later become known as the American Association of University Women. In 1922 the National Association of Deans of Women (NADW) would facilitate a national move towards professionalizing Dean of Women positions and advancing women in higher education. Dean of Men positions would follow by organizing the National Association of Dean of Men (NADM), which would become known as the National Association of Student Personnel Administration (NASPA) in 1952. NASPA and the National Association of Appointment Secretaries (NAAS), established in 1924, would become the leading organizations of student affairs practice today. While student affairs "positions and practice" would lead to professionalizing the field, this would not occur without its problems. It is within the "problems" of the field that diversity and multiculturalism are identified further.

The first Dean of Women was Alice Freeman Palmer at the University of Chicago and her successor was Marion Talbot (Duffy, 2010). Together they founded the American Association of University Women, which would be a significant contribution to gender diversity in higher education institutions across the nation to this day. While gender diversity increased, the ways in which multiculturalism was handled in institutions varied. The process of becoming Dean of Women meant that many of the women faced sexism from men while also enduring stricter controls, such as being forced to live on campus to keep an eye on the students, while the men had the freedom to live outside of campus.

It would take two decades after Alice Freeman Palmer for African Americans to hold the same positions. With the first Morrill Act (1860) and the end of the Civil War (1865), African Americans gained access into American higher education by the establishment of Historically Black Colleges and Universities (HBCU) such as Howard University. In 1922 Lucy Diggs Slowe was the first African American woman to serve as Dean of Women at Howard University. Unlike white women deans, Diggs would encounter sexism and racism. Diggs's colleagues would often forbid her to join their meetings regardless of her title as Dean of Women. When the Dean of Women would have their annual National Association of Deans of Women conference, Diggs would often be relegated to a segregated hotel and then left to enter the host hotel through the back entrance. This set the context of what kind of diversity was acceptable. Diversity and multiculturalism were inclusive of white women deans at specific institutions, yet at the same time the women who occupied these positions were unwilling to expand their notion of racial diversity.

Student Personnel Movement and Diversity

Walter Dill Scott, the 10th president of Northwestern in 1920, would be foundational in establishing student affairs as a profession and field. He earned a PhD in Educational Administration and Psychology in Germany, and he began to teach at Northwestern upon returning to the United States in the early 1900s. Advancing to full professor quickly, he had taken several jobs outside the university to assist in the "psychology of salesmanship and applied psychological tests and measurements to business" (Schwartz, 1997,

p. 25). After World War I ended, he was elected the president of the American Psychological Association and became the president of Northwestern. In his new roles, he began to consider changes in the institution regarding leadership and faculty roles, responsibilities, and how to best serve students (Biddix & Schwartz, 2012).

Having prior experience implementing personnel psychology in the U.S. Army and gaining recognition for his accomplishments, he applied his experience to higher education. Instead of maintaining the gendered dean positions, he created a personnel office. As Schwartz (1997) states, "the personnel office would address enrollment management issues, help increase student satisfaction through the assessment of student needs, and even aid in the job placement of students after graduation" (p. 25). This new approach was a way to evaluate the needs of students so that they could reach their full potential and become active contributors to society.

Personnel psychology was a way to account for each student's characteristics, needs, and development on large or small campuses. Birthed out of the Student Personnel Movement in 1924, the NAAS was established as a leading organization for student affairs practice. In addition, The American Council on Education (ACE) appointed a committee to study student personnel practices in colleges and universities. In 1937, George Zook, head of ACE, published the *Student Personnel Point of View*. The report would document the importance of considering students "as a whole" and was the first to outline the basic functions of student personnel professionals. In 1949, revisions to the document included focus on student growth and development, administration, organizing and governance issues, and development of graduate study for student personnel practitioners. Similar to the deanships, in the Student Personnel Movement, gender diversity was of importance. As personnel offices were predominately run by men, it became clear that there was a need in coeducation to meet the specific demand and concerns of women students in American higher education. At Northwestern, under the advisement of Walter Dill Scott and L.B. Hopkins, gender diversity started with the appointment of Esther McDonald in their personnel department as the "first assistant director for women" (Schwartz, 1997, p. 26).

Overall, diversity in this era was primarily focused on gender, and institutions were undertaking multiculturalism by adapting to an expansion of higher education and coeducation. Due to the wide expansion of institutions, it is a difficult task to capture all diversity and how institutions were adapting to the multiculturalism at the time. However, it is evident that race was not an inclusive priority in this era. Often student affairs practitioners of color were restricted to their practice in their respective race-based institutions and at the national level encountered racist attitudes and perceptions. In the next section, we provide pivotal moments that not only contributed to the expansion of higher education, but that actually bolstered diversity and multiculturalism in these settings.

ACADEMIC REVOLUTION (1945–PRESENT): DIVERSITY TO MEAN DIFFERENT THINGS FOR STUDENT AFFAIRS

Geiger (2011) extends Jencks and Reisman's notion of the Academic Revolution from 1945–1975. He argues, "The thirty years following the end of World War II are possibly the most tumultuous in [the] history of American higher education. Two fundamental movements nevertheless underlie these myriad developments: expansion and academic standardization" (p. 59). We agree and extend the time period to the present day, as diversity and multiculturalism remain in constant flux. Along with diversity and multiculturalism, student affairs has had to adapt and meet the needs of various institutional types and students. Therefore, in this section we focus on The Servicemen's Readjustment Act of 1944, which we argue *expanded higher education,* and The Civil Rights Movement, which in turn *diversified higher education* to address issues of race and ethnicity. We also examine the impact the act has had on student affairs practice. While these acts or laws were intended to be inclusive of marginalized populations, at times, exclusionary acts were practiced due to the national climate of the United States.

Post-World War II, the United States government was contemplating how to best adapt veterans to civilian life (Rumann & Hamrick, 2009). On January 10, 1944, the American Legion's national commander, Harry W. Colmery, put forth The Serviceman's Readjustment Act, commonly known as the GI Bill. Unpopular among the Senate because it would provide access to American higher education, unemployment benefits, and homeownership to veterans, which were widely inaccessible to the average American at the time, it passed on June 12 and was put into law on June 22, 1944 by President Franklin D. Roosevelt (Olson, 1973). The Servicemen's Readjustment Act of 1944 would open the doors of higher education to returning veterans, which resulted in overwhelming numbers of enrollment on college campuses. The increase in college enrollment due to the GI Bill would lead to diverse student populations with various class backgrounds, religious beliefs, and ages. Student affairs was focused on servicing a new population, veterans, and at the same time welcoming new students who were from working class backgrounds (Rumann & Hamrick, 2009). However, returning veterans that were men of color often encountered challenges when seeking to utilize their benefits. This was due to the racial climate of the United States, which was vastly segregated. Black men who wished to enter institutions of higher education were often met with challenges. Herbold (1994) makes this distinction as she states, "The bill broke down class lines in higher education, but inequities of race remained more difficult to dislodge. Although in the abstract the government would pay tuition, that was of little help to blacks who could not enter college, either because of overcrowding at black colleges or inadequate preparation for college-level work" (p. 106). In this context, on college campuses diversity and multiculturalism did not mean people of color received equitable benefits when it came to the GI Bill and American higher education.

To be treated as equal, African Americans spearheaded the Civil Rights Movement in the 1950s to the late 1960s. The goal of the Civil Rights Movement was for African Americans, and more broadly people of color, to gain equitable rights under United States law by ending segregation and discrimination. As one of the largest grassroots movements in the United States, activist groups widely used non-violent and civil disobedience methods to protest for legal and social change. *Overturning Plessy v. Ferguson* (1896), the *Brown v. Board of Education of Topeka* decision stated, "separate educational facilities are inherently unequal" and was one of the first to impact the local, national, and federal government levels (Martin, 1998). It also would ignite other movements, acts, and laws. This was a victory of the Civil Rights Movement, which allowed students of color to gain access into institutions of higher education that they were once legally barred from attending. While by law this court decision banned "separate but equal," it did not prevent de facto segregation in places such as the South. Student affairs would have to adapt to desegregation, but every institution had its own processes. It is important to revisit one of the original points as to the establishment of student affairs. Nuss (2003) argues, "student affairs was originally founded to support the academic mission of the college, and one of the characteristic strengths of American higher education is the diversity among the missions of these institutions" (pp. 65–66). As such, depending on the mission of the university, diversifying in terms of race and ethnicity would take rather longer than expected. Today, student affairs still finds itself in the same predicament. One driving force to resolve the dilemma of diversity and institutional change has been led by student activists at the height of the Civil Rights Movement.

The Free Speech Movement was enacted at the University of California, Berkeley and by Students for a Democratic Society. Influenced by the Civil Rights Movement and the Vietnam War, it was considered the first massive act of civil disobedience in higher education; students challenged the ways in which American higher education was determining their ability to exercise their rights of free speech and academic freedom (Cohen & Zelnik, 2002). Graduate students engaged in civil disobedience. Geiger (2011) states, "the momentum of the academic revolution was checked. The university's relation to its students was profoundly altered from paternalism to exaggerated permissiveness" (p. 61). This shift demonstrates a strict end to what the colonial colleges had established as *loco parentis,* transitioning into students acting on their own behalf. Student affairs would have to adapt to student demands at their respective institutions, which would also help grow student affairs positions to meet the needs of diverse student bodies.

Affirmative Action, also a byproduct of the Civil Rights Movement, was established to provide equal opportunity for people of color, women, and other marginalized groups (Ball, 2000). The 14th Amendment (1868), stating all individuals born in the United States are to be considered citizens and provided equal protection under law, would set the foundation for Affirmative Action. President John Kennedy would be the first to refer to "Affirmative Action" when he issued Executive Order 10925 in 1961. Its main function was to eliminate discrimination in employment practices and public spaces. The *Regents of the University of California v. Bakke* would be the benchmark case in higher education to implement race in college admissions. Specifically, it granted the institution "race" based incentives and a quota system. Alongside Affirmative Action, the Higher Education Act of 1965 would lead to the establishment of Title IV (1972) which would make it illegal to discriminate based on sex or deny access into any education program or federal financial aid services. Following Title IV, the Rehabilitation Act of 1973 provided services to individuals with disabilities in health, education, and social welfare. All these acts and laws helped promote diversity and multiculturalism in higher education and student affairs as a professional field.

The impact the Civil Rights Movement had on student affairs educators and student interactions is twofold. First, it ended *loco parentis* and gave rise to students' legal rights and second, senior student affairs administrators finally became part of the president's cabinet (Gaston-Gayles, Wolf-Wendel, Tuttle, Twombly, & Ward, 2005). Gaston-Gayles et al. (2005) found eight roles that student affairs educators engaged during the Civil Rights era: disciplinarian, advocate, mentor, friend, educator, mediator, initiator, and change agent. By following these roles, professionals found various ways to build student relationships. As previously stated, student affairs emerged out of institutional missions, so the general expectation of these professionals was to address student issues while maintaining peace. Also, it was student affairs professionals' responsibility to help maintain a positive image of institutions of higher education through handling and managing the students. Due to the disciplinarian role, it was difficult for the student affairs educators to play the advocate, mentor, and friend roles, as they wanted to assist the students but also abide by policies of their respective institutions.

Student affairs educators, when engaged in the educator role, helped students use their agency and leverage their voices to be heard effectively by having them address their main concerns and create sustainable solutions. As student affairs educators acted as educators they were simultaneously tasked with being effective mediators. These two roles ensured equitable understanding between students and institutions in which student affairs educators acted as interlocutors. These were by far their most significant roles as they assisted institutions in creating policies and guideline for students. Student affairs educators also advocated for multiculturalism in institutions by recruiting students of color from surrounding communities to create sustainable change. As communities and institutions created partnerships, they gave rise to programs such as TRIO to retain underrepresented students.

Currently, attention to Asian Americans is becoming more significant to student affairs educators and issues of diversity and multiculturalism. Asian Americans have a long-standing relationship in the U.S. and with institutions of higher education. They often experience U.S. society and higher education as being hyper visible or invisible. From the 1800s–1940s, Asian Americans experienced exclusionary practices due The Chinese Exclusion Act and the Asian Exclusion Act. These acts targeted the number of Asian individuals who could immigrate into the U.S. and created hostile climates and stereotypes towards these populations (Suzuki, 2002). In terms of higher education, Asian Americans were initially excluded from Affirmative Action due to the Model Minority Myth. The Model Minority Myth positions Asian Americans as a group that "[overcomes] all barriers of racial discrimination and are more than successful even than whites" in economic and education mobility (Suzuki, 2002, p. 23). This dangerous assumption has made various Asian American groups, specifically Southeast Asians, invisible in higher education. In the profession of student affairs, Asian Americans are greatly underrepresented, and there is a need to have them represented in leadership roles (Suzuki, 2002). Suzuki (2002) recommends that for the student affairs profession to diversify and be inclusive of Asian Americans, the following should occur: "support efforts to diversify the staffs of student affairs units, including efforts to recruit Asian Americans for such positions . . . and provide training to student affairs practitioners on effective approaches to working with Asian American students" (p. 29). This is increasingly important as Asian Americans are the fastest growing ethnic immigrant group in the Unites States, and this growth is reflected across college and university campuses (Brown, 2014).

The multiple and multi-layered roles occupied by student affairs educators were necessary to develop social justice and inclusion. It is a difficult task to document every stage of diversity and multiculturalism for the field of student affairs at every institution in American higher education, but several foundational documents serve to unify the profession.

Three significant documents published in the 1970s laid out the guiding principles of student affairs as a profession. The Council of Student Personnel Associations in Higher Education (COSPA) published "Student Development Services in Postsecondary Education" (1975) and *Student Development in Tomorrow's Higher Education* (1972). The American College Personnel Association published *A Student Development Model for Student Affairs in Tomorrow's Higher Education* (1975). All three documents provide a philosophical foundation for student affairs educators to develop themselves and the institutions and students they serve. Decades later, two of the eldest student affairs professional organizations would collaborate to assist practitioners with the knowledge, skills, and abilities to develop them into holistic professionals. In 2010, ACPA and Student Affairs Administrators in Higher Education (NASPA) developed the *Professional Competency Areas for Student Affairs*. Currently, this document serves as a reference for the field to engage in diversity and multiculturalism as we know it today.

For this chapter, we find two of the 10 competency areas most useful in understanding diversity and multiculturalism: "history, philosophy, and values" and "equity, diversity, and inclusion." These two areas help student affairs educators understand the history of the profession while leveraging knowledge of that history to create learning environments that sustain equity and inclusion across institutional types and student bodies. Up into this point, we have historically documented how diversity and multiculturalism have been present with the birth of American higher education and student affairs as a field. In the next section, considering the two competency areas, we provide a case study of the 1960s Chicana/o Student Movement to pose questions regarding diversity and multiculturalism.

CASE STUDY AS A TOOL TO UNDERSTAND MULTICULTURALISM AND DIVERSITY FOR STUDENT ACTIVISM AND STUDENT AFFAIRS

In a case study, researchers are interested in a group and how its members' involvement in a setting informs practices and understandings (Baxter & Jack, 2008). Program leaders grant researchers access to the groups in a setting of interest. As participant-observers, researchers must remain self-critical and reflective of the experiences individuals undergo. Data is collected on the experiences, encounters, observations, and conversations researchers have with participants. For this section, we turn to a case study focusing on the 1960s Chicana/o Student Movement. Our rationale is threefold. First, Latinx/a/o are the fastest growing ethnic demographic in the U.S. with the lowest educational outcomes at all levels of the educational pipeline (Perez

Huber, Malagón, Ramirez, Gonzalez, Jimenez, & Vélez, 2015). Second, the 1960s Chicana/o Movement is often overlooked in its creation of institutional change led by student activists in higher education. Finally, it is personal to our own experiences as we both identify as Chicana, and this is a part of our student affairs history that informs our practice and research efforts. In this case study, we consider the following: campus climate, institutional responses, and culturally sustaining practices through student activism, which often push student affairs practice.

A Case Study: 1960s Chicana/o Student Movement

At this moment we do not come to work for the university, but to demand that the university work for our people.[2]

"Chicano Power!" "Chicana Power!" "Que Viva la Raza!" Students were chanting and marching to the Chancellor's office at a public research-intensive university in Southern California in the year of 1969. Just a few months prior, high school students had walked out of their high schools in East Los Angeles to protest over 50% of their respective student bodies being forced to drop out or expelled due to their lack of literacy and basic skills to pass their classes. Shortly after the walkouts, protests began all over the Southwest. The Chicana/o college students at their respective campuses were compelled to take action as they felt they had no representation within the faculty, staff, or administration. They also wished to see their experiences and histories reflected in the college curriculum. Aligning themselves with the national Chicana/o Student Movement, 100 Chicana/o students from across the nation met on campus to draft a document titled *El Plan de Santa Barbara: A Chicano Plan for Higher Education* written by the Chicano Coordinating Council on Higher Education as a manifesto for the implementation of Chicano Studies educational programs throughout the state of California. As the students entered the Chancellor's office, they provided copies of the manifesto.

Due to the white male Chancellor's lack of knowledge regarding the surrounding Chicana/o community, he called on three Chicana/o student affairs educators—Jose, a college advisor in the College of Engineering, Monica, and Dolores, a college advisor in the College of Letter and Sciences—to examine the Chicana/o students *El Plan de Santa Barbara* (1969). The Chicana/o professionals were asked to provide recommendations to the Chancellor in a closed meeting with him and the Director of Student Services, also a white male. Feeling conflicted by the request, Jose, Monica, and Dolores read the

---

2. El Plan de Santa Barbara, p. 11.

Student Personnel Point of View (1949), which documented the importance of considering students "as a whole" and outlined their roles as student personnel professionals. In reviewing the *Student Personnel Point of View* (1949) and the *El Plan de Santa Barbara* (1969), they found themselves conflicted between their expectations as student affairs educators and their social positions as Chicanas/os at the university. What the Chicana/o students have written in *El Plan de Santa Barbara* (1969) deeply resonated with their own experiences. Jose, Monica and Dolores specifically outlined the significant points of the manifesto to take into their meeting with the Chancellor:

> Chicanos recognize the central importance of institutions of higher learning to modern progress, in this case, to the development of our community. But we go further: we believe that higher education must contribute to the formation of a complete man who truly values life and freedom...To meet these ends, the university and college systems of the State of California must act in the following basic areas:
>
> 1) Admission and recruitment of Chicano students, faculty, administration, and staff,
> 2) A curriculum program and an academic major relevant to the Chicano cultural and historical experience,
> 3) Support and tutorial programs,
> 4) Research programs,
> 5) Publication programs,
> 6) Community cultural and social action centers.
>
> We insist that Chicano students, faculty, administrators, employees, and the community must be the central and decisive designers and administrators of those programs. We do so because our priorities must determine the nature and development of such programs. Only through this policy can the university and college systems respond efficiently and justly to the critical reality of this society. Through such a policy universities and colleges will truly live up to their credo, to their commitment to diversification, democratization, and enrichment of our cultural heritage and human community.[3]

Jose, Monica, and Dolores were taken aback by these demands, because they were the only Chicana/o student professionals across the university. While this was alarming, they knew they were key leaders for Chicana/o students and the local community. They were committed to developing their Chicana/o students intellectually and socially to become active contributors to U.S. society. These demands made it clear that Chicana/o students did not feel a part of the university, which also made them question their roles as stu-

---

3. Directly taken from El Plan de Santa Barbara (pp. 9–10).

dent affairs practitioners. In reviewing the *Student Personnel Point of View* (1949) they stumbled upon a critical aspect under *Institutional Mores and Policies:*

> The effectiveness of a student personnel program is determined not solely by either its technical quality or its administration and financial structure, but even more by its institutional setting. In an institution where conditions are favorable to the maintenance of friendly, informal working relationships between teachers and students, and where the institutional leaders explicitly support such relationships, effective counseling may be developed far more readily and effectively than would be the case in institutions burdened with an antifaculty attitude established among student leaders.
>
> Personnel workers of all types, particularly those involved in group work functions, need to give continuous attention to the development of positive relationships in their work with student leaders. But, essentially, the institutional leader, the president, must set the standard of such mores. He can accomplish this by making clear his own basic attitudes toward students, teachers, and personnel workers, and the interrelated contributions of each group to the total institutional program of assistance to each student in his efforts to achieve full broad development.[4]

It became evident for Jose, Monica, and Dolores that their Chancellor was neglecting his role and not supporting what they needed to accommodate the diversity and multiculturalism at the university. While they were appreciative of the Chancellor requesting their recommendations, they understood it was the responsibility of the Chancellor to set the university climate right for Chicana/o students. As such, in their meeting with Chancellor and the Director of Student Services, they relied heavily on the student demands to ask the following questions:

- What is the role of the university mission and its leadership in meeting the students' demands to achieve diversity and multiculturalism in this historical context?
- How can student activism best be supported by personnel leaders to meet a balance of student needs and institutional representation?
- How can student activism drive the needs of diversity and multiculturalism for student affairs?
- Every institution has a history of diversity and multiculturalism. How might this case study inform student affair practitioners at their respective institutions?

---

4. Directly taken from Student Personnel Point of View (pp. 34–35).

Through their roles as student affairs educators, Jose, Monica, and Dolores played a critical role in supporting and brokering the diversity and multiculturalism of the student population at the university.

CONCLUSION AND IMPLICATIONS FOR CURRENT STUDENT AFFAIRS PRACTICE

From the start of the colonial colleges to the present day, student affairs has adapted to various institutional types and the diversity and multiculturalism within. The ever-shifting student affairs positions have been created to meet the needs of the institution and the changing student demographics. Our understanding of diversity and multiculturalism, "history, philosophy, and values" and "equity, diversity, and inclusion," helps us understand the history of the profession while simultaneously leveraging knowledge of that history to create learning environments that sustain equity and inclusion across institutional types and student bodies. Moreover, we highlight understanding diversity and multiculturalism through the recognition of student activism.

As exemplified through our case study presentation, student affairs educators helped students use their agency and leverage their voices to be heard effectively by having them address their main concerns and create sustainable solutions. Through facilitating the relationship between the students and the institution, the student affairs educators' dual roles as educators and mediators allowed student activism to aid the university in creating policies and sustainable change for students as well as the start of community partnerships.

Current research highlights the importance of collaboration between students and academic affairs and that relationships with faculty are particularly salient at Minority Serving Institutions (MSIs) where many first-generation faculty of color often take on multiple roles, including as friend and mentor to students (Commodore, Gasman, Conrad, & Nguyen, 2018; Sydnor, Hawkins, & Edwards, 2011). Garcia (2018) argues that institutions such as MSIs can help decolonize their institutions by increasing the "racial, ethnic, cultural, national and religious backgrounds" of not just students but also faculty, staff, and board members (p. 137). Positive interactions and intersections amongst faculty, students, and administrators are key to encompassing diversity, multiculturalism, social justice and inclusion in higher education institutions.

REFERENCES

American College Personnel Association and National Association of Student Personnel Administrators, & Joint Task Force on Professional Standards and Competencies. (2010). Professional competency areas for student affairs practitioners.

American Council on Education. (1937). *The student personnel point of view.* Washington, DC: Author.

American Council on Education. (1949). *The student personnel point of view.* Washington, DC: Author.

Ball, H. (2000). *The Bakke case: race, education, & affirmative action. Landmark Law Cases and American Society.* Lawrence, KS: University Press of Kansas.

Baxter, P., & Jack, S. (2008). Qualitative case study methodology: Study design and implementation for novice researchers. *The Qualitative Report, 13*(4), 544–559.

Biddix, J. P., & Schwartz, R. (2012). Walter Dill Scott and the student personnel movement. *Journal of Student Affairs Research and Practice, 49*(3), 285–298.

Bloland, P. A. (1994). *Reform in student affairs: A critique of student development.* CAPS, Inc., School of Education, University of North Carolina at Greensboro, Greensboro, NC.

Brown, A. (2014). US Hispanic and Asian populations growing, but for different reasons. *Pew Research Center.*

Chicano Coordinating Council on Higher Education. (1971). *El Plan de Santa Bárbara: A Chicano plan for higher education.* La Causa Publications.

Cohen, R., & Zelnik, R. E. (Eds.). (2002). *The free speech movement: Reflections on Berkeley in the 1960s.* Oakland, CA: University of California Press.

Commodore, F., Gasman, M., Conrad, C., & Nguyen, T. H. (2018). Coming together: A case study of collaboration between student affairs and faculty at Norfolk State University. In *Frontiers in Education, 3,* 39. Frontiers.

Delgado Bernal, D. (1999). Chicana/o education from the civil rights era to the present. *The Elusive Quest for Equality, 150,* 77–108.

Duffy, J. (2010). How women impacted the historical development of student affairs. *College Student Affairs Journal, 28*(2), 235.

Eisenmann, L. (Ed.). (1998). *Historical dictionary of women's education in the United States.* Westport, CT: Greenwood Publishing Group.

Garcia, G. A. (2018). Decolonizing Hispanic-serving institutions: A framework for organizing. *Journal of Hispanic Higher Education, 17*(2), 132–147.

Garcia, N. M., & Mayorga, O. J. (2018). The threat of unexamined secondary data: a critical race transformative convergent mixed methods. *Race Ethnicity and Education, 21*(2), 231–252.

Gaston-Gayles, J. L., Wolf-Wendel, L. E., Tuttle, K. N., Twombly, S. B., & Ward, K. (2005). From disciplinarian to change agent: How the civil rights era changed the roles of student affairs professionals. *NASPA Journal, 42*(3), 263–282.

Geiger, R. L. (2011) The ten generations of American higher education. *Johns Hopkins University Press, 3,* 37–68.

Geiger, R. L. (2017). *To advance knowledge: The growth of American research universities, 1900–1940.* Routledge.

Geiger, R. L. (Ed.). (2017). *The land-grant colleges and the reshaping of American higher education.* New York, NY: Routledge.

Giroux, H. A., & Giroux, S. S. (2004). *Take back higher education: Race, youth, and the crisis of democracy in the post-civil rights era.* New York, NY: Macmillan.

Herbold, H. (1994). Never a level playing field: Blacks and the GI Bill. *The Journal of Blacks in Higher Education, 6,* 104–108.

Hevel, M. S. (2016). Toward a history of student affairs: A synthesis of research, 1996–2015. *Journal of College Student Development, 57*(7), 844–862.

Long, D. (2012). The foundations of student affairs: A guide to the profession. In L. J. Hinchliffe, & M. A. Wong (Eds.), *Environments for student growth and development: Librarians and student affairs in collaboration* (pp. 1–39). Chicago: Association of College & Research Libraries.

Martin, W. E. (Ed.). (1998). *Brown v. Board of Education: A brief history with documents* (p. 173). Boston: Bedford/St. Martins.

Nidiffer, J. (2001). *Pioneering deans of women: More than a wise and pious matron.* New York, NY: Teachers College Press.

Nuss, E. M. (2003). The development of student affairs. In S. R. Komives, D. B. Woodard, Jr., & Associates (Eds.), *Student services: A handbook for the profession, 4,* 65–88.

Olson, K. W. (1973). The GI Bill and higher education: Success and surprise. *American Quarterly, 25*(5), 596–610.

Palmer, G. H. (1908). *The life of Alice Freeman Palmer.* New York, NY: Houghton Mifflin.

Peckham, H. H. (1967). *The making of the University of Michigan, 1817–1967.* Ann Arbor, MI: University of Michigan Press.

Perez Huber, L., Malagón, M. C., Ramirez, B. R., Gonzalez, L. C., Jimenez, A., & Vélez, V. N. (2015). Still Falling through the Cracks: Revisiting the Latina/o Education Pipeline. CSRC Research Report. Number 19. *UCLA Chicano Studies Research Center.*

Rumann, C. B., & Hamrick, F. A. (2009). Supporting student veterans in transition. *New Directions for Student Services, 2009*(126), 25–34.

Schwartz, R. A. (1997). How deans of women became men. *Review of Higher Education, 20,* 419–436.

Schwartz, R. A. (1998). Alice Freeman Palmer. In L. Eisenmann (Ed.), *Historical dictionary of women's education in the U.S.* (pp. 317–319). Westport, CT: Greenwood Press.

Schwartz, R. A. (2010). *Deans of men and the shaping of modern college culture.* New York, NY: Palgrave.

Suzuki, B. H. (2002). Revisiting the model minority stereotype: Implications for student affairs practice and higher education. *New Directions for Student Services, 2002*(97), 21–32.

Sydnor, K. D., Hawkins, A. S., & Edwards, L. V. (2011). Expanding research opportunities: making the argument for the fit between HBCUs and community-based participatory research. *The Journal of Negro Education. 79,* 79–86.

Thelin, J. R. (2004). *A history of American higher education.* Baltimore, Maryland: John Hopkin University Press.

Thelin, J. R., & Gasman, M. (2003). Historical overview of American higher education. *Student Services: A Handbook for the Profession, 4,* 3–22.

Wright, B. (1991). The 'untameable savage spirit': American Indians in colonial colleges. *The Review of Higher Education, 14*(4), 429–452.

Zamudio, M., Russell, C., Rios, F., & Bridgeman, J. L. (2011). *Critical race theory matters: Education and ideology.* New York, NY: Routledge.

Chapter 4

MULTICULTURAL AND DIVERSITY COMPETENCE: THEORY AND ITS APPLICATION

Michelle Boettcher, Samantha Babb, & Cristina Perez

Many student affairs graduate programs stress the importance of theory-to-practice, and student affairs educators often have a working knowledge of how identity development theories impact students. However, in the midst of being a "perpetually busy" student affairs educator, the use of theory in one's own development often wanes. This chapter identifies ways in which practitioners can continue to use theory in their own development, beyond their academic programs. Here we provide a brief overview followed by a case study and two sample activities student affairs educators can use on their own or through team or supervision dialogues.

REVIEW OF MAJOR THEORIES

While this chapter is not meant to provide a comprehensive overview of all development theories, it is worthwhile to highlight the areas of identity that theory addresses and how theory informs student affairs practice. Patton, Renn, Guido, and Quaye (2016) provided an excellent overview of social identity development theories. In their work, they divided these theories into the following categories: Racial, Ethnic, Sexual, Gender/Gender Identity, Faith & Spirituality, Disability, and Social Class.

At the heart of many of these theories lies a fundamental understanding of privilege and oppression in modern United States society. In *Teaching for Diversity and Social Justice,* Adams, Bell, Goodman, and Joshi (2007) described oppression as "the interlocking forces that create and sustain injustice" (p. 5). Building on knowledge of a variety of social identities outlined by Patton et al. (2016), this argument suggests that in order to fully engage with our own identities and those of our students, we must first have a baseline understanding of where power resides within our overarching society. We can then map our development on to varying theories. Patton et al. described privilege in two ways: unearned entitlements and conferred dominance, the former outlining the ways in which certain groups maintain both material and abstract privileges that should be expanded to all and the latter outlining the ways in which certain groups maintain power over others.

Working from an understanding that each social identity carries with it the weight of either privilege or oppression, student affairs educators can begin to explore the varying social identity development theories that guide not only the profession, but our understandings of our students and ourselves.

Racial Identity Development

We begin with the identity that carries centuries' worth of institutionalized oppression. It is vital that student affairs educators have a developed understanding of their own racial identity in order to be effective agents of student growth. While our understandings of race are ever changing, Patton et al. (2016) outlined the following racial identity development theories as a baseline for learning about how race impacts the ways we present ourselves in a variety of spaces.

Cross and Fhagen-Smith's (1996) Model of Black Identity Development outlines six sectors which are marked by three distinct patterns that are mapped over an individual's lifetime (socialization, conversion, and recycling/expansion). While this particular model of racial identity development does not suggest that individuals continually progress through it, it does end with a sector that emphasizes "recycling," suggesting that African Americans will continually develop their understanding of themselves as they move throughout adulthood (Patton et al., 2016).

In Helms's (1990, 1997) White Racial Identity Development Model, the author defines only two phases through which White people operate. The first constitutes a space in which White people begin to notice race; Helms explains that this could happen at a variety of stages in life, depending on the individual (Patton et al., 2016). This understanding of White identity development as less specifically linear than some other racial identity development theories rests on the underlying concept of privilege and oppression. Because White people are not oppressed based on their race, and instead enjoy many privileges based on their Whiteness, many are not forced to think about race. As a result, ideas about their Whiteness's impact on their opportunities and success are often realized later in their lifespan. The second phase, evolution of a non-racist identity, is a phase marked by an intentional inclination towards understanding ways in which Whiteness impacts an individual's entire livelihood. Similar to phase one, this phase could happen at any point during a lifespan and is often ongoing and ever-changing.

Ferdman and Gallegos's (2001) Model of Latino Identity Development falls in the space between both racial and ethnic identity development, based on the individual and his or her self-identification with race, ethnicity, and the combination of the two. This model outlines six different orientations that are applicable throughout the lifespan based on the following five factors; "one's 'lens' towards identity, how individuals prefer to identify themselves, how Latinos as a group are seen, how Whites are seen, and how 'race' fits into the equation" (Patton et al., 2016, p. 106). Ferdman and Gallegos in turn suggest understanding of Latino identity can be on going and ever changing or static based on the individual (Patton et al., 2016).

Kim's (2012) Asian American Identity Development Model outlines five stages of identity development for individuals who identify within the Asian American community. This model is intentionally linear in the following sequential order: ethnic awareness, White identification, awakening to a social political consciousness, redirection to Asian American consciousness, and incorporation, which is defined by the embracing of one's Asian American identity across environments both homogenous and heterogeneous (Patton et al., 2016). While individuals may process through the stages of development linearly throughout their lives, the timing of each stage will vary from one individual to the next across the lifespan.

Renn's (2003) Ecological Theory of Mixed-Race Identity Development focused on ecological influences—external factors affecting how individuals identify—and a series of self-identifying labels. Examples of ecological influences included physical appearance, family heritage, cultural knowledge, cultural engagement, and messaging received about identity (Patton et al., 2016). The five identity patterns of Renn's (2003) theory included monoracial identity, multiple monoracial identities, multiracial identity, extra racial identity, and situational identity. In a society with a tendency to categorize individuals into checkboxes, multiracial identity development is complex and can cause a feeling of otherness or not quite belonging in any space. There is a saying in the Latinx community used by those born or primarily raised in the United States who often feel caught in between identities, "ni de aquí, ni de allá," which translates to "from neither here nor there." The complex and layered experiences of Latinx students are often framed by this sense of belonging neither in America nor in their "home" countries.

Sexual Orientation and Gender Identity Formation

In addition to racial identity, sexual orientation and gender identity formation are important considerations for student affairs educators. Bilodeau and Renn (2005) conducted an analysis of LGBTQ+ identity models and highlighted several related specifically to higher education. Focusing on development among college students, the authors highlighted the work of D'Augelli (1994), Evans and Broido (1999), and Rhoads (1994). For the purposes of this chapter and its audience, we will focus on the work of these scholars.

Both D'Augelli (1994) and Rhoads (1994) regarded LGBTQ+ student development as occurring over the lifespan, with a focus on specific processes in specific contexts. Evans and Broido (1999) focused on the coming out process of students in residence halls and described the process as "a very complex phenomenon, mediated by development, but impacted by . . . developmental readiness, motivation, audience, and context" (p. 666).

Bilodeau and Renn (2005) spoke to the importance of institutional context in the experiences of LGBTQ+ identity development. They encouraged student affairs practitioners to reflect on strategic advocacy and the ability to cultivate institutional leadership support for students as a part of the process of serving LGBTQ+students on campus. To the point of this chapter, the authors conclude saying, "Practitioners and scholars have an ethical responsibility to understand what the underlying assumptions of the models are, what each purport to describe, on what populations or premises the models were based, and whose interests are served by different models and their uses" (pp. 36–37).

Multiple Dimensions of Identity

Finally, identity development does not happen compartmentally, and an individual's development in relation to a specific identity is informed by the other identities held by that individual. It is important for student affairs educators to remember that these processes may be happening simultaneously within an individual. For instance, one could actively be processing through stages of Asian American identity development while also experiencing gender identity formation. Hence, following any theory too strictly can be detrimental to understanding ourselves as student affairs educators, and our students. We are all complex containers of identity and experiences, all of which inform how we move through our daily routine.

These social identities do not exist in isolation. Rather, they are in constant communication with one another and serve as a lens through which an individual experiences the world. Given the unbounded impact individuals' collective social identities have on their experience of and contributions to society, it is essential to use theory in practice both for our students and ourselves (Abes, 2016; Abes, Jones, & McKewen, 2007; Jones, 2009; Torres, Jones, & Renn, 2009).

Most existing scholarship stresses the role of social identity theory in student development, which is invaluable in helping students discover themselves (Abes, 2016; Patton et al., 2016). In order to best understand our students and their journeys towards self-actualization, we must engage with social identity critically. "Critically" suggests that we not only engage with theory as educators, but also as learners. How do we student affairs educators use social identity development theories to better understand ourselves? We must understand ourselves in order to guide students through their own journeys to self-understanding. Theory in and of itself is not enough. The work must continue through critical engagement with individual students. So how do we use theory to prepare ourselves for that work?

THE ROLES OF THEORY IN
PROFESSIONAL IDENTITY DEVELOPMENT

Theory informs professional identity development in a number of ways. While students and emerging professionals are discouraged from putting students (or colleagues or themselves) into developmental boxes in a categorical or diagnostic way, theory can serve as a tool for mapping complex identities and circumstances. While not to be followed as a conveyor of absolute truth, theory serves as one of many strategies to understand ourselves and the students with whom we work.

Student development theories outline college as an incubator of change for many students at a time when students can access new, dynamic understandings of themselves and others. While there are a handful of theories that suggest clean-cut and linear development, many theories imply development as an ongoing and non-linear process that continues post-college (Patton et al., 2016; Torres et al., 2009). In turn, many theories suggest that despite studying the development of college students and working to understand a variety of developmental stages, practitioners continue developing after graduation. For instance, Abes et al. (2007) outlined layers of development that are contingent on a variety of contextual influences, including peers, family, norms, stereotypes, and sociopolitical conditions, suggesting that as students move throughout college and eventually post-grad, their understandings of their identities grow and change based on any number of ever-evolving conditions. Student affairs educators are not exempt from the messy forms of self-discovery our students experience on and off campus, but in fact can experience many of the same challenges that we witness with students.

Piskadlo and Johnson (2014) examined the experiences of graduate students and emerging professionals using theory. It is important to acknowledge that the authors used theory to understand the stories that others shared rather than using theory first to project expectations or meanings onto individuals before hearing from them directly. Here we provide examples of ways to use this method intentionally in our work with ourselves and with our students moving forward.

PROFESSIONAL COMPETENCE IN THEORY AND ACTION

In this chapter, we examined the work to be done around various issues as a practitioner and also discussed student collaboration. What does it mean to be both a learner and an educator in the context of a student affairs educator? How can we engage in the hard work of unpacking our own socialization and motives as an ongoing process? In what ways does our engagement in the work serve to model this important process for students?

As ever-growing student affairs educators, it is integral that we push ourselves in deep and meaningful ways toward discovery about our own ways of being, based on our individual lived experiences and our social identities as a collective. For instance, an individual's participation in 10 years of little league impacts his or her approach to work and students, but so do that individual's social class, race, and ability. In fact, all of those factors meld together, consciously or subconsciously, to shape that individual's everyday interactions with his or her students, colleagues, and the institution as a whole.

How might one question the structures, at the institution and beyond, that either provide access or create barriers based on one's collection of social identities and experiences? How are social identities tied to the experiences one is allowed to have? How are social identities tied to the experiences one feels entitled to? How are social identities tied to the ways others expect to experience us?

Individuals with marginalized identities are often very aware of personal and structural impacts of their subordinate identities. The structural hierarchy of identity exists both on and off campuses, and it is both overt and covert. For student affairs educators who maintain a series of dominant identities, it is important to actively examine those identities and their impacts on an individual's navigation of higher education; past, present, and future.

Harro's (2000) Cycle of Socialization is a tool used by many social justice educators to illuminate the ways systemic privilege and oppression impact our varying social identities in day-to-day life. Throughout the activity, participants track the messages they received about their varying social identities throughout their lifespan, and the ways they either upheld or pushed against those messages (Harro, 2000). This activity may be good to review as an individual, or a campus collective, to begin the process of unpacking the messages sent out by society and institutions of higher education that either uphold or dismantle structural inequity.

Theory on the Job: Communicating Student Development

From a theoretical perspective, how can student affairs educators articulate these ideas? In what ways can ideas around identity be incorporated and understood as areas of influence during the college years and beyond? In short, how do we make continued identity development an active practice across functional areas of student affairs?

Here we provide three key questions student affairs educators can use in any situation when thinking intently about the identities of the students, staff, and others with whom they work.

1. Whose voice is missing from this conversation?
2. How have our practices been informed by systemic privilege?
3. How has this current [event, activity, practice, policy, etc.] been vetted by those most directly impacted, including input from across different populations?

Each of these questions requires active engagement with and reflection on student affairs practice and policy. This approach is a shift away from passive awareness toward active and transformative change (Bresciani, Gardner, & Hickmott, 2010; Weiner et al., 2011).

After the questions above are asked, the experience at hand can be reviewed and improved based on input from and assessment of the questions above from more diverse perspectives. These questions can also be used after an event when decisions were made perhaps under tremendous time pressure (crisis, deadlines imposed at the last minute, etc.). This reflective practice using theory related to identity as a lens for review, critique, and revision can help individuals and organizations engage in processes of continuous improvement.

ACPA/NASPA Competencies

The use of theory in practice is consistent with the ACPA/NASPA competencies and, in fact, cuts across competency areas. The Values, Philosophy, and History competency states that at the intermediate level professionals should "teach the principles of the student affairs profession to staff while incorporating the equity, diversity, and inclusion of varying identities and global perspectives" (ACPA/NASPA, 2015, p. 19). The Social Justice and Inclusion competency is focused on social justice work at the foundational, intermediate, and advanced levels. Professional development within this competency focused on the following: "Student affairs educators need to understand oppression, privilege, and power before they can understand social justice. Intermediate and advanced level outcomes reflect social justice oriented applications in practice and then interconnections between leadership and advocacy" (ACPA/NASPA, 2015, p. 14). The development of this competency is important across all levels.

Foundational level outcomes included the ability to "identify systems, engage in critical reflection, and integrate knowledge" (ACPA/NASPA, 2015, p. 30). Intermediate outcomes include the ability to "design programs," "facilitate dialogue," build inclusive teams through hiring practices, and "effectively address bias incidents" (ACPA/NASPA, 2015, p. 31). Finally, at the advanced level, student affairs professionals should be able to "advocate for social justice values in institutional mission, goals, and programs," develop strategic plans for inclusion and an inclusive institutional culture, and "demonstrate institutional effectiveness in addressing critical incidents of discrimination that impact the institution" (ACPA/NASPA, 2015, p. 31)

For instance, let's say the campus activity board wants to plan a week's worth of programming during Pride month to celebrate LGBTQ+ history. As the advisor of the group, you may first examine who already serves on the activity board. Are there any students who identify with the LGTBQ+ community? Do you as their advisor identify within the community? If yes, how open are those students about their LGBTQ+ identity? Is this something that has been openly shared with the group, shared with you in confidence, or are you making assumptions? If no, how do you incorporate members of the LGBTQ+ community in a way that does not burden them to educate their peers or feel tokenizing? As a student affairs educator, how do you hold your knowledge of LGBTQ+ identity development theory with the knowledge that students are experts of their own lives and stories?

Moving forward toward planning programming, you may consider whether the events are relevant for all students who identify within the LGTBQ+ community. This means there are opportunities for students with varying intersecting social identities (race, ethnicity, disability, social class, etc.) to see themselves and their collective of identities represented in the programming (Pryor, Garvey, & Johnson, 2016). One may also consider the materials for the programming and whether the vendors are in support of the LGBTQ+ community. Throughout this entire process, advisors who do not identify within the LGBTQ+ community should constantly be asking themselves, "What am I missing?" When advisors hold dominant identities, they must always be listening to ensure that students feel heard and seen in programming that is meant to represent them.

Case Study: The Student Rep

Kia is an Associate Dean of Student Engagement and is chairing a search committee for the new Associate Dean of Students/Director of Residence Life at a medium-sized public institution in the Southwest. She identifies as a straight, Black, cisgender woman and her direct supervisor, the Dean, is a straight, White, cisgender man. The Dean has already identified three committee members in addition to Kia. They are:

- Sonja, Assistant Director of Residence Life: Sonja is a thirty-five-year-old, cisgender, White woman. Sonja is originally from the East Coast and has been at the institution and in the Southwest for about five years. She lives with her partner, Karen, not far from campus and is an active member of the LGBTQ+ community in the area.
- Robert, Director of Dining: Robert is a fifty-year-old, cisgender, Christian, African American man. He has been at the institution for over 20 years and has two children who have graduated from the institution within the last three years. Robert's children identify as multiracial.
- Carlene, Director of Campus Safety: Carlene is a thirty-seven-year-old, cisgender, Asian woman. Carlene has worked at the institution for 10 years in a variety of roles. She is married, with two children under 10.

The Dean formed this committee with the student experience in mind, and he recognizes that in filling a role that has a lot to do with creating safe and inclusive communities on campus, it is vital that he recruit candidates that have experience with the community and student populations present at the institution. While the institution is still predominantly White, it is located in an area with a high Indigenous population. Kia wants to respect the culture and history of the land, particularly when the individual in this role will sit in on conversations about development and expansion.

1. Whose voice is missing from this conversation?
2. How have practices around the candidate search been informed by systemic privilege?
3. How has this search been vetted by those most directly impacted including input from across different populations?
4. What theories might Kia review in preparing for meeting with the search committee and conducting the search process?

5. What issues might arise during the search, and what theories might be useful to Kia in navigating those issues and challenges?
6. With whom might Kia consult in preparation for this search?

Theory on the Job: Critiquing the Dominant Perspective

Student affairs educators should possess the competence to critique the dominant group perspective present in some models of student learning and development (Bondi, 2012). Therefore, it is incumbent upon them to put these skills into action in support of underrepresented and marginalized students on campus. Theory informs the practice of engaging students as opportunities, issues, and events emerge. Examples include student organization decisions and practices, resident assistant community development strategies, and fraternity and sorority life organizational decision-making, to name a few.

Case Study: The Organizational Tradition

Joseph just started at State University this semester and is excited to get to work as an organization advisor in the student activities office where he is a program coordinator. Joseph is the new advisor to State University's Triathlon Club. Each year the club engages in a number of fundraisers to support its travel to competitions across the country. One fundraiser the organization has historically done is its fall Turkey Trot and Thanksgiving Feast on campus.

In the past few years, the group has encouraged runners to wear costumes and also awards a prize for the best costumes. Joseph is reviewing past years' reports that include photos of various events. He has reports from the past three years, and in the Turkey Trot runs for each of those years there are large groups of runners dressed as both pilgrims and Indigenous People.

The members of the Triathlon Club are historically nearly all White, and that is the case again this year. In fact, the president of the organization, Tad, has been in his role for three years. He has talked about Turkey Trot with Joseph a number of times, and Joseph knows that he is excited about the experience and sees it as a highlight for the year. Joseph wants to engage with Tad first and then the Triathlon Executive Committee to suggest providing more guidance to runners about costumes for this year's run.

1. Whose voice is missing from this conversation?
2. How have practices around this event been informed by systemic privilege?
3. How has this current activity been vetted by those most directly impacted including input from across different populations?

4. What theories might Joseph review in preparing for the conversation with Tad? How might he use information from each to structure the conversation?

5. What theories might be useful to Joseph if the conversation does not go well with Tad, the Executive Committee, or both?

6. With whom might Joseph consult in preparation for this conversation?

Theory on the Job: Translating Theory for Diverse Audiences

For even the most specialized student affairs educators, there is a need to speak to broader and broader audiences (Hirschy & Wilson, 2017). As social media, online engagement, and the ever-present cell phones of audience members, students, etc. continue to impact communication in student affairs and across higher education, speaking to multiple demographic groups, perspectives, and audiences at the same time is essential.

Case Study: An Orientation Session on Civility

Janet is the Assistant Director of orientation at a highly selective institution in the Northeast. She has been in the role for roughly four years, and year after year the orientation team works to put together a session that introduces students to the diversity (and sometimes adversity) they will face while at the institution. Janet sometimes struggles to balance between being the energetic and welcoming committee member while simultaneously critiquing some of the past heinous bias incidents on campus. She knows that while she is a steward of the university, she has a responsibility to share some of the not-so-positive aspects of the institution's history.

This year she would like to create a new program for orientation that can both critique and celebrate the institution's past. However, Janet feels hesitant considering she holds mostly dominant identities and does not have much experience in social justice education.

1. Whose voice is missing from this conversation?

2. How have Janet's and the institution's past practices been informed by systemic privilege?

3. How can this new initiative be vetted by those most directly impacted including input from across different populations?

4. What theories might be relevant for Janet in preparing to plan the new session?

5. What should Janet's initial steps be in creating this new session? When might she start? Who else might she include in the cultivation of such an experience?

6. Create a timeline of Janet's steps toward session creation through the academic year in preparation for a summer session.

Theory on the Job: Building Inclusive Communities

One of the challenges student affairs educators face is helping students (and sometimes parents, alumni, advisors, faculty, staff, and communities) come to terms with their exclusive and exclusionary pasts. Many organizations on campus may be dominated by one particular population or by people holding certain identities (White, male, Christian, straight, etc.). While often organizations (and institutions) share that they want to be more inclusive and diverse, they sometimes struggle to let go of aspects of tradition and history enough to open the doors to welcome others (Bondi, 2012; Patton, 2015).

Case Study: Sorority Recruitment Planning

Camila has worked in the Sorority and Fraternity Life (SFL) office for a year and advises the sorority council. While there have been no public bias or hate-based incidents in the SFL community, Camila recognizes the lack of visible diversity in their membership and the difference in demographic representation from the larger campus community.

During a recruitment-planning meeting, her student leaders express their desire to recruit more diverse members. During the conversation, the focus shifts to the one woman of color in the room, a chapter representative, for her input. She hesitantly shares, "I'm not sure what to do. I like my chapter. I don't know what might get other people to join." The student leaders start to identify a handful of women of color in their chapters and discuss scheduling a photoshoot to use for their marketing campaign. Camila realizes they are about to move on to the next agenda item and feels like they missed the mark in this important conversation.

1. Whose voice is missing from this conversation?
2. How have SFL's practices been informed by systemic privilege?
3. How have the initiative to recruit more diverse members and the photo shoot campaign been vetted by those most directly impacted, including input from across different populations?
4. What theories might be relevant for Camila in responding to the students' plans? How might she bring up those theories in this context?
5. What approach should Camila take to engage students in this conversation? Are there organizational and campus histories she should know to support the discussion? If so, how might she go about learning these things?

6. What are factors that might be impacting the lack of diversity in the sorority community? How do those factors relate to relevant theories?
7. How can Camila help her students better understand the meaning of diversity and inclusion, and the difference between the two terms?

Theory on the Job: Developing Inclusive Paradigms

Institutional history, past participants in the campus culture, and the desire to celebrate tradition emerge not only in organizations, but through campus events as well. When events are coordinated at the institutional level, it can be more challenging to disrupt histories and systems (Stewart-Tillman & Joyce, 2017). Upper-level administrators can be less accessible. Alumni voices (and dollars) are often brought into the conversation as key points of focus. The engagement of legacy students and their parents can play a significant role on campus.

Often those with the clearest view of problematic issues and traditions are those who are new to campus. Unfortunately, they often lack the social and political capital to facilitate change. Additionally, newer student affairs educators may lack the diplomatic and political savvy to be heard and be effective.

Case Study: Homecoming Events for Everyone

Eric works in Student Activities at a private liberal arts institution in the Midwest; he has been in the role for six months. Traditionally, the institution recruits students that are White, upper middle class, and interested in the arts. One of the most popular homecoming events is a museum tour that includes university-sponsored alcohol and a "hunt" for all the best, most famous artwork on campus. Every year students dress up and prepare for their first fancy night around campus and are joined by the many notable artist in the robust Alumni Association.

Recently there has been pushback from some students that the lifestyle that this event evokes and promotes is inaccessible to students who may not be from a certain socioeconomic class. Additionally, most of the art found on the tour was created by wealthy, straight, cisgender, White men. The students concerned with the tour feel that it promotes Whiteness as standard of excellence and creates an environment that stratifies students immediately upon their arrival.

1. Whose voice is missing from conversation about this event?
2. How have practices around this art event been informed by systemic privilege?

3. How has this current event been vetted by those most directly impacted including input from across different populations?
4. What should Eric's primary concerns be with this event?
5. What theories could Eric review to help him prepare for discussions about the issues related to this event?
6. What steps should Eric take to make all students feel welcome?
7. How might Eric navigate the Alumni Association involvement as a new employee?

THEORY: A FRAMEWORK FOR STUDENT AFFAIRS EDUCATOR PROFESSIONAL DEVELOPMENT

It is up to the builder of one's professional identity to determine which tool or tools are needed at a given time. That said, engaging with theory around one's own professional identity is essential (Magolda & Carnaghi, 2014). "Know thyself" is the observation of a general truth espoused by the Greeks that is relevant here. To know who you are as a professional, you must first know who you are as a person.

How do we do this? Read theory. Put yourself and your experiences in the theory. Before turning the lens and critique theory has to offer on others, events, or organizations, examine yourself. Some reflection prompts will get you started:

- Where are the gaps in your knowledge?
- Reflect on mistakes you have made in the past. How do those mistakes and the lessons learned connect with different developmental theories?
- What theories are missing from your repertoire? Who can help you access not only the theories but also the meaning behind and application of those theories?

Going beyond the idea of being at a certain stage today, you may look at where you were or have been at different stages of your life. Engaging in this process on a regular basis can not only help you understand yourself but can provide you with tools to understand your students and where they are at given times (Magolda & Carnaghi, 2014; Patton et al., 2016).

Use theory to identify milestones. These markers in your life might include the ending of your high school relationship in the fall of your first semester, your grandmother's death during your junior year in college, or having to move back home with the parents right after graduation from college as you continued your job search. Of course, there are positive highlights, such as your first-year roommate becoming your lifetime best friend, changing your major in your sophomore year to something you really love, or being elected as the leader of a club or organization that meant a lot to you. All of these things make up who we were and who we have become. Each of these experiences culminates in the professionals we are. Again, here are some prompts to help you begin the process.

- Do a quick review of your college years. What were key highs and lows in your experience?
- What people—friends, faculty, staff, family—played key roles in your experiences (positive or negative)? When? Why?
- How might the experiences you identified in the previous questions fit into the context of theory and your own development?

Now, how do all of those pieces, experiences, moments, and people serve to inform your future development? What are areas where you still need to learn and grow? What are the key issues you face currently? What do you hope to do next in terms of work and life, and how can experiences in your current job set you up for success in what comes next? How might you engage with your supervisor around these thoughts and goals?

It is important to go beyond moments. If we are to be critical practitioners, teachers, supervisors, mentors, advisors, and leaders, we have to intentionally examine ourselves through the multiple lenses of our own identities (Magolda & Carnaghi, 2014; Patton et al., 2016). Sometimes the first step toward being able to do that is to look at others' experiences first in order to make the process a little less personal. With that in mind, we provide the following case study to stimulate your reflection. It is followed by a series of reflective prompts and activities to give you the tools you need to do this work.

Theory and Professional Development: A Case Study

Layla is a cisgender, White woman working as a new professional at a mid-size, regional, rural public institution, Central University (CU). Many students at CU are first-generation students, and the majority of undergraduates come from within three hours of campus to attend the institution. Layla works as a case manager, assisting students in crises ranging from homesickness to loss of a family member, study skills, and eating disorders. Layla's primary role is initiating contact with students then working with them to identify and access the best resources for them on campus and in the community.

Layla attended graduate school at a large, public land-grant institution and undergraduate at a mid-size private school near her family in Chicago.

Both experiences provided Layla with a strong sense of community, whether at home in an area she knew or in her cohort at an institution with seemingly endless school spirit. As a helper at her new institution, Layla is striving to understand the campus and community in order to best assist her students and integrate into the campus environment seamlessly.

Layla's supervisor Ben meets with her early in the fall semester. He asks her to come up with a professional development plan for herself. He says, "I do my best supervision when I know what you are looking for and where you see yourself at the end of the year. The more you share with me, the better I can identify opportunities and support you." He asks Layla to come up with a reflective activity about both her journey before this position and how her past informs her identity as a professional. Finally, he asks her to include goals for the year and what she thinks she may need to achieve those goals.

1. Whose voice is missing from this conversation?
2. How have our practices been informed by systemic privilege?
3. How has this current [event, activity, practice, policy, etc.] been vetted by those most directly impacted including input from across different populations?
4. What might Layla's plan look like? Provide sample reflection questions and incorporate at least one theory in her professional development plan that she will share with Ben.
5. What challenges might emerge for Layla in doing this at a new institution where she is still learning about the history and campus climate? How might she navigate those challenges?
6. What additional information or resources might Ben provide to help Layla write a practical, usable plan with measurable outcomes?

As the case above shows, there can be very intentional and strategic ways to think about how theory informs professional development. The case is designed to afford autonomy to the new professional in choosing a theory and is structured to encourage reflection before theory application. Building on the previous case study, we also provide the additional reflective prompts and activities as tools and strategies to use in your own development or in supervising and working with others.

CONCLUSION

A final comment—while this is structured for new and emerging professionals, it is important for student affairs educators at all levels to engage in ongoing reflection and strategic thinking about their own professional identities. As such, the following were created with all staff in mind—from the entry-level hall director to the Chief Student Affairs Officer. Incorporating these and similar types of activities across a division of student affairs can serve to foster a culture of continuous improvement, a value on individuals as people (not simply in terms of the work they do), and a sense of community and humanity in the difficult labor done by student affairs educators every day.

Putting Theory in the Professional Development of Student Affairs Educators

1. Create a timeline of your identity development. What identities were most salient at different times throughout your professional identity development? You may include all identities that relate to you as a person and inform who you are as a professional including but not limited to ability, ethnicity, gender, race, religious affiliation, sexual orientation, and socioeconomic status. Other identities that may inform who you are and the experiences you have had might include birth order, home environment, etc. Once you have completed your timeline, identify two or three key moments or experiences to share with others. What happened? Why was it significant to you? How does it inform your work today?

2. Your next step is to select a developmental theory that resonates with you. Using the theory framework, you may want to write an autobiography with the title, "How [Theory] Informs Who I am in Student Affairs." Begin mapping your own experiences through the theory from birth to today. Alternatively, map your experiences from the time you started college as an undergraduate through today. It may be interesting for you map both and then compare them to one another. Are there patterns? Can you mark place of specific learning or growth? Share your work with a colleague and have them ask questions about your story to uncover deeper understandings.

3. When applicable, identify and reflect on experiences that moved you from one stage of identity development to the next. What influenced this progression? Was it a specific experience, encounter, conversation, etc.? Were there external influences in this progression? How can your experience inform your support of students moving through different stages of development?

REFERENCES

Abes, E. S. (2016). *Critical perspectives on student development theory.* (New Directions for Student Services, No. 154.) New York: John Wiley & Sons.

Abes, E. S., Jones, S. R., & McEwen, M. K. (2007). Reconceptualizing the model of multiple dimensions of identity: The role of meaning-making capacity in the construction of multiple identities. *Journal of College Student Development, 48*(1), 1–22.

American College Personnel Associates & National Association of Student Personnel Administrators. (2015). *ACPA/NASPA professional competency areas for student affairs practitioners* (2nd ed.). Washington, DC: Author.

Adams, M., Bell, L. A., Goodman, D. J., & Joshi, K. Y. (2007). *Teaching for diversity and social change.* New York: Routledge.

Bilodeau, B. L., & Renn, K. A. (2005). *Analysis of LGBT identity development models and implications for practice.* (New Directions for Student Services, No. 111, pp. 25–39). New York: John Wiley & Sons.

Bondi, S. (2012). Students and institutions protecting Whiteness as property: A critical race theory analysis of student affairs preparation. *Journal of Student Affairs Research and Practice, 49*(4), 397–414.

Bresciani, M. J., Gardner, M. M., & Hickmott, J. (2010). *Demonstrating student success: A practical guide to outcomes-based assessment of learning and development in student affairs.* Herndon, VA: Stylus Publishing.

Cross Jr., W. E., & Fhagen-Smith, P. (1996). Nigrescence and ego identity development: Accounting for differential Black identity patterns. In J. D. Pederson, W. Lonner, & J. Trimble (Eds.), *Counseling across cultures.* Newburg, CA: Sage.

D'Augelli, A. R. (1994). Identity development and sexual orientation: Toward a model of lesbian, gay, and bisexual development. In E. J. Trickett, R. J. Watts, and D. Birman (Eds.), *Human diversity: Perspectives on people in context.* San Francisco: Jossey-Bass.

Evans, N. J., & Broido, E. M. (1999). Coming out in college residence halls: Negotiation, meaning making, challenges, and supports. *Journal of College Student Development, 40,* 658–668.

Ferdman, B. M., & Gallegos, P. I. (2001). Latinos and racial identity development. In C. L. Wijeyesinghe & B. W. Jackson III (Eds.), *New perspectives on racial identity development: A theoretical and practical anthology* (pp. 32–66). New York: New York University Press.

Harro, B. (2000). The cycle of socialization. In M. Adams, W. J. Blumenfeld, R. Castenada, H. W. Hackman, M. L. Peters, & X. Zuniga (Eds.), *Readings for diversity and social justice: An anthology on racism, anti-Semitism, sexism, heterosexism, ableism, and classism* (pp. 15–21). New York: Routledge.

Helms, J. E. (1990). *Black and White racial identity: Theory, research, and practice.* New York: Greenwood Press.

Helms, J. E. (1997). Toward a model of White racial identity development. In K. Arnold & I. C. King (Eds.), *College student development and academic life: Psychological, intellectual, social and moral issues.* New York: Routledge.

Hickmott, J., & Bresciani, M. J. (2010). *Examining learning outcomes in student person-nel preparation programs.* Unpublished manuscript, Department of Postsecondary Educational Leadership, San Diego State University, San Diego, CA.

Hirschy, A. S., & Wilson, M. E. (2017). Student affairs and the scholarship of prac-tice. *New Directions for Higher Education, 2017*(178), 85–94.

Jones, S. R. (2009). Constructing identities at the intersections: An autoethnograph-ic exploration of multiple dimensions of identity. *Journal of College Student Devel-opment, 50*(3), 287–304.

Kim, J. (2012). Asian American racial identity development theory. In C. L. Wijeyesinghe & F. W. Jackson (Eds.), *New perspectives on racial identity development: Integrating emerging frameworks* (2nd ed., pp. 138–160) New York: NYU Press.

Magolda, P. M., & Carnaghi, J. E. (Eds.). (2014). *Job one 2.0: Understanding the next generation of student affairs professionals* (2nd ed.) Lanham, MD: University Press of America.

Patton, A. L. (2015). From individual difference to political analysis: An emerging application of critical theory in student affairs. *Journal of Critical Scholarship on Higher Education and Student Affairs, 2*(1), 5.

Patton, L. D., Renn, K. A., Guido, F. M., & Quaye, S. J. (2016). *Student development in college: Theory, research, and practice.* San Francisco, CA., Jossey-Bass.

Piskadlo, K., & Johnson, C. (2014). Identity and the job one experience. In P. M. Magolda & J. E. Carnaghi (Eds.), *Job one 2.0: Understanding the next generation of student affairs professionals* (2nd ed., pp. 42–54). Lanham, MD: University Press of America.

Pryor, J. T., Garvey, J. C., & Johnson, S. (2017). Pride and progress? 30 years of ACPA and NASPA LGBTQ presentations. *Journal of Student Affairs Research and Practice, 54*(2), 123–136.

Renn, K. A. (2003). Understanding the identities of mixed-race college students through a developmental ecology lens. *Journal of College Student Develop-ment, 44*(3), 383–403.

Rhoads, R. A. (1994). *Coming out in college: The struggle for a queer identity.* Westport, Conn.: Bergin and Garvey.

Stewart-Tillman, K., & Joyce, B. (2017). United front: Engaging issues of diversity across student affairs functional areas. *College Student Affairs Journal, 35*(1), 25–39.

Torres, V., Jones, S. R., & Renn, K. A. (2009). Identity development theories in stu-dent affairs: Origins, current status, and new approaches. *Journal of College Student Development, 50*(6), 577–596.

Chapter 5

WORKING WITH RACIALLY AND ETHNICALLY DIVERSE STUDENTS

Mary Kay Carodine & Naijian Zhang

This chapter takes a strengths-based approach to working with students from racially and ethnically diverse backgrounds. Too often, deficit models limit students and fail to focus on the depth of backgrounds, skills and experiences they bring to college. The complexity of one's identity plays into how one experiences college. The historical context of campuses greatly influences the environment, policies and practices, particularly related to racial and ethnic minority students. The lived experiences and backgrounds of students are also critical factors in their college success. The current campus and national climate play a role in one's experience and education. The awareness, knowledge, and skills needed to support students of diverse racial and ethnic backgrounds are critical to higher education professionals and cannot be overstated.

Multiculturalism is happening on college campuses, and we need to set up campuses and students for success; to have them prepared with the knowledge and skills to work with and learn from others who are different from themselves. Student affairs educators must be equipped with the knowledge and skills to examine campus climate, review policies, use assessment results and develop programs and services that change the fabric of campus to be more inclusive and that model more equitable campuses. Students of marginalized identities are no longer willing to accept the status quo or worse, hostile learning environments. As stated by Howard-Hamilton, Cuyjet, and Cooper (2016), "By recognizing the demographic shift taking place in this country, college campuses can become spaces where everyone belongs and sense that their culture can be embedded in the organizational structure along with other diverse voices" (p. 12). For this change to occur, we need to re-center the conversation on all races and ethnicities instead of maintaining the perspective of White and non-White students which continues to center the work and conversation on White histories, practices and climate. This adjustment will mean that white students, faculty, and staff must examine their identities, privileges and role in the maintenance of the status quo. A fundamental restructuring or re-centering is what is necessary to advance higher education and retain and graduate all students.

Too often, campuses maintain status quo because it is easier or because they don't see the damaging effects on students of color. Physical factors like the absence of photos, artwork and the names of buildings that reflect one's race and identity can have a chilling effect. Similarly, statues and buildings named after people with racist pasts can be damaging and a challenge for institutions to decide how to handle. The organization of residence halls, presence of Greeks and social programs all impact climate for students of color and for White students. Political factors such as student government elections, immigration policies, and campus practices all play into campus climate. The economic background of students is often correlated with race and the first-generation status. Having a lower socioeconomic status may require students to work more, socialize less, and have increased stress as well as feel isolated or excluded. Educational backgrounds and preparedness also vary based on race and the community from which students are coming.

While examining their identities, privileges, and role in the maintenance of the status quo of current campus climate, student affairs educators must develop and possess professional competencies in order to work effectively with racially and ethnically diverse students. ACPA and NASPA (2015) established a common set of professional competency areas for student affairs educators, and one of the competency areas was social justice and inclusion. This competency particularly addresses that student affairs educators must address and acknowledge issues of oppression, privilege, power, and understand oppression, privilege, and power before they can understand social justice. While developing the competency of social justice student affairs educators must seek to include and meet the needs of students from all cultural backgrounds.

Oppression is a devastating control under which the oppressor does not view the oppressed as a human but a thing (Freire, 1987). The *Cambridge English Dictionary* defines oppressor as "someone who treats people in an unfair and cruel way and prevents them from having opportunities and freedom" while the oppressed are "people who are treated in an unfair and cruel way and prevented from having opportunities and freedom." According to Spring (2007) the oppressed people's thoughts and their fate and future are controlled and determined by the oppressor. Moreover, the oppressor creates a dominant environment and an overt and covert system structure which gives little or no freedom to the oppressed people to succeed or be empowered. Bell (1997) identified six characteristics of oppression: (1) oppression has a **pervasive** nature in which social inequality is both woven throughout institutions and embedded within individual consciousness; (2) oppression is **restrictive** and it limits the life opportunities of the oppressed from structure and materials; (3) oppression reflects a **hierarchical** relationship in which the dominant or privileged groups benefit unconsciously from the oppressed groups; (4) "power and privilege are relative" and "individuals hold multiple complex and cross-cutting social group memberships that confer relative privilege or disadvantage differently in different context (Collins, 1990, cited in Bell, 1997, p. 3), oppression signifies **complex, multiple, cross-cutting relationships**; (5) "oppressive beliefs are **internalized** by victims as well as perpetrators" (p. 4); and (6) oppression is manifested through a **shared and distinctive characteristic of "Isms"**—for example, racism, classism, or sexism.

An effective approach to understanding the oppression, privilege, and power for student affairs educators is to study the theory of oppression and increase their awareness of what role they play in situations involving the powerful and the powerless. Walking away from the conflict between the powerful and the powerless means one sides with the powerful (Freire, 1987). Student affairs educators must not only understand oppression, privilege, and power but also empower the racial and ethnic minority students to change their perception that being different from the majority is dysfunctional so that they are able to define their own identities and cultural backgrounds instead of having the oppressor do so for them (Spring, 2007). Student affairs educators may also employ the theory of three-stage developmental response to oppression (Alschuler, 1986) to examine where they stand concerning their understanding of oppression. The three stages include (1) magical conforming in which people conform with the society and believe the problems of the oppressed are unresolvable and their situations are hopeless due to fear of change; (2) naïve reforming at which people blame the oppressed and believe the oppressed deviate from the rules of the society and system; and (3) critical transforming in which people employ critical intellectual skills to analyze the system that creates unequal power and oppression, and themselves in ways they have oppressed others and been victimized "by their active collusion in supporting the conflict-producing rules and roles" (p. 493).

COMMON EXPERIENCES AND ISSUES FOR MANY STUDENTS OF COLOR

Common themes across racially diverse students which can greatly affect success in college include: (a) immigration status and reasons for immigrating, (b) generational status (i.e., if students are immigrants or if their parents are), (c) language skills/being bi-lingual and the need to interpret for family, (d) experiences being told that one is "not enough" based on language, color, country of origin, etc., (e) being told that one isn't an American based on his or her skin color or perceived race, (f) socioeconomic status which often impacts the need to work, quality of primary and secondary schooling and pressures to support family, (g) educational attainment of parents and family/first-generation status for some, and (h) perceived religion based on skin color. While not all the factors listed are directly related to race, they are often related to the experience of students of color.

Coming to college as a student of color from a majority White community, coming to college as a person of color from a predominantly minority community, coming to college as a White student from a majority White community and coming to college as a White student from a predominantly minority community can be drastically different experiences and influence racial awareness and identity. The experience is also different whether a student is attending a predominantly White institution (PWI), historical Black college or university (HBCU), Hispanic serving institution (HSI), minority serving institution (MSI) or community college. Given the situations described above student affairs educators must develop their professional competency in social justice and inclusion so as to work effectively with each of these students who possess unique personal, cultural and racial experiences.

BLACK AND AFRICAN AMERICAN STUDENTS

Black students began earning college degrees as early as 1834; however, access to college has been a fight that has played out in the legal system, on campuses and in policies (Fleming, 1976). In 1954 the Supreme Court ruled, in *Brown v. Board of Education* and other cases, that separate but equal (or racial segregation within public education) was unconstitutional (Bowles & DeCosta, 1971, Ogletree, 2004). The history of slavery, segregation and exclusion can still be felt for many students and on many campuses (Shuford & Flowers, 2016). This context is important to consider in educating and supporting Black and African American students.

As professionals, it is important to interrogate one's own perspectives, experiences, knowledge, and biases related to supporting Black and African

American students. The lack of information and misinformation often influence the way student affairs educators do their work and view campuses. As with all identities, it is important for students to be able to self-identify their race and ethnicity. Immigrants from countries in Africa or parts of the Caribbean may identify with their country of origin. Other students may not know their ethnic background, often due to ancestors brought to the US against their will, and may prefer terms like Black or African American. Others may use terms based on their ethnicity like Haitian American. The dramatic changing demographics of the United States in recent years also suggest that the African American/Black student population on college campuses has become more diverse than before. This population includes students from the African diaspora, Haitian, Jamaican and of other Afro-Caribbean descent whose history, immigration and needs may be different from those of traditional African American/Black students. Being multilingual or feeling bi-cultural as an immigrant can create a distinctly different experience with race and racial identity.

Overall, family is very important to Black and African American students. Extended family is an important part of this structure (Suizzo, Robinson, & Pahlke, 2008). Because African Americans are more likely than White students to be low-income and first-generation college students, it has been suggested that they should break away from their family and friends from home in order to be successful. Research has also shown that close relationships from home with friends and family can hinder college students of color (Guiffrida, 2005b). Contrastingly, high achieving students described families as their most important asset regardless of socioeconomic status while low achieving students or those who leave college were more likely to have families who are critical of their educational goals and environment (Guiffrida, 2006, Harper, 2012). This finding supports how important it is for educators to discuss the role of family for African American students and help them negotiate a relationship that supports their academic success while also maintaining a relationship with their family.

Much of the foundational research on African American students took a deficit approach. The lower retention and graduation rates of African American students were often blamed on the lack of academic preparedness, and programs were often focused on this. When controlling for variables like SAT, high school GPAs and socioeconomic status, the academic performance of Black students was still lower, thus suggesting that there are additional factors besides the often blamed academic underpreparedness (Guiffrida, 2006). These results support a holistic approach to supporting African American students and examining campus climate issues. More recent work has focused on student success instead of taking a deficit approach.

Some of the developmental tasks that Black and African American should handle for academic, personal, and professional success include developing identity, racial and ethnic identity, and interdependence as well as fulfilling affiliation needs, succeeding intellectually, developing spiritually, and developing social responsibility. (McEwen, Roper, Bryant, & Langa, 1990, Shuford & Flowers, 2016). In addition to the developmental tasks outlined for students, it is critical to examine a campus' role in the success of African American students. Some of the success strategies include getting involved in cultural student organizations, historically Black Greek organizations (National Panhellenic Council), professional associations, and advocacy groups. Identifying faculty/staff mentors is also a major contributor to college success, particularly if the mentors are Black or described as willing to go above their normal responsibilities and are culturally aware (Guiffrida, 2006). Students described African American faculty as more willing to "go above and beyond to assist students in succeeding at college" by (a) providing students with comprehensive academic, career, and personal advising; (b) actively supporting and advocating for students at college and at home; and (c) demonstrating beliefs in students' academic abilities" (Guiffrida, 2005a, p. 710). All professionals should be willing to serve as mentors and develop the competency to do so. Research indicates that African American students who have positive attitudes about self are more likely to progress in their racial identity development (Scottham, Cooke, Sellers, & Ford, 2010). Providing opportunities and experiences for African American students to develop in their cultural awareness and knowledge along with their racial identity encourages their growth, retention and graduation.

Harper (2012) examined the factors and lessons learned from successful Black male students and graduates. Participants in this study described parents who viewed college as the path to economic and social uplift. Their families viewed attending college as non-negotiable. Many also had at least one influential teacher who pushed them to attend college. Attending pre-college programs on campuses also gave successful Black male students greater exposure and influenced their expectations for higher education. Additionally, these students were involved in high school and continued their campus involvement which developed their leadership skills and expanded their network of peers and faculty and staff, all of whom were sources of support. According to Dr. Robert M. Franklin, President of Morehouse College, "We know that providing positive success messaging, group mentoring, the careful monitoring of progress, compassionate ministering when wounds must be address, and the strategic investment of money to support academic progress work" (Harper, 2012, p. 2).

Transition programs into college were also a positive factor because they had exposure to resources at the institution, took an introductory class or two, met upper class students and faculty/staff who are Black, and helped them acclimate to predominantly White campuses before the rest of students arrived for fall (Harper, 2012). Active engagement on campus aided in their academic performance via time management, interactions with academically-driven peers, relationships with faculty advisors, and a network of peers to study with and provide support.

Interestingly, the students in this study were not engaged in a structured mentoring program but rather had close relationships with high level administrators and faculty, often through their involvement and leadership positions. These Black men experienced instances of racism and what Harper and colleagues termed "onlyness" in which students felt a "profound sense of pressure to be the spokesperson or ambassador for people of color in general and Black men in particular" (Harper, 2012, p. 13). The students in this study developed skills and strategies to respond productively to racism and became "skilled at simultaneously embarrassing and educating their peers through the thoughtful act of calmly questioning their misconceptions" (Harper, 2012, p. 13). These lessons can be applied to all Black students. Much can be learned from engaging with and studying successful African American students to provide more support, messaging and celebration of accomplishments.

ASIAN AMERICAN AND PACIFIC ISLANDER STUDENTS

Asian Americans are the most recent group to immigrate to the United States in unprecedented numbers. This is in addition to the large number of Chinese immigrants during the 1800s. As a result of many military, economic, and political events (Min, 2006, Spring, 2010; Wright, 1987) between 1970 and 1980, the United States received "a steady stream of Asian immigrants and refugees" (Hsia & Hirano-Nakanishi, 1989, p. 22). The racial and ethnic group of Asian Americans and Pacific Islanders include East Asians, Southeast Asians, South Asians, and Pacific Islanders. The term Asian American and Pacific Islander (AAPI) and similar terms are pan-ethnic terms that are imperfect and often politicized (Park & Poon, 2016). The racial/ethnic grouping can be beneficial for advocacy, gaining resources, and politics yet it can also hide the deeply distinct cultures, languages and needs. Differences include immigration status, generational status, socioeconomic status, cultural identities, educational levels and religions among many others.

Some ethnic groups have come to the United States for graduate and professional education and have stayed and had a stable experience. Other ethnic groups "have been deeply shaped by their experiences as primarily refugee populations (e.g., Cambodian, Lao, Vietnamese, Hmong) who experienced tremendous hardship in leaving war-torn lands" (Park & Poon, 2016, pp. 113–114). Within other ethnic groups, there is great within-group diversity often depending on the circumstances of immigration, skill and economic level, and generational status. When statistics for Asian Americans and Pacific Islanders are viewed in their totality, the stark differences become invisible and often ignore the "severe educational disparities" for some groups (Park & Poon, 2016; Buenavista, Jayakumar & Misa-Escalante, 2009). For example, South Asians and Taiwanese Americans have the highest rates of college attainment while Southeast Asian Americans and Pacific Islanders have some of the lowest college attainment (CARE, 2008). South Asian students (including Indian, Pakistani, and Bangladeshi) may be forgotten in this grouping or may identify as Asian American. While there may be some shared experiences, again uniqueness of individuals and cultures cannot be overlooked.

Because of the perceived acculturation and high academic and professional performance of Asian Americans, the term "model minority" was coined with the intention to praise the accomplishments of Japanese Americans while suggesting that other racial and ethnic minority groups should strive to do the same (Peterson, 1966, cited in Wong, & Halgin, 2006). This stereotype has affected the experience of AAPI students including funneling into STEM (science, technology, engineering and math) fields, expectations of good grades, failure to consider mental health needs and lack of consideration of the diverse identities and experiences that comprise this group. As described by Pendakur & Pendakur (2012), "the model minority mythology positions APIAs as well-adjusted, well-mannered, smart, hardworking, and from financially well-off families, cloaking the very real struggles and challenges these students face on college campuses" (Choi, Rogers, & Werth, 2007; Yeh, 2002, 2004) (p. 38). The complexity of the AAPI experience ranges from being viewed as "perpetual foreigners," "honorary Whites," excluded from campus conversations about race, hesitant to seek support for mental health or academic support, assumed by many campuses to be succeeding due to the lack of disaggregation of data about the diversity of AAPI success and challenges, to being highly engaged, culturally aware and proud students.

Asian Americans generally value their family and collectivism (Kim, Atkinson, & Umemoto, 2001). The values of considering the family, making sacrifices, and following your elders is very significant to them. In addition, "group interests and goals should be promoted over individual interests and goals" (Kim, Atkinson, & Umemoto, 2001, p. 575). The culture of higher education is often very individualistic, and students are viewed as being the sole decision makers about their careers. This stance negates the culture of collectivism and valuing family expectations which many AAPI students consider in career and other choices. The pressure of balancing expectations from family and community with expectations of friends and with self-expectations can be overwhelming for students.

High levels of enrollment and persistence by AAPI students collectively should not override the fact that special assistance and education about one's identity and culture is still needed. Too often, campus conversations about race focus on African American students and Whites and possibly Hispanic-Latinx students with the exclusion of AAPI students which further reinforces the invisibility of issues and the perceived lack of importance of AAPI students in conversations about race. AAPI students are sometimes victimized or ostracized by their non-Asian peers. A given student may be the "only" AAPI student (or one of very few) in the classroom, residence hall, or other campus environments and experience pressure to perform.

One of the opportunities for supporting AAPI students includes developing bridge programs that assist in transition to college, mentoring, academic preparations, and community-building (Pendakur & Pendakur, 2012). Culturally competent academic and career advising as well as counseling services by professionals who are trained about AAPI students can make a profound impact on the success and development of AAPI students. Creating spaces for AAPI students to connect with students of their same culture(s) helps them thrive in college and develop in their identity. Engagement can occur through cultural organizations, Asian American or South Asian Greek letter organizations, multicultural affairs, programming and curricular offerings (Museus, 2013; Museus & Yi, 2014).

AMERICAN INDIAN STUDENTS

While each tribal nation maintains its own traditions, customs and languages, "historical and social elements shared by all tribes influence the development of Native American college students" (Bitsoi, 2016, p. 164). The deculturalization by the European conquerors, the systematic and government-sanctioned oppression of Native culture, and the historical trauma all are part of the historical context that affects American Indians. The importance of tribal sovereignty stems from this. The issues that have the most impact on the development of American Indians are "history, self-identification with tribal culture with the institution or community, and the prevalence of American Indian culture in the environment" (p. 164).

In the United States, there are 566 tribal nations as well as 70 tribal nations recognized by state governments (Bureau of Indian Affairs [BIA], 2015; Bitsoi, 2016). Just like other racial and ethnic groups, the diversity within American Indians and tribes makes it difficult for colleges to understand the experiences and needs of the students. Higher education professionals must be committed to learning more about American Indian students and how to help them succeed in college.

In order to best support and educate American Indian and Native students, student affairs educators must first educate themselves on the values, beliefs and traditions of individual American Indian students. "They should attempt to understand how students self-identify as American Indians and help them make choices that align with their cultural values," ideally using research on American Indian students (Bitsoi, 2016, pp. 177-178). College should set up ways for students to stay true to their values. "At the core of Native values are communal concerns (including adherence to tradition), responsibility for family and friends, cooperation and tribal identification" (LaFramboise, Heyle, & Ozer, 1990, cited in Bitsoi, 2016, pp. 169-170). These values can conflict with values of individualism, materialism and competition that may be exhibited by other students, particularly White students. Student affairs educators must understand American Indian students need a place or places on campus where they can belong and feel a sense of safety and comfort, particularly when considering that the choices (including career) they make "can be based on Native values and may not necessarily be in line with the majority-oriented societal values prevalent in the college environment" (Bitsoi, p. 170). Some of the core values that many American Indians hold include "sharing, cooperation, noninterference, present-time orientation, being versus doing, extended-family orientation, respect, harmony and balance, spiritual causes for illness and problems, group dynamics, and the importance of the tribe" (Bistoi, 2016, p. 170). Besides understanding and considering American Indian students' values while helping them student affairs educators also pay attention to their language, culture, cultural identity, genealogy, worldview, self-concept as an American Indian, and enrollment in a tribe (Horse, 2005).

Forms of alienation detracted from persistence (Taylor, 1999), and the factors that contributed to the alienation were "stereotypes, hostility, lack of respect, thoughtless comments, aloneness, lack of role models, and lack of institutional support" (Bitsoi, 2016, p. 175). A lack of diversity, support and role models affects American Indian students in similar ways as other marginalized students. Student affairs educators must counteract this by learning from and about American Indian students including their individual experience and their tribal affiliation, examine policies and practices to ensure inclusion, build supportive communities, encourage familial involvement, and continue to collect more data to best inform one's work.

LATINX AMERICAN STUDENTS

The Hispanic-Latinx population is growing in the United States and in college. Latinxs will become the largest minority group in the United States by 2060, moving from 17% of the current population to 31% (Ennis, Rios-Vargas, & Albert, 2011). This shift in population will influence the higher education landscape, policies, practices, and services. Some of the factors to consider for Latinx students include "time of immigration, precollege educational environments, extended family units, family history with higher education," identity development, and campus climate (Hernandez & Ortiz, 2016, p. 83). The national and global climate, immigration policies, and campus demographics will also influence the work occurring on campus. It is important to note that the term *Latinx* is used in this chapter as it is a more inclusive term that is gender inclusive and includes people whose ethnic origins are from the Caribbean, Central America and South America while it does not have the governmental overlay of Hispanic (Spring, 2010).

The diversity of identities within this population is significant. Students within this population may define themselves by their ethnicity, such as Columbian, by pan-ethnic terms like Cuban American, politicized terms like Chicano/Chicana, or Hispanic as tracing their origin back to Spain. Students who are Afro-Latino balance multiple identities as do others based on immigration or refugee status, socioeconomic status, abilities, sexuality, and many more. The history of Latinx ethnic groups is unique and often complicated, which plays into the identity and experience of Latinx college students. The largest Latinx populations in the United States are Mexican Americans (63%), Puerto Ricans (9.2%) and Cubans (3.5%), but it is important to recognize that the populations are drastically different depending on the location (Ennis et al., 2011). For example, "nearly one third of all Latinxs in Florida are Cuban" (Hernandez & Ortiz, 2016, p. 85). The majority of other Latinx ethnic groups have come to the United States within the past 25 years due to political unrest and have faced many of the same "economic, cultural and language barriers faced by the immigrants before them" (Hernandez & Ortiz, 2016, p. 86). The history of immigration and immigration policies have influenced the experience for Latinxs and their path to college.

There are several common factors related to Latinx students including: immigration status and reasons for immigrating, generational status, socioeconomic status, educational attainment of parents and family, other major intersectional identities, and the communities one comes from. Students who have been minority in their hometown and/or schools can have a drastically different experience than students who come from a predominantly Latinx community. Students who have immigrated in their mid to late teens also experience college in unique ways. For many students, they may feel bicultural in circumstances where they are American born and their parents are immigrants; this often causes students to wrestle with facets of their identity until they become more resolved about how they self-identify.

Many Latinx families experience poverty as immigrants, and then their families achieve greater economic security with subsequent generations. As such, "generational status influences other sociological factors related to Latinxs, such as educational attainment, familial influence and structure, bilingual skills, and Spanish language use" (Hernandez & Ortiz, 2016, p. 86). Spanish is often the primary language at home for first generation immigrants and sometimes second generation. Students as children may be the translators for their families including in areas of health care and education. The further from immigration, the more likely that Spanish use has diminished which can have a negative effect on students' identity and not feeling Latinx enough, particularly if others around them speak Spanish (Delgado Bernal, 2001; Torres, 2003). Being bilingual can give students a sense of identity, comfort, and help in the job market (Delgado Bernal, 2001). Additionally, as recent immigrants, Latinxs likely have a collectivist view on family and may have extended family staying together. There is a strong sense of responsibility to family that can influence how Latinx college students balance facets of their life and identity. Latinx students may experience micro-aggressions related to political anti-immigrant sentiments that have them labeled as "illegal immigrants," uneducated, or all as Mexican (Hernandez & Ortiz, 2016). This racism and discrimination influences how Latinx students experience college.

The number of Latinx students has increased steadily to the point that they comprise 16.5% of the undergraduate population (National Center for Education Statistics, 2013). What is different about students of this ethnic group than students from other ethnic groups is that almost half of Latinx students begin higher education in a community college, though these numbers are decreasing as more students are starting at four-year institutions (Fry & Thomas, 2013). These students are also more likely to attend part-time, go to a less selective college, and be the first in their families to attend college (ibid.). Given this information, it is important to consider ways to expand college access, aspiration, and affordability for Latinx students.

One of the significant ways to increase Latinx college attendance includes college access programs that begin as early as middle school and involve the families for support and awareness. According to Excelencia in Education (2015), of Latinx students who took the ACT and attended a four-year institution 78% were retained from their first to second year in college and were just one percent behind White students. Financial awareness is also important. For Latinx students who are undocumented, the cost of attendance varies from in-state tuition and scholarships to paying out-of-state/international student rates. The more an institution can provide easily accessible and multi-lingual information for students and their families, the more they can support the access, retention and graduation of Latinx students.

As mentioned above, students who develop and strengthen their ethnic identity, pride, and salience perform better in college. Students who participate in cohort programs for Latinx students have higher GPAs, experience pride, affirmation and acceptance of their Latinx identity as well as are more engaged in their community and develop bicultural leadership (Case & Hernandez, 2013; Cerezo & Chang, 2013). Some other critical supports for Latinx students include study and time management skills, mentoring, financial literacy, cohort models, student engagement in Latinx student organizations, and leadership opportunities.

MULTIRACIAL STUDENTS

The presence and awareness of multiracial or mixed-race students have increased since the 1990s as students became more vocal and as the national multiracial movement advocated for the federal government to change how it defined and collected data to be more inclusive (Renn & Johnston-Guerrero, 2016). According to the National Center for Education Statistics (2014), 2.9% of college students marked themselves as Two or More Races. In addition to this, students are required to mark first if they are Hispanic/Latino and then select one or more racial categories, thus illustrating the social construction of race which is fluid. It is critical that the identities of multiracial students are not rolled up into a multiracial category for data collection purposes as it negates the diversity of multiracial identities. For example, a student who is White and Asian American will likely have a different experience than a student who is Black and Latinx. Campuses should give students the opportunity to define their racial and ethnic identity rather than only allow them to check one box.

Society tends to want people to fit into neat boxes, and a "multiracial person's existence challenges the rigidity of racial lines that are a prerequisite for maintaining the delusion that race is a scientific fact" (Root, 1996, p. 7). This results in experiences of people asking, "What are you?" or trying to negate one aspect of a mixed-race person's race. Maria Root (1996) describes a Bill of Rights for Racially Mixed People which, in many ways, is foundational to future research and support for multiracial students. The Bill of Rights states:

I have the right
> not to justify my existence in this world
> not to keep the races separate within me
> not to be responsible for people's discomfort with my physical ambiguity
> not to justify my ethnic legitimacy

I have the right
> to identify myself differently than strangers expect me to identify
> to identify myself differently than how my parents identify me
> to identify myself differently than my brothers and sisters
> to identify myself differently in different situations

I have the right
> to create a vocabulary to communicate about being multiracial
> to change my identity over my lifetime – and more than once
> to have loyalties and identify with more than one group of people
> to freely choose whom I befriend and love. (p. 7)

The Bill of Rights highlights the often-felt tension between internal definitions and external pressures. Physical appearance receives a lot of attention for multiracial students as people try to categorize them, tell them whether they "belong" in a group, and only recognize part of their racial identity. Participants in a study by Talbot (2008) had difficulty expressing what it is like to be a biracial student in a mono-cultural world. Biracial/multiracial students are sometimes confronted with having to choose one aspect of their identity over another (ibid.), or not feeling accepted in mono-racial spaces on campus (King, 2008; Renn, 2004). In a study by Museus, Lambe Sarinana, Lee and Robinson (2016), students describe the invalidation of their racial identities and being told by others that they were not of their race or that they were "not really" a part of that group since they were multiracial. Renn and Johnston-Guerrero (2016) identified three themes for multiracial students: "the desire to identify themselves rather than be placed in categories by others, the role of racism (largely related to physical appearance) in multiracial identity, and the role of peers and peer culture in school and college experiences related to race" (p. 188).

Multiracial students benefit from campuses that promote healthy racial identity development for mixed race students and account for their identity in programs and services (Renn & Johnston-Guerrero, 2016). Programs and services should be culturally open and inclusive while acknowledging the similarities and differences among student of all backgrounds. Programs and services that are monoracial should recognize that multiracial students may be included and need to be recognized in the language and planning. The approach to any program or service for students of color must take into account that many students do not fit neatly into one race or ethnicity (ibid.). Faculty and staff should be trained to be inclusive of mixed-race students and to lead conversations related to this lived experience. Other action steps to serve multiracial students include conducting audits of existing programs, developing programs and groups exclusively focused on multiracial students, identifying role models on campus and in the community, including curricular opportunities to explore mixed race identities, and conducting a campus audit (ibid.). Multiracial students should have the opportunity to examine the various components of their racial and ethnic identity to self-determine their identity.

ARAB AMERICAN STUDENTS

The previous section on multiracial students illustrates the social construction of race and the great variability of experience and the significance of physical appearance for many students. Also, evidence in this is that the framing of race in America is still being centered around Whiteness. Little is researched or written about Middle Eastern and Arab American students. The current racial categories in admissions, census or other surveys are confusing because many of the students in this section do not identify with any of the categories.

The first Arab Americans who immigrated to the United States in 1880–1945 were predominantly Christian and came for economic opportunity and mostly worked as laborers (Naber, 2000). Later immigrants were typically well-educated Muslim (Moradi & Hasan, 2004). Because government officials classified Arabs according to multiple and conflicting categories and the ways that Arab immigrants identified themselves did not correspond with the U.S. categories, the visibility and understanding of this community is low. Naber (2000) identified four central paradoxes that shape Arab American identity. These are:

> The first paradox is that Arab Americans are a complex, diverse community, but are represented as a monolith in popular North American media images. The second paradox is that Arab Americans are simultaneously racialized as white and non-whites. The third paradox is that Arab Americans are racialized according to religion (Islam) rather than biology (phenotype). The fourth paradox involves the intersection between religious forms of identity that Arab immigrants bring to the US and the racial forms of identity that structure US society. (p. 37)

As the paradoxes indicate, Arab Americans are racialized, viewed as a monolithic group, and stereotyped in a way that assumes religion based on skin color. Perceived discrimination and actual experiences of discrimination and prejudice were found to have direct links with psychological distress for

Arab Americans. (Moradi & Hasan, 2004). With the sample of Arab Americans, the link between self-esteem and perceived discrimination was mediated fully by perceived control (Moradi & Hasan, p. 425). As with other groups, the complexity and diversity of the experience of Arab Americans and other students is not accounted for on college campuses and in lived experience. More research and campus programs and services are needed related to this group of students.

WHITE STUDENTS

In many books, articles and research studies related to race and college students, White students are only considered as the comparison to students of color. This framing continues to examine development, success and climate from a lens centered on Whiteness. In order to create open and inclusive college campuses, White students must be a part of changing campus climate and examining self in the process. Because of the current and historical framing, White students do not often "see" their race because it is the majority and assumed in most circumstances. "Many White students feel confused about how to have a positive White racial identity while simultaneously understanding a history of racism in the United States" (Linder, 2016, p. 208). They also often don't understand their role in addressing racism and where and how to act. Faculty and staff must educate, challenge and support White students' racial development and examine their own identity and understanding of race.

The changing demographics and the rise in racial acts of discrimination accentuate this need. According to the National Center for Education Statistics (2014), from fall 1976 to fall 2014 the percentage of White students fell from 84 percent to 58 percent. Like the other racial/ethnic groups, there is significant intra-group diversity ranging from recent immigrants to students who chart their heritage to the Mayflower. Regardless of other marginalized identities like socioeconomic status, sexuality or disability, White students remain a privileged group in the United States and this must be included in education. White children are often socialized to be "color-blind" with the idea that not seeing or discussing race is a positive thing when indeed it leaves White students unprepared about how to discuss race (Linder, 2016). Due to this socialization, White students often do not recognize Whiteness as a race or culture; part of this is due to the pervasiveness of White culture in campus traditions, policies, curricula, and programs (Harper & Hurtado, 2007; Rankin & Reason, 2005; Reason & Evans, 2007). Similarly, much of the scholarship about White racial identity development only explores identity in the context of racism and White privilege (Linder,

2016). More recent work strives to examine "Whiteness independently of other races and for assuming all White people grow and develop as antiracist allies" (Linder, 2016, p. 216; Hardiman, 2001; Rowe, Bennett & Atkinson, 1994; Sabnani, Ponterotto & Borodovsky, 1991). White racial identity and the experience of White college students cannot be separated from membership in a privileged group.

Goodman (2011) describes the characteristics of a privileged or dominant group of (a) normalcy, (b) superiority, (c) cultural and institutional power and domination, and (d) privilege. She notes that "there are also significant variations among forms of oppression and among individuals" (p. 12). The dominant group of White people serves as the point of reference and becomes "normal" and define what is right and wrong. "These cultural norms become institutionalized and establish policy and practice" (ibid.). Everything that is different from this de facto is viewed as not normal or wrong. This sense of normalcy then gets translated into superiority such as the White (European) books and music being viewed the standard for classroom education. Since the dominant groups creates the systems, rules and structures, these values and beliefs become the infrastructure which rewards the dominant group and disadvantages the marginalized groups. The structures are maintained through interpersonal, institutional and cultural systems, often without individuals being aware of this perpetuation and the exclusion of other views and identities (ibid.). Finally, privilege is derived for the dominant group, in this case, White students. This system gives them unearned privileges just because of their group membership. Some examples of this are the assumption that they were admitted on their own merit, lack of singling out in class based on their race, and having most professors and administrators look like them and likely support their values and beliefs.

For individuals from privileged groups, they are affected by being a part of this dominant group and a society structured around their identity. Often, there is a lack of awareness of the role that race plays in social structures. Goodman (2011) states that some of the common traits for individuals from privileged groups are (a) lack of consciousness, (b) denial and avoidance of oppression, (c) sense of superiority and entitlement, (d) multiple identities and experiences of privilege, and (e) resistance to seeing oneself as privileged. One of the biggest challenges in the education of White students related to race/ethnicity is reducing the resistance to be open to conversations and education about history, facts, and lived experiences. Because of the ever-presence of Whiteness, many White students are not aware of their race and its impact, while students of color can see the system of advantage and disadvantage. A related example would be a White student not thinking about race discrimination in the society while a student of color would be dramatically aware of lack of resources and being treated unfairly due to their skin color while growing up when a teacher says, "you can succeed like everyone else if you work hard."

Because of this longstanding lack of awareness, the confrontation of privilege and inequity can be challenging for White people, and they often want to avoid the discomfort or the conversation. White students may go through their entire college experience without learning about oppression, privilege and racial identity; this would be a failure on the part of colleges if we don't educate students about the broader social system. As student affairs educators, we need to encourage White students to lean into their discomfort and internal conflict. This means exploring the divide between "being uncomfortable" and thus avoiding conversations and the lived experience of students of color who are embroiled in daily experiences related to race. Related to this, Blacks are more likely to see the daily indignities and the system of institutionalized policies and practices while Whites are more likely to see racism as individual acts. (Goodman, 2011). Finally, being privileged is often equated to intentionally discriminating against someone as opposed to understanding the broader system which gives power to those in the dominant group and disadvantages the marginalized group. Often, Whites don't feel privileged and may have other disadvantages based on other identities, so they often deny the privilege that comes from being White. The difference between individual acts of racism and benefitting from a system without doing anything to change it must be explored with White students.

To fully educate White students in college, we need to ensure that they understand their identity, their privilege and how to work and empower others from diverse racial and ethnic backgrounds. Deep dialogue and meaningful interactions by White students with students of color will enhance their learning and ideally empower them to create change. White students need to be prepared to examine social systems and work with a diverse team to change the power structure and create a more inclusive environment.

KEY SKILLS FOR STUDENT AFFAIRS EDUCATORS

In working with students from racially and ethnically diverse backgrounds, student affairs professionals must balance the cultural knowledge they have with general helping skills to support students individually and collectively. Staff must also be attuned to their own racial/ethnic identity, biases and gaps in knowledge and comfort. In addition, they must be confident and competent enough to engage White students with the change that needs to occur and help them work as allies. The ability to use appropriate and powerful questions can help students reflect and make meaning of their growth and college experience (Harper, 2012). This also helps keep a pulse on campus issues and connect students with resources. Compassion, empathy and vulnerability are all part of being a culturally competent professional. Linder and Cooper (2016) promote a step beyond multicultural competence, stating, "Critical consciousness advances multicultural competence by requiring educators to stay critically engaged, understanding the complex ways in which power, context, and constantly shifting identities influences ways students experience campus environments" (p. 318). This requires continued engagement and self-assessment. Some of the strategies listed by Linder and Cooper are: continually work to make the unconscious conscious; create identity-explicit, not identity-exclusive, spaces; approach work from a "yes, and . . ." perspective; address racial battle fatigue, compassion fatigue, and vicarious trauma; stay abreast of current issues; and seek out critically conscious communities (pp. 386-389).

The connection between student affairs and academic units, particularly ethnic studies, cannot be overstated. The academic grounding and learning about one's culture is a significant opportunity in college. Professionals must have assessment and evaluation skills to examine the qualitative and quantitative data available to make informed decisions. These skills and perspective will also allow one to see where the data may be biased or not disaggregated to understand the variance for different racial and ethnic groups. Finally, higher education professionals must have a strong understanding of the First Amendment and how it interacts with protests, diversity and goals of inclusive excellence.

RECOMMENDATIONS

1. Student affairs educators have a responsibility to educate themselves about all racial and ethnic groups and maintain a posture of lifelong learning as the nuances, needs and experiences of students will evolve and change as will the campus climate and broader landscape.
2. Student affairs educators must develop their helping skills in culturally responsive ways so that they can listen and ask questions to support and educate all students.
3. Student affairs educators must interrogate their own racial/ethnic identity and how that influences their lens and work. It is also vital to examine one's biases, blind spots, and stereotypes and lean into the discomfort to challenge them.
4. Student affairs educators must learn about and be aware of how social, political, and historical forces shape student engagement and educational opportunity (Park & Poon, 2016). It is imperative to understand issues of social justice.

5. Student affairs educators must learn advocacy skills and allyship to magnify the strengths and needs of students. The understanding of when and how to bring students into this advocacy matters. It is equally important the student affairs educators understand their role at the institution and that position is likely as educator and student advocate and not of activist, particularly against the institution, but also in general. One should interrogate their professional role and their personal actions.

6. Staff and faculty must learn to discern when programs and services should be for a specific racial/ethnic population, when it should be for students of color and when the diversity and inclusion program should engage students of all racial and ethnic identities.

7. Student affairs educators must look for partnership with ethnic studies and similar programs like sociology and political science, to have more blended learning that teaches the history and current research about identity groups. Partnering with multicultural affairs offices is also an important component to ensure a web of services, education and support.

8. Finally, student affairs educators must take ownership for creating environments and cultures that include and empower all students, but with special emphasis on students of color. They must examine policies and procedures. This change will benefit the whole community.

REFLECTION QUESTIONS

1. How are you feeling after reading about the disparate experiences and treatment of students of various racial/ethnic backgrounds?

2. What are some areas of learning for you related to students of racially diverse backgrounds? What steps can you take to further your learning?

3. How might you begin to help White students or staff participate in dialogues about race/ethnicity, traditions, and climate in a way that educates them and allows them to explore their privileged identity, potential guilt, and the complexity/intersections of their identities?

CASE STUDY

The queer students of color on your campus have expressed outrage that the LGBTQ+ student organization has not been inclusive nor supportive of their needs. The cultural centers and the students who frequent them have also been described as unwelcoming, very gendered in their approach and homophobic. The queer students of color have organized, reached out to the media, and planned a protest and march to the main administration building. In their materials, they have also expressed disdain for student health care services, the counseling center, housing and recreational sports. Please reflect on your role and possible responses to the situations below:

1. There are 1–2 students in the group that you know. In your role as a newer professional who has a relationship with a couple of students in the organized groups, what role would you play?
   a. How would you communicate with the division of student affairs leadership about your relationship and possible role?
   b. How might you reach out to the students you know?
   c. How would you balance your role of student support and advocacy with your role as a university agent?
2. As someone who doesn't know much about the issues and identities and/or feels fairly uncomfortable, what role might you play?
3. Several of the students who are highly involved or work in your area talk about how the students should be expelled and are morally wrong. How would you proceed?
4. Your best friend on campus works in multicultural affairs and is deeply hurt by the comments about the cultural centers and/or the LGBTQ+ student organization that they advise. How do you interact with them?
5. The work that your campus and you have been doing related to students of color and campus climate has been predominantly or narrowly focused simply on race/ethnicity with minimal consideration to the intersection of identities like gender, sexuality, disabilities, or immigration status. How might you help the group to regroup and examine scope and the intersection of identities?

REFERENCES

ACPA/NASPA. (2015). *Professional competency areas for student affairs educators.* Washington, DC: Author.

Alschuler, A. S. (1986). Creating a world where it is easier to love: Counseling applications of Paulo Freire's theory. *Journal of Counseling and Development, 64,* 492–496.

Bell, L. A. (1997). Theoretical foundations for social justice education. In M. Adams, L. A. Bell, & P. Griffin (Eds.), *Teaching for diversity and social justice* (pp. 3–15). New York, NY: Routledge.

Bitsoi, L. L. (2016). Native American college students. In M. J. Cuyjet, C. Linder, M. F. Howard-Hamilton, & D. L. Cooper (Eds.), *Multiculturalism on campus: Theories, models and practices for understanding diversity and creating Inclusion* (pp. 164–185). Stylus Publishing, LLC, Sterling, VA.

Bowles, F., & DeCosta, F. A. (1971). *Between two worlds: A profile of Negro education.* NewYork: McGraw-Hill.

Buenavista, T. L., Jayakumar, U. M., & Misa-Escalante, K. (2009). Contextualizing Asian American education through critical race theory: An example of U.S. Philipino college student experiences. *New Directions for Institutional Research, 2009*(142), 69–81.

Bureau of Indian Affairs. (2015). What we do. Retrieved from https://www.bia.gov /bia/ots/what-we-do

CARE (National Commission on Asian American and Pacific Islander Research in Education). (2008). *Asian Americans and Pacific Islanders—facts, not fiction: Setting the record straight.* New York: NY: Author.

Case, K. F., & Hernandez, R. (2013). "But still, I'm Latino and I'm proud": Ethnic identity exploration in the context of a collegiate cohort program. *Christian Higher Education, 1*(12), 74–92.

Cerezo, A., & Chang, T. (2013). Latina/o achievement at predominantly White universities: The importance of culture and ethnic community. *Journal of Hispanic Higher Education, 12*(1), 72–85.

Choi, J. L., Rogers, J. R., & Werth, J. L. Jr. (2007). Suicide-risk assessment with Asian American college students: A culturally informed perspective. *The Counseling Psychologist, 20*(10), 1–31.

Delgado Bernal, D. (2001). Learning and living pedagogies of the home: The mestiza consciousness of Chicana students. *Qualitative Studies in Education, 14*(5), 623–639.

Ennis, S. R., Rios-Vargas, M., &Albert, N. G. (2011). The Hispanic population: 2010. The United States Department of Commerce. Retrieved from https://www .census.gov/prod/cen2010/briefs/c2010br-04.pdf

Excelencia in Education. (2015). Growing what works database. Retrieved from http://www.edexcelencia.org/growing-what-works

Fleming, J. E. (1976). *The lengthening shadow of slavery: A historical justification for affirmative action for Black in higher education.* Washington, DC: Howard University Press.

Freire, P. (1987). *Pedagogy of the oppressed.* New York, NY: Continuum.

Fry, R., & Thomas, P. (2013, April 23). An uneven recovery, 2009-2011: A rise in wealth for the wealthy; declines for the lower 93%. Pew Research Center. Retrieved from http://www.pewsocialtrends.org/files/2013/04/wealth_recovery _final.pdf

Goodman, D. J. (2011). *Promoting diversity and social justice: Educating people from privileged groups* (2nd ed.). New York: Routledge.

Guiffrida, D.A. (2005a). Othermothering as a framework for understanding African American students' definitions of student-centered faculty. *The Journal of Higher Education, 76*(6), 701–723.

Guiffrida, D. A. (2005b). To break away or strengthen ties to home: A complex question for African American students attending a predominantly White institution. *Equity and Excellence in Education, 38*(1), 49–60.

Guiffrida, D. A. (2006). Preparing and supporting African American college students. *VISTAS Online.* Walz, G. R. & Bleuer, J. C. American Counseling Association.

Hardiman, R. (2001). Reflections on White identity development theory. In C. L. Wijeyesinghe & B.W. Jackson III (Eds.), *New perspectives on racial identity development: A theoretical and practical anthology* (pp. 108–128). New York, NY: New York University Press.

Harper, S. R. (2012). *Black male student success in higher education: A report from the National Black Male College Achievement Study.* Philadelphia: University of Pennsylvania, Center for the Study of Race and Equity in Education.

Harper, S. R., & Hurtado, S. (2007). Nine themes in campus racial climates and implications for institutional transformation. *New Directions for Student Services, 2007*(120), 7–24.

Hernandez, S., & Ortiz, A.M. (2016). Latinx college students. In M. J. Cuyjet, C. Linder, M. F. Howard-Hamilton, & D. L. Cooper (Eds.), *Multiculturalism on campus: Theories, models and practices for understanding diversity and creating inclusion* (pp. 83–111). Sterling, VA: Stylus Publishing, LLC.

Horse (Kiowa), P. G. (2005). *Native American identity.* (New Directions for Student Services, 61–68). San Francisco, CA: Jossey-Bass.

Howard-Hamilton, M. F., Cuyjet, M. J., & Cooper, D. L. (2016). Understanding multiculturalism and multicultural competence among college students. In M. J. Cuyjet, C. Linder, M. F. Howard-Hamilton, & D. L. Cooper (Eds.), *Multiculturalism on campus: Theories, models and practices for understanding diversity and creating inclusion* (pp. 11–21). Sterling, VA: Stylus Publishing, LLC.

Hsia, J., & Hirano-Nakanishi, M. (1989, November/December). The demographics of diversity: Asian Americans and higher education. *Change,* 39–47.

Kim, B. S. K., Atkinson, D. R., & Umemoto, D. (2001). Asian cultural values and the counseling process: Current knowledge and directions for future research. *Counseling Psychologist, 29*(4), 570–603.

King, A. R. (2008). Student perspectives on multiracial identity. In K. A. Renn & P. Shang (Eds.), *Biracial and multiracial students* (*New Directions for Student Services, No 123,* pp. 33–41). San Francisco: Jossey-Bass.

LaFramboise, T. D., Heyle, A. M., & Ozer, E. J. (1990). Changing and diverse roles of women in American Indian cultures. *Sex Roles, 22*(7-8), 455–476.

Linder, C. (2016). Working with White college students to understand and navigate White racial identities. In M. J. Cuyjet, C. Linder, M. F. Howard-Hamilton, & D. L. Cooper (Eds.), *Multiculturalism on campus: Theories, models and practices for understanding diversity and creating inclusion* (pp. 208–231). Sterling, VA: Stylus Publishing, LLC.

Linder, C., & Cooper, D. L. (2016). From cultural competence to critical consciousness. In M. J. Cuyjet, C. Linder, M. F. Howard-Hamilton, & D. L. Cooper (Eds.), *Multiculturalism on campus: Theories, models and practices for understanding diversity and creating inclusion* (pp. 379–392). Sterling, VA: Stylus Publishing, LLC.

McEwen, M. K., Roper, L. D., Bryant, D. R., & Langa, M. J. (1990). Incorporating the development of African American students into psychosocial theories of student development. *Journal of College Student Development, 31*(5), 429–436.

Min, P. G. (2006). Asian immigration: History and contemporary trends. In P. G. Min (Ed.), *Asian Americans: Contemporary trends & issues* (pp. 7–31). Thousand Oaks, CA: Pine Forge Press.

Moradi, B., & Hasan, N. T. (2004). Arab American persons' reported experiences with discrimination and mental health: The mediating role of personal control. *Journal of Counseling Psychology, 51*(4), 418–428.

Museus, S. D. (2013). Asian Americans and Pacific Islanders: A national portrait of growth, diversity, and inequality. In S. D. Museus, D. C. Maramba, & R. T. Teranishi (Eds.), *The misrepresented minority: New insights on Asian Americans and Pacific Islanders, and their implications for higher educations* (pp. 11–41). Sterling, VA: Stylus.

Museus, S. D., Lambe Sarinana, S. A., Lee, A. L., & Robinson, T. (2016). A qualitative analysis of multiracial students' experiences with prejudice and discrimination in college. *Journal of College Student Development, 57*(6), 680–697.

Museus, S. D., & Yi, V. (2014). Asian American college students. In P. A. Sasso & J. L. DeVitis (Eds.), *Today's college students: A reader* (pp. 45–56). New York: Peter Lang.

Naber, N. (2000). Ambiguous insiders: An investigation of Arab American invisibility. *Ethnic and Racial Studies, 23*(1), 37–61.

National Center for Education Statistics. (2013). Projections of education statistics to 2021. Retrieved from https://nces.ed.gov/pubs2013/2013008.pdf.

National Center for Education Statistics. (2014). Digest of education statistics. Retrieved from https://nces.ed.gov/programs/digest/d15/tables/dt15_306.10.asp

Ogletree, C. J. (2004). *All deliberate speed: Reflections on the first half century of Brown vs. Board of Education.* New York: W. W. Norton & Company.

Park, J. J., & Poon, O. A. (2016). Asian American and Pacific Islander students. In M. J. Cuyjet, C. Linder, M. F. Howard-Hamilton, & D. L. Cooper (Eds.), *Multiculturalism on campus: Theories, models and practices for understanding diversity and creating inclusion* (pp. 112–140). Sterling, VA: Stylus Publishing, LLC.

Pendakur, S., & Pendakur, V. (2012). Let's get radical: Being a practitioner-ally for Asian Pacific Islander American college students. In D. Ching, & Agbayani, A. (Eds.), *Asian Americans and Pacific Islanders in higher education: Research and perspectives on identity, leadership, and success* (pp. 31–55). Washington, DC: National Association of Student Personnel Administrators (NASPA),

Peterson, W. (1966, January 6). Success story: Japanese American style. *New York Times Magazine,* p. 11.

Rankin, S. R. & Reason, R. D. (2005). Differing perceptions: How students of color and White students perceive campus climate for underrepresented groups. *Journal of College Student Development, 46*(1), 43–61.

Reason, R. D., & Evans, N. J. (2007). The complicated realities of Whiteness: From color blind to racially cognizant. *New Directions for Student Services, 2007*(120), 67–75.

Renn, K. A. (2004). *Mixed-race college students: The ecology of race, identity, and community.* Albany, NY: SUNY Press.

Renn, K. A., & Johnston-Guerrero, M. P. (2016). Biracial and multiracial college students. In M. J. Cuyjet, C. Linder, M. F. Howard-Hamilton, & D. L. Cooper (Eds.), *Multiculturalism on campus: Theories, models and practices for understanding diversity and creating inclusion* (pp. 186–207). Sterling, VA: Stylus Publishing, LLC.

Root, M. P. P. (1996). A bill of rights for racially mixed people. In M. P. P. Root (Ed.), *The multiracial experience: Racial borders as the new frontier* (pp. 3–14). Thousand Oaks, CA: Sage Publications.

Rowe, W., Bennett, S. K., & Atkinson, D. R. (1994). White racial identity models: A critique and alternate proposal. *Counseling Psychologist, 22*(1), 129–146.

Sabnani, H. B., Ponterotto, J. G., & Borodovsky, L. G. (1991). White racial identity development and cross-cultural counselor training: A stage model. *Counseling Psychologist, 19*(1), 76–102.

Scottham, K. M., Cooke, D. Y., Sellers, R. M., & Ford, K. (2010). Integrating process with content in understanding African American racial identity development. *Self and Identity, 9,* 19–40.

Shuford, B. C., & Flowers, L. A. (2016). African American college students. In M. J. Cuyjet, C. Linder, M. F. Howard-Hamilton, & D. L. Cooper (Eds.), *Multiculturalism on campus: Theories, models and practices for understanding diversity and creating inclusion* (pp. 141–163). Sterling, VA: Stylus Publishing, LLC.

Spring, J. (2007). *Wheels in the head: Educational philosophies of authority, freedom, and culture from Confucianism to human rights* (3rd ed.). New York, NY: McGraw-Hill.

Spring, J. (2010). *Deculturalization and the struggle for equality: A brief history of the education of dominated cultures in the United States* (6th ed.). Boston, MA: McGraw-Hill.

Suizzo, M., Robinson, C., & Pahlke, E. (2008). African American mothers' socialization beliefs and goals with young children: Themes of history, education, and collective independence. *Journal of Family Issues, 29*(3), 287–316.

Talbot, D. (2008). Exploring the experiences and self-labeling of mixed-race individuals with two minority parents. In K. A. Renn & P. Shang (Eds.), *Biracial and Multiracial Students (New Directions for Student Services, No 123)* (pp. 33–41). San Francisco: Jossey-Bass.

Taylor, J. S. (1999, November). America's first people: Factors which affect their persistence in higher education. Paper presented at the annual meeting of the Association for the Study of Higher Education, San Antonio, TX.

Torres, V. (2003). Influences on ethnic identity development of Latino college students in the first two years of college. *Journal of College Student Development, 44,* 532–547. University of Southern California. *The equity scorecard: Balancing educational outcomes.* Retrieved from https://rossier.usc.edu/the-equity-scorecard-balancing-educational-outcomes/.

Wong, F., & Halgin, R. (2006). The "model minority": Bane or blessing for Asian Americans? *Journal of Multicultural Counseling and Development, 34*(38–49).

Wright, D. J. (1987). Minority students: Developmental beginnings. In D. J. Wright (Ed.), *Responding to the needs of today's minority students (New Directions for Student Services, No. 38)* (pp. 5–21). San Francisco: Jossey-Bass.

Yeh, T. L. (2002). Asian American college students who are educationally at risk. In M. K. McEwen, C. M. Kodama, A. N. Alvarz, C. Liang, & S. Lee (Eds.), *Working with Asian American college students (New Directions for Student Services, no. 97)* (pp. 61–72). San Francisco, CA: Jossey-Bass.

Yeh, T. L. (2004). Issues of college persistence between Asian and Asian Pacific American students. *Journal of College Student Retention, 6*(1), 81–96.

Chapter 6

SUPPORTING COLLEGE STUDENTS WITH VARIOUS NEEDS

Matthew R. Shupp, Mindy Suzanne Andino,
Jacqueline S. Hodes, & Martin Patwell

Vincent is a 28-year-old Indian American returning to college after serving two tours in Iraq and Afghanistan. He was called into active duty in the middle of his junior year. At that time, he was an undeclared student, yet was hoping to major in psychology. During his time in Iraq and Afghanistan, Vincent was injured by an improvised explosive device. In order to save his life, medical personnel needed to amputate his left leg. He received numerous recognitions from the military for his bravery and valor and was honorably discharged from service three years ago. Since that time, Vincent has completed physical therapy and has been fitted with a prosthetic device. He still prefers to walk with crutches rather than use the prosthetic device. He also sought out counseling immediately returning home from service after having a violent outburst and anxiety attack during the Fourth of July festivities. He has been diagnosed with Post-Traumatic Stress Disorder, however his insurance will no longer cover the cost of his counseling sessions. Because of this dilemma, Vincent hopes to seek out free counseling services on campus as long as he is able to schedule appointments in the evenings. Vincent works full-time to support his wife and one-year- old daughter. Due to his work schedule, Vincent requires a very specific schedule of courses (online, on most evenings, or on weekends) as well as support services open and available in the evenings. He is taking advantage of the G.I. Bill and other financial aids provided to veterans. Now returning to college, Vincent plans to major in political science. He finds that he is one of the oldest students in class, which often makes it hard to relate with his peers.

Jules is a first-year student who moved 3,000 miles away from home to attend a large, public, urban institution. She is extremely close to her family and was born and raised in a small, conservative town. Yet, Jules' family has always encouraged her to "follow her dreams" of becoming a speech pathologist. This institution's speech pathology program is ranked as one of the best in the nation. Jules has questioned her sexual orientation from a very young age, yet was always hesitant to talk with her family about it given the conservative environment of her home town. She is interested in becoming more involved in the LGBTQ+ community at her progressively inclusive institution. Still, Jules has turned to drinking—sometimes to excess—in order to cope with the exploration of her sexual identity. Her college has a reputation for being a "party school" and was recently featured in the national news for not adequately responding to several sexual assault allegations.

Bonnie is an international student from Ukraine who arrived on campus three days before the International Services Office and Orientation Team expected her. She speaks very little English, and the staff were surprised to see that she requires use of an electronic wheelchair due to a congenital illness. The campus is recovering from several acts of vandalism and anti-Semitic protests that occurred the semester prior to Bonnie's arrival. The hate groups assembled due to the institution's nationally recognized status as one of the most welcoming institutions for study-abroad and international student experiences. Although Bonnie has a small friend group, she recently assumed an executive board position in the International Students Club and appears to be adjusting well to her new home in the United States. She struggles in many classes due to the language barrier. She is resistant to receiving academic assistance from campus support offices for fear of appearing "weak," as she is not accustomed to asking for help.

Mia identifies as a transgender female who is preparing for gender-affirming surgery. She is a biology major with the hopes of attending medical school at one of the most competitive and prestigious institutions in the country. Mia has very little family support and was kicked out of her home during her sophomore year of high school after coming out as gay to her family. Mia lived with friends until her high school graduation. Due to her lack of family support, Mia has accrued a large amount of student financial debt and faces unmet needs for the upcoming school year. She enjoys the chess and anime clubs on campus and has a supportive peer environment. Mia's institution does not yet have a preferred name policy, and Mia is exhausted at having to explain that her legal name is "Mike," but she identifies as Mia.

As a reader of this text, from the brief vignettes shared above, how might you go about supporting each of these students? How has each of these students experienced campus life? What similarities exist between them? How might their experiences differ from one another? What else might you want or need to know in order to best support each of these students?

From a purely cognitive perspective, we might encourage the use of the Council for the Advancement of Standards (CAS) in Higher Education as well as the ACPA (College Student Educators International) and NASPA (Student Affairs Administrators in Higher Education) Professional Competencies in Student Affairs that cite practitioners' need of "essential knowledge, skills, and dispositions expected of all student affairs educators" (2015, p. 7). Furthermore, the ACPA/NASPA Professional Competencies in Student Affairs call for an "active orientation" (p. 4) toward student development that helps us think critically and act accordingly. Institutional responses have often served these populations by focusing on one particular aspect, yet what might be the drawback of focusing on one piece of individuals' identity? How do we honor students holistically?

It is equally important to examine our understanding of our identities if we are to be fully engaged with others. The aspect of self-awareness embedded within multicultural competence is paramount in order for us to gain the knowledge and skills to help other individuals. Therefore, before you read this chapter, we ask that you engage in the following reflective exercise. Your honest reflection is an important component to fully engaging with the concepts we propose throughout the chapter.

Who are you? How do you identify? If asked this question, how might you answer? What characteristics would you focus on? For example, you may focus on gender, your profession, a hobby, whether or not you are a parent or sibling, etc. Consider your answers and jot a few of them down below:

_____

_____

_____

_____

What did you come up with? Typically, when asked, individuals tend to focus on surface level characteristics. Although completely appropriate and not untrue, often these identifiable characteristics do not address the underlying complexities that make each of us.

Figure 1, based on Stanley Herman's illustration of a cultural iceberg (1978), illuminates the complexities of an individual's identity. The tip of the triangle is a visual representation of our outward appearance to others. It is

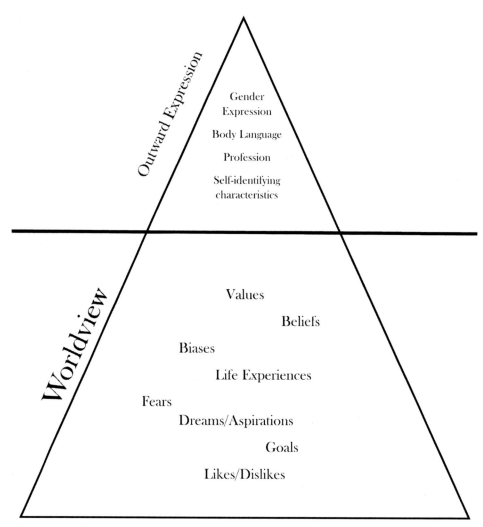

Figure 1. Adapted from Herman, S. N. (197). TRW Systems Group. In Wnedell L. French and Cecil H. Bell, Jr. *Organisational [sic] Development: Behavioral [sic] Science Interventions for Organisational [sic] Improvement,* 2nd ed., p. 16.

the social mask put forth that others see, including our body language, gender expression, language, and tone of voice. The base of the triangle includes the aspects embedded within the larger concept of our identity. Some of these aspects might include a person's beliefs, values, biases, life experiences, fears, dreams, aspirations, and feelings. These pieces are often hidden or not easily identifiable to others. These pieces, over time, come together to form our true, authentic selves. Each of us is made up of our life experiences that shape how we see the world and interact with others.

These types of illustrations are certainly not new, but they visually demonstrate an important concept: in most of our daily interactions, individuals see surface level representations of one another. Who we truly are—our authentic self—lies underneath the surface. And what often makes us who we truly are has emerged over a lifetime of lived experiences. Herein is the complexity. How we respond to the world around us is dictated by who we truly are, yet very few individuals present more than surface-level representations of themselves. More so, "who" we are and "how" we present ourselves to the world are often misaligned.

What is on the surface level is informed by our worldview, developed from learned ways of perceiving life events and the environment around us (Brown & Landrum-Brown, 1995). Differing worldviews impact how we receive and make meaning of life's experiences. Through this perspective, life events are far less important than how a person interprets and makes meaning of those experiences.

Let's revisit the initial question: Who are you? If asked this question, and considering the life experiences that have shaped your view of the world, how might you answer now? What characteristics would you focus on? Consider your answers and jot down a few of them below:

_____

_____

_____

_____

Higher education has grown in its diversity, however, colleges and universities have not kept up with this change in order to best meet the needs of the rapidly growing diverse population. Therefore, this chapter is both a reminder and a challenge; it reminds us to continually center our work around students' lived experiences and challenges us to find successful ways to do so. The student demographic in higher education is rapidly evolving. This evolution necessitates faculty and student affairs educators' response to be grounded in an understanding of the intersectional nature of student's identities as well as to employ multiculturally sensitive and effective intervention strategies while working with all college students.

Our approach to our practice must not be reactionary and haphazard but intentional and focused. To focus on one aspect of the student's identity dismisses the holistic process of student development and, in turn, limits our ability to adequately and appropriately support students. Yet institutions of higher education, perhaps out of necessity, have a long history of established affinity centers which often focus on and call attention to one aspect of students' identities. While the inclusion of affinity centers is not inherently negative, the danger comes when the community assumes that all individuals within one shared identity have the same lived experience.

Indeed, students do not function in a vacuum. For example, if Vincent, Jules, Bonnie, or Mia visited the Office of Academic Advising for an appointment, how might we work with each of them? Although each of them may be seeking the same outcome (i.e. assistance with course scheduling for the next semester), they all bring with them a worldview consistent with their own lived experience. What would we need to know in order to inform our practice and best support each student? Their need for academic advisement and their intersecting identities are not mutually exclusive, at least we do not believe them to be so. The purpose of this chapter, therefore, is to address how to effectively support the needs of all students while calling attention to specific populations that have been traditionally marginalized and underserved in our current system of patriarchy and white supremacy.

Given the ever-increasing diversity of our student body, gaining the necessary helping proficiencies to be most successful in our positions may appear to be a daunting task. To center our students via one primary identity may expedite a student affairs educator's ability to quickly identify the skills necessary to aid this student, yet it diminishes the complexity of the person's intersecting identities when doing so. For this reason, the concept of intersectionality (Crenshaw, 1995) will be woven throughout the content of this particular chapter as we highlight a number of populations that may exist on our campuses. Intersectionality is a term coined by Kimberle Crenshaw in 1989. Originally used to explain the experiences of Black women, intersectionality has become ubiquitous when discussing student development, examining students' numerous intersecting identities, and their lived experience on college campuses. Although robust, this chapter is certainly not complete; rather, we believe it illustrates the need for continued dialogue as it relates to identity, intersectionality, and support systems on college campuses. Colleges and universities have seen an increase over the last two decades in the variety of students they serve. Campus environments (public, private, religiously-affiliated, etc.) impact student development as much as the development of their intersecting identities. The chapter highlights the following populations:

- LGBTQ+ students
- International students
- Women college students
- Students in low socioeconomic class (SES)
- Students with disabilities
- Veteran students

Each section provides a brief historical context identifying how these sub-populations of students have traditionally been served. The chapter addresses salient information that frames the readers' understanding behind the unique needs each sub-population of students face as they navigate their higher education experience. Each section contains questions for the reader to pause and reflect upon. Questions such as "What services does your current institution have in place to support this group of students?" and "How might your current institution provide services in order to positively impact students' experiences?" will help the reader to critically reflect upon these important concepts. Finally, each subsection concludes with considerations and recommendations that the reader could potentially implement in order to best assist these students.

LGBTQ+ STUDENTS

Overview of Salient Issues

At the writing of this chapter, there is a great deal of unrest and divisiveness within the country. A white supremacist rally in Charlottesville, VA recently resulted in the death of a rally protestor and numerous additional individuals injured. Racist and anti-Semitic beliefs and violent rhetoric, vaguely concealed under the guise of the freedom of speech, is not something new in higher education or our country. Yet, in 2018, it appears there has been a regression from cultural competence that falls far below even a basic level of political correctness. Hate, to some, appears to be a natural and preferred reaction to difference and the driving force behind an alt-right agenda. Many of our students within the LGBTQ+ community have experienced this same type of marginalization throughout their lifetime, including experiencing it on our campuses. According to the National LGBT Health Education Center, approximately nine million individuals in the United States identify as gay, lesbian, bisexual, or transgender. As such, more and more of an institution's student body identifies as LGBTQ+. Yet, many individuals within this community, including trans-folx and trans persons of color, in particular, face the greater risk of violence or sexual assault than their non-LGBTQ+ peers (Green & Wong, 2015). Stress often resulting from discrimination or needing to work harder to receive the same level of care is higher within the LGBTQ+ population, which can lead to self-medicating tendencies, including higher use of substances than the general population (LGBTQ Addiction Guide, n.d).

Over the last two decades, colleges and universities nation-wide have provided institutional resources that aid in the retention of marginalized students. For example, over 100 LGBTQ+ affinity centers exist on college campuses (Henshaw, n.d.). Likewise, additional support services, including gender-neutral housing, student clubs, and diverse campus programming have created a greater sense of inclusion for many traditionally marginalized students. Although higher education has made inroads when it comes to addressing the safety and inclusion of LGBTQ+ students on campus, more can still be done. In August 2017, Donald J. Trump, the 45th President of the United States, sent out a series of tweets announcing a ban on transgender individuals from serving in the military. This announcement dismantled much of the gender identity and sexual orientation equity work done in the US. It has set a tone in our country that students sharing an identity within the LGBTQ+ spectrum are "less than." These actions essentially undo the Office of Civil Rights's (OCR) previous edicts as stated in their *Dear Colleague* letters.

The implications of the military ban on trans-serving personnel cannot go understated. Removing LGBTQ+ individuals' access to the military limits educational opportunities and essentially denies educational access to the LGBTQ+ community. This example, above all else, is a social justice issue, and student affairs educators must be steadfast in our advocacy for students at both a micro and macro level. What might we do to increase greater access to higher education for the LGBT+ population, specifically trans-individuals? How might we best assist our LGBTQ+ students ensuring a safe and equitable campus climate?

Recommendations and Service Interventions

We implore institutions to look deeply and critically at their current policy as it relates to LGBTQ+ students and work to shift higher education's culture to one of greater inclusivity and understanding. Shifting cultural norms—any cultural norms—is difficult and takes time. We encourage institutions to engage in campus-wide climate surveys to assess the members' overall experience of connectedness. The climate survey can help an institution develop system-wide goals focused on increasing safety and inclusiveness. Some of these changes could include diversifying admissions materials and creating gender-neutral housing policies. Likewise, institutions should implement preferred-name policies, which affirm members of the LGBTQ+ community true, authentic self. Ongoing diversity training, with a focus on inclusive LGBTQ+ practices, is essential for all members of the campus community. Moreover, institutions should include gender-affirming language within institutional mission statements and policies and create dedicated spaces that destigmatize gender non-confirming and non-gender binary individuals.

People are often resistant to change. What might we change in our daily interactions to create greater inclusivity in our student affairs practice? To begin, we must acknowledge that we don't know what we don't know. Our experiences matter. Yet, so do the experiences of our students, and, often times, these experiences vastly differ from our own. Next, we must commit to broadening our understanding of issues impacting our most marginalized students. For example, we must educate ourselves on the nuances of identity. This can be accomplished by developing an understanding that gender identity, sexual orientation, and biological sex are separate, distinct aspects of an individual's identity. Next, we must utilize our privilege in ways that elevate marginalized voices. Only when we begin to infuse new behaviors into our daily practice will growth occur. One example of a behavior change is for student affairs educators to share their gender pronouns, both publicly and in email signatures. "Hello! My name is _____. My pronouns are he/him/his; she/him/her; they/them; ze/zir, etc. . . ." creates several responses. We have experienced confusion from students, wondering why we would verbalize our pronouns to students. This level of inquisitiveness creates teachable moments to educate students. In addition, students can be asked and encouraged to share their name and pronouns. Be mindful that, if not utilized appropriately, this type of exercise may inadvertently out a student not yet comfortable being out to the public. Therefore, challenge by choice. Affirming students' true identity from the beginning creates a greater sense of investment in their lived experience and may increase their overall retention in their collegiate pursuits.

Reflection Questions

Utilizing Jules' vignette at the beginning of the chapter, what programs, policies, and services are available on your campus to support students who claim this identity? Would your response differ if you were working with Mia? How might Jules' and Mia's situations be similar/different? What additional programs, policies, and services could be available on any campus to positively support students who claim these identities?

INTERNATIONAL STUDENTS

Overview of Salient Issues

There are approximately 1,044,000 international students attending colleges and universities in the United States, mainly from China, India, South Korea, Saudi Arabia, and Canada (Institute of International Education, 2016). These students contributed $24.7 billion to the U.S. economy in 2012-2013 through tuition and other living expenses and make up four percent of the total U.S. higher education population (Gautam, Lowery, Mays, & Durant, 2016). Despite their large contribution to the U.S. economy, international students face many challenges in the college environment, including barriers to language proficiency, social life, cultural adaption, academics, and finances (Gartman, 2016).

One of the biggest challenges international students face is their Language proficiency that affects their social and academic development. Generally, language barriers, social cues, and cultural norms tend to be difficult for most international students. Although international students may find faculty approachable and nice, communicating issues or asking class questions does not always yield positive results. Accents, pronunciation, and rate of speech make communicating difficult even though the students have studied English in their home country prior to beginning school (Wu, Garza, & Guzman, 2015).

This barrier can affect the social life of international students, as they are less likely to make friends with American students, and they may experience a sense of discrimination. They are also likely to feel different from everyone else and feel that they do not belong. Language proficiency also plays a role in the academic barrier that international students experience—in addition to having difficulty with the different teaching styles, different ways in which students relate to professors, and different structures in lesson delivery (Gartman, 2016). Differing academic cultural practices ranging from essay writing structure, plagiarism, and assessments to the interaction between staff and students influences how an international student experiences college (Mackinnon & Manathunga, 2003).

For international students language barriers can lead to difficulties connecting with roommates, completing group projects, and fulfilling basic needs such as ordering food. Being able to communicate effectively in the language of the university facilitates international students' academic and social life; they socialize better, have higher self-esteem levels, and feel less annoyed due to their accent or racial background (Contreras-Aguiree & Gonzalez, 2017; Lee, Park, & Kim, 2009). American colleges and universities remain as the leading destination for thousands of students around the world (Mamiseishvili, 2012) and as such practitioners must respond to the diverse and changing needs of international students. Practitioners must not rely on the typical qualities of this student type. An international student with a learning disability or one who is struggling being away from home for the first time can pose challenges with which staff and faculty are not familiar. It is important that every institution have protocols for assisting and helping international students succeed; these protocals include recognizing intersecting identities.

Recommendations and Service Interventions

For college student affairs educators there are several ways campuses can better serve the international student population. This means that every educator on the campus should be advocating for these students. In order to best serve, all staff and faculty must understand the challenges students face. Encouraging and facilitating collaboration between offices of international student services and other academic departments of support are uncomplicated ways that student affairs practitioners can create a welcoming environment for international students. Examples of such encouragement and collaboration include creating an English program to support ESL language learners; embracing and appreciating the diversity these students bring by learning from them and not always about them; and understanding that tutoring and counseling are of the utmost importance. A suggestion for practice would be using in-service, seminars, or professional development days to host open workshops on how to best serve international students, hosted by the international student support office (Mamiseishvili, 2012; Wu, Garza, & Guzman, 2015). Some campuses have created affinity groups for international faculty and staff. These groups also serve as resources for international students. Practitioners should also be aware of supportive organizations in the region that may be able to assist these students off-campus or that would be willing to partner with the school. Once the greater campus understands the obstacles this group of students may face, they can better tailor their academic methods and support to accommodate them. Overall, "persistence of international students should not be viewed as the responsibility of only international student advisors. Instead, it should become a joint responsibility of a broader campus community" (Wu, Garza, & Guzman, 2015).

The financial burden on international students is something not often considered by college student affairs practitioners. International students struggle with the stress of out-of-state tuition costs, a lack of access to loans and scholarships, and not being able to work off-campus (Gartman, 2016). Additionally, international students face out-of-state fees, living expenses, and potentially fluctuating visa costs. The cost of activities, cultural excursions, and museum tours may be cost prohibitive. In some cases the cost to return to their home country is so prohibitive that international students are at a loss for housing over breaks when residence halls may be shut down. At some universities, residence life and housing professionals strategically pair international students with domestic student roommates and sometimes even try to room them with a student who is relatively close to campus. This provides the opportunity for the domestic student to bring the international student home over breaks. Even if campus housing is open during breaks, international students may find that dining services are not operating or operating on a limited schedule, and public transportation to grocery stores is limited if not nonexistent. In some parts of the country calling a cab or using a bus or train may not be an option. One way to support international students is to create a "family" adoption program. Host families from the university community or local community are paired with international students and serve as a resource for them. This mitigates some of the issues of access to resources and can help to decrease the feeling of homesickness. Additionally, these interactions help international students learn the host country customs, traditions, and colloquialisms.

Continuing with the concept of intersectionality, international students who identify as a student with a disability face unique challenges. Access and support services may be different in their country of origin. Let us revisit our international student, Bonnie. Bonnie has intersecting identities of being an international student, a woman, and a student with a disability. For international students, disability support services and accommodations may be very different in their home country. For some individuals, the US process of receiving accommodations may be overwhelming, more advanced, or less advanced. With a potential language barrier and intersecting identities to navigate, this process can prove daunting to students.

Another challenge faced by international students is cultural adaptation. International students often struggle with the idea of individualism versus collectivism, a lack of common interests with U.S. students, and different beliefs about communication and friendship. These cultural differences have led to misunderstandings, misperceptions, and discrimination. Two other challenges faced by international students are the lack of a transportation system around universities and differences in religion (Gautam et al., 2016).

Some of the ways that student affairs educators can help international students is by having a comprehensive set of resources available for these students, such as up-to-date websites with different language options and ongoing orientations that can allow students to become aware of the resources available to them. Programs that allow international students to interact with domestic students can help with the social and cultural barriers as well as opportunities for scholarships and part-time jobs that can help with their finances (Gartman, 2016). International students should also have the option of being able to go to a healthy social space, where they can interact with other international students to make them feel at home (Gautam et al., 2016). Although not all, many campuses have an international student office and may even have a lounge.

One population, similar to international students, is the group of students who participate in study abroad programs for either a semester or a year and then return to their home campus. Participating in study abroad is touted as a transformative experience that immerses students in a culture uniquely different from their own. College student affairs educators need to be aware of the difficulties this population faces as they transition back to campus. This may also be true for veterans who are transitioning back to the US. Students may struggle with connecting with their previous classmates who do not have this shared lens or experience. Problems and issues that were important before their abroad experience are insignificant in comparison. For example, for some students a current issue of concern may be obtaining the newest fashionable outfit or bag, but for a student who just returned from a third world country in which a significant portion of the population may not have had access to shoes, obtaining the latest fashion item may feel insignificant.

Reflection Questions

What programs, policies, and services are available on your campus to support students who claim this identity? What programs, policies, and services could be available on any campus to positively support students who claim this identity? In reading through the third vignette at the start of the chapter, what challenges might Bonnie face as a student leader on campus and how might you best support her?

WOMEN STUDENTS IN HIGHER EDUCATION

The intersection between feminist theory and the historical, social, professional, and institutional contexts of higher education sheds light on the educational process and how it frequently tracks, underserves, or discriminates against women.

Glazer, Bensimon, & Townsend (1993, p. 1)

Overview of Salient Issues

A Historical Overview

Women have multiple identities, which are shaped by a number of factors: race, ethnicity, age, class, culture, sexual orientation, motherhood, etc. Although women constitute more than half of the population, within the patriarchal structure of U.S. society, women have been historically subjected to prejudice and discrimination as well as a disadvantaged status (Sue & Sue, 2016). This is also true for women college students.

The history of women on college campuses provides context for understanding the current issues facing women students. The earliest university women's commissions were formed in 1968 at the University of California, Berkeley and the University of Chicago (Allan, 2011; Freeman, 1973). Although they were not limited to research universities, these institutions in particular initiated commissions on the status of women as a means of responding to demands for them made by women and to "demonstrate their good faith efforts" toward enhancing the status of women on campus (Glazer-Raymo, 1999, p. 66). Commissions were part of a growing number of women-focused higher education groups, including undergraduate and graduate women's caucuses, consciousness-raising groups, and academic discipline-related groups for women such as Committee W of the American Association of University Professors (Allan, 2011; Rossi & Calderwood, 1973).

In response to a second wave of feminism within higher education, many women's centers were founded in the 1970s and 1980s (Pasque & Nicholson, 2011). Oberlin College of Ohio was the first coeducational institution in 1833, yet women's centers did not emerge until approximately 140 years later. Although not all women's centers are the same, typically the focus has been on providing services and programs that empower and support women to achieve equality. The role of women's centers (also referred to as "gender centers" or similar terms) has evolved over time to include issues of gender exploration, sexual assault and domestic violence advocacy, Title IX issues, transgender identities, counseling, leadership training, and scholarship support, to name a few. The list is exhaustive and varies depending on the mission and motivation behind the formation of the center on that campus. If your institution has a women's center on campus, can you articulate the resources this center provides to the larger community?

Title IX, Sexual Assault, and Sexual Violence

Women on college campuses face issues unique to their gender identity. Allan (2011) stated that for women, "the most vital policy instrument to mediate women's relationship with higher education was the passage of Title IX of the Education Amendments of 1972 (renamed the Patsy T. Mink Equal Opportunity in Education Act in 2002) prohibiting discrimination based on sex in educational programs receiving federal funds and requiring institutional audits" (p. 8).

The U.S. Department of Education's Office of Civil Rights (OCR) reinterpreted and expanded Title IX of the Education Amendments of 1972 between 2011 and 2016 (Beavers & Halabi, 2017). This reinterpretation has resulted in colleges changing procedures and policies and an increase in reporting of violations. Historically, although many people may have thought Title IX only applied to equity in athletics, there are multiple ways in which this legislation has impacted education for women students, including greater access to higher education, increased career education, ample education opportunities for pregnant and parenting students, challenging of gender stereotypes in the classrooms, and expedited responses to sexual harassment allegations (Chadband, 2012).

Although inroads have been forged prohibiting sex discrimination on college campuses, there is still work to be done, specifically as it relates to women college student sexual assaults. Carey, Dunrey, Shepardson, & Carey (2015) identify that today's college women are five times more likely than other women to be sexually assaulted. According to the National Sexual Violence Resource Center (2015), one in five women—compared to one in 16 men—experience sexual assault during their college years. Although this is an issue faced by both women and men, it is disproportionately experienced by women students. The shame, embarrassment, and guilt felt by the victims, along with the stigma of sexual assault, are barriers to the reporting of assaults to police and caregivers and to the recovery and healing process of victims (Miller, Canales, Amacker, Backstrom, & Gidycz, 2011).

These disproportionately negative experiences for women college students manifest themselves in other ways, as well. Sexual violence, which occurs to 20–25% of women on college campuses, is correlated to eating disorder symptoms (Groff Stephens & Wilke, 2016). With the advancement of technology and the unrealistic societal expectations of the "perfect" body, eating disorders such as anorexia nervosa and bulimia nervosa are increasing on college campuses. This is partially the result of maladaptive coping behaviors that occur when the number of developmental transitions surpass coping behaviors. The effect is an increase in health risk behaviors. Individuals, specifically women college students with body image issues, are more likely to engage in eating disorder behaviors to cope with other issues such as sexual violence.

Although academia has become more inclusive of women, including women college students, faculty members and administrators articulated in an *ASHE Higher Education Report* special issue (Allan, 2011) that a "chilly climate" is still very prevalent for women college students. A chilly climate is when one gender portrays itself as dominant over another. In the study, the categories of chilly climate analyzed included: male peers taking over leadership in small group activities; sexually suggestive stories, jokes, or humor; male students "hogging air time" in class; males making disparaging remarks about women's behaviors; and men ignoring female ideas or input (Allan, 2011). The findings of this study reveal that behavior suggesting one gender is dominant over the other not only still exists in American higher education, but also results in an unsafe learning environment for women college students. More attention to understanding and preventing chilly classroom behaviors is important.

Faculty and administrators play a crucial role in not only recognizing but also working to change these negative patterns of behavior. Specifically, Jones (2010) found that social climate is something that faculty and administration need to be aware of in order to keep women in nontraditional majors. "While many women have the abilities necessary to succeed in STEM majors, the milieu of the academic departments at many universities—including the expectations, assumptions, and values that guide the actions of professors, staff members, and students—may make women feel unwelcome" (Jones, 2010, p. 62). Regardless of academic discipline, student affairs practitioners also must ensure that all students on campus are receiving appropriate support in achieving their academic goals.

Cyberbullying

Digital technology has changed the way social interactions occur in society. Cyberbullying among young adults and college students is present in about 10–15% of the student population and is a rising issue facing college students, especially those with marginalized identities (Selkie, Kota, Chan, & Moreno, 2015). Defined as electronic harassment or online aggression, cyberbullying is an emerging threat to college women ages 18–25 and "can include any willful and repeated harm inflicted through the use of computers, cell phones, and other electronic devices. It can also be an aggressive intentional act carried out by a group or an individual, using electronic forms of contact, repeatedly and over time against a victim who cannot easily defend him or herself" (Patchin & Hinduja, 2006, p. 149). In a recent study conducted by Selkie et al. (2015) of 265 women college students age 18–25, 27% of the women experienced cyberbullying in college. Women students who have experienced cyberbullying report higher levels of depression, suicidal thoughts, increased emotional distress, externalized hostility, and delinquency compared to others who have not. Similarly, college women who cyberbully others also have a higher rate of depression, anxiety, and increased substance use (Selkie et al., 2015).

In this 18–25 age group, cyberbullying is seen as more acceptable than physical bullying, but less acceptable than verbal bullying. Selkie et al. (2015) found that some of the motivations for engaging in this behavior include an imbalance of power, entertainment value, and retaliation. Depression and alcohol use are also on the rise as a consequence of cyberbullying. About 30% of college students have been diagnosed with depression, and nine percent contemplated suicide in the last year. This population is at risk for suicide due to depression and heavy alcohol use (Selkie et al., 2015).

Recommendations and Service Interventions

College student affairs educators can assist and support women students in many ways on campus and need to be aware of both the external and internal environments of the campus. First and foremost, as educators, we must be acutely aware of the behavior we model for others through our words and actions. Sexism can be overt (i.e., blatantly unequal and unfair treatment), covert (i.e., unequal, harmful treatment conducted in a hidden manner, such as gender-biased hiring practices for student leadership positions), or subtle (i.e., unequal treatment that is so normative that it is unquestionably accepted [Sue & Sue, 2016]). We must put in the emotional labor to identify, disrupt, and challenge sexism on campus.

In today's society and with the fluctuation of Title IX laws, it is difficult for women to navigate the sexual reporting process. The support of educated and dedicated advocates on college campuses is crucial to the resiliency of college women. Student affairs educators must educate themselves on the resources available to students and the mandated reporting process. As stated earlier, sadly, sexual violence is an act disproportionately experienced by women in college. In our pursuit of students' holistic development, and based on the findings of Groff Stephens and Wilke (2016), "individuals working with victims of sexual violence (e.g., victim advocates, counselors, social workers, etc.) should be routinely asking questions about eating habits and providing information to students on resources for treatment and health services when appropriate" (p. 45). Eating disorders can be both chronic and pervasive, even life-threatening. Early interventions, such as connecting a student with health services or psychological services could be life-saving acts. It is important for "health and mental health providers working with victims to be aware of the potential for engaging in disordered eating or purging behaviors, especially among those who have experienced more severe forms of sexual violence" (Groff Stephens & Wilke, 2016, p.45). With depression and alcohol use on the rise as a result of cyberbullying, following up with those who are on the receiving end of the bullying is critical.

It is imperative that student affairs educators have access to—and take part in—training such as mental health first aid, Title IX reporting, and cyberbullying awareness and intervention strategies. By no means is this an exhaustive list. Consider the issues present on your campus. What training or professional development might you need to engage in? What resources are available to women on your campus?

Women students may have difficulties articulating or discussing the intersections of their identity even when prompted by well-intentioned student affairs educators. It is imperative to remember that while supporting this population, student affairs educators must help women students identify their need for assistance and find the appropriate space to explore their intersecting identities.

Reflection Questions

In reflecting on each of the vignettes featured at the beginning of the chapter, how might understanding issues facing women help you better advise and support each student? What programs, policies, and services are available on your campus to support students who claim this identity? What programs, policies, and services could be available on any campus to positively support students who claim this identity? What can you do as a student affairs educator to address the issue of a "chilly campus" for women students?

STUDENTS IN LOW SOCIOECONOMIC STATUS (SES)

Overview of Salient Issues

As access to higher education has increased, so has the number of college students who are from low socioeconomic families. There have always been students on campus who have struggled financially, but previous to the Servicemen's Readjustment Act in 1944 and the first Higher Education Act in 1965, the numbers were extremely small.

The enactment of the Servicemen's Readjustment Act (GI Bill) in 1944 and the Higher Education Act of 1965 were the beginning steps to increasing financial access to a college education for those who could least afford the cost (Haynes & Bush, 2011; Stewart & Colquitt, 2015). In 1972, Federal legislations, including the National Direct Student Loan (currently known at the Federal Perkins Student Loan) and Basic Educational Opportunity Grant (known since 1980 as the Pell Grant Program), allowed for loans to low-income students based on expected family contribution. Perkins loans offer low-interest loans with long repayment terms (Haynes & Bush, 2011) and Pell Grants are loans that do not need to be repaid (Stewart & Colquitt, 2015).

As college has become more important to success, affording college has become increasingly prohibitive regardless of the ability to obtain financial aid. The recession beginning in 2007 sent a collective message to young people and their families who watched unemployment rates soar and experienced the loss of income and secure employment. This devastating event increased the need for a college education. Where once high school graduation was the key to success, now the college degree has become a necessity and is seen as a way to enhance the prospect of obtaining employment

(Jury et al., 2017). Recently, there has been more attention and focus on the needs of college students who are "under-resourced" and food/housing /resource insecure (Carnevale, Smith, & Strohl, 2010; Engle & Tinto, 2008; Goldrick-Rab, 2016a; Jury, 2017; Walpole, 2003).

Gone are the days when a "poor college student" meant that you had to work in the campus dining hall or deliver pizzas to be able to contribute to your tuition, room, board, and supplies. It was possible, with the help of some financial aid and grants to "work your way through college." Now, the challenges for college students in low SES mean living *without*–without books, food, living accommodations, and often working to support family members (Goldrick-Rab, 2016a). Even students who might be considered "middle income" are feeling the financial pressures of paying the bill each semester. According to The College Board (2016), the cost of attendance is increasing at alarming speeds. The financial aid system fails to estimate a realistic family contribution and the actual cost, including opportunity costs of attending college (Goldrick-Rab, 2016b). For example, at the time of this writing, a cell phone or some type of mobile device is a necessity for college students and no longer a luxury. For many college students, their cell phone is their computer and their access to on-line learning platforms, institutional information, and class assignments.

Students from low-income families have the same dreams as most college students–to obtain a degree and to have long-term occupational choices. A college education was historically a way to move into the middle class and, before that, a high school diploma was sufficient (Bjorklund-Young, 2016). Currently, the high school diploma is not enough, making college degree completion even more important (Carnevale, Smith, & Strohl, 2010). But, students who come from low-income families are often underrepresented on college campuses and face equity issues on a daily basis (Walpole, 2003). The intersection of minoritized racial and ethnic identities and low socio-economic status create additional challenges for students.

There are many access challenges for students from low-income families. Once those challenges are met and solved, at least for the first year of college, the challenges continue as students engage in their college experience. Challenges for low-income students can be many, ranging from lack of funds for food, books, clothes to basic supplies (Goldrick-Rab, 2016a). Students often work more than one job and are sending money from their wages and their student loans to family members who are financially struggling. Students from low-income backgrounds also face a lack of social capital, the networks that help them obtain information, experiences, and assistance (Bjorklund-Young, 2016). Low SES students are often not able to access co-curricular opportunities and events or academic support experiences on campus (Engle & Tinto, 2008; Walpole, 2003).

Recommendations and Service Interventions

How can student affairs educators support students from low-income backgrounds? The ACPA/NASPA Professional Competencies (2015) can help guide us in developing the skills needed to respond to this complex issue for students. Certainly, the foundational skills in the Social Justice and Inclusion and Advising and Supporting competencies can be developed to aid each of us in developing thoughtful and strategic supports, interventions, programs, and policies. Understanding one's own social class privilege is important for student affairs educators. Examples of class privilege range from being able to visit a doctor for a check-up, moving out of your home voluntarily and into another home, to the ability to call in sick to work (Killermann, 2012; Rios, 2015).

In the past few years, colleges and universities have responded to help low-income students. Many institutions have developed sophisticated resource pantries, aid for students coming from the foster care system, accommodations and services for homeless students, and support/interventions and academic/social coaching for students (Bjoklund-Young, 2016; Goldrick-Rab, 2016a). As institutions look at retention and completion rates for students, many are realizing that a small balance on a student bill is relative. Many institutions have established programs that "close the financial gap" for low income students (Kruger, Parnell, & Wesaw, 2016). Colleges and universities must think "outside the box" to help students. Directing students to on-campus job opportunities or scholarship opportunities can be ways to assist students in earning money and decreasing their debt load.

As student affairs educators, we want to pay attention to the signs that students may be struggling financially. We cannot jump to conclusions when a student may fall asleep during a student organization meeting or eats food while standing in line to pay for their items. Students who once were on time for their on-campus work-study position and now are consistently late or not showing up may be trying to juggle the work-study job, their classes, and another off-campus job. Or they may not be able to put gas in their car or afford the transportation cost to come to campus. Students who are violating the guest policy in a residence hall may not have a place to live. Student affairs educators can be helpful in partnering with both on-campus and off-campus resources to help find assistance for students in need.

There are institutional responses to helping low-income students to succeed. Creating a structured first-year experience, developing and emphasizing academic support, more intrusive advising, constructing a plan for and valuing participation in co-curricular events and programs, and reviewing barriers for low-income students are all approaches to help retain and graduate low-income students. Student Affairs educators can advocate for these experiences and opportunities on their campuses (Engle & Tinto, 2008).

Reflection Questions

In reflecting on Mia's story in the opening vignettes, how might under-standing issues facing women help you in advising and supporting each student? What are tangible ways you might be able to offer Mia support? How might you advocate for policies and programs that might help Mia and others who are experiencing financial insecurity? What programs, policies, and services are available on your campus to support students who claim this identity? What programs, policies, and services could be available on any campus to positively support students who claim this identity?

STUDENTS WITH DISABILITIES

In September 2016, The Chronicle of Higher Education *acknowl-edged that, according to* The National Center for Learning Disabilities, *"Roughly 11 percent of college students have a disability . . . and about two-thirds of that group suffer from one or more so-called invisible dis-abilities, such as learning disabilities, ADHD (attention-deficit hyper-activity disorder), and mental-health and emotional disabilities. . . . Students who need help don't always ask for it—nationwide, only 17 percent of college students with learning disabilities receive accommoda-tions, according to the National Center for Learning Disabilities."*(Gose, 2016)

Overview of Salient Issues

The ADA-Implications for Service Providers

In 1990, the year the Americans with Disabilities Act (ADA) was passed, a career as a Disability Services director became possible for many, promis-ing a vehicle to impact the lives of a whole class of students who had lacked access to college. While Section 504 of the Rehabilitation Act (of 1974) had made accommodations in workplaces and on college campuses part of fed-eral law, the adoption of the ADA's broad scope and publicity made a col-lege education a reality for people with disabilities.

Today, students with disabilities are evident on every college campus and the role of the ADA in social change is apparent. Nevertheless, there are still areas of contention for those who envision a career in disabilities services, which make careers in this field both challenging and deeply rewarding. Furthermore, many students with disabilities still face a difficult transition from high school to college due to a continuing confusion about the differ-ent disability laws governing K–12 and college.

To be clear, the ADA was only intended to provide access to the same educational opportunities as non-disabled students have always been afforded. At the high school level on the other hand, students with disabilities are subject to different laws that ensure academic success. Accommodations which were designed to give students an equal opportunity at success in high school were only supposed to provide access to programs, services and opportunities in college.

The interactive process that is reiterated in the ADA Amendments Act (2010) requires students with disabilities to self-identify and advocate for themselves as a college student. The case by case approach to addressing students' problems under the ADA is intended to create an environment that is close to a clinical interaction but can easily become a tug of war between competing interests who often do not speak the same language. To some faculty and administrators the word "accommodations " can be construed as an attempt by students to game the system; students approach the process hoping for a sympathetic ear, but fear their attempts at accommodation will be misunderstood as singling them out for special treatment. While the law has made attending college easier for students with disabilities, social norms have not changed apace to make the process of fitting in as smooth as it should be.

Recommendations and Service Interventions

On college campuses, students with visible disabilities are the most readily accommodated. Those students with invisible disabilities, who "look normal," often feel like they face the most discrimination. One reason for this is that society has been forced (via federal and state laws) to accommodate in the most obvious ways; curb cuts, accessible buses, etc. But for non-visible disabilities all manner of obstacles exist, unknown until they become a problem. For staff and faculty the issues are: How do we not unintentionally discriminate in a course or program design and how do we communicate our desire to be helpful?

Most introductory courses in disability awareness talk about language that the college staff member needs to learn (terms like "student with a disability, wheelchair user, and Deaf student"), but for all other purposes there is no universal blueprint. Competence as a student affairs educator will be measured by how well we listen and put ourselves in that person's shoes. When confronting situations wherein the disability is not an obvious factor, we will have to test ourselves with subtle feelings about people with disabilities. Does this person expect different treatment because that has been the norm? Are they using the disability to influence us to decide in their favor? How do we help negotiate between competing claims, making sure we are not discriminating, even when we have no intention of doing so?

The best time to refer students to campus professionals is when there is a question of legal rights. It is up to the disability office to confer legitimacy on the documentation of disability and the request of an appropriate accommodation (modification of policy or procedure). While it is not okay to ask students if they have a disability, we can certainly include the disability office on a list of referral sources we make available to students. Each person with a disability will require unique services. As professionals, it is important to understand the accommodations available, yet be aware that what worked for one student may not work for all.

Planning events that include accessibility and communicating that intention are critical. A statement on every event announcement offering assistance for people who have questions about accessibility is a minimum step that shows students and visitors the university has considered their needs and welcomes their participation. Moving forward, familiarizing ourselves with standard accommodations (how to find interpreters, where to look for captioned videos, ensuring accessible venues) will make the response to enquiries more professional.

Policy changes that keep abreast of current legal cases on campuses are a must for college administrators. Integrating such information onto campuses requires coordination and a willingness to overcome resistance from entities that see change as undermining the balance of power. Making college campuses welcoming places for people with disabilities does not mean making different rules for the disabled. However, policies which unintentionally discriminate should be reevaluated to allow for more latitude as long as those allowances do not undermine the purpose or value of the program.

For college administrators the key is to strike a balance. Understanding the changing needs of students and the advances in case law while ensuring the safety of persons and integrity of programs is an ongoing job. Even if therapy animals are permitted in the residence hall, for example, their owners must abide by the code of conduct. Some rules were created, however, without full consideration for health issues or the full range of human performance capabilities, including temporary injuries. When we learn more about differences in learning and physical performance we will learn to be more empathetic in how we apply the rules.

A Disabilities Studies Perspective

Disabilities Studies (DS) is a relatively new field that has arisen in the last decades to bring understanding and cultural awareness to the concerns of people with disabilities. The purpose of disabilities studies is to make it known that the society itself, not the person, is the source of the handicapping condition. According to Litvak (1994), "Disability Studies both emanates from and supports the disability rights movement, which advocates for civil rights and self-determination. This focus shifts the emphasis away from intervention/treatment/remediation paradigm, to a social/cultural/political paradigm" (p. 24).

The need for a Disability Studies perspective on campuses becomes evident when we contrast the profile of people with disabilities with other "underrepresented" minorities. People with disabilities differ from other marginalized groups in significant ways. For example, although the majority of students with disabilities have learning problems in traditional classrooms, they as a group are not often considered in efforts to increase their role in universities' enrollment planning. Nor are major efforts underway to increase pedagogical approaches to meet the needs of "differently abled learners." Author Jay Dolmage (2017) argues only 10% of the students who get accommodations in high school receive them in college due to the culture of independence, measurement, competition, and comparison.

Further, in the vast majority of university settings, most students with disabilities do not like to be recognized as being disabled and prefer anonymity. The act of self-identification and self-advocacy usually comes forced, only when the need arises for modifications to the programs, policies, or practices that create discrimination. This reluctant attitude does not necessarily imply shame or lack of self-respect, although that too is an issue. Most students with disabilities would naturally prefer to live their lives without consciously thinking about their disability. It is when the institution and its employees ignore the needs of students with disabilities that that issue needs to come up at all. "Nothing about us without us" is a common clarion call from disability advocates and activists to decision-makers. One of the objectives of activist movements is to encourage incorporation of "Universal Design" into architecture, course design, communications, and other pedagogical practices. It is the role of the disability services professional to help move the university forward in including disabilities in consideration of policies and practices that might otherwise exclude them. It is only when universities are forced to adjust practices in place to include disabled people that they see it as a "cost," in Dolmage's terms. When it is a built-in part of the plan, additional features are an investment.

Disabilities Studies offer us the opportunity to emerge from a theoretical inquiry with a changed perception about ourselves and what constitutes our own version of normal. Along with Queer Studies, it allows us to shrug off the burden of hyper-masculinity or idealized femininity that afflicts our culture. And Disabilities Studies offer something else: an opportunity to broaden what we value in humanity. In the early 1900's many states had "ugly laws" that prevented people with disabilities from active involvement in society. We are only half a century from socially accepted and government supported euthanasia practices, and practices involving sterilization of the disabled is still common in some countries. The United States Senate along with Uzbekistan, Libya, and a few other countries has yet to ratify the UN Declaration of Rights for People with Disabilities.

Some in Disability Studies would want disabled people on college campuses to inhabit the same space as LGBT+—that is, to create a force for themselves. ASAN, a group of Asperger's students, advocate this type of model, which has led the LGBT+ movement from acceptance to a re-thinking of gender role in considering the design of public spaces on many college campuses in the United States. Organizations like DREAM (Disability Rights, Education, Activism, and Mentoring) enable college students with disabilities to share resources, news and, activist ideas (http://www.dream-collegedisability.org/).

Veterans with Disabilities

Veterans who have physical disabilities require the same accommodations as other disabled students but due to their history they may be reluctant to ask for help. Like athletes or students who have disabilities due to accidents, veterans are unused to needing help and some may resist your attempts at solicitation. More recently, veterans have come to campus after being subjected to battlefield incidents that cause closed head injuries or may experience Post Traumatic Stress Disorder after traumatic experiences. Veterans with cognitive disabilities may experience memory loss, inattention, mood swings, and other cognitive concerns. These symptoms along with age differences will make it more difficult for veterans to fit in. For those students, student affairs educators may need help from professionals to assist them. Most campuses have offices that deal with veterans affairs, either a special staff member in key offices like financial aid or fully staffed separate centers just for veterans. Being aware of those services and having a liaison with that office can be invaluable for you in working successfully with veterans. Acknowledging our limitations in understanding the veteran's special circumstances and referring them to another veteran will often ease the tension both parties could be feeling at first meeting.

Ultimately, we measure success by helping students find meaningful employment, although this is rarely discussed in college counseling or services training. The issue is not simply a matter of steering students towards the career center in their senior year. As one alumni participant in a large study stated, "Participants mentioned that staff members from the University's Office for Persons with Disabilities offered informal support by providing employment references or friendly advice. The universities could, however, provide more formal transitional support, such as offering sessions on résumé writing, interviewing, and job searching, all specifically geared to address the particular challenges faced by persons with disabilities" (Gillies, 2012). Partly these challenges exist due to the past 25 years of the ADA. Since raising expectations among people with disabilities and encouraging millions to attend college, we have not continued to meet the needs of those students when it comes to dealing with the social restrictions and discrimination inherent in a shrinking job market. Unemployment of people with disabilities is a major issue not only within the disability community but in terms of the impact on health care, the ongoing debate over social security longevity and society's movement toward a more humane and positive acceptance of difference.

Reflection Questions

How might you approach this work with an intersectional lens? How do you determine when you might refer a student to the Office of Disability Services? Reflecting upon the vignettes at the beginning of the chapter, what would you take into consideration when advising and supporting Vincent? How might your work be similar or different when working with Bonnie?

PROFESSIONAL COMPETENCY

The ACPA/NASPA Professional Competency Areas for Student Affairs Educators (2015) identifies the area of social justice and inclusion as a key tenet to guide our practice. The social justice and inclusion competency includes "the knowledge, skills, and dispositions needed to create learning environments that foster equitable participation of all groups while seeking to address and acknowledge issues of oppression, privilege, and power" (ACPA/NASPA, 2015, p. 14). Understanding the complexity of the intersection of lived identities is critical to meeting this professional competency. This understanding is important for student affairs educators as they engage in the construction of services, supports, programs, and interventions for students. Creating services, supports, programs, and interventions with an eye and sensitivity to intersectional identities can result in a more inclusive learning environment and campus community.

The Social Justice and Inclusion professional competency also calls for "student affairs educators who have a sense of their own agency and social responsibility that includes others, their community, and the larger global context" (p. 14). It is imperative that student affairs educators engage in professional development opportunities and critical self-reflection to learn and understand more about their own power and privilege and the intersection of their lived identities. It is important for educators to learn about systems of oppression and ways those systems disadvantage and advantage various groups of people. Then educators can begin to advocate for change. A commitment to developing competence in the area of social justice and inclusion will enhance one's professional identity as a student affairs educator and simultaneously help to create a more inclusive learning environment both in and out of the classroom.

In order to enhance one's practice in social justice and inclusion, student affairs educators can begin by 'seeking to meet the needs of all groups, equitably distributing resources, raising social consciousness, and repairing past and current harms on campus communities" (p. 14). Understanding intersectional identities and the lived identities of students is essential for good practice in student affairs. Although students may present with a primary identity, their other lived identities are difficult to separate from the problem and the potential solution. The focus on the "whole student" is a fundamental value in student affairs practice and can be embraced fully by a commitment to understanding and valuing the intersectionality of identity.

We began this chapter by introducing you, the student affairs educator, to four students—Vincent, Jules, Bonnie and Mia. Each student is facing challenges as they navigate their college experience. How can we assist each of these students? How can we use what we know and what we learn to contribute to student success?

For example, in working with Mia who identifies as a transgender female, we want to also understand that she is confronting financial issues having been "cut off" by her family. We do not know her previous socio-economic status but we know that she now has financial concerns. We know that directing Mia to the office of financial aid will be an important first step. But we can also help Mia by directing her to resources on campus for underserved and under-resourced students. Helping Mia to know about resources such as scholarship funds, an on-campus or off-campus resource pantry, and other support programs can help her bridge some of the financial gap. We can be helpful to Mia by advocating with our colleagues and supervisors for a preferred name policy. We might be able to find areas where Mia can have an unofficial or chosen name (email address, student identification card) and brainstorm with her about ways to inform her professors about her chosen name as they access class rosters and the student information system. She will also need some assistance from student affairs educators as she investigates medical schools and prepares her resume for potential employment.

Vincent and Bonnie might both benefit from having a relationship with the staff in the Office of Disability Services. As a student affairs educator you might want to refer them to the office so that they can determine if they can utilize the programs and support offered. Vincent might find that he would prefer to get support from the Veteran's Center or directly from the counseling center. He might also find connection with other older and returning adult students through a club or organization. Bonnie seems to have engaged in a leadership role and may find that she is able to connect with and find support from the student affairs staff in the student involvement area. It might benefit her to have relationship with the staff in the International office as she manages the complexity of international study.

In our work with Jules, we want to understand the many issues she is facing. She is in the process of "coming out," living far from family, and struggling with alcohol use at a key transition time. A referral to the counseling center might be initially appropriate but Jules might need support in other ways too. For example, she might be willing to attend an LGBTQ+ event if she didn't have to go by herself. We might be able to connect her with an orientation leader who might be open to supporting Jules in this way.

> As we understand students' lived experiences, both those they disclose and those that they do not identify or do not yet know, we can be intentional in providing programs, services, supports, and interventions to help students succeed. As mentioned at the start of the chapter, there are a myriad of student identities to consider and address. Although a student may claim or identify with one primary identity, the intersection of all identities must be considered when developing university and college supports, services, programs, and policies. It is through this critical lens that we implore all professionals to explore their work with students. Students' unique intersecting identities demand a distinctive and individualized approach to our practice in order to ensure the success of all students.

REFERENCES

ACPA/NASPA. (2015). *Professional competency areas for student affairs educators.* Washington, DC: Author.

Allan, E. J. (2011). Special issue: Women's status in higher education—equity matters. *ASHE Higher Education Report, 37*(1), 1–163.

Beavers, J. M., & Halabi, S. F. (2017). Stigma and the Structure of title IX Compliance. *Journal of Law, Medicine, & Ethics, 45,* 558–568.

Bjorklund-Young, A. (2016). *Family income and the college completion gap.* Johns Hopkins University School of Education. Retrieved from http://edpolicy.education .jhu.edu/family-income-and-the-college-completion-gap/.

Brown, M. T., & Landrum-Brown, J. (1995). Counselor supervision: Cross-cultural perspectives. In J. G. Ponterotto, J. M. Casas, L. A. Suzuki, & C. M. Alexander (Eds.). *Handbook of multicultural counseling* (pp. 263–286). Thousand Oaks, CA: Sage.

Carey, K. B., Dunrey, S. E, Shepardson, R. L., & Carey, M. P. (2015). Incapacitated and forcible rape of college women: Prevalence across the first year. *Journal of Adolescent Health, 56*(6), 678–80.

Carnevale, A. P., Smith, N., & Strohl, J. (2010). *Help wanted: Projections of job and education requirements through 2018.* Lumina Foundation.

Chadband, E. (2012). Nine ways title IX has helped girls and women in education. *NEA Today.* Retrieved from http://neatoday.org/2012/06/21/nine-ways-title-ix-has -helped-girls-and- women-in-education-2/.

Contreras-Aguiree, H. C., & Gonzalez, E. Y. (2017). Experiences of international female students in U.S. graduate programs. *College Student Journal, 51*(1), 33–46.

Council for the Advancement of Standards in Higher Education. (2015). *CAS professional standards for higher education* (9th ed.). Washington DC: Author.

Crenshaw, K. (1995). Mapping the margins: Intersectionality, identity politics, and violence against women of color. In Crenshaw, K., Gotanda, N., Peller, G., & Thomas, K. (Eds.), *Critical race theory: The key writings that formed the movement* (pp. 357–383). New York, NY: The New Press.

Dolmage, J. (2017). *Academic ableism: Disability and higher education.* Ann Arbor, MI: University of Michigan Press.

Engle, J., & Tinto, V. (2008). *Moving Beyond Access: College Success for Low-Income, First-Generation Students.* Washington, DC: The Pell Institute. Retrieved from http://files.eric.ed.gov/fulltext/ED504448.pdf.

Freeman, J. (1973) The origins of the women's liberation movement. *American Journal of Sociology, 78*(4), 792–811.

Gartman, K. D. (2016). Challenges of international students in a university setting. *MPAEA Journal of Adult Education, 45*(2), 1–7.

Gautam, C., Lowery, C. L., Mays, C., & Durant, D. (2016). Challenges for global learners: A qualitative study of the concerns and difficulties of international students. *Journal of International Students, 6*(2), 501–526.

Gillies, J. (2012). University graduates with a disability: The transition to the workforce. *Disability Studies Quarterly, 32*(3). Retrieved from http://dsq-sds.org/issue/view/95

Glazer, J. S., Bensimon, E. M., & Townsend, B. K. (1993). *Women in higher education: A feminist perspective.* Needham Heights, MA: Ginn Press.

Glazer-Raymo, J. (1999). Taking stock: Perspectives on women and leadership in higher education in the UK and the US. *Society for Research into Higher Education News, 41,* 8–10.

Goldrick-Rab, S. (2016a, August 28). What colleges can do right now to help low-income students succeed. *The Chronicle of Higher Education.* Retrieved from http://www.chronicle.com/article/What-Colleges-Can-Do-Right-Now/237589.

Goldrick-Rab, S. (2016b). Paying the price. Chicago: The University of Chicago Press.

Gose, B. (2016, September 18). Disability experts debate merits of universal design. *The Chronicle of Higher Education.* Retrieved from http://www.chronicle.com/article/Disability-Experts-Debate/237780.

Green, A., & Wong, A. (2015, September). LGBT students and campus sexual assault. *The Atlantic.*

Groff Stephens, S., & Wilke, D. J. (2016). Sexual violence, weight perception, and eating disorder indicators in college females. *Journal of American College Health, 64*(1), 38–47. doi:10.1080/07448481.2015.1074237.

Haynes, R. M., & Bush,V. B. (2011). Student financial aid practice. In N. Zhang & Associates (Eds.), *Rentz's student affairs practice in higher education* (pp. 396–429). Springfield, IL: Charles C Thomas.

Henshaw, A. (n.d.). LGBT college statistics. Retrieved from http://www.campus explorer.com.

Herman, S. N. (1978). TRW Systems Group. In Wendell L. French & Cecil H. Bell, Jr., *Organisational Development: Behavioural Science Interventions for Organisational Improvement* (2nd ed., p. 16). Upper Saddle River, New Jersey: Prentice Hall.

Institute of International Education. (2016, January). Open doors data. Retrieved from https://www.iie.org/Why-IIE/Announcements/2016-11-14-Open-Doors-Data

Jones, J. (2010). Closing the gender gap. *Civil Engineering* (08857024), *80*(7), 60-63.

Jury, M., Smeding, A., Stephens, N. M., Nelson, J. E., Aeleniei, C., & Darnon, C. (2017). The experience of low-SES students in higher education: Psychological barriers to success and interventions to reduce social-class inequality. *Journal of Social Issues, 73*(1), 23–41.

Killerman, S. (2012). *30+ examples of middle-to-upper class privilege.* Retrieved from http://itspronouncedmetrosexual.com/2012/10/list-of-upperclass-privilege /#sthash.772BEIov.SZYOcmUa.dpbs.

Kruger, K., Parnell, A., & Wesaw, A. (2016). *Landscape Analysis of Emergency Aid Programs.* Washington, DC: NASPA. Retrieved from https://www.naspa.org /images/uploads/main/Emergency_Aid_Report.pdf.

Lee, S. A., Park, H. S., & Kim, W. (2009). Gender differences in international students' adjustment. *College Student Journal, 43*(4), 1217–1227.

Litvak, S. (1994). Disability studies vs. disability policy studies. *Disability Studies Quarterly, 14*(2).

MacKinnon, D., & Manathunga, C. (2003). Going global with assessment: What to do when the dominant culture's literacy drives assessment. *Higher Education Research & Development, 22*(2), 131–144.

Mamiseishvili, K. (2012). International student persistence in U.S. postsecondary institutions. *Higher Education, 64*(1), 1–17. doi:10.1007/s10734-011-9477 -0.

Miller, A., Canales, E., Amacker, A., Backstrom, T, & Gidycz, C. (2011). Stigma threat motivated nondisclosure of sexual assault and sexual revictimization: A prospective analysis. *Psychology of Women Quarterly, 35*(1), 119–128.

National Sexual Violence Resource Center (2015). Statistics about sexual violence: Info & stats for journalists. Retrieved from https://www.nsvrc.org/sites/default /files/publications_nsvrc_factsheet_media-packet_statistics-about-sexual-violence _0.pdf

Pasque, P. A., & Errington Nicholson, S. (Eds.). (2011). *Empowering women in higher education and student affairs: Theory, research, narratives and practice from feminist perspectives.* Sterling, VA: Stylus and American College Personnel Association.

Patchin, J. W., & Hinduja, S. (2006). Bullies move beyond the schoolyard: A preliminary look at cyberbullying. *Youth Violence & Juvenile Justice, 4,* 148–169.

Rios, C. (2015, December 9). Did you do these 6 activities today?: Then you've got class privilege. Retrieved from https://everydayfeminism.com/2015/12/everyday -class-privilege/.

Rossi, A. S., & Calderwood, A. (Eds.). (1973). *Academic women on the move.* New York, NY: Russell Sage Foundation.

Selkie, E. M., Kota, R., Chan, Y., & Moreno, M. (2015). Cyberbullying, depression, and problem alcohol use in female college students: A multisite study. *Cyberpsychology, Behavior and Social Networking, 18*(2), 79–86. doi:10.1089 /cyber.2014.0371.

Stewart, D. & Colquitt, K. Y. (2015). Privileged access: Higher education's unfulfilled promise. In P. A. Sasson & J. L. DeVitis (Eds.), *Today's college students: A reader* (201–211). New York: Peter Lang.

Sue, D. W., & Sue, D. (2016). *Counseling the culturally diverse: Theory and practice.* Hoboken, NJ: John Wiley & Sons, Inc.

The College Board. (2016). *Trends in college pricing 2016.* Author. Retrieved from https://trends.collegeboard.org.

Walpole, M. (2003). Socioeconomic status and college: How low SES affects college experiences and outcomes. *The Review of Higher Education, 27*(1), 47–23.

Wu, H., Garza, E., & Guzman, N. (2015). International student's challenge and adjustment to college. *Education Research International,* 1–9. doi:10.1155/2015 /202753. Retrieved from https://www.hindawi.com/journals/edri/2015/202753/

Chapter 7

ETHICAL AND LEGAL ISSUES FROM A MULTICULTURALISM, DIVERSITY, AND SOCIAL JUSTICE PERSPECTIVE

LaWanda Ward & David H. K. Nguyen

Society expects higher education to produce well-rounded graduates who are ready to solve the world's problems and make valuable contributions as law-abiding citizens. College is not only "a space for transformative knowledge production that challenges dominant discourses and ways of operating in and beyond the academy" (Patton, 2016, p. 335), but also one of the most prevalent societal institutions where the citizenry learns democratic principles of equality, social justice, and fairness. However, the reality is that the American higher education system fails to assist students in examining "their own racial biases and racist attitudes which result in racist college graduates who later become racist professionals, lawmakers, institutional leaders, teachers, and so on" (p. 324).

Consequently, racial inequity continues to thrive within institutions of higher education due to racism and White supremacy's hegemonic order that are operating in a normative manner through curriculum, policies, research, students, administrators, staff, and faculty (Patton, 2016). The existence of racial inequity, social injustice, and exclusion of minoritized students in higher education has been challenging to administrators' positions and practices from an ethical and legal standpoint. Although some efforts have been made to improve the condition for minoritized students in multiple areas at the higher education institution, transformative changes that result in racial equality, social justice, and inclusion continue to be an elusive quest.

This chapter uniquely approaches legal and ethical issues in student affairs from multicultural, diversity, and social justice perspectives informed by Critical Race Theory (CRT). CRT is a legal based theoretical framework that emerged in the mid-1970s as a challenge to mainstream notions of race, racism, and racial power in American society. It "is an exciting, revolutionary intellectual movement that puts race at the center of critical analysis. Race has no necessary epistemological valence, we are told, but depends on the context and organization of its production for its political effects" (Jones, 2009, p. 17). Delgado and Stefancic (2017) ground CRT in three main tenets. First, racism is the norm and not the exception to the rule in U.S. society. Daily, people of color experience offensive language and actions influenced by stereotypes and presumptions, which are created and (re)produced through societal institutions such as family, education, the work place, and legal system. Second, the thesis of interest convergence or material determinism, coined by one of CRT's founders, law professor, and activist, Derrick Bell, occurs when the maintenance or elevation of White people is undisturbed by people of color gaining access to societal resources. The 1954 Supreme Court case *Brown v. Board of Education* demonstrates an example of interest convergence with its ruling that separate but equal is illegal. Bell (1980) argued that instead of *Brown* being a civil rights triumph, it occurred because White people with resources had a political agenda more so than intentions of bringing educational equity to Black and Brown communities. Specifically, the U.S. government aimed to maintain its political status as a world leader and the display of Black people being beaten and mistreated in the international news jeopardized the nation's position. Finally, the third principle is the social construction thesis which is recognizing that race and its meaning can shift and confirm to allow the greatest benefits to those perceived and designated as White depending on societal relations and political complexities (Delgado & Stefancic, 2017).

Critical Race Theory in Higher Education

CRT probes the legal system and questions its established and accepted foundational doctrines such as equality theory, legal reasoning, and neutrality in constitutional law (Delgado & Stefancic, 2017). CRT has expanded beyond the legal field and emerged in various disciplines such as sociology, political science, and education. Since Ladson-Billings and Tate (1995) used CRT to critique the experiences of students of color in the K-12 sector, many scholars have used CRT in primary and secondary education settings to question normalized practices, prompt discussions about equity and inclusion, and produce research that illuminates education violence (Mustaffa, 2017) inflicted upon people of color through seemingly innocuous policies and procedures. In higher education, CRT is employed to expose "the challenges associated with moving the academy forward in a way that explicitly names racism/White supremacy in areas such as college access, curriculum, and policy" (p. 2). In the next section, specific attention is given to how scholars engage CRT in research.

Various but consistently aligned presentations of CRT's tenets (Delgado & Stefancic, 2017; Ladson-Billings & Tate, 1995; Solórzano & Yosso, 2002) have emerged since CRT's inception. "The strategies it deploys can be used by scholars working on issues of gender, class, ability, and other forms of human difference" (Ladson-Billings, 2004, p. 57). A combination of five CRT tenets identified by sociology scholars have been used to critique education including higher education (Solórzano, 1997, 1998; Solórzano & Delgado Bernal, 2001; Solórzano & Yosso, 2000, 2001, 2002). These tenets served as the guiding principles for this writing because each tenet highlights an area that is usually overlooked or minimized as social justice advocates seek resolution to inequities in higher education. The first tenet is the centrality of race and racism and their combined "impact on the structures, processes, and discourses within a higher educational context" (Yosso, Parker, Solórzano, & Lynn, 2004, p. 3). While institutions of higher education tout being places of inclusion and acceptance of difference, there continues to be policies implemented and experiences that happen on college campuses that can be attributed to race and racism.

The second tenet is to "challenge dominant ideology that supports the deficit theorizing prevalent in educational and social science discourse" (Solórzano & Yosso, 2002, p. 156). Calling out and naming White privilege gives voice to practices that are perceived as unfair and are valuable engagements that expose and rectify inequities in the academy. Also, rejecting "the claims that educational institutions make toward objectivity, meritocracy, colorblindness, race neutrality, and equal opportunity" (Yosso et al., 2004, p. 4) provides a platform to question the methods of selection in admissions policies. Ignoring how structural and systemic racism in K-12 education impacts the readiness and eligibility of students of color disproportionately for higher education must be addressed.

The third tenet acknowledges the lived histories and experiences of people of color, which are categorized as "the centrality of experiential knowledge" (Yosso et al., 2004, pp. 3-4). Higher education did not become an open and inclusive space on its own terms but instead by the people of color with forceful and at times painful efforts through the legal system to demand equal treatment that is guaranteed under the Constitution. Counterstories challenge and correct the dominant accounts of how people of color entered higher education.

Tenet four is a call to action for individuals who teach, write, and advocate for social justice with a specific focus on strategies that will end oppression and racism (Garcia et al., 2011; Yosso et al., 2004). In addition, tenet five promotes interdisciplinary perspectives being used for the expansion of information gathering, which provides depth to analysis (Solórzano & Yosso, 2000). Incorporating scholarship from sociology, law, communications studies, and other disciplines broadens the scope of exploration which results in exhibiting how education issues do not occur in isolation.

CRT has been used to critique issues in higher education such as affirmative action cases (Solórzano & Yasso, 2002; Yosso, Parker, Solórzano & Lynn, 2004), experiences of Black faculty members (Patton & Catching, 2009), doctoral educational experiences of students of color (Gildersleeve, Croom & Vasquez, 2011), qualitative research, (Parker, 1998), and higher education as a system (Gildersleeve, Croom, & Vasquez, 2011; Parker, 1998; Patton, 2016; Patton & Catching, 2009; Solórzano, & Yasso, 2002; Yosso et al., 2004). Race-conscious admissions policies are situated within the larger political and social context of access to higher education; therefore, a critical race analysis serves as a catalyst to demonstrate how racism and White supremacy are embedded and perpetuated through institutional policies. As a theoretical tool of inquiry for ethical and legal issues in higher education, CRT is appropriate because scholars who utilize it can explain the law's role within historical and contextual reasoning to advocate for racial justice. Additionally, CRT provides a legal lexicon that can demonstrate how the law is malleable and can create value conflicts for student affairs educators. Because those who utilize CRT in their scholarship and social justice efforts understand that law and ethics are influenced by societal systems such as higher education, there is value in discussing how student affairs educators arrive at various decisions.

Ladson-Billings (2004) advocates "The promise of CRT is that it can be deployed as a theoretical tool for uncovering many types of inequity and social injustice—not just racial inequity and injustice" (p. 61). Because of its genesis in law, CRT is a common tool used by legal and non-legal educators whose approaches to social justice are embedded in eradicating racialized systems and structures. Ladson-Billings (2004) outlined at least three ways that CRT's application to multicultural education has a meaningful impact:

> (a) it theorizes about race while also addressing the intersectionality of racism, classism, sexism and other forms of oppression; (b) it challenges Eurocentric epistemologies and dominant ideologies such as meritocracy, objectivity, and neutrality; and (c) it uses counterstorytelling as a methodological and pedagogical tool. (p. 245)

Student affairs educators are expected to address ethical and legal issues in higher education since their roles' inception at colleges and universities. However, the higher education landscape has evolved from historically White, cisgender male, and heteronormative institutional profiles due to the inclusion of marginalized and minoritized populations. Hence, new ways of problem solving and influencing student values must match diverse campuses. Critical race multiculturally competent student affairs educators recognize that campus community members' intersectional identities command collaborative consideration of how shared values and ethics are determined due to varying power dynamics. While much advocacy for critical race analyses in student affairs comes from minoritized people of color, White student affairs educators have also advocated for CRT's to better understand the impact of race and racism in their experiences. For example, Erkel (2015) professes that a critical race awareness contributes to her own self-reflections about the role of Whiteness in her life, and it informed her research with racially diverse undergraduate students at a Historically White Institution (HWI).

CRT and its Progenies

Additional racialized critical frameworks, LatCrit (Latinx), Tribal Crit (Indigenous), AsianCrit (Asians and Asian Americans), and KanakaCrit (Native Hawaiians) are developed from CRT to expand racial experiences beyond the Black-White binary. It is important to recognize that the additional lenses parallel the essence and themes of CRT and "these frameworks aim to produce richer and more focused analyses of racism in the experiences of various minoritized peoples and communities" (Museus, Ledesma, & Parker, 2015, p. 20). Furthermore, Critical Race Feminism (CRF) and Queer Theory expose the ways in which power and oppression are embedded in the social constructs of gender, gender identity, and sexual identities, CRF and Queer Theory emerged. CRF shares the tenets of CRT with an additional opportunity for scholars to expose how White supremacy contributes to racially gendered experiences, thereby illuminating how minoritized women of color's experiences are unique. For example, collegiate Black women experience racism differently than Black men and sexism differently than White women (Patton & Ward, 2016).

"Queer Theory acknowledges the interplay of sexuality, gender, race, class, culture, and other identities that significantly impact the changing nature of lived realities" (Patton, 2011, p. 81). The application of Queer Theory challenges the binary of sexual orientation by rejecting identity labels that essentialize individuals. Additionally, Queer Theory calls out the ways in which heterosexuality and patriarchy maintain power and oppress those who resist them. "Queer theorists assert that gender and sexuality are socially constructed identities and that how one understands and names their experiences with these social constructions is mediated both internally and externally by the self and environment" (p. 81).

The few described theories above are not exhaustive renderings of ways to approach the study of higher education nor are they fully illuminated. Our descriptions are truncated due to space limitations. Therefore, it is important to note that entire chapters and voluminous books are dedicated to explicating these theories and numerous others. Overall, CRT and its progenies offer a more nuanced and transdisciplinary engagement with ethics, law and policy issues.

In the following sections, the authors use a critical race multicultural competence to discuss four challenges that student affairs educators encounter on campus. Select topics include free speech, admissions, employment, safety, and equal access to university facilities. Our approach analyzes only a limited number of legal and ethical challenges that student affairs educators encounter at various levels of responsibility. Patton, McEwen, Rendon, and Howard-Hamilton (2007) recommended the use of CRT as a constant lens for at least three invaluable benefits in daily student affair practice:

> professionals approach their work with an awareness of the existence of race and the different ways that people experience racial realities. They also are clear about the ways in which race continues to reproduce societal inequities. Last, they understand how the intersection of race with other social identities presents a clearer picture that is necessary for working with individual students. (p. 49)

Multiculturalism and Characteristics of Multicultural Competent Student Affairs Educators

Student affairs educators with multicultural competence will intentionally seek out ways to "explore multicultural considerations in all aspects of their work. This exploration ultimately leads to a reconceptualization of what is viewed as core attitudes, knowledge, and skills" (Pope, Reynolds, & Mueller, 2004, p. 129). One must have self-awareness of beliefs, values, and biases. "Self-knowledge and knowledge of relevant ethical principles, values, codes, and legal considerations" (Pope, Reynolds, & Mueller, 2004, p. 130) are two knowledge types that must be part of a student affairs educator's ethical decision-making process. Before one can adequately articulate and address issues, there should be reflection on one's own positionality because "self-knowledge means understanding the personal context, including cultural values and assumptions, which influences the decision-making process" (p. 130).

Critical Race Theory as a Multicultural Heuristic for Legal and Ethical Issues

Ladson-Billings (2004) suggested CRT as a "multicultural heuristic" to "challenge traditional notions of diversity and social hierarchy" (p. 57) in a discussion about the politics of K-12 multicultural education. In the following sections, we employ the critical race multicultural competence to discuss key issues in higher education that affect its transformation. This layered tool can yield self-reflection that prompts student affairs educators to acknowledge and become "aware of their own racial identities, honestly evaluate themselves in terms of their understanding of race and racism, and recognize how their knowledge, awareness, and racial identity influence their decisions, policies, and interactions with students from diverse backgrounds" (Patton et al., 2007, p. 49). Gaining insight into what influences shape and contribute to one's thought process about student affairs matters is necessary for substantive change. Also, knowing and understanding how hegemonic Whiteness standards and perspectives are traditionally used to make decisions that oppress and marginalize individuals based on race, gender, sexual orientation, ability and other intersecting identities is important. This critical understanding informs student affairs educators how to strategize and engage in dialogues that will not only counter status quo approaches, but also result in transformative results.

Realistically, "the very nature of academic environments continues to perpetuate multiple characteristics that excuse White [and non-White] students from seriously taking time to examine the role of race (their own and others) in their lives" (Reason & Evans, 2007, p. 67). Students, as well as key administrators whose advice and guidance are sought in making transformative decisions and policies, should be challenged to examine the role of race and racism in the maintenance of inequality in higher education institutions. The next section discusses attorneys who work within the academy and student affairs educators who are responsible for carrying out conduct and compliance policies.

College and University Legal Counsel

"Human beings—including lawyers—make assumptions about people based on ingrained, generally unconscious stereotypes that may have little or no basis in reality" (Silver, 2006, p. 435). Therefore, a critical race multicultural competence is also a necessity for lawyers who work within and around higher education. Their intellectual abilities and knowledge of law are needed to reframe the ways in which legal interpretations and facts are approached regarding situations. The formalistic approach to legal issues "limits the intellectual independence of broadly educated lawyers" and, detrimentally at times, "enables the rapid delivery of a product, such as the application of syllogistic reasoning to recurring situations falling under well-known rules" (Delgado & Stefancic, 2005, p. 49). For example, the response of many public institution administrators that they cannot deny access to alt-right or White nationalist speakers to speak on campuses reinforces the myth that all speech is created equal in its impact. Institutional responses that suggest alternative meetings for more and countering speech to occur during assaultive speech events "is a weak remedy to a powerfully exclusionary practice" (Moore & Bell, 2017, p. 99). University attorneys who have embraced their institutions' diversity and inclusion statements would seem to be personally and ethically in conflict with status quo maintaining responses which define assaultive speech that public institutions are compelled to allow within campus communities as deserving of First Amendment protection General counsel, aware of the unrelenting persistence of assaultive speech, may find the narrow interpretation of hate speech problematic for and frustrating to address in dignity affirming campus communities. Documented accounts of racialized verbal and behavioral violence on college campuses should be the guide for drafting dignity inclusive policies (Koopman, 2014).

CRT allows the social and humanistic characteristics of an individual's story to be a centralized component of one's quest for justice. Legal narratives that entail historical and contemporary "social science can provide CRT with data and theoretical frameworks to support key empirical claims. Social psychology and sociology can help to explain how race constructs key aspects of social experience—for example, the role of race in suspicion of African Americans as potentially criminal and the use of excessive force by law enforcement" (Carbado & Roithmayr, 2014, p. 149). Similarly, in the higher education context, the racialized harassment experiences of minoritized people of color are explained when they are disproportionately interrogated by campus or local police for their mere presence on campus or occupying academic spaces in which Whites do not perceive them as belonging.

Instead of perpetuating colorblindness and dismissing or minimalizing the significance of inextricable social identities that impact the way individuals are treated in society, lawyers should be creating new narratives that are supported by social science and uncovering the normalized ways that stereotypes and biases are used to make decisions. Student affairs educators who regularly speak to university and college attorneys should encourage lawyers to assess their own biases and acknowledge the ways in which thinking like a lawyer—thinking White paradigm (Moore, 2008) is limited in application and results in more harm than benefit.

Community standards staff, Title IX administrators along with college and university attorneys who develop and enhance a critical race multicultural competence will approach and analyze legal issues and legal interpretations more critically (Brooks, 1994). Their analysis would "entail a two-pronged inquiry that asks (1) whether a rule of law or legal doctrine, practice, or custom subordinates' important interests and concerns of racial minorities and (2) if so, how is this problem best remedied?" (p. 3). Responses to these questions can lead to transformative institutional initiatives that serve more students including those in the margins.

Ethics in Higher Education

There is a myriad of situations that student affairs educators encounter daily. Being guided by a critical race multicultural ethical competence to issues can be helpful in recognizing how systems and structures stymie progress that is consistent with diversity, equity values, and institutional goals. Simply, "ethics is the identification of values—what we ought to do—while the law is the expression of values in social rules what we have to do" (Chabon & Morris, 2004, as cited in Anderson, 2007, p. 33).

Higher education and student affairs educators are provided with ethical principles by two major professional organizations, the College Student Educators International and the National Association of Student Personnel. While each entity covers the individual and institutional expectations for ethical behavior, "both professional codes call for respect for diversity as central to their ethical principles or values" (Pope, Mueller, & Reynolds, 2004, p. 126). For a more concise discussion, the content in this chapter is contextualized by the definition of *ethics* "as conduct based on values that guide the actions of the members of the institution" (Goonen & Blechman, 1999, p. 3). "Until now, the ethics of student affairs have been presented and implemented under the presumption of value-neutral or universal perspectives, when in fact such cultural neutrality is unlikely and may even be undesirable" (Dalton, 1993 as cited in Pope et al., 2004, p. 128).

A critical race multiculturally competent educator seeks to explore and interrogate the ways in which White hegemonic approaches define student affairs' values and exclude multiple perspectives. With an understanding of how Whiteness operates in an unacknowledged and normalized manner, student affairs educators are equipped to implement programs and policies that disrupt and potentially eradicate exclusionary and oppressive campus cultures. Student affairs educators are in constant motion intellectually, hence, they must maintain a mental agility for questions, incidents, and dilemmas that arise. An intentional focus on the decision-making process of student affairs educators is necessary as they encounter various issues that require their attention, action, and implementation. "The task of addressing ethical concerns in higher education has only become more delicate, complex, and demanding as campuses have grown and changed" (Pope et al., 2004, pp. 121–122). Equipped with a social justice sensibility such as CRT, student affairs educators can address the sensitive and unique needs of their students.

While legal and ethical issues can each separately fill up numerous chapters, the discussion of the two together is also appropriate because "legal issues seem to constitute the frame for our [student affairs] work, while ethical considerations bring substance or meaning to what we do" (Pope et al., 2004, pp. 121–122). Student affairs educators should not consider ethics and legal issues as independent variables but as a *cause and effect* of one another in many situations. Cognizant of the campus culture transformations needed to reach inclusive and equity goals, student affairs educators have used scholarship to employ their colleagues to be responsible for Title IX oversight as they will be more ethical in their approaches for issues that plague higher education institutions. For example, ethical and legal issues can be applied to sexual assault on campus as Buzo (2017) pointed out, "compliance, alone, is not enough to reduce sexual assault occurrences. To change rape culture, institutions of higher education must have educational programming that is engaged and direct" (p. 215). Buzo also called to task institutions by explaining their complicity in not making necessary changes. "Sexual assault policies cannot truly support survivors until universities acknowledge that they wittingly or unwittingly benefit from being lenient with perpetrators and silencing survivors" (p. 215). An examination of the root causes of sexual assault on campus and trainings that connect to students' lives are critical. Using a critical race feminist multicultural competence, Harris and Linder (2017) advocate for transformative changes in sexual violence prevention that includes the voices and needs of racially gendered survivors whose lived realities, due to disproportionately limited societal power, influence their responses and institutional needs. "In order to begin addressing the pervasiveness of sexual violence on our campuses, higher education educators first need to be brave enough to look at the ways that our procedures might be perpetuating rape culture through minimal and outdated compliance approaches" (Buzo, 2017, p. 216).

In the remaining sections the authors discuss four issues that justify and compel a critical race multicultural competence in the student affairs profession. These matters impact students' experiences from entry into and exit from institutions of higher education.

Race-Conscious Admissions: Diversity in Context

In higher education and society as a whole, master narratives that promote diversity through colorblind ideologies versus color conscious initiatives for redressing historical exclusion present a tension within the race-conscious admissions debate. Two ideologies of the construct diversity have become institutionalized in the public's rhetoric about equality efforts. One is that "diversity ideology represents White elites' taming of what began as a radical fight for African-American equality," and the other is "the ideology of 'diversity' was a neoliberal response to the reactionary blowback against affirmative action" (Herring & Henderson, 2011, p. 632). Both forms of ideologies for racial diversity are flawed because neither has substantially moved society in a direction of inclusion and equality (Ward, 2017).

Bell (2003) problematized diversity by describing it as a distraction to the achievement of racial justice, voicing four key concerns, and engaging discussions about race, racism and higher education admissions policies through a critical race analysis. To support his four reasons, Bell gave specific exemplars for each one based on the 2003 University of Michigan cases, *Gratz v. Bollinger* and *Grutter v. Bollinger*. First, diversity allows lawmakers and the process of the legal system to ignore how race and class impact applicants' eligibility to higher education. Bell argued that his interest convergence thesis, in which people of color only receive benefits when Whites are not disenfranchised by the gains, is manifested through the justices' and lawmakers' lack of recognition for a history of discrimination that continues to impact people of color's advancement, specifically in higher education. An example of interest convergence in the Michigan cases is how the argument to rectify past racial discrimination as an obstacle to access higher education was replaced with advocacy to improve the employability prospects for White students due to being exposed to people of color (Ward, 2017).

Second, "diversity invites further litigation by offering a distinction without a real difference between those uses of race approved in college admissions programs, and those in other far more important affirmative action policies that the Court has rejected" (Bell, 2003, p. 1622). Litigation possibilities are increased by the Court's fragmented opinions in both *Gratz* and *Grutter*. Bell (2003) cautioned excitement over the diversity rationale being interpreted as a resolution to reverse discrimination claims because he predicted more lawsuits in the future based on the dissenting opinions in *Grutter*. His forecast is confirmed with a White woman, Abigail Fisher, suing the University of Texas-Austin in 2008 over alleged race discrimination and Asian Americans also claiming racially discriminatory admission practices by Harvard University and the University of North Carolina-Chapel Hill in 2014. Fisher's case was determined twice by the Supreme Court, 2013 and 2016. The Harvard and Chapel Hill lawsuits have the potential to reach the high court and race-conscious admissions could be ruled unconstitutional. Race-conscious admissions are in a precarious state with the Supreme Court's majority justices being vocal opposers of race as a consideration factor and rejecting the rationale that racial diversity in campus communities is a compelling state (institution) interest.

The third critique is "diversity serves to give undeserved legitimacy to the heavy reliance on grades and test scores that privilege well-to-do, mainly White applicants" (Bell, 2003, p. 1622). Bell discussed meritocracy by using Justice Thomas' opinion in Grutter that concurs in part and dissents in part. Thomas explained that he is anti-affirmative action due to his perspective that race-conscious programs and others like them are a violation of the U.S. Constitution. He personally believes that affirmative action programs are an impediment to Blacks achieving in society and stigmatizes people of color by the perception that they were not qualified for educational admittance or employment. Justice Thomas pointed out the fact of alumni's children being specially admitted is evidence of a non-meritocratic process, yet this group does not draw near as much needed attention. Several studies reveal that legacy admits have a disproportionately higher probability of admission than non-legacies at elite institutions and are disadvantageous to Asian American applicants (Leong, 2016). Bell also demonstrated how financial disparities disproportionately impact the ability of students of color to afford resources that can enhance their standardized test scores. "The standardized tests are retained for the convenience of the schools even though they privilege applicants from well-to-do families, alumni children, and those born into celebrity" (Bell, 2003, p. 1631). Limited resources to afford tutors for college preparation tests or access to the "best performing" schools are disproportionately weighted against students of color in comparison to their White peers (Ward, 2017).

Fourth, Bell (2003) pointed out the substantial challenges that prevent applicants from entering college are not financially addressed. Funding diversity programs does not add to the resolution of the P-12 issues. To support this view, Bell explained how economic hardships on people of color impact all areas of their lives including quality education in the K-12 setting. He concluded with a harsh criticism of diversity as not being an effective practice for the admission of students of color, but rather "it is a shield behind which college administrators can retain policies of admission that are woefully poor measures of quality, but convenient vehicles for admitting the children of wealth and privilege" (p. 1632).

Building on Bell's (2003) assertion that diversity is a distraction, Nunn (2008) argued diversity as a social justice tool does not adequately work but instead creates no catalyst for racial inequities to be resolved. Because the Supreme Court ruled quotas, set-asides, and racial balancing methods as unconstitutional, the process of colleges and universities intentionally assessing their campuses for students, faculty, and administrators of color is contentious and any numerical measures implemented to address low numbers could result in lawsuits (Ward, 2017).

Heavy criticism from the disagreeing justices of diversity in *Gratz* and *Grutter,* meeting the strict scrutiny standard of diversity being a compelling state interest for race-conscious admissions, and the lack of definition for critical mass are evidence that the use of race in higher education admissions is not settled. Further proof of this turmoil is the Court's acceptance of hearing *Fisher v. University of Texas* twice. *Fisher* has been described as a strategic project of Whiteness (Donner, 2016). A critical race analysis recognizes that despite Abigail Fisher not being qualified for admission to the University of Texas at Austin, a master narrative and stock story reinforced by society and law was created about her case. Fisher's argument centered on the mythical belief of unqualified students of color being unfairly admitted instead of qualified White applicants (Donner, 2016). The sense of entitlement that Whites view themselves in possession of many of the opportunities and resources in American society stems from the historical establishment of Whiteness as a valuable commodity (Harris, 1993; Ward, 2017). "Whites have come to expect and rely on these benefits [set of assumptions, privileges and benefits that accompany the status of being White], and over time these expectations have been affirmed, legitimated, and protected by the law" (Harris, 1993, p. 1713). Harris connected race, property, and law to reflect the historical creation and modern-day maintenance of Whiteness as a subordinating power in society.

Beyond the Gender Binary: Inclusive Practices for Transgender Students

A national debate about bathroom bills and the rights of lesbian, gay, bisexual, and transgender (LGBT) students to access facilities of their choice persists, especially for transgender students, in the education system including higher education (*Seamus Johnston v. University of Pittsburgh*, 2015). The 2016 *Dear Colleague Letter* issued by the U. S. Department of Justice & U. S. Department of Education Office for Civil Rights clarified how to understand and respect non-gender binary people. Therefore, the rescission of this document in 2017 perpetuates the gender- and hetero-normative society in which we live. The term transgender encompasses a wide spectrum of expressions within the notion of gender identity (Beemyn, Curtis, Davis, & Tubbs, 2005). The larger category of transgender as well as more specific labels are commonly used to identify individuals who reject the gender binary of male and female, and the labels also encompass many forms of fluidity within gender expression and/or identity (Beemyn et al., 2005; Boucher, 2011; Cook-Daniels, 2010; Diamond & Butterworth, 2008). We heed the caution that "language and categories are insufficient to capture the fluid nature of the various permutations of gender identities, expressions, and embodiments that show up in various spatial and temporal locations" (Nicolazzo, 2017, p. 7). Therefore, while for this chapter transgender is defined as an umbrella term that commonly defines those who do not identify within the gender binary of male and female and/or the gender they were biologically assigned, it should not be understood as a ubiquitous concept.

Individuals may question their gender assigned at birth and question their gender identity, such as if they identify as female, male, or gender-variant (Lorber, 1996; McKinney, 2005). Consequently, people may explore their gender identity while in college, or may have done so prior to entering college, and are in the process to transition from their biological sex to their psychological gender (Beemyn, Curtis, Davis, & Tubbs, 2005; Bilodeau, 2005; Schneider, 2010). Studies on the experiences of the LGBT community have only been conducted recently. According to a study conducted by The National Center for Transgender Equality (2016), 24% of transgender students left higher education because of the discrimination they experienced while on campus. This departure occurs because many transgender individuals decide to come out as transgender or gender non-conforming while attending a college (Beemyn, 2005a; Beemyn, 2005b). Transphobic behavior exhibited by peers, faculty, and administrators results in transgender students dealing with hostility, harassment, and discrimination on campus but not feeling comfortable to report those incidents (Beemyn, 2005a; Beemyn, 2005b; Evans et al., 2010). Unfortunately, many higher education institutions fail to provide transgender students with resources and services that meet their most basic needs; meanwhile, faculty and staff members are uneducated about transgender issues (Beemyn, 2008; Beemyn, 2012; Beemyn & Pettitt, 2006; Case, Kanenberg, Erich, & Tittsworth, 2012). Furthermore, campus communities do very little to acknowledge transgender as a population outside of the lesbian, gay, bisexual and transgender (LGBT) community umbrella, which leads them to believe that colleges and universities continue to reinforce the gender-binary of male and female (Beemyn, 2005b; Butler, 1999; Hart & Lester, 2011; Lees, 1998; Lorber, 1996; Roof, 2002).

A positive or negative campus environment impacts the ability of a student to succeed academically and graduate (Evans et al., 2010). Critical race muliculturally competent student affairs educators would analyze all the data shared above and be adamant in their advocacy of why higher education institutions must provide support services that help improve the campus environment experience for all students. Additionally, they would conduct research to fill in gaps about transgender students' collegiate experiences. The scholarship of critical race multiculturally competent student affairs is necessary since most research groups focus on transgender students' experiences based on their sexual orientation and not on their gender identity. This erroneous focus results in minimal information being known about the campus environment specifically for transgender students (Beemyn, 2005a; Beemyn, 2005b; Beemyn et al., 2005; Nicolazzo, 2017). However, some research has shown that transgender students experience a hostile and unwelcoming campus environment due to the amount of discrimination, isolation, and harassment they experience in higher education, as well as the limited availability of support services that meet their needs (Agans, 2007; Case et al., 2012; Evans, 2002; Evans et al., 2010; McKinney, 2005; Schneider, 2010).

The 2016 *Dear Colleague Letter on Transgender Students* was a new guidance to help improve the campus environment for transgender students. This guidance was in response to state legislation that required students to use bathrooms and locker rooms based on their biological sex and not their gender identity. To comply with Title IX, schools "will not exclude, separate, deny benefits to, or otherwise treat differently on the basis of sex any person" (U. S. Department of Justice & U. S. Department of Education Office for Civil Rights, 2016, p. 3). Gender identity was then included as part of the sex definition for Title IX compliance, and the guidance clearly stated that schools must treat transgender students as they would treat cisgender students (U. S. Department of Justice & U. S. Department of Education Office for Civil Rights, 2016). The *Dear Colleague Letter* also afforded other rights, such as schools and colleges must not have required transgender students to (1) complete a year's worth of medical treatment, including counseling, before recognizing their gender identity as their sex; (2) provide identification documents that match their sex with their gender identity; (3) use resources and services that are for cisgender individuals, and do not meet the needs of transgender students; and (4) use facilities, such as restrooms and locker rooms, or join athletic teams or student organizations based on their biological sex instead of based on their gender identity (U. S. Department of Justice & U. S. Department of Education Office for Civil Rights, 2016). In addition, schools and colleges must have addressed discrimination and hate crimes against transgender students in a prompt manner that would not result in transgender students leaving the institution. These measures reflect efforts to reduce the hegemony of hetero cis-patriarchy practices embedded in governmental policies. However, in February of 2017, the new administration rescinded this guidance because it believes gender identity is not part of the definition of sex as stated in Title IX, and decisions of inclusion and anti-discrimination should be left to the states and court systems. It is the federal government's role to uphold the country's values of equality and justice for all; yet, without a critical race analysis coupled with cisgender, transformative solution are elusive and prone to do more injury than aid.

Higher education institutions have made little to no progress to provide resources and services specific for transgender students that are based on their gender identity, and not their sexual orientation (Erbentraut, 2016). Furthermore, faculty and staff continue to be uneducated about transgender issues and the experiences of transgender students on campus. When the

U. S. Department of Justice (DOJ) and the U. S. Department of Education Office for Civil Rights (OCR) (2016) issued their *Dear Colleague Letter on Transgender Students* indicating that higher education institutions must provide services, resources, and accommodations to transgender students based on their gender identity and not on their biological sex, the perception given was that many schools and colleges needed to amend their current practices to meet the new federal guidance. In other words, transgender students were not being provided access to resources and services that met their needs, as well as rights based on their gender identity and not their biological sex (Erbentraut, 2016). Now that the 2016 *Dear Colleague Letter* has been rescinded, rights and educational experiences of transgender students will be further violated. A critical race multicultural competence regarding how the law impacts transgender students would reflect an understanding that even with "vigorous efforts of gay and lesbian activists and theorists and the recent, apparent broadening of public support for gays and lesbians informal civil rights structures, the legal status of gay, lesbian, bisexual, and transgendered individuals remains largely unequal and unprotected" (Hutchinson, 2000, p. 1358). Additionally, "the success or failure of efforts to achieve legal equality for gays, lesbians, bisexuals, and transgendered individuals will depend in large part on how scholars and activists in this field [law] address questions of racial identity and racial subjugation" (p. 1359). We would add student affairs to Hutchinson's profession list of those who are doing work that impacts LGBTQ college students. Hutchinson argues that an intersectional approach is needed to ensure that "the racial effects of heterosexism" (p. 1361) do not exclude minoritized members of color in LGBTQ community. Legally, colleges and universities do not have to provide resources and equal access to public facilities to transgender students based on their gender identity, however the choice not to do so results in relapsing into practices of the past that yield isolation and create unwelcoming environments. It is the responsibility of student affairs educators and their institutions to support student success for all students and work to unlearn gender binary approaches to offering services and programming. Under the current national executive branch, institutions do not have to comply with the 2016 *Dear Colleague Letter,* yet a critical race multicultural competence yields an ethical commitment within institutions and educators to provide the most supportive, inclusive, and accessible learning environment for transgender students.

The Hegemony of Whiteness in Campus Free Speech Discourse

CRT legal scholars define assaultive speech as "words that are used as weapons to ambush, terrorize, wound, humiliate, and degrade" (Matsuda,

Lawrence, Delgado, & Crenshaw, 1993, p. 1). In a thought-provoking and status quo challenging writing about free speech in society and higher education, the scholars expressed the purpose of their work:

> As a pragmatic response to the urgent needs of students of color and other victims of hate speech who are daily silenced, intimidated, and subjected to severe psychological and physical trauma by racist assailants who employ words and symbols as part of an integrated arsenal of weapons of oppression and subordination. (p. 7)

Their work is even more relevant 25 years later. A so-called alt-right movement has gained momentum with the election of the 45th U.S. president who has not condemned their White supremacy messages. Colleges and universities stand at a crossroad with right-wing rallies and White nationalist speakers invited to speak by student organizations on their campuses. Hateful incidents are not new to the academic landscape; hence this new resurgence demonstrates an updated strategy in which status quo defenders are utilizing the First Amendment as a cloak for domination and suppression. A critical race multicultural competence about assaultive speech that is labeled free speech on college campuses is aligned with campus community aspirations of inclusive dignity (Koopman, 2014) and racial harassment free learning environments.

Campus administrators who espouse the goal of ensuring all speakers access to their campuses to talk about a range of problematic topics from White nationalism to the disproved theory of racist science regarding people of color and their intelligence compared to Whites, have received criticism from students, alums, faculty, staff, and outside interest groups. Concerned factions challenge the allowance of anti-inclusive and assaultive rhetoric on campuses because the messages conflict with egalitarian institutional values and missions. Student affairs educators who employ a critical race multicultural competence to free speech issues in the community understand that transforming campus cultures does not begin with concerns about speakers invited to campus but instead encompasses "introducing ideas, facilitating discussion and encouraging reflections on race as part of everyday student affairs practice" (Erkel, 2015, p. 161). Campus community discussions should center around a critique of the ways in which "the first amendment is employed to trump or nullify the substantive meaning of the equal protection clause, that the Constitution mandates the disestablishment of the ideology of racism" (Matsuda et al., 1993, p. 15).

When student affairs educators employ a critical race multicultural competence that narrow and equity deficient interpretations of law stymie their ability to regulate "hate speech," they challenge this restriction by invoking their institution's values, mission, and overall ethos of inclusivity. The power to define hateful speech different from hate speech is a powerful discourse strategy rooted in thinking like a lawyer—thinking White paradigm that results in dominant group members being able to continuously express racialized assaultive discourse without recourse. In higher education, First Amendment protection for assaultive expression results in students of color being limited in their full engagement of educational experiences. Additionally, the recognition that certain speech is assaultive, while simultaneously advocating for its First Amendment protection, renders the creation and implementation of campus community civility policies impotent.

However, student affairs educators with a critical race multicultural competence understand "that the best way to teach ethics and values to students is through what we say and the choices we make" (Fried & Young as cited in Pope et al., 2004, p. 137). Hence, modeling credence for ethics and legal interpretations that reflect an inclusive and dignity affirming campus community is key. Student affairs educators also understand that their role must be on the front line advocating for policy changes to address situations that prohibit students of color from having full access to and benefit from academic and extracurricular activities. Student affairs educators who understand the severity of the emotional and psychological impact on minoritized community members can demonstrate a critical race multicultural competence in decision making by affirming that "fascist gatherings [and speakers] *by their very presence* pose a threat to" [campus community] "spaces of work and learning" (Figueroa & Palumbo-Liu, 2017) and therefore efforts to reframe the First Amendment protection around assaultive speech is a priority. Ultimately, educating campus communities that when race is placed at the center of analysis, instead of assaultive speech rights, the possibility of creating a racially inclusive educational learning environment is increased and so is the eradication of all oppressive forms of subordination (Matsuda et al., 1993).

Employment Discrimination in Student Affairs

Many newly minted higher education and student affairs graduates and current professionals engaged in job searches may likely encounter challenges based on the nebulous and subjective concept of "fit." The normativity of the dominant culture's expectations of appearance and behavior of applicants can outweigh and conflict with institutions' promotion of diversity and inclusion. Most higher education institutions tout commitments to diversity and inclusion through various marketing outlets, yet a critical race multicultural competence observes the reality that the student enrollment, curriculum, professors and staff continue to be predominantly White. This overwhelming Whiteness manifests as White supremacist practices that operate as the norm (Patton, 2016). Whiteness is a societal construct that is created, sustained, and justified by social, legal, education, and economic institutions with a normalized and invisible mode of operation (McLaren & Torres, 1999). The hegemony of Whiteness manifests itself in employment when qualified candidates are denied employment offers because they are not perceived, consciously or unconsciously, to align with office norms and values. This unspoken screening process finds solace in the concept of "fit" and results in disproportionately discriminating against members of marginalized communities.

One would assume that anti-discrimination laws, specifically Title VII which prohibits discriminatory practices ranging from hiring to termination, is a deterrent to exclusionary behaviors. However, Title VII applied rigidly to a perceived wrongful employment action, such as hiring, firing or demotion, makes it difficult to prove that "fit" is a cloaked method for discrimination because courts are reluctant to allow the effects of historic and current systemic exclusionary behavior towards marginalized populations to serve as evidence (Nguyen & Ward, in press). Narrow constructions of Title VII require direct or indirect evidence of discriminatory intent on an employer for a claim of discrimination to move forward. A critical race multiculturally competent student affairs educator understands that the hegemony of Whiteness cloaks itself in concepts like "fit" which serve as a difficult barrier to establish that racially gendered discrimination was the motivation behind not hiring a qualified candidate. They also know that employment laws interpreted with a narrow focus do not yield equitable court decisions. In addition to hiring discrimination, work place microaggressions are not unlawful. Microaggressions are daily comments and behaviors, overt and covert, which negatively impact the experiences of minoritized people of color (Pierce, 1970; Sue, 2010). "One of the enduring problems of dismantling oppression in the academic workplace is that microaggressions, though consistently destructive, are not always prohibited under civil rights law" (Lukes & Bangs, 2014, p. 3). Hence, a student affairs applicant who files a lawsuit about microaggressions is highly unlikely to obtain a successful court decision. Due to legal shortcomings to address employment discrimination practices, such as hiring decisions based on "fit," institutional transformation is a key solution to addressing hegemonic cultures of Whiteness.

Within the study of environments and human interactions there has been a focus on the positive and negative results of combining human characteristics and values inside various spaces (Lewin, 1935, 1952; Parsons, 1909). Specifically, "fit has been a central concept in organizational theory literature since the 1960s when person-environment fit models became prevalent" (Kezar, 2001, p. 86) by the works of numerous researchers. "Fit" is described as relevant within organizational research because prior studies have revealed, "individuals were most successful and satisfied when their skills, aptitude, values, and beliefs matched the organizations" (p. 87). In a student affairs context, the profession prides itself on being inclusive and welcoming individuals who will add value to department missions because of their unique perspectives and experiences. Hence, the importance of interrogating how and in what ways "fit" becomes a proxy for discrimination in higher education and student affairs (Nguyen & Ward, in press).

Two key criticisms have emerged regarding the concept of organizational fit (Kezar, 2001). First, historically marginalized people are challenged with how to best present themselves to be viewed as the right fit for positions (Carbado & Gulati, 2000). Second, there is an increased likelihood of assimilation because of the expectation to meet some unspoken criteria that may not align with one's own unique expression and values (Kezar, 2001). Hence, institutions of higher education hiring practices should reflect efforts to be cognizant of their own existing environments and interrogate what message they embody and communicate to those seeking employment. This critical assessment of "fit" is warranted because it may be difficult for marginalized candidates to present themselves in an authentic way that will be considered the right "fit" for an organization. Job "fit" can be perceived and articulated in different ways which should heighten the sense of awareness for decision makers. Work environments that are encumbered with a "culture of hegemonic collegiality," that is, "a set of norms that demand that subordinated groups conform their behavior and interactions to the expectations of the group in power in order to 'get along'" (Cho, 2006, p. 812), can be stressful and result in premature departures. Student affairs divisions in which racial profiles and the office cultural expectations are steeped in the hegemony of Whiteness result in isolation and early departures of staff of color.

Conclusions and Case Study

The authors began the chapter with a proposition that "Higher education serves as a space for transformative knowledge production that challenges dominant discourses and ways of operating in and beyond the academy" (Patton, 2016, p. 335). Higher education and student affairs graduate preparation programs contribute to transformative knowledge being shared and effectively used by graduates when they are intentional with infusing discussions about race and racism in all courses and not just the diversity focused ones. The use of a critical race multicultural competence to teach provides student affairs faculty with a theoretical framework that promotes self-reflection in students that can lead to better engagement with other students as well as positively influence decisions for ethical and legal issues.

Additionally, "faculty need to 'walk the talk' in emphasizing the importance of diversity in their teaching. That is, students want to see diversity integrated into course content and pedagogy-and see it reflected in faculty's personal and professional lives" (Pope et al., 2004, p. 175).

Reflecting agreement with Pope et al. (2004) regarding the development of "*multicultural skills* requires occasions to practice specific behaviors, tasks, and interventions" (p. 183); the authors have developed a case study with an opportunity for users of this text to discuss possible solutions informed by a critical race multicultural competence. "Case studies encourage consideration of multiple perspectives, allow simulations of real-life practice, and yet simultaneously reduce anxiety because the stakes are not nearly as high as in an actual work situation" (p. 183). There are no "right" answers; therefore, readers are encouraged to focus on exploring the power dynamics and centering race and inextricable intersecting identities as relevant factors when addressing the case study questions.

Case Study

Bell University is a four-year public institution located in a small college town about 45 minutes from a metropolitan city. Approximately 30,000 students are enrolled in undergraduate and graduate programs combined. The student demographic is touted as diverse, and the student affairs division has a mission of promoting social justice through programs that recognize the uniqueness of students from all walks of life. The student affairs unit is searching for a Vice President. The search committee is comprised of three men and four women. All three men are White and cisgender; two women are Black cisgender, and queer; one woman is cisgender and Native American; and one woman is cisgender and White. All members are able-bodied by society's ability standards. After reviewing approximately 50 applications, the committee selects ten candidates for phone interviews. After conducting the phone interviews, four candidates are invited to campus. The candidates are from diverse backgrounds. One cisgender, gay, White man, one cisgender, heterosexual, White woman, one cisgender, gay, Black woman and a cisgender, heterosexual, woman from Iran. The campus interviews consisted of two full days of meetings and presentations. At the end of the interviews, the search committee convened to discuss the candidates' qualifications.

Each search committee member ranked their preferences in order, and a discussion ensued. One of the White men commented, "Our division has over 50 people in it and having someone with stellar supervisory experience is non-negotiable." One of the queer Black women responded, "I agree, however, our need to add diversity to a predominately White men staff is important be . . ."; before she could continue another White man interrupted,

"White men are constantly under attack! We go through the diversity trainings to learn to say the right things and it isn't enough. What else can we do to show that we deserve jobs in student affairs!" The Native American woman stated, "No one is saying White men should not have jobs. We should all be concerned about our students voicing concerns about not having folks who look like them to talk with and advocate for their unique needs." The room fell silent for a while.

1. What information is considered in this discussion that is not in the fact pattern but as a result of a critical race multicultural competence?
2. Do all the individuals involved equally share in the power dynamics of hiring decisions? Why or why not?
3. What solutions would you propose? Why?
4. If this case study occurred on your campus, would you suggest the same solutions? Why or why not?

Pope et al. (2004) recommends a discussion about one's campus to "challenge you to more fully understand the implications for campus policy, state law, ethical standards, community expectations and demographics, administrative procedures, and the endless possible reactions and views of the various constituent groups involved" (p. 189). The more knowledge individuals have about institutional policies and culture, the better equipped they are to gain benefit from the case study.

REFERENCES

Agans, L. J. (2007). Beyond the binary: Gender, identity, and change at Brandeis University. *The College Student Affairs Journal, 26*(2), 201–207.

Anderson, N. (2007, 25 September). Ethics and ethnicity: Essentials of best practices for our students. *The ASHA Leader.*

Beemyn, B. G. (2005a). Making campuses more inclusive of transgender students. *Journal of Gay & Lesbian Issues in Education, 3*(1), 77–87.

Beemyn, B. G. (2005b). Trans on campus: Measuring and improving the climate for transgender students. *On Campus with Women, 34*(4).

Beemyn, B. G. J., (2008). *Ways that U.S. colleges and universities meet the day-to-day needs of transgender students* (PDF document). Retrieved from: http://www.transgender law.org/college/guidelines.htm.

Beemyn, G. (2012). The experiences and needs of Transgender community college students. *Community College Journal of Research and Practice, 36,* 504–510.

Beemyn, B. G., Curtis, B., Davis, M., & Tubbs, N. J. (2005). Transgender issues on college campuses. *New Directions for Student Services, 111,* 49–60.

Beemyn, B.G., Pettitt, J. (2006). How have trans-inclusive non-discrimination policies changed institutions? *GLBT Campus Matters, 2*(6), 12.

Bell, D. (1980). Brown v. Board of Education and the interest convergence dilemma. *Harvard Law Review, 93,* 518-533.

Bell, D. (2003). Diversity's distractions. *Columba Law Review, 103,* 1622.

Bilodeau, B. (2005). Beyond the gender binary: A case study of two transgender students at a Midwestern research University. *Journal of Gay & Lesbian Issues in Education, 3*(1), 29–44.

Boucher, M. J. (2011). Teaching "Trans Issues": An intersectional and systems-based approach. *New Directions for Teaching and Learning, 125,* 65–75.

Brooks, L. R. (1994). How do you define critical race theory? In D. A. Brown (Ed.), *Critical race theory: Cases, materials, and problems* (pp. 2–9). St. Paul, MN: Thomson West.

Butler, J. (1999). *Gender trouble: Feminism and the subversion of identity* (2nd ed). New York, NY: Routledge.

Buzo, C. (2017). Ethical approaches to compliance. *Journal of Character, 18*(3), 215–220.

Carbado, D. W., & Gulati, M. (2000). Working Identity. *Cornell Law Review, 85*(5), 1259–1308.

Carbado, D. W., & Roithmayr, D. (2014). Critical race theory meets social science. *Annual Review of Law & Social Science, 10,* 149–167.

Case, K. A., Kanenberg, H., Erich, S. A., & Tittsworth, J. (2012). Transgender inclusion in university nondiscrimination statements: Challenging gender-conforming privilege through student activism. *Journal of Social Issues, 68*(1), 145–161.

Chabon, S. S., & Morris, J. F. (2004, February 17). A consensus model for making ethical decisions in a less-than-ideal world. *ASHA Leader,* 18–19.

Cho, S. (2006). Unwise, untimely, and extreme: Redefining collegial culture in the workplace and revaluing the role of social change. *UC Davis Law Review, 39,* 805–857.

Cook-Daniels, L. (2010). Thinking about the unthinkable: Transgender in an immutable binary world. *New Horizons in Adult Education and Human Resource Development, 24*(1), 63–70.

Delgado, R., & Stefancic, J. (2005). *How lawyers lose their way: A profession fails its creative minds.* Durham, NC: Duke University Press.

Delgado, R., & Stefancic, J. (2017) *Critical race theory: An introduction* (3rd ed.). New York: New York University Press.

Diamond, L. M., & Butterworth, M. (2008). Questioning gender and sexual identity: Dynamic links over time. *Sex Roles, 59,* 365–376.

Donner, J. K. (2016). Lies, myths, stock stories, and other tropes: Understanding race and Whites' policy preferences in education. *Urban Education, 51*(3), 343–360.

Erbentraut, J. (2016, Feb. 2). College campuses are more Trans-inclusive than ever, but still have a long way to go. *Huffington Post.* Retrieved from: http://www.huffingtonpost.com/2015/05/18/trans-friendly-colleges_n_7287702.html.

Erkel, S. E. (2015). Dialogue matters: Applying critical race theory to conversations about race. In S. K. Watt (Ed.), *Designing transformative multicultural initiatives: Theoretical foundations, practical applications, and facilitator considerations* (pp. 153–163). Sterling, VA: Stylus Publishing.

Evans, N. J. (2002). The impact of an LGBT safe zone project on campus climate. *Journal of College Student Development, 43*(4), 522–538.

Evans, N. J., Forney, D. S., Guido, F. M., Patton, L. D., & Renn, K. A. (2010). *Student development in college: Theory, research, and practice.* San Francisco, California: Jossey-Bass.

Figueroa, M., & Palumbo-Liu, D. (2017, September 8). Why Berkeley's battle against white supremacy is not about free speech. *The Nation.* Retrieved from https://www.thenation.com/article/why-berkeleys-battle-against-white-supremacy-is-not-about-free-speech/

Garcia, G. A., Johnston, M. P., Garibay, J. C., Herrera, F. A., & Giraldo, L. G. (2011). When parties become racialized: Deconstructing racially themed parties. *Journal of Student Affairs Research and Practice, 48*(1), 5–21.

Gildersleeve, R. E., Croom, N. N., & Vasquez, P. L. (2011). "Am I going crazy?!": A critical race analysis of doctoral education. *Equity & Excellence in Education, 44*(1), 93–114.

Goonen, N. M., & Blechman, R. S. (1999). *Higher education administration: A guide to legal, ethical and practical issues.* Westport, CT: Greenwood Press.

Harris, C. I. (1993). Whiteness as property. *Harvard Law Review, 106*(8), 1710–1791.

Harris, J. C., & Linder, C. (Eds.). (2017). *Intersections of identity and sexual violence on campus: Centering minoritized students' experiences.* Sterling, VA: Stylus Publishing.

Hart, J., & Lester, J. (2011). Starring students: Gender performance at a Women's college. *NASPA Journal about Women in Higher Education, 4*(2), 193–217.

Herring, C., & Henderson, L. (2011). From affirmative action to diversity: Toward a critical diversity perspective. *Critical Sociology, 38*(5), 629–643.

Hutchinson, D. L. (2000). Gay rights for gay Whites: Race, sexual identity, and equal protection discourse. *Cornell Law Review, 85*(5), 1358–1391.

Jones, R. A. (2009). Philosophical methodologies of critical race theory. *Georgetown Law Journal & Modern Critical Race Perspective, 1*(17), 17–39.

Kezar, A. (2001). Investigating organizational fit in a participatory leadership environment. *Journal of Higher Education Policy and Management, 23*(1), 85–101.

Koopman, N. (2014). Inclusive dignity and land reform in South Africa. *Scriptura, 113,* 1–8.

Ladson-Billings, G. (2004). New directions for multicultural education: Complexities, boundaries, and critical race theory. In C. A. M. Banks (Ed.), *Handbook of research on multicultural education* (pp. 50–65). San Francisco, CA: Jossey-Bass.

Ladson-Billings, G. J., & Tate, W. F. (1995). Toward a theory of critical race theory in education. *Teachers College Record, 97*(1), 47–68.

Lees, L. J. (1998). Transgender students on our campuses. In R. L. Sanlo (Ed.), *Working with lesbian, gay, bisexual and transgender college students: A handbook for faculty and administrators* (pp. 37–43). Westport, CT: Greenwood Press.

Leong, N. (2016). The misuse of Asian Americans in the affirmative action debate. *UCLA Law Review Discourse, 64,* 90–98.

Lewin, K. K. (1935). *A dynamic theory of personality.* New York, NY: McGraw-Hill.

Lewin, K. K. (1952). *Field theory in social science: Selected theoretical papers.* London, United Kingdom: Tavistock.

Lorber, J. (1996). Beyond the binaries: Depolarizing the categories of sex, sexuality, and gender. *Sociological Inquiry, 66*(2), 143–159.

Lukes, R., & Bangs, J. (2014). A critical analysis of anti-discrimination law and microaggressions in academia. *Research in Higher Education Journal, 24,* 1–15.

Matsuda, M. J., III Lawrence, C. R., Delgado, R., & Crenshaw, K. W. (1993). *Words that wound: Critical race theory, assaultive speech, and the first amendment.* Boulder, CO: Westview Press.

McKinney, J. S. (2005). On the margins: A study of the experiences of transgender college students. *Journal of Gay & Lesbian Issues in Education, 3*(1), 63–75.

McLaren, P., & Torres, R. (1999). Racism and multicultural education: Rethinking 'race' and 'whiteness' in late capitalism. In S. May (Ed.), *Critical multiculturalism: Rethinking multicultural and antiracist education* (pp. 42–76). New York, NY: Routledge.

Moore, W. L. (2008). *Reproducing racism: White space, elite law schools, and racial inequality.* Lanham, MD: Rowman and Littlefield Publishers.

Moore, W. L., & Bell, J. M. (2017). The right to be racist in college: racist speech, White institutional space, and the First Amendment. *Law & Policy, (39)*2, 99–120.

Museus, S. D., Ledesma, M. C., & Parker, T. L. (2015). Racism and racial equity in higher education. *ASHE Higher Education Report, 42*(1), 1–112.

Mustaffa, J. B. (2017). Mapping violence, naming life: A history of anti-Black oppression in the higher education system. *International Journal of Qualitative Studies in Education, 30*(8), 711–727.

National Center for Transgender Equality. (2016, December). 2015 U.S. transgender survey executive summary. Retrieved from: http://www.aglp.org/images/USTS -Executive-Summary-FINAL.pdf.

Nicolazzo, Z. (2017). *Trans* in college: Transgender students' strategies for navigating campus life and the institutional politics of inclusion.* Sterling, VA: Stylus Publishing.

Nguyen, D. H. K., & Ward, L. W. (2018). Innocent until proven guilty: A critical interrogation of the legal aspects of "job fit" in higher education. In B. J. Reece, V. T. Tran, E. N. DeVore, & G. Porcaro (Eds.), *Debunking the myth of job fit in higher education and student affairs.* Sterling, VA: Stylus Publishing.

Nunn, K. (2008). Diversity is a dead-end. *Pepperdine Law Review, 35*(3), 705–732.

Parker, L. (1998). 'Race is race ain't': An exploration of the utility of critical race theory in qualitative research in education. *International Journal of Qualitative Studies in Education, 11*(1), 43–55.

Parsons, F. (1909). *Choosing a vocation.* Boston, MA: Houghton, Mifflin and Company.

Patton, L. D. (2016). Disrupting postsecondary prose: Toward a critical race theory of higher education. *Urban Education,* 1–28.

Patton, L. D. (2011). Perspectives on identity, disclosure and the campus environment among African American gay and bisexual men at one historically Black college. *Journal of College Student Development, 5*(1), 77–100.

Patton, L. D., & Catching, C. (2009). 'Teaching while Black': Narratives of African American student affairs faculty. *International Journal of Qualitative Studies in Education, 22*(6), 713–728.

Patton, L. D., McEwen, M., Rendón, L., & Howard-Hamilton, M. F. (2007), Critical race perspectives on theory in student affairs. *New Directions for Student Services,* pp. 39–53.

Patton, L. D., & Ward, L. W. (2016). Missing Black undergraduate women and the politics of disposability: A critical race feminism perspective. *The Journal of Negro Education, 85*(3), 330–349.

Pierce, C. (1970). Offensive mechanisms. In F. Barbour (Ed.), *The black seventies* (pp. 265–282). Boston, MA: Porter Sargent.

Pope, R. L., Reynolds, A. L., & Mueller, J. A. (2004). *Multicultural competence in student affairs.* San Francisco, CA: Jossey-Bass.

Reason, R. D., & Evans, N. J. (2007). The complicated realities of Whiteness: From color blind to racially cognizant. *New Directions for Student Services, 120,* 67–75.

Roof, J. (2002). Is there sex after gender? Ungendering/the unnameable. *The Journal of the Midwest Modern Language Association, 35*(1), 50–67.

Schneider, W. (2010). Where do we belong? Addressing the needs of Transgender students in higher education. *The Vermont Connection, 31,* 96–106.

Silver, M. A. (2006). The professional responsibility of lawyers: Emotional competence, multiculturalism and ethics. *Journal of Law and Medicine, 13,* 431-438.

Solórzano, D. G. (1997). Images and words that wound: Critical race theory, racial stereotyping, and teacher education. *Teacher Education Quarterly, 24,* 5–19.

Solórzano, D. G. (1998). Critical race theory, race and gender microaggressions, and the experiences of Chicana and Chicano scholars. *International Journal of Qualitative Studies in Education, 11,* 121–136.

Solórzano, D. G., & Delgado Bernal, D. (2001). Examining transformational resistance through a Critical Race and LatCrit framework: Chicana and Chicano students in urban context. *Urban Education, 36*(3), 308–342.

Solórzano, D. G., & Yosso, T. J. (2000). Towards a critical race theory of Chicana and Chicano education. In C. Tejeda, C. Matinez, Z. Leonardo, & P. McLaren (Eds.), *Chartering new terrains of Chicana(o)/Latina(lo) education* (pp. 35–65). Cresskill, NJ: Hampton Press.

Solórzano, D. G., & Yosso, T. J. (2001). Critical race and Latcrit theory and method: Counter-storytelling. *International Journal of Qualitative Studies in Education, 14*(4), 471–495.

Solórzano, D. G., & Yosso, T. J. (2002). A critical race counter-story of race, racism, and affirmative action. *Equality & Excellence in Education, 35*(2), 155–168.

U. S. Department of Justice, & U. S. Department of Education Office for Civil Rights. (2016, May 13). *Dear colleague letter on Transgender students.* Washington, D.C. Retrieved from: http://www2.ed.gov/about/offices/list/ocr/letters/colleague -201605-title-ix-transgender.pdf?_cldee=Y2xvdmVVAYWNwYS5uY2hlLmVVkd Q%3d%3d&utm_source=ClickDimensions&utm_medium=email&utm _campaign=P2P%202016.

U. S. Department of Justice, & U. S. Department of Education Office for Civil Rights. (2017, February 22). *Dear colleague letter.* Washington, D. C. Retrieved from: https://www2.ed.gov/about/offices/list/ocr/letters/colleague-201702-title-ix .docx.

Ward, L. W. (2017). An all-White enterprise: How the normalcy of White privilege is maintained in U.S. Supreme Court race-conscious admissions oral arguments. *Thresholds in Education, 40*(1), 21–39.

Yosso, T. J., Parker, L., Solórzano, D. G., & Lynn, M. (2004). From Jim Crow to affirmative action and back again: A critical race discussion of racialized rationales and access to higher education. *Review of Research in Education, 28,* 1–25.

Chapter 8

TOWARD A MODEL OF INCLUSIVITY FOR RACIALLY AND CULTURALLY DIVERSE STUDENTS ON COLLEGE CAMPUSES: IMPLICATIONS FOR RESEARCH AND PRACTICE

Mary F. Howard-Hamilton, Naijian Zhang, & Stephanie Bambrick

Fortunately, your generation has everything it takes to lead this country toward a brighter future. I'm confident that you can make the right choices—away from fear and division and paralysis, and toward cooperation and innovation and hope.

> Barack Obama (2017), Commencement Address, Rutgers University, New Brunswick, New Jersey, May 15, 2016 (Kelly-Gangi, 2016)

According to the U.S. Census Bureau, the next 50 years will be marked by the continued growth of racial and ethnic diversity. By 2060, it is projected that the United States will no longer be a country with a single majority and will become a "minority-majority nation." It is estimated that over the next 40 years the non-Hispanic White population will comprise less than 50 percent of the U.S. population, the Hispanic population more than 25 percent, the Black population around 14 percent, the Asian population around nine percent, two-or-more races population around six percent, and the Native Hawaiian and Other Pacific Islander populations, American Indian, and Alaska Native populations each representing one percent of the total U.S. population (Colby & Ortman, 2014). This estimate projects a unique stage in the recent changes to U.S. demographics, and research has noted that "[t]he 2014 school year marked the first time in U.S. history that the majority of elementary and secondary schoolchildren were children of

167

color—Black, Latinx, Asian, or American Indian" (Tatum, 2017, p. 2). The anticipated demographic shift in the United States population will inevitably be reflected within the landscape of higher education, including our college and university environments. Throughout this chapter, readers will note terminology that is now being used by diverse groups such as Latinx, Latin@, African American or Black, and lastly, "minoritized," which has replaced "people of color" or "minority." The term "minoritized" (Harper, 2012; Ogbu, 1990) will be used in this chapter to describe racial and ethnic individuals "to signify the social construction of underrepresentation and subordination" (p. ix). Individuals are not born into minority status nor are they minoritized in every social environment, instead "they are rendered minorities in particular situations and institutional environments that maintain an overrepresentation of one racial group and its dominant cultural norms" (Harper, 2012, p. ix).

DIVERSITY AND CAMPUS CLIMATE

Minoritized students are increasing in number thus there are protests, such as Black Lives Matter, and voices being heard because of systemic racism reflected in the educational organizational structure (Mwangi, Thelamour, Ezeofor, & Carpenter, 2018). Within the first two decades of the 21st century, the United States has witnessed the two-term administration of Barack Obama, first African American president; the polarizing presidential election of Donald Trump; the legalization of same-sex marriage; litigation challenging the Deferred Action for Childhood Arrival (DACA) program; and policy concerning the rights for transgender individuals. Diversity, broadly defined, has become a topic of national discussion and invited a deeper exploration of how higher education environments can evolve into becoming inclusive spaces and not mirror society at large, which has produced exclusionary dialogue, policies, practices, and systemic challenges

- The reality of an increasingly diverse society has created an accelerated agenda for colleges and universities to embrace dynamic change in the student population on their campuses. Although many these institutions have committed to creating administrative positions that promote inclusiveness, physical centers for minoritized or marginalized groups, and hiring diverse faculty and staff, patterns of exclusivity still exist. In fact, increased cultural diversity has arguably provoked some of the episodes of intolerance we have seen on campuses across the nation. These incidents of prejudicial hatred are not isolated or limited in number, and are notably exacerbated when social media

(Tynes, Rose, & Markoe, 2013) intersects with the distribution of bigotry, for example, young men belonging to Sigma Alpha Epsilon at The University of Oklahoma can be found on You Tube singing a racist chant "There will never be a N . . . in SAE."

- Three weeks after the start of the 2017 school year, Drake University students found a Swastika carved into a campus elevator and racial slurs scribbled on the whiteboard of an African American student (Taylor, 2017).
- In September 2017, fliers were posted on University of Louisville's and Stockton University's campus recruiting students to join White supremacist groups on campus (Novelly, 2017).
- Eighteen fraternity members were removed from academic participation and the fraternity was expelled from Syracuse University after a discriminatory initiation video was leaked. The video showed members of the fraternity spouting racist, homophobic, and misogynistic language.
  (https://www.jbhe.com/2018/04/student-newspaper-exposes-racist -fraternity-initiation-video-at-syracuse-university/)

Incidents such as these occur collectively thousands of times on college campuses throughout an academic year. While these instances of bigotry have seen measurable responses from administrators, institutions, and police attempting to quash hostilities, the academic landscape has certainly been impacted by this surge of intolerance. In spite of this, campuses nationwide continue to commit themselves to educating students, faculty, and staff on the importance of creating and promoting spaces that facilitate introspective discourse, purposeful programming, and enlightened learning as it relates to diversity.

Research on Higher Education Racial and Cultural Campus Climate

Despite the best efforts of higher education institutions, marginalized populations continue to report that they lack a sense of belonging on campus (Cabrera, 2019; Mwangi et al., 2018; Tatum, 2017; Watt, 2015a). Black students' experience on predominantly White campuses was the focus of a qualitative study in which the researchers found four overarching themes: "(a) perceptions of Blackness on campus, (b) campus racial climate mirroring societal racial climates, (c) experiencing and engaging in movements on campus and (d) impact of racial climate on future planning" (Mwangi et al., 2018, p. 462). The narrative in the first theme dealt with microaggressions that were unwarranted perceptions of distrust and fear projected by White students toward Black students. As discussed previously in this chapter, the Black students in this study shared that the national racial climate "was a clear reflection of issues going on in their lives and on their campuses" (Mwangi et al., 2018, p. 463). The Black students felt the impact of the societal racial incidents occurring across the country which had come to affect them personally and made for "a very raw experience" as one participant stated (Mwangi et al., 2018, p. 465). The lack of concern among their White peers was perplexing and disheartening. However, their overall experiences empowered them to become agents of change as noted in the last theme: The struggles that Black students experience on college campuses are not only of ideological importance, but also found to impact emotional and psychological health, which are already concerns for most students during their college experience (Banks, 2010).

Unfortunately, racial discrimination is inevitable when there is a confluence of different individuals in any given environment. Banks (2010) found that "college hassles mediate the association of racial discrimination and depressive symptoms" (p. 30). In other words, the environment and the preponderance of daily micro-assaults for minoritized students can impact their personal and academic success in college (Banks, 2010). Nuñez (2009) conducted a longitudinal national study of Latino students which found a diminished sense of belonging to an institution created by overt and covert forms of exclusion, such as marginalization, discrimination and stereotyping. Perez (2017) noted similar results in his study with Latino men in which they became ideal college students when academic and social engagement were attained. Latin@s comprise the largest ethnic minority population in the United States yet they are woefully underrepresented as full-time students in colleges and universities (Dueñas & Gloria, 2017). Collecting data from Latin@ students, Dueñas and Gloria (2017) found that "belonging mediated the relationships of cohesion and congruity with mattering" (p. 891). Thus, Latin@ students need connections to peers on campus to be successful.

Studies conducted by Rankin and Reason (2005) and Johnson et al. (2007) found that African American and Latino students at predominantly White institutions were more likely to view the environment as racist and tended to perceive campus climates less favorably than their White counterparts. African American women find that the intersectionality of race and gender, or "living in two worlds" (Hannon, Woodside, Pollard, & Roman, 2016, p. 658), is particularly challenging because the question arises whether a situation encountered on campus is due to racism or sexism (Hannon et al., 2016).

In a mixed-methods study conducted by Nguyen, Chan, Nguyen, and Teranishi (2017) the researchers explored the campus experiences of Asian American and Pacific Islander students at UCLA (University of California,

Los Angeles). Their research attempted to address an obvious gap in the literature, as most studies on campus racial climate focus primarily on the African American and Latino student experiences. The data revealed similarities with other minoritized groups, finding that, "despite attending a compositionally diverse institution, Asian American students still experienced racism and lower levels of belonging" (Nguyen et al., 2017, p. 3).

Another group which tends to be disregarded in such studies are American Indian students, evidently because their "families and tribal leaders often question the extent to which predominantly White colleges and universities can contribute to positive outcomes for their students" (Lundberg, 2014, p. 263). American Indian students, in the fall of 2016, comprised 0.8 percent of all college students, which is comparable to their overall representation in the United States (Piper, 2019). Using the National Survey of Student Engagement (NSSE), data from 647 American Indian students from predominantly White institutions was studied and found that when student success is supported, and if there is a positive interpersonal environment, the students succeed (Lundberg, 2014). This can be a daunting task when many campuses are ill equipped to create an environment for American Indian students that is both culturally sensitive and racially diverse. The specific challenges for this population are socioeconomic oppression, academic preparedness, variation in cultural values and norms, and lack of support from significant family and friends (Keith, Stastny, & Brunt, 2016). In addressing the variety of challenges American Indian students face, it is the responsibility of colleges and universities to create safe spaces and train personnel to reduce the institutional barriers those students are forced to navigate. An example of a university that is dedicated to keep a promise made to American Indians is Harvard University, whose 1650 charter "specifies that the university's purpose is 'the education of English and Indian youth'" (Piper, 2019, p. A43). This promise was not officially honored until 1970 when Harvard established the American Indian Program to prepare members of the Navajo Nation to become teachers in their respective communities (Piper, 2019). This practice is an example of how institutions can integrate American Indian perspectives and influence, and would improve the campus culture of colleges and universities with significant native student populations or large American Indian communities near them.

Multiracial and biracial students are growing in number on college campuses (Harris, 2017; Harris & BrckaLorenz, 2017; Museus, Lambe Sariñana, & Ryan, 2015). Multiracial women face racial stereotypes on campus from White and other minoritized students because there is a desire to place them into the binary frame of Black or White (Harris, 2017). This in turn causes multiracial women to believe in racist stereotypes about monoracial students of color (Harris, 2017). Issues impacting biracial students are lower quality of interaction and less engagement on predominantly White campuses (Harris & BrckaLorenz, 2017). Although there are limited studies on multiracial and biracial students, the research shows that these groups experience alienation and marginalization on campus as well. Themes that emerged in Museus, Lambe Sarinana, Yee, and Robinson's (2016) study of multiracial students' experiences with prejudice and discrimination in college were issues related to a need to place them in one specific racial ethnic category thus invalidating their other identities. Additionally, multiracial students face overt and covert marginalization because there is a lack of understanding or invalidation of the racial identities chosen which could lead to exoticization or objectification of "their unique or different backgrounds and phenotype" (Museus, Lambe Sarinana, Yee, & Robinson, 2016, p. 691) and pathologizing of multiracial individuals assuming that they are psychologically imbalanced and confused about their identities. These issues can impede the cognitive and psychosocial growth of multiracial students during the most critical developmental period in their lives.

In addition to the extant literature on the perception and experience of race on campuses is a growing body of literature that focuses on the experiences of other marginalized groups such as women and LGBTQ students. The research indicates that women have a long-standing history of experiencing what has been described as a "chilly" campus climate (Hall & Sandler, 1982). Although much of the research focuses on the classroom experiences of female students, the results reveal that women often find campus environments to be less inviting, less supportive and less attuned to their needs (Allen & Madden, 2006; Hall & Sandler, 1982; Hart & Fellabaum, 2008). Similarly, the research surrounding LGBTQ students reveals that these students often experience acts of discrimination and harassment culminating in an overall hostile campus experience (Hong, Woodford, Long, & Renn, 2016; Rankin, Weber, Blumenfeld, & Frazer, 2010; Stewart, & Howard-Hamilton, 2015). This is particularly important because research has shown that deeper issues emerge when the intersections of race, gender, and sexual orientation, which are integral parts of the students' identity, are attacked (Means, 2017; Patton, 2011). Research findings regarding the experiences of minoritized LGBTQ students have demonstrated that they have been especially marginalized at predominantly White institutions (Means, 2017; Stewart & Howard-Hamilton, 2015). Finding a place within the White LGBT community has not been meaningful and there is no sense of belonging because of cisgender queer privilege (Kirk & Okazawa-Rey, 2010). What is meant by cisgender queer privilege is that White men are accepted because of their dominant race and gender identity thus submerging their sexual identity. Patriarchy is prevalent in this society and can leave minoritized gay individuals powerless. Patton (2011) found that Black LGBTQ students are even further ostracized because the terms used to describe their sexual identities do not resonate with their sense of self. "Terms such as sexually free, same gender loving, woman who loves women, or man who loves men are all labels that expand beyond the typical LGBTQ designations" (Patton, Kortegast, & Javier, 2011, pp. 177-178). Seeking refuge outside of the LGBTQ environment can be a challenge for minoritized LGBTQ students because their Black peer group may not accept them due to culturally-rooted homophobia which compounds with the experience of dealing with bias within the university environment overall (Goode-Cross & Good, 2009; Means, 2017).

Comparatively, White millennial students report that they rarely feel "excluded at school or work because of race or ethnicity (10 percent) while 23 percent of respondents of color said they often felt excluded in those settings" (Tatum, 2017, p. 23). Rather than living in a post-racial and color-blind society as many people hoped leading up to and after the Obama administration, Tatum (2017) says we are in a color-silent society in which we purposely avoid talking about racial and ethnic differences. Cabrera (2014) analyzed "White male college student narratives regarding racial joking" (p. 1) in which he found that the men were comfortable and oblivious to the offensive nature of the jokes and rationalized why they could share them with other White people. Furthermore, the men viewed minoritized groups as overly sensitive to racial jokes and could not understand the severity of their actions.

MULTICULTURAL COMPETENCY

Prompted by the shift towards multicultural competency development, the past two decades have been marked by an increasing number of campus climate assessments at institutions across the country (Bensimon, 2012). Colleges and universities have committed themselves to the task of creating diverse and comfortable learning environments for all students, and continue the push for assessment (Hurtado, Carter & Kardia, 1998). Although well intended, these assessments lack a clear focus. In a content analysis of over 100 campus climate studies, researchers Harper and Hurtado (2007) found that most studies did not have an agreed upon definition of campus climate nor the components and participants that comprise climate. They also found discrepancies in the way these assessments were conducted in terms of methodology, as well as the internal or external influence of researchers. Finally, the study revealed that more often than not the results of campus climate assessments were not readily accessible nor were they shared beyond the campus (Harper & Hurtado, 2007).

As previously noted, part of the push for data can be attributed to the emphasis organizations such as the American College Personnel Association (ACPA), and the National Association of Student Personnel Administrators (NASPA) are placing on assessment. In an era where knowledge is power, institutions are placing research and assessment at the forefront of their work. While the benefits of campus climate studies are profuse, scholars are beginning to remind colleges and universities the purpose of these studies "to improve student learning [and] the quality of the undergraduate experience" (Wehlburg, 2008, p. 2). The findings generated by these assessments are a first step in understanding the current climate, but unless the information gained is converted into institutional action, its value is lost (Hurtado, Griffin, Arellano, & Cuellar, 2008).

MODEL OF INCLUSIVITY FOR DIVERSE STUDENTS ON COLLEGE CAMPUSES

Why the Need for a Model?

In 2014, the American College Personnel Association (ACPA) and the National Association of Student Personnel Administrators (NASPA) assembled the Joint Task Force of Professional Competencies to review and revise the existing competencies that guide professionals working in student affairs. In 2015, these two organizations unveiled the revamped Professional Competency Areas for Student Affairs Educators, which included the renaming of the competence formerly known as "Equity, Diversity and Inclusion" to Social Justice and Inclusion (ACPA/NASPA, 2015). The revision was not simply nominal, but was reflective of the shift that the task force charges practitioners to make in practice. As is evidenced by the literature, student affairs professionals must now move beyond the passive awareness of diversity issues to a more active stance of fostering change (ACPA/NASPA, 2015). These competencies construct the dispositions and skills necessary to achieve the goal of social justice—"full and equal participation of all groups in a society that is mutually shaped to meet their needs" (Bell, 2013, p. 21). Although organizations like the ACPA and NASPA provide the framework for practice, the competencies themselves are not comprehensive enough to describe and explain the current climates of student populations nor do they offer strategies for institutional transformation. Institutions must turn to a model of inclusivity to conceptualize their existing environments and construct a plan for systemic and systematic development.

Student affairs educators are beholden to the needs of their students and as such are obligated to approach their work through a multicultural lens.

This prerequisite for ethical practice stems not only from organizations such as ACPA and NASPA, but also from the learning outcomes associated with a diverse campus environment. Broadly defined, these outcomes include "habits of mind or skills for lifelong learning, competencies for a multicultural world, and achievement, inclusive of retention and degree attainment" (Hurtado et al., 2012, p. 50). Educators and professionals have the ability to challenge students to think critically, to engage in problem solving, and to reflect on new information and situations. These skills, honed in a diverse environment, cultivate individuals who practice flexible, self-directed, and complex thinking, which allows for lifelong learning in an ever-changing world (Hurtado et al., 2012). The second outcome, multicultural competency, is bolstered when students are taught through inclusive practice that supports circumspection and appreciation for the differences of others (Gutmann, 2004). A diverse campus environment grants students the opportunity to develop a more realistic worldview, open to new information and experiences, which has been shown to reduce individual prejudice and encourage advocacy for social justice and inclusion (Zuñiga et al., 2005). Researchers have now begun exploring the connection between campus climates and achievement outcomes. The data indicates that individual satisfaction with campus climate has a positive influence on retention and degree completion for Latino/a, White, Asian and African American students (Museus et al., 2008). Taken together, these three outcomes are necessary for students to experience success while in college and upon graduation, but in order for the outcomes to be realized campus diversity must first exist.

The Authentic, Action-Oriented, Framing for Environmental Shifts (AAFES) Method

An important question that must be answered is "how can higher education intentionally create inclusive environments where its community members have the possibility of being more fully human?" (Watt, 2015a, p. 25). The Authentic, Action-Oriented, Framing for Environmental Shifts (AAFES) method, developed by Watt (2015a), is a social change process tool for faculty, administrators, and students in higher education. The author states that there are two key terms that are integral to the processing of environmental shifts: (1) Difference, spelled with a capital "D," which is "having dissimilar opinions, experiences, ideologies, epistemologies and/or constructions of reality about self, society, and/or identity (Watt, 2015a, p. 24), and (2) multicultural initiative which is "any type of program and/or a set of strategies that promotes skill development to better manage Difference on a personal, institutional, community, or societal level (Watt, 2015a, p. 26). The AAFES method takes into consideration Difference and multicultural initiatives to create space for all voices to be heard to create an organic process that encourages the development of skills "to withstand the controversies associated with Difference" (Watt, 2015a, p. 26).

The AAFES method shifts the responsibility of deconstructing systemic oppression from minoritized populations, transferring the dismantling process to individuals who have authority or dominant identities (Watt, 2015a). The theoretical underpinnings of AAFES are Freire (2017) and Hooks (1994) in which the authors discuss the importance of transformation and liberation so that critical reflection, dialogue, and action can take place. Watt (2015a) has noted six primary assumptions to the AAFES method:

1. There is a pathology or social illness linked to the subjugation of marginalized people by a dominant group and is deeply embedded in the culture of the campus. This pathological behavior impacts how individuals communicate and make decisions on a daily basis.
2. There must be dialogue, open communication, and constructive facilitation of the process in order for the deconstruction of toxic environments and the reconstruction of egalitarian communities.
3. There must be a personal connection to the deconstruction of social issues that impacts the individual intellectually and emotionally, providing individual as well as ideological motivation.
4. There will be an awakening for all community members and the college/university when multicultural initiatives are implemented that invite all voices around the decision-making table.
5. There must be a universal shift in the environment for change to occur that includes individuals as well as the overall system itself.
6. "Increasing the capacity of community members/citizens to engage skillfully [with] Difference equips people with the skills to face [a] culture that is ever changing and nebulous" (p. 30).

As Watt (2015a) noted, in order for the AAFES method to be adopted and put into practice, administrators, faculty, and staff must be collaborative, conscious of their biases, and reflect continuously on the impact their work is having on the entire community. The final qualities of this process for transformative multicultural initiatives according to Watt (2015a) are: (1) that the authentic practitioners listen deeply, think about their own positionality, and participate authentically in difficult dialogues, (2) that there be an action-oriented process that allows everyone to "sit with dissonance, engage in difficult dialogue, and continuously seek critical consciousness" (p. 33), and (3) that there is a deconstruction and reconstruction process that takes into account environmental shifts. Overall, the AAFES method "identifies qualities of process that higher education institutions can use to improve their approach to managing cultural change" (Watt, 2015a, p. 37). When introducing any type of change within an institution that will shift the power away from the privileged groups and create an environment of equity and inclusion there will inevitably be resistance from the dominant group. This resistance will require that those engaged in the transformation process recognize the behaviors that will surface when having conversations with those from privileged identities.

The Privileged Identity Exploration Model dissects and expounds upon eight defenses that surface within privileged individuals when a dissonance-provoking stimulus (DPS) is introduced (Watt, 2007). The three components and eight behaviors are: denial, deflection, and rationalization, which are under the Recognizing Privileged Identity component; intellectualization, principium, and false envy connected with Contemplating Privileged Identity component; and last, under the Addressing Privileged Identity component, are the benevolence and minimization behaviors (Watt, 2007).

A DPS can be unfamiliar information or new content that, in the Recognized Privileged Identity phase, can be rejected, denied, or shifted to another person via deflection, and in these processes "people are not conscious of their emotion or thought process" (Watt, 2015b, p. 46). When their emotion and thoughts are awakened, they are Contemplating Privileged Identity. Emotional awakening behaviors are minimization, or the downplaying of the DPS impact, and rationalization of explanations to justify the DPS, followed by intellectualization to scientifically legitimize the DPS. Moving into the next defensive posture, Addressing Privileged Identity, individuals will try to equalize their relationship with others who they may have stereotyped with kind expressions and compliments which is generalized as false envy. Another defensive posture is principium, which is a principle or value presented that invalidates the DPS or may be an act of benevolence to cloak the DPS. Overall, "this model identifies the normal reactions that people often display as they attempt to incorporate ideas that challenge the very structure of their beliefs and values" (Watt, 2015b, p. 55). As administrators, faculty, and students are faced with the task of creating supportive and inclusive environments for marginalized and minoritized individuals, it is imperative that they first recognize, challenge, and acknowledge defensive reactions. Recognizing these defensive behaviors is an essential skill that will lead to heightened self-awareness which "strengthens the capacity of people to stay in the difficult dialogues that are necessary for reconstructing environments that are more inclusive" (Watt, 2015b, p. 55).

CREATING AN INCLUSIVE CAMPUS

The Ideal Campus

An ideal campus environment achieves the goal of creating a " welcoming environment where all students—inclusive of the growing diversity of identities in American higher education—are affirmed and supported as learners" (Pope, Reynolds & Mueller, 2014, p. 116). A review of the literature highlights five main components that are crucial to creating an environment where all students can thrive.

The first is what is often referred to as compositional diversity, or "the numerical representation of individuals from diverse social identities among students, faculty staff and administrators" (Hurtado et al., 2012, p. 64). Scholars agree that for culture change to take place, an institution must possess a critical mass of diverse students, faculty, and staff to generate increased opportunities for interactions with a diverse array of individuals (Chang, Astin, & Kim, 2004; Gurin, Dey, Hurtado, & Gurin, 2002; Hurtado et al., 2008; Pike & Kuh, 2006). The second is the need for multicultural competency among all academic professionals. According to Pope et al. (2014), this requires the individual mastery of three different components—awareness, knowledge and skills. Important to note is the idea that multiculturalism is the responsibility of the entire community, not just student affairs staff. Diversity initiative should be central to the mission of the institution and reflected in enrollment, learning initiative, and curricular and co-curricular programs (Delgado & Stefancic, 2017).

The third component necessary for the ideal campus environment is diversity content embedded within the curriculum. Research has shown that taking classes related to diversity issues positively affects cross-cultural interactions and helps students to develop critical perspectives (Hurtado, Alvarez, Guillerom-Wann, Cuellar, & Arellano, 2012; Nuñez, 2009). In a similar vein is the fourth component of the idyllic environment: diversity and equity programming. As diversity in the classroom fosters positive interactions and critical thinking, so too does diversity programming in the co-curricular sphere. It is important for students to engage with diversity outside of the classroom as it brings together like-minded individuals and allies, encouraging the development of interpersonal peer relationships (Strange & Banning, 2015). Lastly, the ideal institution is one committed to continual and ongoing assessment. Campus climate research is essential in assisting institutions to understand where they are presently, how effective interventions have been, and where change efforts need to be focused moving forward (Jackson, 2006; Pope et al., 2014).

Best Practices for Campus Cultural Transformation

In order to achieve an ideal campus environment, an institution must first be committed to diversity and inclusivity at all levels. Jayakumar and Museus (2012) state that "colleges and universities that engage in inquiry aimed at achieving equity, create and maintain collectivist values, integrate students' backgrounds and communities into campus life, and construct inclusive educational environments will move closer to attaining equity-oriented campus cultures" (p. 21). This work is the shared responsibility of all parties—administrators, faculty, staff, and students alike. Despite this reality and the need for pervasive commitment, student affairs professionals and offices are often charged with the task of creating multicultural change (Pope et al., 2014). A review of the literature suggests the following as best practices for student affairs educators in order to better engage in meaningful multicultural change initiatives.

Programming and Services

Student affairs professionals are uniquely positioned to support students in a co-curricular setting where they can provide opportunities for students to experience diversity in a non-academic environment (Strange & Banning, 2015). Best practices require practitioners to implement programming that has clear educational purpose and defined outcomes (Hurtado et al., 2012). It is also crucial for the coordination of programming campus-wide. Research indicates that participation in co-curricular diversity programs has been shown to reduce prejudice, improve cognitive development, and increase civic engagement (Bowman, 2010, 2011; Denson, 2009; Hurtado et al., 2012). Furthermore, involvement in such activities encourages students with marginalized identities while simultaneously developing allies for those individuals (Hurtado et al., 2012; Mayhew et al., 2016).

> - *Example: Create a service-learning program focused on diversity initiatives in partnership with multiple offices.*

Relationship Building

In their role, student affairs educators serve as "resocializing agents for students from multiple social identities groups teaching students to recognize prejudice, understand the sources of conflict, and interrupt unthinking social behaviors" (Hurtado et al., 2012, p. 84). They have the capability to empower students through interpersonal validation, which fosters student development and social adjustment (Hurtado et al., 1998; Hurtado et al., 2012). In addition to the relationships student affairs educators build with students, they are also conduits for interpersonal interactions between students and their peers. These formal and informal peer-to-peer interactions enhance student outcomes, counteract marginalizing experiences, and increase sense of belonging (Banks, 2009; Hurtado et al., 1998; Nuñez, 2009). Student affairs educators are also charged with coalition building among various stakeholders, educators, administrators, and faculty in order to advance campus-wide diversity initiatives (Broadhurst et al., 2016; Cuyjet, Linder, Howard-Hamilton, & Cooper, 2016).

- *Example: Connect leaders of student organizations that share a similar purpose and goals.*

Advocacy

The university setting can sometimes be cumbersome and difficult to navigate for students, and thus requires advocacy on the part of practitioners. This advocacy can take the form of serving as an advisor to a student organization, mentoring individual students, mediating between students and administrators, and empowering students to be agents of change (Broadhurst et al., 2016). Students who feel disenfranchised by an institution or the systems within it often feel impotent and do not know how to go about asking for the support they need. This in turn positions student affairs educators in a role to ensure all students have a voice and a "place at the table where decisions that affect them are made" (Harrison, 2014, p. 167).

- *Example: Recommend the creation of identity-explicit spaces on campus.*

Research and Assessment

The more recent trend in higher education has placed diversity and inclusion at the center of most institutions. This shift in focus has brought with it the creation of new offices such as Vice President or Vice Provost for Diversity and Inclusion, and the development of multicultural programs with attention being paid to evaluating the impact of these initiatives (Harper & Hurtado, 2007; Smith & Parker, 2005). Part of ensuring a program, office, or functional area is effectual in assessing the level to which they achieve the intended learning outcomes. Practitioners must continually engage in research to understand the experiences of the students they serve and to inform and improve future efforts (Hart & Fellabaum, 2008). Furthermore, professionals need to document and report the findings of their assessments so that fellow practitioners can benefit from the results as well.

Another method of gauging the cultural climate on campus is to use an assessment tool such as The Equity Scorecard (Bensimon, 2012) which is a process or way of thinking and observing the campus environment which instills in observers " the expertise, know how, and self-efficacy to produce equity outcomes within their classrooms, departments, and institutions (p. 26).

The University of Southern California Race and Equity Center (2019) conducts national studies on minoritized students and has created the National Assessment of Collegiate Campus Climates (NACCC), a survey that asks salient questions about equity and race at the institution. Using an assessment conducted either by campus leaders or a consultant off campus is a useful tool to identify and measure issues prevalent within the environment and coursework, as well as estimating the effort needed to overcome challenges.

- *Example: Identify faculty, staff, and students as potential members of an equity committee to create an assessment (e.g. Equity Score Card), conduct a campus climate study, and disseminate the findings. The final outcome would be the implementation of recommendations from the study.*
- *Example: Evaluate and revamp departmental policies to identity language or areas that are exclusive.*

The most important work is to shift institutions from providing diversity and inclusion programming on campus to a complete immersion process of valuing and implementing diversity and inclusion initiatives throughout the campus system (Watt, 2015b). Institutions cannot be divided when implementing diversity initiatives. There must be a "dynamic social change process" (Watt, 2015b, p. 15) which is a multi-level approach to social change recognizing "the reality that the dynamic social change process requires all campus community members to work together from their particular professional roles" (Watt, 2015b, p. 15).

CONCLUSION

Will our campuses, communities, and society become welcoming and non-toxic environments for everyone so that they can become fully human and express their authentic selves? The challenge and responsibility is with individuals on college campuses who have the tools, energy, time, resources, and influence to engage in dialogue, reflection, and action to transform people, places, and spaces. Everyone on campus is a cultural change agent and it only takes a single person to create a ripple that will extend beyond impacting a few to empowering many. This is a process that will require a considerable amount of personal, emotional, and intellectual development for everyone involved in the transformation of a given institution's environment. Freire stated that "those who authentically commit themselves to the people must re-examine themselves constantly. Conversion to the people required a profound rebirth. Those who undergo it must take on a new form of existence; the can no longer remain as they were" (2017, p. 61). Prepare to become undone by the experience of empowering others to be change agents engaged in an equitable environment.

CASE STUDY

The Student Leadership Honorary

Pluto College is a public institution of 13,000 located in a medium-sized city in the Midwest. It was founded in 1910 and has an active and successful student affairs program for its student body, virtually all of whom are of typical age with a racial/ethnic demographic population of 60% White, 20% African American, 10% Latinx, 5% international, and 5% other. The majority of the students are enrolled full time and about half of the students live on campus with the remainder living in private apartments close to the campus. There is a lively on campus social life, and many student organizations do positive work in the community. Students have close relationships with the administration and retention rates are high. Most students are proud of attending Pluto College.

The Cardinal Guild is the most prestigious student leadership community for students at Pluto College, and this group has been active on the campus for almost 70 years. The current members select the new initiates each year, and when the new group is announced, it is one of the highlights at a campus wide symposium each spring, presided over by the President of Pluto College. Pictures of the new members of Cardinal Guild are placed in a special display in the Union, and remain there for many years.

Judy Ferver is the Director of Programs for New Students at Pluto and has held that position for three years. She is a hardworking and creative professional who has earned the respect and admiration of top student leaders at Pluto for her many accomplishments and her friendly, supportive approach. She was asked by Cardinal Guild to become its adviser when a faculty member, who had been its adviser for 22 years, retired last year. She accepted the invitation to be the advisor and consulted with her predecessor prior to his departure. The conversation was engaging, however, there were very few notes, data, or selection materials provided when they met.

Judy discovered, much to her dismay, that the process of selecting the 25 new members of Cardinal Guild each Spring was very flawed. While the published criteria for being selected included grades, service, and major leadership positions, she found that new members were often selected on the basis of campus political affiliations and friendships. She also noted that the current members were highly protective and secretive about how they selected new members and did not invite her into the discussion about applicants. Due to the respect she has garnered on campus, she has been approached by several minoritized students individually, who have, in confidence, communicated their bitterness about the unfair nature of the selection process for this most prestigious honor. The examples they shared with Judy confirmed her fears of racial division being a factor.

Judy reported her experiences to the Dean of Campus Life, who in turn, reported to the Vice President for Student Affairs. She shared her concerns with the Dean, who had been at Pluto for a long time. He shrugged his shoulders and told her it has always been politically charged, and that she ought to leave it alone.

Case Analysis and Questions to Consider

As you examine the issues in this case it is important to remember that change should occur at the top of the administrative level. Blaming the victims, or in this case the minoritized students who are asking to be included in the honorary society, is not the primary focus because they should be observed as individuals who are marginalized in a toxic environment.

1. How should Judy proceed? Who are her allies in this situation?
2. What theoretical frameworks should Judy use as reflection tools?
3. How can Judy use the Authentic, Action-Oriented Framing for Environmental Shifts (AAFES) Model to help Pluto College assess the campus climate?
4. What institutional or programmatic policies should she read and possible revise?
5. What proactive programs should she suggest for the students, staff, and faculty?
6. How will she begin the listening and communication process to change systematic oppression at Pluto College?

REFERENCES

ACPA: College Student Educators & NASPA–Student Affairs Administrators in Higher Education (2015). *ACPA/NASPA professional competency areas for student affairs educators*. Washington, DC: Authors.

Allen, E. J., & Madden, M. (2006). Chilly classrooms for undergraduate students: A question of method? *The Journal of Higher Education, 77*, 684–711.

Banks, K. H. (2010). African American college students' experience of racial discrimination and the role of college hassles. *Journal of College Student Development, 51*(1), 23–34.

Bell, L. A. (2013). Theoretical foundations. In M. Adams, W. Blumenfeld, C. Castaneda, H. W. Hackman, M. L. Peters, & X. Zuniga (Eds.), *Readings for diversity and social justice* (3rd ed., pp. 21–25). New York, NY: Routledge.

Bensimon, E. S. (2012). The Equity Scorecard: Theory of change. In E. M. Bensimon & L. Malcom (Eds.), *Confronting equity issues on campus: Implementing the Equity Scorecard in theory and practice* (pp. 17–44). Sterling, VA: Stylus.

Bowman, N. A. (2010). College diversity experiences and cognitive development: A meta-analysis. *Review of Educational Research, 80*(1), 4–33.

Bowman, N. A. (2011). Promoting participation in a diverse democracy: A meta-analysis of college diversity experiences and civic engagement. *Review of Educational Research, 81*(1), 29–68.

Cabrera, N. L. (2014). But we are not laughing: White male college students' racial joking and what this says about "post-racial" discourse. *Journal of College Student Development, 55*(1), 1–15.

Cabrera, N. L. (2019). *White guys on campus: Racism, White immunity and the myth of "post-racial" higher education.* New Brunswick, NJ: Rutgers University Press.

Chang, M. J., Astin, A. W., & Kim, D. (2004). Cross-racial interaction among undergraduates: Some consequences, causes, and patterns. *Research in Higher Education, 45*, 529–553.

Colby, S. L., & Ortman, J.M. (2014). *Projections of the size and composition of the U.S. population: 2014 to 2060,* Current Population Reports. U.S. Census Bureau. Washington, DC.

Cuyjet, M. J., Linder, C., Howard-Hamilton, M. F., & Cooper, D. L. (Eds.). (2016). *Multiculturalism on campus theory, models, and practices for understanding diversity and creating inclusion* (2nd ed.). Sterling, Va.: Stylus Pub.

Delgado, R., & Stefancic, J. (2017). *Critical race theory: An introduction* (3rd ed.). New York, NY: New York University Press.

Denson, N. (2009). Do curricular and cocurricular diversity activities influence racial bias? A meta-analysis. *Review of Educational Research, 79*(2), 805–838.

Dueñas, M., & Gloria, A. M. (2017). ¿Pertenezco a esta Universidad? The mediating role of belonging for collective sefl-esteem and mattering for Latin@ undergraduates. *Journal of College Student Development, 58*(6), 891–906.

Freire, P. (2017). *Pedagogy of the oppressed: 50th anniversary edition.* New York: Bloomsbury Academic.

Goodman, K. M. (2017). The effects of viewpoint diversity and racial diversity on need for cognition. *Journal of College Student Development, 58*(6), 853–871.

Gurin, P., Dey, E. L., Hurtado, S., & Gurin, G. (2002). Diversity and higher education: Theory and impact on educational outcomes. *Harvard Educational Review, 72*, 330–367.

Gutmann, A. (2004). Unity and diversity in democratic multicultural education: Creative and destructive tensions. In J. A. Banks (Ed.), *Diversity and citizenship education: Global perspectives* (pp. 71–97). San Francisco: Jossey-Bass.

Hall, R. M., & Sandler, B. R. (1982). *The classroom climate: A chilly climate for women?* Washington, DC: Association of American Colleges.

Hannon, C. R., Woodside, M., Pollard, B. L., & Roman, J. (2016). The meaning of African American college women's experiences attending a predominantly White institution: A phenomenological study. *Journal of College Student Development, 57*(6), 652–666.

Harper, S. R. (2012). Foreword. In S. D. Museus & U. M. Jayakumar (Eds.), *Creating campus cultures: Fostering success among racially diverse student populations* (pp. ix–xi). New York: Routledge.

Harper, S. R., & Hurtado, S. (2007). Nine themes in campus racial climates and implications for institutional transformation. In S. R. Harper & L. D. Patton (Eds.), *Responding to the realities of race on campus. New directions for student services.* San Francisco: Jossey-Bass.

Harper, S. R., & Simmons, I. (2019). *Black students at public colleges and universities: A 50-state report card.* Los Angeles: University of Southern California Race and Ethnicity Center.

Harris, J. C. (2017). Multiracial women students and racial stereotypes on the college campus. *Journal of College Student Development, 58*(4), 475–491.

Harris, J. C., & BrckaLorenz, A. (2017). Black, white, and biracial students' engagement at differing institutional types. *Journal of College Student Development, 58*(5), 783–789.

Harrison, L. (2014). How student affairs professionals learn to advocate: A phenomenological study. *Journal of College and Character, 15,* 165–177.

Hong, J. S., Woodford, M. R., Long, L. D., & Renn, K. A. (2016). Ecological covariates of subtle and blatant heterosexist discrimination among LGBQ college students. *Journal of Youth and Adolescence, 45,* 117–131.

hooks, b. (1994). *Teaching to transgress.* New York: Routledge.

Hurtado, S., Alvarez, C. L., Guillermo-Wann, C., Cuellar, M., & Arellano, L. (2012). A model for diverse learning environments. In J. Smart & M. Paulsen (Eds.), *Higher Education: Handbook of Theory and Research, 27,* 41–122.

Hurtado, S., Carter, D. F., & Kardia, D. (1998) The climate for diversity: Key issues for institutional self-study. In K. W. Bauer (Ed.), *Campus climate: Understanding the critical components of today's colleges and universities.* (New directions for institutional research, No. 98, pp. 53–63). San Francisco: Jossey-Bass.

Jackson, B. W. (2006). Theory and practice of multicultural organization development. In B. B. Jones & M. Brazzel (Eds.), *The NTL handbook of organization development and changes: Principles, practices, and perspectives* (pp. 139–154). San Francisco, CA: Pfeiffer.

Johnson, D. R., Soldner, M. Leonard, J. B., Alvarez, P., Inkelas, K. K., Rowan-Kenyon, H., & Longerbeam, S. (2007). Examining sense of belonging among first-year undergraduates from different racial/ethnic groups. *Journal of College Student Development, 48,* 525–542.

Jayakumar, U. M., & Museus, S. D. (2012). Mapping the intersection of campus cultures and equitable outcomes among racially diverse student populations. In S. D. Museus & U. M. Jayakumar (Eds.), *Creating campus cultures: Fostering success among racially diverse student populations* (pp. 1–27). New York: Routledge.

Keith, J. F., Stastny, S. N., & Brunt, A. (2016). Barriers and strategies for success for American Indian college students: A review. *Journal of College Student Development, 57*(6), 698–714.

Kelly-Gangi, C. (2016). *Quotable wisdom: Barack Obama.* Sterling: New York.

Kirk, G., & Okazawa-Rey, M. (2010) Identities and social locations: Who am I? Who are my people? In M. Adams, W. J. Blumenfield, C. Castaneda, H. W. Hackman, M. L. Peters, & X. Zuniga (Eds.), *Readings for diversity and social justice* (pp. 8–14). New York, NY: Routledge.

Lundberg, C. A. (2014). Institutional support and interpersonal climate as predictors of learning for Native American students. *Journal of College Student Development, 55*(3), 263–277.

Mayhew, M. J., Rockenbach, A. N., Bowman, N. A., Seifert, T. A., Wolniak, G. C., Pascarella, E. T., & Terenzini, P. T. (2016). *How college affects students: 21st century evidence that higher education works* (Vol. 3). San Francisco: Jossey Bass.

Means, D. (2017). "Quaring" spiritually: The spiritual counterstories and spaces of Black gay and bisexual male college students. *Journal of College Student Development, 58*(2), 229–246.

Museus, S. D., Nichols, A. H., & Lambert, A. D. (2008). Racial differences in the effects of campus racial climate on degree completion: A structural equation model. *Review of Higher Education, 32*(1), 107–134.

Museus, S. D., Sariñana Lambe, S. A., & Ryan, T. K. (2015). A qualitative examination of multiracial students' coping responses to experiences with prejudice and discrimination in college. *Journal of College Student Development, 56*(4), 331–348.

Museus, S. D., Sariñana Lambe, S. A., Yee, A. L., & Robinson, T. E. (2016). A qualitative analysis of multiracial students' experiences with prejudice and discrimination in college. *Journal of College Student Development, 57*(6), 680–697.

Mwangi, C. A. G., Thelamour, B., Ezeofar, I., & Carpenter, A. (2018). "Black elephant in the room": Black students contextualizing campus racial climate within U.S. racial climate. *Journal of College Student Development, 59*(4), 456–474.

Nguyen, M. H., Chan, J., Nguyen, B. M. D., & Taranishi, R. T. (2017). Beyond compositional diversity: Examining the campus climate experiences of Asian American and Pacific Islander students. *Journal of Diversity in Higher Education, 11*(4), 484–501. doi: 10.1037/dhe0000071

Novelly, T. (2017, September 21). White nationalist recruiting fliers posted around University of Louisville's campus. *The Courier-Journal.* Retrieved from https://www.courier-journal.com/story/news/education/2017/09/21/university-louisville-white-nationalist-fliers/689119001/

Nuñez, A. M. (2009). Latino students' college transition: A social and intercultural capital perspective. *Harvard Educational Review, 79*(1), 22–48.

Ogbu, J. U. (1990). Minority education in comparative perspective. *Journal of Negro Education, 59*(1), 45–57.

Patton, L. D. (2011). Perspectives on identity, disclosure, and the campus environment among African American gay and bisexual men at one historically Black college. *Journal of College Student Development, 51*(1), 77–100.

Patton, L. D., Kortegast, C., & Javier, G. (2011). LGBTQ millennials in college. In F. A. Bonner II, A. F. Marbley, & M. F. Howard-Hamilton (Eds.), *Diverse millennial students in college: Implications for faculty and student affairs* (pp. 193–209). Sterling, VA: Stylus.

Perez II, D. (2017). In pursuit of success: Latino male college students exercising academic determination and community cultural wealth. *Journal of College Student Development, 58*(2), 123–140.

Pike, G. R., & Kuh, G. D. (2006). Relationships among structural diversity, informal peer interactions and perceptions of the campus environment. *The Review of Higher Education, 29,* 425–450.

Piper, J. (2019, January 18). Program directors keep old promises to American Indians. *The Chronicle of Higher Education,* p. A43.

Pope, R. L., Reynolds, A. L., & Mueller, J. A. (2014). *Creating multicultural change on campus.* San Francisco: Jossey-Bass.

Rankin, S. R., & Reason, R. D. (2005). Differing perceptions: How students of color and White students perceive campus climate for underrepresented groups. *Journal of College Student Development, 46,* 43–61.

Rankin, S. R., Weber, G., Blumenfeld, W., & Frazer, S. (2010). *2010 state of higher education for lesbian, gay, bisexual, and transgender people.* Charlotte, NC: Campus Pride.

Smith, D. G., & Parker, S. (2005). Organizational learning: A tool for diversity and institutional effectiveness. *New Directions for Higher Education, 131,* 113–125.

Stewart, D-L., & Howard-Hamilton, M. F. (2015). Engaging lesbian, gay, and bisexual students on college campuses. In S. J. Quaye & S. R. Harper (Eds.), *Student engagement in higher education: Theoretical perspectives and practical approaches for diverse populations* (pp. 121–134). New York: Routledge.

Strange, C. C., & Banning, J. H. (2015). *Designing for learning: Creating campus environments for student success* (2nd ed.). San Francisco: Jossey Bass.

Sue, D. W., Arredondo, P., & McDavis, R. J. (1992). Multicultural counseling competencies and standards: A call to the profession. *Journal of Counseling and Development, 70,* 477–486.

Tatum, B. D. (2017). *Why are all of the Black kids sitting together in the cafeteria?* New York: Basic Books.

Taylor, K. (2017, September 19). Swastika, racial epithet found at Drake University spark investigation. Retrieved from https://www.nbcnews.com/news/nbcblk/swastika-racial-epithet-found-drake-university-spark-investigation-n802651

Tynes, B. M., Rose, C. A., & Markoe, S. L. (2013). Extending campus life to the internet. Social media, discrimination, and perceptions of racial climate. *Journal of Diversity in Higher Education, 6*(2), 102–114.

Watt, S. K. (2007). Difficult dialogues, privilege and social justice: Uses of the privileged identity exploration (PIE) model in student affairs practice. *College Student Affairs Journal, 26*(2), 114–126.

Watt, S. K. (2015a). Authentic, action-oriented, framing for environmental shifts (AAFES) method. In S. K. Watt (Ed.), *Designing transformative multicultural initiatives* (pp. 23–39). Sterling, VA: Stylus.

Watt, S. K. (2015b). Privileged Identity Exploration (PIE) Model revisited: Strengthening skills for engaging difference. In S. K. Watt (Ed.), *Designing transformative multicultural initiatives* (pp. 40–57). Sterling, VA: Stylus.

Wehlburg, C. M. (2008). *Promoting integrated and transformative assessment: A deeper focus on student learning.* San Francisco, CA: Jossey-Bass.

Zuñiga, X., Williams, E. A., & Berger, J. B. (2005). Action-oriented democratic outcomes: The impact of student involvement with campus diversity. *Journal of College Student Development, 46*(6), 660–678.

Chapter 9

USING CULTURALLY APPROPRIATE
INTERVENTION STRATEGIES IN PRACTICE

Saundra M. Tomlinson-Clarke & Ebelia Hernández

The growing need to address multicultural and diversity issues in higher education coincided with the changing demographic landscape of the United States population. The diversity index, representing the proportion of the non-white college student body (i.e., Black/African American, Latino/Hispanic, American Indian, Asian, Pacific Islander, multiracial) recently reached 75 percent at many institutions of higher education (U.S. News & World Report, 2017). Also, increased enrollment among women students has continued to contribute to changing demographic profiles on college campuses, with many of the nation's colleges and universities reporting a student body that is predominantly female (Freeman, 2004). "Life in most American colleges and universities today is an immersion in human diversity in many of its forms" (Dalton & Crosby, 2013, p. 281). Multicultural initiatives driven solely by structural diversity, however, will not ensure that students are exposed to or benefitting from learning resulting from cross-cultural interactions. Instead, colleges and universities will continue to mirror the ongoing challenges associated with an increasingly culturally diverse society. The recent resurgence of racism, sexism, and homophobia in society is evidenced on campuses, with renewed attention to civil rights and human rights. With an increase in campus diversity, student affairs professionals are charged with an ongoing challenge to promote students' academic, social and moral development. There is a growing need to engage leaders for social justice with the dispositions, competencies and skills for using culturally appropriate intervention strategies to affect student-learning outcomes. Important in developing and using culturally appropriate intervention strategies is the clarification of related terms (e.g., *multiculturalism, diversity, social justice, identity*) that are commonly and often interchangeably used in practice. Key terms are discussed within the context of developing culturally appropriate intervention strategies designed to prepare individuals with competencies and skills for productive citizenry in a complex and interconnected world.

MULTICULTURALISM, DIVERSITY AND SOCIAL JUSTICE

Multiculturalism has been used synonymously to denote race, ethnicity and nationality, as well as to describe an approach for developing cultural competence (Sue & Sue, 2016). Conceptualized within the historical and sociopolitical context of the United States, the term multiculturalism has been used to refer to five racial-ethnic groups; four of which are identified as racial-ethnic minority groups (i.e., Asian, Black/African, Latino/Hispanic, Native American or indigenous people who have historically resided in the continental United States and its territories), and Caucasians/Europeans are identified as the majority group (Arredondo, Toporek, Brown, Sanchez, Locke, Sanchez, & Stadler, 1996; Sue & Sue, 2016). Also used as a method of analysis in cross cultural encounters, multiculturalism refers "exclusively to narrowly defined culture-specific categories such as nationality or ethnicity," whereas multiculturalism used as a generic perspective or theoretical framework provides a sociocultural context for examining self and others, and includes "broadly defined social system variables such as ethnographics, demographics, status, and affiliation..." (Pedersen, 1991, p. 7). A broad and inclusive definition of multiculturalism eliminates the focus on a "difference approach" and promotes perspectives that encourage cultural self-awareness, cultural self-development and a deeper understanding of culturally diverse others (Sciarra, 1999). An inclusive definition also expands notions of multi-cultural beyond multi-ethnic and multi-national to include "demographic variables (e.g., age, sex, place of residence), status variables (e.g., social, educational, economic), and affiliations (formal and informal) as well as ethnographic variables such as nationality, ethnicity, language, and religion," making multiculturalism generic in all interpersonal interactions (Pedersen, 1991, p. 7). Multiculturalism from an inclusive perspective is multidimensional, embracing interrelated aspects of personal identity (Duan & Brown, 2016).

Diversity also has been used when referring to dimensions of personal identity, individual differences, and shared identity (Arredondo et al., 1996; Arredondo & Glauner, 1992). Often referred to as cultural diversity, dimensions of diversity include age, gender, sexual orientation, ableism, identity, language, social status, religion, and "socially created life environments" and their intersections (Arredondo et al., 1996; Duan & Brown, 2016). Consequently, diversity and multicultural are terms that are often used synonymously in the literature.

"Personal identity is cultural identity . . . and a powerful organizer of people's lives" (Thomas & Schwarzbaum, 2006, p. 1). Cultural identity, therefore, is comprised of the interrelated dimensions of diversity. Arredondo and Glauner (1992) proposed a model of personal identity and the interrelated dimensions that offers a flexible and fluid framework for exploring multiple identities and the intersections of these identities that make up personal identity. The model uses three broad dimensions or categories that list characteristics that may be part of an individual's identity. *Dimension A* characteristics are based on Equal Employment Opportunity (EEO) and Title VII of the Civil Rights Act of 1964. These characteristics are described by Arredondo and Glauner (1992) as most likely to be fixed and are also the characteristics that are most often used to stereotype others, reinforce culturally biased assumptions and create barriers to interpersonal and intercultural relationships. *Dimension B* characteristics represent the many aspects of the human experience and include factors such as education, region, work experience, religion, spirituality, and interpersonal relationships. *Dimension B* variables can be used to connect individuals that may differ along *Dimension A,* creating homogenous groups that might otherwise be perceived as different if based solely on salient characteristics (i.e., race/ethnicity, gender). Unique to this model of personal identity is *Dimension C,* which includes the interaction of contextual factors such as historical sociopolitical considerations that occur over a span of time, and the effects of an era on interactions among and between individuals and groups. The Zeitgeist defines an era and the cultural moments that impact identity by transforming the way we think about ourselves as well as our relationship to others. Using a complex model of personal identity assists in understanding the ways in which individuals are unique and like no others (individual identity), similar to other groups in some respects (group identity), and similar to all individuals in other respects (universal identity) (Sue & Sue, 2016). A multi-dimensional framework for exploring diversity in identity also is useful in challenging assumptions about culture, and exploring ways in which individuals and groups might connect to one another. For example, work experience or recreational interests (*Dimension B*) might be used to build rapport between and within groups within the sociopolitical context of the 21st century (*Dimension C*) rather than groupings created from fixed, binary and socially constructed categories used to define social identity (e.g., race/ethnicity, gender, sexual orientation).

CULTURAL COMPETENCE AND SOCIAL JUSTICE IN PRACTICE

Critical to developing cultural competence is the ability to understand historical and sociopolitical contextual factors, and dynamics of power and oppression between racial-ethnic/cultural groups (Ratts, Toporek, & Lewis, 2010). Sue and Sue (2013, 2016) asserted the importance of conceptualizing cultural competence as a fluid and ongoing process or journey rather than a set of skills that are fixed. Although cultural competence (attitudes/beliefs, knowledge and skills) is necessary, Sue and Sue (2016) cautioned that these components alone are not sufficient to ensure that practice is culturally appropriate or effective when working in culturally diverse settings. Practice guided by a multicultural philosophical orientation assumes cultural competence as an aspirational goal, and cultural humility as critical to effective interpersonal interactions.

Cultural humility is defined as "a way of being" as demonstrated by "an accurate view of self" in relation to others (intrapersonal dimension) and an ability to be "other-oriented" with openness to other beliefs, values, worldview and cultural identities (interpersonal dimension) (Hook, Davis, Owen, Worthington, & Utsey, 2013, pp. 353-354). Identified as a characteristic of leaders for social justice, humbleness is reflected through cultural humility (Chung & Bemak, 2012). Cultural humility can be conceptualized as an extension of Ponterotto's work on the multicultural personality. Ponterotto and Associates (Ponterotto, 2010; Ponterotto, Costa-Wofford, Brobst, Spelliscy, Mendelsohn Kacanski, Scheinholtz, & Martines, 2007) also identified five dispositions of the multicultural personality: *cultural empathy, open-mindedness, emotional stability, social initiative* and *flexibility*. These components are psychometrically robust and are associated with cross-cultural adaptability and intercultural effectiveness (Kealey & Protheroe, 1996).

Developing self-awareness and openness to cultural and social identities are pre-requisites for developing an ability to use reflective thinking to understand situations from multiple perspectives, and to develop and use culturally appropriate intervention strategies to facilitate the overall growth and development of learners across the developmental lifespan. The connection between diversity and morality is exemplified in Fitzgerald's (2000) definition of cultural competence:

> It is about developing the ability to 'see' a situation from multiple perspectives and, if necessary, to reconcile them. It is about developing multiple potential interpretations and using critical reflective thinking to choose which alternatives are most likely to provide effective strategies for care. It is about using such understandings to become more competent and effective professionals. (pp. 184–185)

Concepts and definitions from culturally responsive pedagogical theory and practice also can be used to inform higher education practice. Ladson-Billings (2014) describes *cultural competence* as "the ability to help students appreciate and celebrate their cultures of origin while gaining knowledge of and fluency in at least one other culture" and *sociopolitical consciousness* as "the ability to take learning beyond the confines of the classroom . . . to identify, analyze, and solve real-world problems" (p. 75). These abilities and competencies are essential to developing and using culturally appropriate intervention strategies in practice. Learning must extend beyond the confines of classroom to co-curricular experiences designed to increase students' multicultural interactions.

A social justice agenda advances multiculturalism and diversity initiatives beyond *theorizing* to *acting* on behalf of individuals and groups who are systemically oppressed and marginalized in society. Effective implementation of social justice implies an action-oriented approach to achieving multiculturalism and diversity. The relationship between multiculturalism, cultural competence, and social justice is demonstrated through competencies that include leadership, social change agents, advocacy, accessing and negotiating systems, interdisciplinary skills and risk (Chung & Bemak, 2012). Social justice action requires developing attributes, competencies and skills that support social justice work and include: (1) capacity for commitment and appreciation for human suffering, (2) nonverbal and verbal communication skills, (3) maintaining a multi-systems perspective, (4) individual, group, and organizational interventions, (5) knowledge and use of the media, technology, and the internet, and (6) assessment and research skills (Kiselica & Robinson, 2001). Therefore, utilizing culturally responsive initiatives informed by a social justice agenda assumes (1) developing multicultural and advocacy competencies, and (2) engaging in "alternative helping roles" in delivering culturally responsive individual and systemic interventions and strategies that assist individuals and groups to achieve optimal well-being and overall learning and development.

DIVERSITY AND CAMPUS CLIMATE

Perceptions of the Campus Climate

A positive racial climate has been related students' willingness and ability to engage in critical thinking associated with equity and social justice (Henry, Fowler, & West, 2011). Perceptions of the campus climate are directly influenced by social identity, impacting students' level of engagement, interactions and experiences (Ancis, Sedlacek, & Mohr, 2000; Nelson Laird

& Niskodé-Dossett, 2010). For example, Black and Latino students attending predominantly White institutions reported dissatisfaction with the perceived lack of diversity among the faculty (Lee, 2010), and tended to perceive the overall campus climate less favorably than did White students (Rankin & Reason, 2005). Women students have historically experienced the college environment as less welcoming, with the negative effects of the "chilly climate" well documented (Britton & Elmore, 1977; Hall & Sandler, 1982; Ossana, Helms, & Leonard, 1992; Pascarella, Hagedorn, Whitt, Yeager, Edison, Terenzini, & Nora, 1997). The negative outcomes of the "chilly" campus climate on overall development are exacerbated for women of color attending predominately White institutions (Brown, 1994; Buck, 2001, Jackson & Sears, 1992). LGBTQ students described their experiences on campus as "neither positive nor inclusive" (Tetreault, Fette, Meidlinger, & Hope, 2013, p. 949) with oppressive collegiate experiences resulting in a lack of participation in campus activities, decreased academic development (Rankin, 2004, 2005) and delayed identity development (Garvey & Rankin, 2015). Often ignored in the higher education literature when considering multicultural and diversity initiatives is the accessibility of services within the collegiate community (Barris, 1980). Although 11 percent of college students are reported to have a disability (USDOE, 2016), campus services are often inaccessible, creating barriers to student engagement that compromise holistic approaches to college student development (Forrest & Fitchen, 2003).

Student Engagement and Cross-Cultural Interactions

Student engagement in diversity initiatives results in both direct and indirect gains in overall development (Denson & Chang, 2009; Glass, Glass, & Lynch, 2016; Harper & Yeung, 2013; Milem & Umbach, 2003). Although White students were more likely to engage in campus co-curricular activities and more likely to express campus support for diversity, they were less open to cross-cultural interactions when compared with students of color (Glass, Glass, & Lynch, 2016). Also, White students may report an awareness of racism, but are less likely to report that racism has personally affected their life (Yang, 1992). Exposure to culturally diverse interactions may be limited, and White student are less likely to have explored their racial identity, or to acknowledge privilege as a function of their race (McIntosh, 1998; Sue & Sue, 2016). Whiteness and white privilege are identified as barriers that prevent White Americans from understanding the impact of race and racial interactions in society (Helms, 1990; Spanierman, Poteat, Beer & Armstrong, 2006; Sue & Sue, 2016; Tatum, 1992). It is often difficult to successfully engage individuals in social justice advocacy and commitment when they have not recognized or experienced oppression and marginalization, and may feel that they are not responsible for inequities in society (Dalton & Crosby, 2013; Yang, 1992). There is an important distinction to be made between being responsible for societal inequities, and recognizing a personal responsibility to engage in actions that promote equity and social justice. Cross-racial interactions and settings that promote meaningful engagement are associated with positive student outcomes (Bowman & Park, 2015). To be meaningful and transformative, culturally appropriate intervention strategies must be intentional, providing opportunities for all individuals to have access to safe spaces to engage in authentic participation (Watt, Golden, Schumacher & Moreno, 2013). Re-envisioning multicultural centers within a framework of intersectionality creates learning environments that promote inclusion, engaging students in cross-cultural interactions (McShay, 2017).

EDUCATIONAL APPROACHES
ADDRESSING CULTURAL DIVERSITY

Too often intervention strategies may be targeted toward difference, increasing the likelihood that the difference is perceived as the focus of the problem or concern and not as a dimension of personal identity to be embraced and affirmed. When multiculturalism or diversity is identified as the source of the problem, interventions are typically designed to reduce tensions and conflict by using strategies to increase tolerance and harmony. This type of intervention strategy may be perceived as an attempt to have members of an identified cultural community "fit in" with the mainstream. This approach is neither proactive nor culturally appropriate. Rather, such an approach is more likely to be perceived as a remedial intervention designed to silence discontent. Holistic initiatives are proactive and culturally appropriate in that "difference" is not identified as the source of the problem, rather strategies are developed in concert with a pre-established mission aimed toward educational equity and culturally-shared learning. Culturally appropriate interventions are "culturally engaging," acknowledge intersectionality, promote inclusion and maximize opportunities to engage students in intercultural relationships that facilitate student intellectual, identity and moral development (McShay, 2017).

Dalton and Crosby (2013) identified three educational approaches that are used in addressing cultural diversity in higher education. Each of the approaches has distinct goals, which result in different outcomes for members of the campus community. The diversity approach examines human differences with goals of promoting positive attitudes and behaviors towards those who are different, with an emphasis on teaching polite and respectful behavior towards others. Equated with a hospitality approach, a diversity approach teaches respect and tolerance, with a goal of peaceful co-existence as the primary moral basis. Although respect and consideration on culturally different others may be achieved, attitudes and beliefs about difference and inclusion may remain unchallenged, as does the tendency toward protecting one's self-interest. The diversity approach is typically fostered through diversity programming such as workshops, classes, and leadership training.

The *multicultural educational approach* is designed to assist individuals in gaining a deeper understanding of cultures through campus initiatives and programming. In addition to exploring aspects of culture inclusive of identity, language, and communication styles, the multiculturalism approach includes a focus on power and oppression for historically privileged and marginalized groups that have led to discrimination and prejudice. The underlying assumption of the multicultural educational approach is to help develop good citizenry for a democratic and global society. Appreciation of culturally diverse values and beliefs (i.e., appreciation of differences) are critical for facilitating authentic dialogue and engagement within a culturally diverse environment. Dalton and Crosby (2013) suggested that the multiculturalism approach for developing campus wide initiatives can result in moral relativism, whereby individuals misunderstand the appreciation of difference to mean that "anyone's beliefs and behaviors must be treated as equal in worth or truth as any others" (p. 284). This misrepresentation that all beliefs and actions are valued interfers with authentic cross-cultural interactions.

Pluralism is the third educational approach described by Dalton and Crosby (2013) and is described as

> . . . the process of educating future citizens to acknowledge differences and to search for common ground with others – striving for empathic understanding; cultivating and open for possible transformation of their own beliefs and practices; and working toward eliminating injustice and suffering. It is, therefore, a social achievement that goes beyond welcoming and tolerance by being rooted in purposeful and resolute action. (p. 285)

Through resolute action, individuals engage in actions that promote social justice and equity by addressing issues of power and oppression in social injustice. As a moral basis for social inclusion, a pluralism approach increases opportunities to engage in ongoing difficult dialogues that facilitate individuals' growth and development toward personal transformation and institutions toward transformative change. A pluralism approach fits well with goals for global citizenry in an increasingly interconnected and interdependent world.

CAMPUS ECOLOGICAL CULTURE:
CREATING NETWORKS FOR INTERVENTIONS

The ecological culture has been used to describe a group's or individual's location on earth and how one relates to the environment (Vontress, 1986). Bronfenbrenner's ecological systems approach (1979; 1986) provides a deeper understanding of individuals and communities within a cultural context. "Ecological models encompass an evolving body of theory and research concerned with the processes and conditions that govern the lifelong course of human development in the actual environments in which humans live" (Bronfenbrenner, 1994, p. 37). The proposed ecological model of campus systems (Figure 1) aligns with a model of personal identity (Arredondo & Glauner, 1992) and provides opportunities to explore the influences on personal identity with the institution's learning environment by examining the: (a) interpersonal interactions with others such as family, friends, peers, classmates, faculty, and staff that may influence social identities, which are inclusive of race/ethnicity, gender, sexuality, sexual orientation, and ability (i.e., microsystem); (b) interactions between microsystems, which include in-and-out of class learning and co-curricular experiences (i.e., mesosystem); (c) social, cultural, and political institutional structures and policies (i.e., exosystem); (d) societal culture, values and beliefs (i.e., macrosystem); and (e) the time or year in which the systems are influenced (i.e., chronosystem). An ecological perspective creates an inclusive model that enables diverse individuals and communities to be perceived as equally valuable and responsible in multicultural-diversity and social justice initiatives (Tomlinson-Clarke & Ota Wang, 1999) in addition to providing a way to analyze networks for culturally appropriate intervention strategies that maximize learning and development.

Exploring campus ecology using network analysis provides a way to explore complex patterns of connections and interactions (Glass, Glass, & Lynch, 2016). Culturally appropriate intervention strategies that are infused into multiple in-and-out of classroom learning opportunities increase the likelihood that student sharing will occur in multiple networks, thereby increasing cross-cultural exchanges within and between social identity groups (Denson & Chang, 2009) benefitting student learning. Using intergroup and diversity dialogues exposes students to new beliefs and ideas, and increases the likelihood that experiences will be shared through ongoing student formal and informal interactions. Student engagement utilizing a network approach is maximized through (a) collaborative programing designed to reduce silos, and (b) the use of disassociative networks, decreasing the tendency for individuals to connect solely on the basis of perceived similarity (Glass, Glass, & Lynch, 2016). The goal with a network approach is to encourage cross-cultural interactions, facilitate dialogues and increase peer

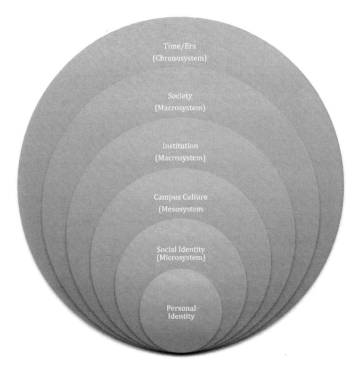

Figure 1. Campus Ecological Systems Model.

engagement between heterogeneous and within homogenous groups (networks of analysis).

USING CULTURALLY APPROPRIATE INTERVENTION STRATEGIES

Based on Sue and Sue's (2016) framework for developing multicultural interventions, we propose six foci for culturally appropriate intervention strategies that are informed by an ecological perspective and are designed to create learning and development to foster diversity and inclusion for the campus community. A social justice framework guides campus-wide initiatives with goals and interventions that increase opportunities for interpersonal exchanges and intrapersonal growth. The six foci for intervention strategies include:

1. *Individual* provides diverse opportunities to challenge and acquire cognitive, affective and behavioral learning associated with personal cultural competence and commitment for diversity and social justice advocacy.

2. *Group* increases engagement in cultural dialogues between and within social identity groups in the microsystem, focusing on associative and disassociative networks to increase learning and moral development.
3. *Professional* encourages critical thinking and reflection to ensure that ethical standards and codes are culturally responsive, challenging and disrupting ethnocentric and culture bound practices.
4. *Organizational* provides opportunities to align the mission, vision and practices of divisions within the institution with a social justice agenda designed to promote equity.
5. *Institutional* examines traditions, structures, customs, policies, and programs that privilege some while marginalizing others. An institutional focus provides the overarching mission that frames the focus for interventions at all levels.
6. *Societal* keeps the mission and goals of the institution relevant to the social issues, preparing students as productive citizens.

Diversity work that is guided by a data-driven model identifies the focus of intervention and networks for engagement, and ensures that culturally appropriate intervention strategies are used (Glass, Glass, & Lynch, 2016; Sundt, Cole, & Wheaton 2017).

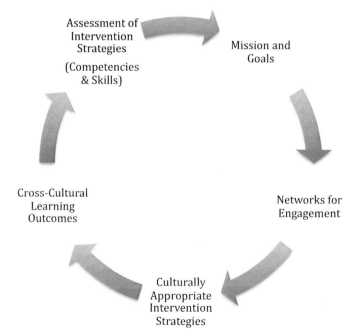

Figure 2. Model for Using Culturally Appropriate Intervention Strategies.

IMPLICATIONS FOR STUDENT AFFAIRS PROFESSIONALS

Cheatham and Associates (1991) emphasized the social obligation of student affairs professionals to provide culturally appropriate programming that promotes student educational and intellectual development. Socially just student affairs practice requires intentional cultural appropriate intervention strategies to disrupt systemic oppression perpetuated through institutional traditions, policies, procedures and practices that privilege some while disadvantaging others. Campus initiatives must be culturally appropriate in order to facilitate ongoing opportunities to "[enhance] knowledge, understanding, and creativity while improving interpersonal interactions and relationships" (Henry, Fowler, & West, 2011, p. 690). In addition to campus environments that are supportive for students, Strayhorn and Johnson (2017) called attention to diversity and inclusion as critical components in developing holistic initiatives that are beneficial to faculty and staff as well. Holistic and culturally appropriate interventions are connected to institutional missions and goals for developing the cultural competency and moral integrity of all members of the campus community. Using culturally appropriate intervention strategies also requires engaging campus networks, evaluating learning outcomes among campus professionals as well as students, and assessing the effectiveness of the intervention strategies for ongoing change and improvement (see Figure 2). Therefore, culturally appropriate intervention strategies in practice require that student affairs professionals remain actively engaged in an ongoing process of developing professional, cultural and social justice advocacy competencies. A professional, philosophical orientation that supports advocacy, inclusion and leadership for social justice assumes an understanding identity from a multidimensional rather than a binary perspective. Kendall and Wijeyesinghe (2017) stressed that intersectionality informs practice for work with a variety of social groups, inclusive of individuals with multiple privileged identities, and the relationship between identities and social location that serves to oppress or privilege individuals and groups.

Using culturally appropriate intervention strategies in professional practice also requires an understanding of the purpose and desired outcomes (cognitive, interpersonal or intrapersonal dimensions of learning and overall student development). Due to the varied and changing roles of student affairs however, practitioners may not have acquired the professional development competencies and skills needed to provide culturally appropriate educational interventions to students differing in identity and experience (Cuyjet, Longwell-Grice, & Molina, 2009). The ability to use culturally appropriate intervention strategies in practice to positively influence diverse collegiate environments is directly connected to personal and professional competencies. *Professional Competencies and Standards* developed by the

ACPA/NASPA Joint Task Force (2010) described 10 professional competencies that are useful for guiding student affairs practice. These competencies may have been developed as part of graduate education and training, however, also require continuous learning. Cultural competencies, which include cultural awareness and attitudes, cultural knowledge, and cultural skills, are assumed to be central and fundamental to the successful development and implementation of culturally appropriate intervention strategies for practice (Sue & Sue, 2016). Student affairs professionals must commit to a multicultural journey to developing cultural competence that includes understanding their own worldviews, as well as cognitive, emotional and behavioral resistance to diversity training (Sue, 2013; Sue & Sue, 2015) to effectively disrupt the status quo and facilitate culturally appropriate learning opportunities for students. As Jansen (2016) so profoundly articulated in a discussion of transformative leadership and social justice,

> . . . leadership is inevitably about identity. Nobody comes to work as a coldhearted automaton divorced from history, passion, memory and self. It is important, therefore, to be conscious of how your identity shapes your choices and preferences; of how unknowingly you might be seen to be "hanging out" with those who look or pray like you, or come from where you do. Nothing wrong with that, but in divided organizations your role as leader is to bridge divides, to break through accepted ways of knowing and associating by demonstrating a more inclusive lifestyle such that what followers see is not a rigid, ethnocentric, static, exclusive leadership is on display. You have multiple identities, and how they intermesh in leadership practice—not simply statement—is an important component of your credibility as a leader. (Foreword, p. x)

The challenge is developing and engaging campus leadership (i.e., faculty, staff, student leaders) in culturally appropriate intervention strategies that are consistent with the clearly articulated social justice mission and goals of the institution.

Questions

1. In your own words, define multiculturalism, diversity, and social justice. Which of these three do you feel you are working most towards? What challenges and supports do you think you need to help continue your development?
2. Perceptions about campus climate vary by social identities. As you reflect on your own perceptions about your campus climate, how do you feel about your own campus's climate? In what ways might your social identities contribute to this?

3. It is noted earlier in the chapter that "it is often difficult to successfully engage individuals in social justice advocacy and commitment when they have not recognized or experienced oppression and marginalization, and may feel that they are not responsible for inequities in society (Dalton & Crosby, 2013; Yang, 1992)." How have you seen this resistance towards social justice work play out when working with students? What strategies have you employed to address this issue?

4. Oftentimes, the focus of student affairs professionals is on the development of students, but various scholars noted throughout the chapter emphasize the importance of our own continuous learning towards cultural competence. What opportunities (e.g., conferences, events, or staff trainings) do you have available for you to attend to support your continued growth? What other activities might you do to continue your own learning?

Case Study

Understanding of self is a critical component for development of professional practice that is culturally competent. Recall that cultural competency is defined as an understanding and appreciation of one's own culture, and fluency in at least one other culture (Ladson-Billings, 2014). Also consider the foundational outcomes listed in the Social Justice and Inclusion (SJI) professional competency, which includes "engaging in critical reflection to understand one's prejudices and biases," and "identify[ing] systems of socialization that influence one's multiple identities and sociopolitical perspectives and how they impact one's lived experiences" (ACPA/NASPA, 2015, p. 30). You are your own case study, and your task is to assess your own cultural competency by engaging in critical reflection of who you are (e.g., biases, beliefs, identities) and how you are influenced by the various levels of the environment in which you engage in, both personally and professionally. This case study activity is best done with another person or with a group, all who will do the following steps:

1. Copy the Campus Ecological Systems model (Figure 1) presented earlier in the chapter using a full sheet of paper.
2. Starting at the center circle, Personal Identity, write down the multiple identities you hold, including those that are thrust upon you.
3. The next layer is the Microsystem. Who do you have important personal and/or professional relationships with that you connect with on a consistent basis? List these individuals in this layer.
4. Next, consider how these individuals interact with each other. You might realize you have different social circles, each serving a different

purpose for you both professionally and personally. Plot out these connections in your Mesosystem layer in your chart.

5. Fill out your Macrosystem by considering the prevailing social norms, values, and beliefs you are living out today. What are the political issues that you see affecting your work and personal life? What pop culture references do you feel represent prevalent values in our society today?

6. As you complete your final layer, Chronosystem, think of the major national and world issues, events, and innovations that have affected you and the generation of people your age, from your childhood to today.

Now that you have completed your own diagram, take a moment and reflect. What identities seem to be the most salient for you? Did you consider race, ethnicity, gender, social class, and/or ability? Are privileged and marginalized identities present in your diagram?

Next, share your diagram with another person, or have a group discussion, and discuss your diagrams. As you share, consider the similarities and differences you have in your diagrams. Ask each other the significance or meaning of certain people or events noted on their diagrams.

This exercise aims to engage in developing your cultural competency by gaining an appreciation for your own cultural background, which can start by plotting out your cultural self. What cultures (ethnic, religious, sexual identity, etc.) do you see illustrated in your chart? Do you see how your cultures might influence each layer of your ecosystem, from friends who share the same cultural background (microsystem) to recognizing how events that occurred during your lifetime (chronosystem) might have influenced society's view of your culture as well as your own?

This exercise also allows for you to work on your cultural competency by improving your fluency in a culture that is not your own. As you engage in discussion about others' diagrams, you might also learn how others live their cultural lives through the many layers in their own ecological systems. You might recognize similar people or events on others' diagrams and realize their significance and impact as substantially different (or the same) than yours, as well as learn about diverse lived experiences due to differences in age, privileges, challenges, and environments.

REFERENCES

American College Personnel Association & National Association of Student Personnel Administrators. (2010). *ACPA/NASPA professional competency areas for student affairs practitioners.* Washington, DC: Authors.

American College Personnel Association & National Association of Student Personnel Administrators. (2015). *ACPA/NASPA professional competency areas for student affairs educators.* Washington, DC: Authors.

Ancis, J. R., Sedlacek, W. E., & Mohr, J. J. (2000). Student perceptions of campus cultural climate by race. *Journal of Counseling & Development, 78,* 180–185.

Arredondo, P., & Glauner, T. (1992). *Personal dimensions of identity model.* Boston, MA: Empowerment Workshops, Inc.

Arredondo, P., Toporek, R., Pack Brown, S., Jones. J., Locke, D. C., Sanchez, J., & Stadler, H. (1996). Operationalization of the multicultural counseling competencies. *Journal of Multicultural Counseling and Development, 24,* 42–78.

Barris, R. (1980). Changing campuses: Mainstreaming and accessibility of higher education. In J. P. Hourihan (Ed.), *Disability: The college's challenge* (pp. 9–16). United States Bureau of Education for the Handicapped, Project for Handicapped College Students. New York, NY: Teachers College, Columbia University.

Britton, V., & Elmore, P. B., (1977). Leadership and self-development workshop for women. *Journal of College Student Development, 18,* 318.

Brown, S. (1994). Images of me: A model to promote retention of Black female students on predominantly White campuses. *Journal of College Student Development, 35,* 150–151.

Bowman, N. A., & Park, J. J. (2015). Not all diversity interactions are created equal: Cross-racial interaction, close interracial friendship, and college student outcomes. *Research in Higher Education, 56,* 601–621.

Bronfenbrenner, U. (1979). The ecology of human development: Experiments by nature and design. Cambridge, MA: Harvard University Press.

Bronfenbrenner, U. (1986). Recent advances in research on the ecology of human development. In R. K. Silbereisen, K. Eyferth, & G. Rudinger (Eds.), *Development as action in context: Problem behavior and normal youth development* (pp. 287–309). Heidelberg and New York: Springer-Verlag.

Bronfenbrenner, U. (1994). Ecological models of human development. In International Encyclopedia of Education (2nd ed., Vol. 3., pp. 1643-1647). Oxford, UK: Elsevier. Reprinted in M. Gauvain, & M. Cole (Eds.), *Readings on the development of children* (2nd ed., 1993, pp. 37–43). New York, NY: Freeman.

Buck, G. F. (2001). *"White privilege": Discrimination and miscommunication: How it affects/effects underrepresented minority (groups) on college campuses.* (ERIC Document Reproduction Service No. ED453748).

Cheatham, H. E., & Associates. (1991). *Cultural pluralism on campus.* Washington, DC: ACPA Media Board.

Chung, R. C.-Y., & Bemak, F. P. (2012). *Social justice counseling: The next steps beyond multiculturalism.* Thousand Oaks, CA: Sage.

Cuyjet, M. J., Longwell-Grice, R., & Molina, E. (2009). Perceptions of new student affairs professionals and their supervisors regarding the application of competencies learned in preparation programs. *Journal of College Student Development, 50,* 104–119.

Dalton, J. C., & Crosby, P. C. (2013). Diversity, multiculturalism, and pluralism: Moving from hospitality and appreciation to social inclusion on campus and beyond. *Journal of College & Character, 14,* 281–287.

Denson, N., & Chang, M. J. (2009). Racial diversity matters: The impact of diversity-related student engagement and institutional context. *American Educational Research Journal, 46,* 322–353.

Duan, C., & Brown, C. (2016). *Becoming a multiculturally competent counselor.* Thousand Oaks, CA: Sage.

Fitzgerald, M. (2000). Establishing cultural competency for mental health professionals. In V. Skultans & J. Cox (Eds.), *Anthropological approaches to psychological medicine: Crossing bridges* (pp. 184–200). Great Britain: Athenaeum Press.

Forrest, K. D., & Fichten, C. (2003). Overcoming unintentional barriers with intentional strategies: Educating faculty about student disabilities. *Teaching of Psychology, 30,* 270–276.

Freeman, C. (2004). *Trends in educational equity of girls & women: 2004 Institute of Education Sciences* (NCES 2005–016). U.S. Department of Education. Washington, DC: National Center for Education Statistics.

Garvey, J. C., & Rankin, S. R. (2015). The influence of campus experiences on the level of outness among trans-spectrum and queer-spectrum students. *Journal of Homosexuality, 62,* 374–393.

Glass, K., Glass, C. R., & Lynch, R. J. (2016). Student engagement and affordances for interaction with diverse peers: A network analysis. *Journal for Diversity in Higher Education, 9,* 170–187.

Hall, R. M., & Sandler, B. R. (1982). *The classroom climate: A chilly climate for women?* Washington, DC: Association of American Colleges.

Harper, C. E., & Yeung, F. (2013). Perceptions of institutional commitment to diversity as a predictor of college students' openness to diverse perspectives. *Review of Higher Education: Journal of the Association for the Study of Higher Education, 37,* 25–44.

Helms, J. E. (Ed.). (1990). *Black and White racial identity: Theory, research, and practice.* Westport, CT: Greenwood.

Henry, W. J., Fowler, S. R., & West, N. M. (2011). Campus climate: An assessment of students' perceptions in a college of education. *Urban Education, 46,* 689–718.

Hook, J. N., Davis, D. E., Owen, J., Worthington Jr., E. L., & Utsey, S. O. (2013). Cultural humility: Measuring openness to culturally diverse clients. *Journal of Counseling Psychology, 60,* 353–366.

Jackson, A. P., & Sears, S. J., (1992). Implications of an Africentric worldview in reducing stress for African American women. *Journal of Counseling & Development, 71,* 184–190.

Jansen, J. (2016). Race, justice and leadership in education in the aftermath of atrocity. In S. M. Tomlinson-Clarke & D. L. Clarke (Eds.), *Social justice and transformative learning: Culture and identity in the United States and South Africa* (pp. ix–xiii). New York, NY: Routledge.

Kealey, D. J., & Protheroe, D. R. (1996). The effectiveness of cross-cultural training for expatriates: An assessment of the literature on the issue. *International Journal of Intercultural Relations, 20,* 141–165.

Kendall, F. E., & Wijeyesinghe, C. L. (2017). Advancing social justice work at the intersections of multiple privileged identities. *New Directions for Student Services, 157,* 91–100.

Kiselica, M. S., & Robinson, M. (2001). Human dramas of social justice work in counseling. *Journal of Counseling & Development, 79,* 387–397.

Ladson-Billings, G. (2014). Culturally relevant pedagogy 2.0: A.K.A the remix. *Harvard Educational Review, 84,* 74–84.

Lee, J. A. (2010). Students' perceptions of and satisfaction with faculty diversity. *College Student Journal, 44,* 400–412.

Martin, D. (2014). Good education for all? Student race and identity development in the multicultural classroom. *International Journal of Intercultural Relations, 39,* 110–123.

McIntosh, P. (1989, July/August). White privilege. Unpacking the invisible knapsack. *Peace and Freedom,* 10–12.

McShay, J. C. (2017). Engaging students at the intersections through multicultural centers: An application of the culturally engaging campus environment model. *New Directions for Student Services, 157,* 25–34.

Milem, J. F., & Umbach, P. D. (2003). The influence of precollege factors on students' predispositions regarding diversity activities in college. *Journal of College Student Development, 44,* 611–624.

Nelson Laird, T. E., & Niskodé-Dossett, A. S. (2010). How gender and race moderate the effects of interactions across difference on student perceptions of the campus environment. *The Review of Higher Education, 33,* 333–356.

Ossana, S. M., Helms, J. E., & Leonard, M. M. (1992). Do "womanist" identity attitudes influence college women's self-esteem and perceptions of environmental bias. *Journal of Counseling & Development, 70,* 402–408.

Pascarella, E. T., Hagedorn, L. S., Whitt, E. J., Yeager, P. M., Edison, M. I., Terenzini, P. T., & Nora, A. (1997). Women's perceptions of a "chilly climate" and their cognitive outcomes during the first year of college. *Journal of College Student Development, 38,* 109–124.

Pedersen, P. B. (1991). Multiculturalism as a generic approach to counseling. *Journal of Counseling & Development, 70,* 6–12.

Ponterotto, J. G. (2010). Multicultural personality: An evolving theory of optimal functioning in culturally heterogeneous societies. *The Counseling Psychologist, 38,* 714–758.

Ponterotto, J. G., Costa-Wofford, C. I., Brobst, K. E., Spelliscy, D., Mendelsohn Kacanski, J., Scheinholtz, J., & Martines, D. (2007). Multicultural personality dispositions and psychological well-being. *The Journal of Social Psychology, 147,* 119–135.

Rankin, S. (2004). Campus climate for lesbian, gay, bisexual and transgender people. Diversity Factor, 12(1), 18–23. Retrieved from http://www.researchgate.net /publication/233681325_Campus_Climate_for_Lesbian_Gay_Bisexual_and _Transgender_People

Rankin, S. R. (2005). Campus climates for sexual minorities. *New Directions for Student Services, 111,* 17–24.

Rankin, S. R., & Reason, R. D. (2005). Differing perceptions: How students of color and White students perceive campus climate for underrepresented groups. *Journal of College Student Development, 46,* 43–61.

Rankin, S., Weber, G., Blumenfeld, W., & Frazer, S. (2010). *2010 state of higher education for lesbian, gay, bisexual & transgender people.* Charlotte, NC: Campus Pride.

Ratts, M. J., Toporek, R. L., & Lewis, J. A. (2010). *ACA advocacy competencies: A social justice framework for counselors.* Alexandria, VA: American Counseling Association.

Sciarra, D. T. (1991). *Multiculturalism in counseling.* Itasca, IL: F. E. Peacock.

Spanierman, L. B., Poteat, V. P., Beer, A. M., & Armstrong, P. I. (2006). Psychosocial costs of racism to Whites: Exploring patterns through cluster analysis. *Journal of Counseling Psychology, 53,* 434–441.

Strayhorn, T. L., & Johnson, R. M. (2017, March). Most promising places to work in student affairs. *Diverse: Issues in Higher Education.* Retrieved from www.diverseeducation.com

Sue, D. W. (2015). *Race talk and the conspiracy of silence. Understanding and facilitating difficult dialogues on race.* Hoboken, NJ: Wiley & Sons.

Sue, D. W., & Sue, D. (2013). *Counseling the culturally diverse: Theory and practice* (6th ed.). Hoboken, NJ: Wiley & Sons.

Sue, D. W., & Sue, D. (2016). *Counseling the culturally diverse: Theory and practice* (7th ed.). Hoboken, NJ: Wiley & Sons.

Sundt, M. A., Cole, D., & Wheaton, M. (2017). Using data to guide diversity work and enhance student learning. *New Directions for Student Services, 159,* 93–103.

Tatum, B. D. (1992). Talking about race, learning about racism: The application of racial identity development theory in the classroom. *Harvard Educational Review, 62,* 1–24.

Tervalon, M., & Murray-Garcia, J. (1998). Cultural humility versus cultural competence: A critical distinction in defining physician training outcomes in multicultural education. *Journal of Health Care for the Poor and Underserved, 9,* 117–125.

Tetreault, P. A., Fette, R., Meidlinger, P. C., & Hope, D. (2013). Perceptions of campus climate by sexual minorities. *Journal of Homosexuality, 60,* 947–964.

Thomas, A. J., & Schwarzbaum, S. (2006). *Cultural & Identity: Life stories for counselors and therapists.* Thousand Oaks, CA: Sage.

Tomlinson-Clarke, S., & Ota Wang, V. (1999). A paradigm for racial-cultural training in the development of counselor cultural competencies. In M. Kiselica (Ed.), *Confronting prejudice and racism during multicultural training* (pp. 155–167). Alexandria VA: American Counseling Association.

U.S. Department of Education, National Center for Education Statistics. (2016). *Digest of Education Statistics, 2015* (2016-014).

U.S. News & World Report (2017). *Campus ethnic diversity.* Retrieved from https://www.usnews.com/best-colleges/rankings/national-universities/campus-ethnic-diversity

Vontress, C. E. (1986). Social and cultural foundations. In M. D. Lewis, R. L. Hayes, & J. A. Lewis (Eds.), *An introduction to the counseling profession* (pp. 215–250). Itasca, IL: Peacock.

Watt, S. K., Golden, M., Schumacher, L. A. P., & Moreno, L. S. (2013). Courage in multicultural initiatives. *New Directions for Student Services, 144,* 57–68.

Yang, J. (1992). Chilly campus climate: A qualitative study on White racial identity development attitudes. U.S. Department of Education (ERIC). Retrieved from https://www.google.com/search?q=Yang%2C+J.+%281992%29.+Chilly+campus+climate%3A+A+qualitative+study+on+White+racial+identity++development+attitudes.+&ie=utf-8&oe=utf-8&client=firefox-b-1

Zirkel, S., & Cantor, N. (2004). 50 years after Brown v. Board of Education: The promise and challenge of multicultural education. *Journal of Social Issues, 60,* 1–15.

Chapter 10

MULTICULTURALISM, DIVERSITY, SOCIAL JUSTICE, AND INCLUSION: EVIDENCE-BASED PRACTICE IN STUDENT AFFAIRS

V. Barbara Bush & Shani Barrax Moore

Accountability is the operative word for higher education in the current political climate, particularly in relation to student affairs. Colleges and universities are being pressured by local and governmental agencies, coordinating boards, and accrediting agencies to provide evidence that students are actually learning during their time in higher education. Student affairs has been challenged particularly on this front because student outcomes are more difficult to measure. How can we measure student learning outside the classroom with the same accuracy with which we can determine whether a student has mastered a specific curricular outcome? In response to the need for evidence, student affairs has developed objectives starting with the Student Learning Imperative to show that learning outcomes can be achieved.

At the same time, we respond to the need for accountability and evidence of learning, student affairs educators are called to take leadership in multiculturalism, diversity, inclusion and social justice. How do student affairs educators use evidence to establish practice that addresses these areas? In this chapter, we will explore how student affairs practitioners can establish and maintain evidence-based practice that is responsive to multiculturalism, diversity, inclusion, and social justice.

DEFINITIONS

What is Evidence-Based Practice?

When referring to evidence-based practice, it is helpful to understand the origins of the term, evidence-based. This term was used by the British epidemiologist Archie Cochrane in the early 1970s and applied to medicine (Po, 1998). The practice was described as "a problem-solving approach to practice that is based on the systematic and conscientious identification of and use of current best evidence when caring for patients" (Ciliska, DiCenso, Melnyk, & Steder, 2005, p. 185). In short, experts in the area used evidence of best practice to establish guidelines for their professional practice in health disciplines.

Evidence-based practice may have different meanings, depending on the context. It could be (1) based on best practice or it could be (2) evidence providing the basis for practice and decisions made by practitioners (Creamer, Mutcheson, Sutherland, & Meszaros, 2013). In either case, evidence gained through research and assessment can be critical to sound decision making.

In education, generally, evidence-based "refers to any concept or strategy that is derived from or informed by objective evidence" (Evidence-based Practice in Education, n.d.). In this case, evidence involves utilization of data collected during research, the expertise of educators, as well as measures used by school or college, instructor, and student performance to fit student needs (McCormick, Kinzie, & Korkmaz, 2011). The terminology "data-driven" is often used to anchor decisions in "evidence." The results of these processes are most often used for improvement of practice. In higher education, specifically, evidence-based practice calls to mind those approaches we use to determine whether certain practices are in line with guidelines set aside for accreditation, certification, assessment, and compliance. These guidelines are, presumably, set after extensive research on effective practice.

What is Evidence-Based Practice in Student Affairs?

Student affairs has long been responsible for the out-of-classroom learning of college students. In fact, the document Learning Revisited (NASPA) stressed the importance of outcomes data that could be used as evidence of learning taking place on campus. Much of this work was spurred by the climate of accountability in higher education as well as the rest of the country. In order to continue funding of certain efforts, legislatures were demanding evidence that the funds were being used for what they determined to be educational necessities. This was necessary because some of these funding decision makers had no idea how providing student support, programs, and activities related to what they considered the core outcome of the university—student learning. Student Affairs has responded by stating that assessment should be part of the educational culture. Assessment results become the evidence necessary to make decisions, plan and implement practice required by the National Association of Student Personnel (NASPA, 2017) and the American College Personnel Association (ACPA) (ACPA, 2017).

Upon review, we find that the literature addressing evidence-based practice in student affairs has almost exclusively focused on assessment and learning outcomes. The first allusion to the importance of assessment came with *The Student Personnel Point of View of 1949* (ACPA, 1949). However, the call for evidence of college outcomes being connected with governmental and accrediting bodies did not become as pervasive until the 1980s. Aside from the inherent funding issues, student affairs found that assessment was critical in gaining an understanding of student needs as well as providing effective programs (Ryder & Kimball, 2015). The missing piece may be the cycle of how results of the assessment are used to improve practice. We conduct assessment, we use the outcomes to justify the existence of our programs, and we may or may not use the results directly to inform practice.

MODEL FOR EVIDENCE-BASED
PRACTICE IN STUDENT AFFAIRS

Evidence-based practice in student affairs must follow a theory-to-practice loop facilitated by constant assessment. First there is the research which serves as evidence gathered from the theoretical model of specialists in the field or current practice. The decisions made for practice come from research and evidence. After the practice is implemented, there must be assessment which in turn provide more evidence. Using the resulting evidence, the cycle starts once more to create a continuous loop. The model is based on the elements of continuous improvement (Blimling et al., 1999).

The model addressed in this chapter is a continuous loop as shown in Figure 1. Another illustration of this cyclical process is the Bresciani cycle (Bresciani, Zelna, & Anderson, 2004) which provides an illustration for assessment. Student affairs educators are charged with using their knowledge of theory, best practice, their own or other professionals' experiences as research (EVIDENCE). They then make decisions as to how practice should reflect what they learn from this research (DECISONMAKING-PRACTICE). When the practice is completed, professionals create a means by which they can measure the effectiveness of that practice (ASSESSMENT-EVIDENCE) which leads back to step one. An example would be the planning of a professional development workshop. The responsible professional would research theory about how professionals learn, how other colleges and

Figure 1. Cycle of Evidence-Based Practice in Student Affairs.

universities plan their professional development, and their own and other experiences with these workshops. In an assessment model, the professional might conduct a needs assessment to provide more evidence that they can use for the implementation phase. The next step would be the decision to implement the program through a specific design. When the program is implemented, the professional will have established input factors as to the level of knowledge participants have in relation to the workshop content. At the end of the initiative, the professional would measure outcomes in relation to the input factors. The evidence gained from the outcomes allow the professional to take into consideration not only learning, but also elements that are needed to improve the next workshop (RESEARCH-EVIDENCE).

USING EVIDENCE-BASED PRACTICE IN STUDENT AFFAIRS FOR MULTICULTURALISM, DIVERSITY, INCLUSION, AND SOCIAL JUSTICE LEARNING

To meet the needs of student affairs educators in pursuit of effective engagement with difference—whether via cultural competence, proficiency, or humility—diversity and inclusion practitioners in higher education have developed assessment processes to ensure that learning and development opportunities achieve desired educational outcomes. Diversity and inclusion practitioners can be effective partners with student affairs in developing processes to achieve these outcomes (Association of American Colleges and Universities, 2015). The process would begin with identification of problematic gaps and the student-centered knowledge, skills, and abilities needed to address them. If the learning objective is to cultivate a more inclusive campus climate, the desired outcomes should determine how inclusion is defined and measured. For example, will inclusion in terms of student leadership indicate inclusive student engagement? Will evidence-based data such as existing policies, programs, and practices be used to determine active inclusion or passive exclusion? Should there be corresponding faculty or staff diversity and inclusion measures to provide students with reflections of themselves in the campus environment? These questions may often vary by type and size of institution, geographic location, accrediting agency, and funding sources. However, a key consideration for any institution should be the strategic goals, objectives, and desired outcomes based on evidence.

One such approach to considering assessment strategy can be found in the National Association of Diversity Officers in Higher Education (NADO-HE) Standards of Professional Practice for Chief Diversity Officers (CDOs). These standards are useful for clarifying the scope of the work of CDOs, but they also provide a framework for administrators and institutions to align the work of CDOs with approaches to multiculturalism, diversity, social justice and inclusion (National Association of Diversity Officers in Higher Education, 2014). The standards take into account social identity characteristics (i.e., race/ethnicity, gender, age, sexual orientation, disability, religion, national and geographic origin, language use, socioeconomic status, first generation, veteran/military, and political ideology) with focal groups (faculty, students, staff, administrators, trustees, alumni, and others) around core areas necessary for institutionalizing multiculturalism, diversity, social justice, and inclusion such as:

- Recruitment and retention
- Campus climate
- Curriculum and instruction
- Research and inquiry
- Intergroup relations and discourse
- Student/faculty/staff achievement and success
- Leadership development
- Nondiscrimination
- Procurement/supplier diversity
- Institutional advancement
- External relations
- Strategic planning and accountability (Worthington, 2012).

These twelve standards set forth by NADOHE all have application to and implications for student affairs educators in their approach to evidence-based practice in terms of multiculturalism, diversity, inclusion, and social justice.

Best Practice or Data-Centered Evidence in Multiculturalism, Diversity, Inclusion and Social Justice that can be used in Student Affairs Professional Development

As student affairs practitioners began to realize the importance of identity-based considerations on student development practice, the need for professional development around issues of diversity and inclusion became increasingly critical. The evolution of competencies needed to develop students from multiple backgrounds has resulted in a more intentional approach to evidence-based professional development for both student and academic affairs professionals (Gansemer-Topf & Ryder, 2017; Pope, Reynolds, & Mueller, 2004). This evolution has moved from what was once known as cultural sensitivity in the early days of racial integration, to cultural competence and cultural proficiency as a strategy for engaging with differences (Lindsey, Robins, & Terrell, 2009), and cultural humility as an advanced tool for self-reflection and self-assessment (Tervalon & Garcia, 1998). In all cases and approaches, the goal is to engage effectively with identity-based difference in a way that is inclusive, affirming, and contributes to positive identity authoring for students.

The Use of Evidence-Based Practice to Promote Inclusive Thought and Practice

Because diversity and inclusion practitioners are tasked with meeting the needs of student affairs educators who engage in facilitating success for students of multiple backgrounds, the need for development of appropriate professional development has increased. Universities are attempting to fill the knowledge, skill, and ability gaps that can potentially hinder student retention, matriculation, and engagement. While such markers are often the measures of success, competency building should also include the integration of the evidence-based standards set by the Council for the Advancement of Standards in Higher Education (CAS) that task programming and initiatives with cultivating cognitive complexity, intrapersonal development, interpersonal competence, civic engagement and practical competence (CAS, 2015). However, many professionals developing and executing these programs had not yet submitted themselves to the level of reflection and inquiry around multiculturalism, diversity, social justice, and inclusion that would mitigate their ability to do so for the students they serve (Association of American Colleges and Universities, 2015).

In its call for registrants to its 2017 Alcohol, Other Drug, and Campus Violence Prevention Conference, the National Association of Student Personnel Administrators (NASPA) urged student affairs administrators to attend workshops and presentations that would "identify sources and repositories for identifying evidence-based risk factors, protective factors, and practices" (NASPA, 2017a, Learning Objectives section, para. 4) that would support learning about those topics. In fact, "evidence-based practice" is a terminology used throughout the descriptions of professional development and best practices.

EXAMPLES OF EVIDENCE-BASED PRACTICE IN STUDENT AFFAIRS

NASPA and the American College Personnel Association (ACPA), both national student affairs professional development organizations, set criteria for recognition of exemplary student affairs practice. NASPA has an Equity, Inclusion, and Social Justice Division for the purpose of attending to these issues within the profession. The Association presents awards annually for colleges and universities that show achievement in creating welcoming and inclusive campus environments. Excellence Awards are given in the areas of international, multicultural, gender, LGBTQ, spirituality, and related areas. Criteria for these awards include the following:

- Application of available or emerging theoretical models,
- Application of practical research, and
- Application of program assessment. (NASPA, 2017, "NASPA Awards.")

It is notable that these criteria provide evidence in the evidence-based practice loop. NASPA also maintains an annual institute focused on equity and inclusion (NASPA, 2017, Equity, Inclusion, and Social Justice section).

ACPA created the Strategic Imperative for Racial Justice and Decolonization in 2016 with the goal of "reducing the oppression of communities of color" through providing "leading research and scholarship; tools for personal, professional, and career development; and innovative praxis opportunities" (ACPA, 2017, "Strategic Imperative for Racial Justice and Decolonization" for ACPA members). They also give individual awards such as the Voice of Inclusion Medallion, to student affairs educators who have created programs and practices that promote multiculturalism, diversity, and social justice. (ACPA, 2017, "Voice of Inclusion Award"). The Association's focus on research, scholarship, and practice indicates an evidence-based approach.

Training: A Potential Model for Staff Training

This portion of the chapter will present a potential model of how evidence-based practice can be operationalized by student affairs educators in cooperation with campus diversity officers through a staff training process. As a potential model of evidence-based practice, the process starts when a student affairs unit requests an assessment of unit staff training needs from a department responsible for diversity or multicultural training. This could be an office of diversity and inclusion, a multicultural center, or other entity responsible for creating more equitable and inclusive campuses. The student affairs and diversity and inclusion department engage in a thorough consultation to determine areas of desired growth and skill-building for the training. At this point, a pre-assessment (EVIDENCE) should be conducted to determine baseline existing competencies, knowledge, skill, and awareness level of staff related to inclusion, multiculturalism, diversity, and/or social justice, as well as the staff's assessment of the organizational/unit culture and climate. To supplement this effort, instruments such as the *Intercultural Development Inventory or IDI* may provide additional perspective on participants' individual and collective orientation to difference (Hammer, 2012), and can subsequently serve as another measure of the impact of the training.

In this pre-assessment stage, focus group data could also be collected to provide more qualitative detail and insight. From these activities, facilitators should focus on themes that emerge from the data, particularly those themes that emerge in the areas of inclusion, multiculturalism, and social justice topics. It may also be helpful to collect data from different levels in the organization to gather what may be varied or congruent perspectives from administrators, supervisors, and line staff.

After pre-assessment, the proposed training model would move to curriculum development. Ideally, the curriculum should be designed to establish capacity-building for broader awareness and to focus heavily upon responses to identity-based critical incidents that occur in student affairs units. The need to provide for self-reflection and awareness cannot be understated and should be explicitly communicated by practitioners both before and during the training. Authentic and safe spaces for self-reflection and exploration of difficult topics such as bias, privilege, and systemic inclusion and exclusion should be provided.

Student affairs units often have time constraints that make it difficult to provide such a thorough and extensive exploration. That is why it is critical for unit managers to ensure support of the time and effort from senior administrators. Conversations between managers and senior administrators may include identification of the student affairs educators seeking the training, and the degree of direct student interaction they have on a daily basis. For example, those engaged in direct student service delivery may receive a more comprehensive training curriculum that includes long-term and sustained engagement. Those who are involved in more administrative roles may receive more introductory training introducing them to basic concepts that encourage shared language and broadened perspectives. A focus on intended outcomes, accountability measures, and expectations and how they fit within departmental goals should be clear.

The next phase of the proposed training is delivery. It is recommended that training designed to build capacity for multiculturalism and inclusion be conducted in small groups with no more than 30 to 40 participants in each session. Within this framework, small group activity is encouraged to minimize the potentially overwhelming nature of voicing one's perspectives in larger groups. Smaller groupings of six to eight within this larger group may be appropriate for especially sensitive disclosure and discussion. Opportunities for reflection via a journal or some other mechanism is recommended, because some participants may prefer to process privately instead of in groups. Journals may also provide a record of changes in awareness and competency for outcomes measurement.

The following is an example of a multi-module training curriculum designed for student affairs educators by an office of inclusion and diversity. In preparation for the modules, it is recommended that larger units form cohorts according to specific employee characteristics such as direct or indirect student contact, reporting structures, and job function. It would be preferable to avoid placing staff into groups that include both the staff member and the person to whom that member reports. Ideally, cohorts can help the training facilitators to tailor the discussion to specific roles and provide more practical application of the material. As training modules continue, evidence gained from the modules can be incorporated into programs, policies, and practices of the unit.

- **Module 1: Diversity and Cultural Humility for Inclusive Community Building:** As an introductory workshop, this module can be designed to explore diversity, cultural humility, self-reflection, and identity, and their application to staff's professional roles. Participants can be guided to examine the role of invalidations on climate and community building, and validations as a tool for building community and inclusion.
- **Module 2: Bias Awareness, Socialization, and Identity Development:** Relative to bias awareness, under our proposed model par-

ticipants can be given the opportunity to explore their own biases, and how these biases may be influenced by socialization, through instruments developed for this purpose. Identity development, with a focus on internal and external authoring, can be introduced at this stage to demonstrate the importance of intentionally inclusive environments in positive student development.

- **Module 3: Inclusive Language, Communication, and Triggers:** Following bias awareness opportunities, a next session could be designed explore micro-aggressions and the role of language, communication, and socialization in inclusion and exclusion, and how these factors contribute to authoring identity, experience, and student success.
- **Module 4: Privilege and Allyship:** Moving further in the proposed model, training can be developed so that participants can be introduced to various types of privilege and how they are manifested in theirs and others' lives. This module would focus on an examination of privilege, collusion, and positional power, and necessary efforts to practice allyship and apply intentional inclusion strategies.
- **Module 5: Change Leadership and Action Planning:** The final module in the proposed model would explore what organizational change looks and feels like, indicators of progress, and how individuals can use spheres of influence to enact change.

After completing the participation phase of the staff development strategy, participants can then begin to apply these new perspectives and approaches to their practice.

Training: Impact Measurement and Institutionalization

Continuing the evidenced-based approach, student affairs departments can begin to develop several strategies for measuring the impact of the training (ASSESSMENT). Such strategies may include several areas including an assessment of departmental culture for inclusive practices, continued efforts toward bias awareness and change leadership, among others. A post-assessment can be offered after the training at various points such as immediately after training delivery, and perhaps three to six months after to determine application of the knowledge, skills, and abilities to student affairs practice. Such ongoing assessment may also help to identify additional training needs and strategic direction as student affairs practitioners continue to practice intentional inclusion.

Continuous assessment is a recommended practice for sustaining diverse and inclusive student affairs program delivery, which includes receiving feedback from intended program participants to determine if program objectives are met. Participation under the proposed model will prime other student affairs units to engage in the same process and, eventually, this process could spread to larger areas of the university. Creating and maintaining a partnership with the university's multicultural/diversity and inclusion unit is recommended because they can assist with the longer-term process. Such an expanded evidence-based approach can empower student affairs staff and will position the university to better serve its students.

STUDENT AFFAIRS SCENARIO FOR
EVIDENCE-BASED PRACTICE

What has been presented in the previous section is a model for developing an evidence-based multiculturalism, inclusion, diversity, and social justice professional development program. To provide additional guidance on how the described model may be utilized in student affairs, the following scenario is provided.

Carlos is the director of student programs on the campus of Welcome University, a small campus of 7,000 students located in the Midwest. He has been in the position for six months. His most recent work experience was at State University, a large, urban university on the west coast with a student population of around 30,000. He was director of student activities at that institution. At State University, he hired 50% of a staff of 25 activities advisors and provided training for them. The staffing at Welcome is much different in that his staff consists of an assistant director, four activities coordinators, two graduate assistants, and two support staff members, all white.

Welcome University is proud of its mission and goals which include providing opportunities for campus engagement for a diverse student body. However, it is not until recently that the institution has increased its recruitment efforts of Black and Latino students, and the university has just begun to create programmatic support for other identities such as sexual orientation. The student population is currently 75% White, 10% Black, 10% Latino, and 2% Asian or Pacific Islander. The remaining 3% of their population identifies as "other," which includes their growing multiracial population and some international students. While their representation of international students had begun to increase over the last ten years, external sociopolitical factors have resulted in a recent decline in international student enrollment. To stay competitive and keep pace with the changing landscape of higher education and the students they wish to attract, the university created an office of diversity and inclusion that works collaboratively with their equal opportunity office.

Recently, several Black and Latino students met with Carlos about the nature of planned activities. They believed that current campus events do not reflect the culture of students who are not white. At his former institution, Carlos conducted an annual student needs assessment before any programs were planned for the academic year. At Western, he has discovered that the Black and Latino students graduated from high schools and with excellent reputations and a more diverse student body, and that students who identified as Asian and Pacific Islander were beginning to request more culturally relevant programming. His most recent assessment also revealed the need for more support for LGBT students. For most of these students, programming met their needs in high school and supported their involvement in campus life and they expected the same level of programming from a large university with demographics reflective of the external population. His Western staff had approached these students from what he considered to be a culturally-relevant perspective based upon student needs and experiences and had received training to expand their capacity to do so. As a result, they also worked collaboratively with identity-based student organizations and Western's multicultural affairs staff and had begun to support the creation of additional programming and resources for LGBT (lesbian, gay, bisexual, and transgender), Muslim, and non-traditional students.

Because of his educational background in higher education and his experience in student affairs, Carlos saw immediately the need for training of all student activities staff at Welcome University. The training would be designed to increase the cultural awareness, cultural competency, and cultural humility of staff, with the goal of providing more culturally-relevant student programming. He employed the services of the campus office of diversity and inclusion to design and develop the training. How can evidence-based practice be utilized to address Carlos' goals of a more multiculturally-competent staff? The responses to this case will be made using a combination of the evidence-based decision-making model and the steps illustrated in Figure 1 on page 212. These steps are numbered as follows:

Research

1. Review existing data. There are voluminous literature and research on cultural similarities, differences, and their implications on program delivery. Much of this literature addresses student needs and preferences by race, gender and gender identity, sexual orientation, and ethnicity. With the assistance of the diversity and inclusion practitioner, Carlos can identify applicable literature and use it in developing a needs assessment for the staff that will help achieve the goal of more culturally-relevant programming. Carlos discovered that the diversity and inclusion practitioner had conducted similar training workshops at Welcome and at other institutions, and Carlos had also worked with diversity practitioners at his previous institution to help develop and deliver training for his staff. In this scenario, if the institution has previously conducted a climate survey or any other assessment to determine the experiences and needs of students, use of such data will be helpful to potentially determine both institutional capacity and the cumulative effect of the university's programs, policies, and practices on the university's student population. Collection of these data can also take the form of benchmarking, or studying what programs other institutions have developed in pursuit of similar goals.

2. Perform a staff pre-assessment. A pre-assessment of staff knowledge will uncover baseline competencies in the areas of inclusion, multiculturalism, diversity, and social justice that are important for the training design. Such a pre-assessment may choose to measure individual and collective awareness of areas such as privilege, bias, cultural humility, and other specific topics. Carlos and the diversity and inclusion practitioner may choose to use an instrument such as the *Intercultural Development Inventory* (Hammer (2012) to determine individual and collective perspectives regarding difference overall and for those participating in the training.

If data from an instrument do not already exist, pre-assessment should include a survey to determine how the staff views the campus climate regarding multiculturalism, diversity, inclusion, and social justice—both for themselves and students. How does the staff feel about the new campus initiatives and the move toward more diversity and intentional inclusion? How do these feelings impact their sense of campus community? How prepared do they feel personally and professionally to meet the needs of the changing demographics? What incidents or programs on campus may support their perspectives?

Such data can contribute to the development of a curriculum that meets participants' needs. For example, if the assessment shows a lack of understanding about the dynamics of privilege, perhaps the training will include such elements as privilege walks or other activities designed to bring personal experience with privilege to the surface for discussion. Such exercises are meant to help participants reflect upon their own experiences and how they may affect their interactions with those who are different. If participants tend to minimize the importance difference in an effort to build community and see everyone as the same, the training may help them understand the role of identity development in the way students may experience programs and service differently to make them more culturally relevant.

Decision Making

1. Share and discuss the pre-assessment results with staff. Carlos must discuss the results of the needs/pre-assessment with the staff in order to secure their engagement in the process. This includes implications of the data that would be applicable to curriculum development. Transparency is vital throughout the process to strengthen trust, cultivate buy-in, and develop a collective understanding of the need for and desired outcomes of the training. This discussion may be difficult and yield multiple questions from staff, so it will be helpful to have a representative of the diversity and inclusion office present. Ideally the representative will be the one delivering the training in order to minimize discomfort and assure participants of the safe space that will be created for them to explore these perspectives throughout the process.

2. The director helps to develop the curriculum and scope of training in collaboration with the diversity and inclusion practitioner. Using timing considerations and the availability of staff to fully participate, Carlos and the diversity and inclusion practitioner determine the nature and scope of the intervention, appropriate curricular materials, and the length and modality of the training. He must keep in mind staff responsibilities including schedules, workload, and work-life balance. Working in tandem with the practitioner—who may know the intended material but not the staff, their daily duties, or strengths and limitations—will be critical to training success. This ensures that the training will not be viewed as an "add on" to their work, but as a benefit to their roles and part of a process towards continuous improvement that will enhance their students' collegiate experience. Senior administrators must understand the importance of the training and explicitly express and provide support. Ideally, the curriculum includes modules similar to those outlined earlier that provide enough time to learn, process, and apply the material over an extended period of time. This both helps to avoid participant burnout and devotes the amount of time necessary for them to be able to effectively synthesize the material and not just "check the box" that they have completed diversity training—a common pitfall that often does not yield changed behavior, perspectives, or different results.

Practice

1. Delivery of the training is completed. The training is scheduled at an appropriate time allowing full participation, which may require consideration of the appropriate time of day or year. Ground rules or other group agreements should be determined at the outset to create clear participation expectations. It should begin with "getting to know you" activities introductions that allow time for staff to build trust and feel comfortable about the level of vulnerability and authenticity needed to benefit from the experience. Small groups should be used as appropriate to encourage disclosure and discussion. The importance of trained diversity and inclusion practitioners familiar with leading and facilitating such discussions cannot be overstated. While some student affairs professionals may think their awareness of their practice is enough to guide the process, diversity and inclusion practitioners with familiarity of the specific content are critical so that all participants are guided through the process at a rate acceptable to their learning. Issues of multiculturalism, inclusion, diversity, and social justice can evoke strong emotional responses in participants, and facilitators can help in mitigating negative short-term and long-term outcomes.

2. Staff are intentional. Staff should be fully present during the training (ideally without distractions such as phones, computers, and other means by which they can "check out") and devote full attention to all activities while reflecting upon their reactions to training content. Ground rules will ideally help participants express authentic perspectives and emotions throughout; and journaling in some form is encouraged. Supervisors should be held accountable for their own objectivity, and facilitators should help to ensure that no retaliation occurs for expression of authentic perspectives as part of the training process. This may require long-term engagement and post-training support from the diversity and inclusion practitioner and potentially human resources as perspectives, challenges, and concerns may be raised that can affect the culture of the unit.

Assessment (Evidence)

1. Post-training assessment is conducted. An assessment of learning from the training will be anonymously conducted on the last day and again three months after. The results should be shared with both the diversity and inclusion practitioner and Carlos. The initial assessment should evaluate intended objectives, learning outcomes, and ideas for application of the new information to the work environment. The immediate responses to this outcomes assessment should capture both their feelings and perspectives regarding the experience combined with initial learning. This will be helpful for Carlos in determining both their willingness to engage in further discussions about diversity, inclusion, and multiculturalism, and their ability to apply it. The longer-term assessment will better capture application of the new information to their work environment and determine any additional training needs to help them advance their application. Such trainings should not be conducted in a "one and done" manner. As programs, policies, practices, people are ever-changing, continuing these discussions will help staff to meet those needs effectively.

2. Application of the learning is evidenced. This is where true practice is applied to these experiences. The daily activity of the staff should reflect active learning from the workshop. Participants may wish to create an individual action plan that details what they aspire to do differently as a result of the new information acquired, with desired outcomes. Ideally, the staff should be better able to respond to student programming needs, evaluate their existing practices to assess for active inclusion, consider new policies that may better serve their students, and consider with whom to collaborate both inside and outside the university to integrate perspectives that may better reflect those of their students. A by-product of this evidence-based practice will be that staff who plan future programs will better understand the importance of their own use of evidence. They will have gained competency in effective program planning for inclusion, equity, multiculturalism, diversity, and social justice.

3. Practice assessment is reviewed annually and as new staff is hired. This process starts again at the beginning of each academic year and whenever new staff are hired. Learning outcomes are ongoing, and applications during the work experience are expected and measured, which will enhance this learning. Staff should be able to articulate how and what they are doing differently and the outcomes they observe as a result—these may take the form of student engagement, retention, academic performance, or other outcomes. Ideally, the student programming staff will position the university to better serve its students. As the director, Carlos should employ student assessment methods yielding increased satisfaction among ALL students—not just those historically underrepresented - regarding programs and activities.

Scenario Questions

- How can Carlos's experiences enhance his ability to lead others in this area?
- What skills, abilities, and knowledge may his staff possess that can help move the student affairs division towards more intentional inclusion?
- What higher education and student development research can be used to provide evidence for practice?
- How can Carlos sustain this initiative within the university community?
- What support does he need from upper-level administration?
- How can Carlos provide ongoing data regarding the effectiveness of his division in improving campus climate?
- How can Carlos build a climate of evidence-based practice among his staff?

- What incentives and rewards can he provide for ongoing learning among his staff?
- How can Carlos create a culture of accountability for his unit's programs, practices, policies, and people?
- Are there technological and data-driven supports that will keep evidence-based reporting viable in student activities?

Questions for Personal and Institutional Reflection

- Does my institution as a whole support principles of inclusion, equity, multiculturalism, social justice and diversity? What evidence exists to support your claim?
- Do I, as a student affairs educator, have the will to ensure staff and student competency in the areas of multiculturalism, diversity, inclusion, and social justice learning? What will it take for me to do so?
- What are the risks and rewards of embarking on a diversity, inclusion, multiculturalism, and social justice journey? How might I navigate and leverage them both for desired outcomes?
- How might I respond to peers, colleagues, and even students who may not see the benefit of diversity, inclusion, multiculturalism and social justice? What evidence would I use to support my claims?
- How do I acquire the skills to educate others in these areas?
- Who within the campus community can support my learning? How can I navigate potential barriers to my development in this area?

In reflecting upon the answers to these questions, student affairs educators will actually be conducting the personal and institutional assessment which may be necessary for lasting change. Self-reflection is a step that cannot be omitted when working with others to develop a practice supportive of multicultural, diversity, inclusion, and social justice learning—this includes an awareness of one's existing knowledge and experiences, and perspectives, and those that may be lacking for desired outcomes. Some may call this a "reality check" for both the institution and the student affairs educator. While sometimes difficult, it allows student affairs educators to be an example to others and build coalitions for support and action.

RECOMMENDATIONS

Student affairs educators planning to utilize evidence-based practice to promote equity-minded intentional inclusion and pursuit of multiculturalism, equity, and social justice should consider the following recommendations:

1. Take advantage of personal and professional learning and development (Research/Evidence): In addition to professional development opportunities primarily focused upon student affairs, professionals should seek out training, professional development, and learning communities that are focused on topics such as diversity, multiculturalism, inclusion, equity, privilege, and/or social justice. These may be through professional associations and resources such as:

- NASPA Multicultural Institute
- National Conference on Race and Ethnicity in American Higher Education (NCORE)
- White Privilege Conference
- Social Justice Training Institute
- Critical Race Studies in Education Association Conference
- White Men as Full Diversity Partners

Student affairs professionals should also engage in critical self-reflection and inquiry around their own perspectives, interactions, experiences, and biases (EVIDENCE).

2. Seek out CDO or related offices (RESEARCH): If your institution has a chief diversity officer, cultural centers, diversity and inclusion committees, or any other entity with the knowledge, skills, and abilities to provide support and capacity building for inclusion, equity, and social justice, you want to consider working with them. These entities may be able to provide training, workshops, program analysis, or provide other evidence-based services to assist with multiculturalism, diversity, social justice or inclusion.

3. Learn your institution's diversity, equity, inclusion, and multiculturalism goals and expectations (RESEARCH): Before engaging in evidence-based practice, student affairs practitioners must first understand how these concepts are being addressed, defined, and valued in your institution. Are the goals primarily expressed by way of compositional diversity through admissions and recruitment efforts? Are inclusion and student success determined by retention and matriculation of historically underrepresented or marginalized students? Is the institution primarily concerned with compliance and meeting federal mandates? Has the institution indicated whether capacity building for inclusion is part of its strategic efforts? Expressed and implied institutional expectations (or lack thereof) may serve as helpful starting points for determining the role that student affairs should play in the larger institutional landscape as it relates to diversity, equity, inclusion, and multiculturalism.

4. Identify existing or relevant data (RESEARCH): To implement an evidence-based approach, professionals must have data that can provide insight into strengths, opportunities, and gaps related to multiculturalism, inclusion, equity, and diversity. Data from commonly-used tools such as the *National Survey of Student Engagement* and the corresponding *Community College Survey for Student Engagement* in two-year institutions can help to identify starting points. Fact books and other data provided by university institutional research departments can provide baseline data from which student affairs practitioners can glean composition, retention and matriculation insights. If a chief diversity officer or similar role or office exists on your campus, determine what data they have or intend to collect regarding inclusive climates. These data can provide useful perspectives around evidence-based multiculturalism, diversity, social justice, and inclusion strengths, opportunities, gaps, and needs.

5. **Identify your own sphere of influence and capacity (RESEARCH/EVIDENCE):** Should you as a student affairs educator decide to answer the call to multiculturalism, diversity, equity, and inclusion efforts, the first question is: What *can* I do and what am I *willing* to do? These are critical questions that determine not only one's sphere of influence, but also the boundaries and capacity one has to affect change in these areas. It should be noted that deciding to address these topics is not for the faint of heart—particularly if one chooses to do it well. Student affairs practitioners should resist the temptation to seek out only the "low hanging fruit," because that may do harm by creating a false sense of success or achievement of these goals.

The recommendations stated here all involve the first phase of the evidence-based practice related to multiculturalism, diversity, inclusion, and social justice. They also present the next phase of the implementation or practice. How are you using the evidence you found to meet your learning goals? The third phase involves assessment. This assessment provides evidence that can be used for future programs and activities. In practice the loop, the evidence you have gathered from your assessment becomes part of the future planning.

CONCLUSION

Student affairs educators are expected to provide for the holistic growth of students through knowledge of student development theory as well as through their daily interactions with students. Researchers (Astin, 1977/1997; Pascarella & Terenzini, 1991) showed us that the college experience has a significant effect on students. The out-of-classroom experiences of students with regard to how they view the world is affected by the college environment. Student affairs practitioners have a responsibility to provide environmental learning experiences that include the understanding and awareness of diversity and inclusion. They are expected to use theoretical frames, assessment, and research to provide evidence that students learn and develop from their interventions. In the absence of evidence, it is impossible to determine when goals are met, practices are effective, and efforts are yielding returns. Long-term strategies that include scaffolding, broad engagement, and clear measures of accountability and desired outcomes must be employed.

Efforts towards positive and productive outcomes for multiculturalism, equity, inclusion and social justice are never achieved through reaching a specific destination, they are more akin to a continuing journey where the changing student demographics, external sociocultural factors, institutional foci and goals, and personnel changes require continuous looping through the process of research, decision-making, practice, and assessment. When student affairs practitioners decide to commit to the process of evidence-based practice on multiculturalism, diversity, inclusion, and social justice—whether personally or departmentally—the result is a meaningful contribution to ensuring that all students who pursue educational attainment can do so in environments that support, affirm, and integrate multiple perspectives into the student development process.

REFERENCES

American College Personnel Association (ACPA). (1949). *The student personnel point of view.* Washington, DC: Author.

American College Personnel Association. (2017). ACPA strategic imperative for racial justice and decolonization. Retrieved from http://www.myacpa.org/sirjd #SIRJ%20History

Association of American Colleges and Universities. (2015). *Committing to equity and inclusive excellence: A campus guide for self-study and planning.* Washington, D.C.: AAUP. Retrieved from https://www.aacu.org/sites/default/files/Committing toEquityInclusiveExcellence.pdf

Astin, A. (1977). *What matters in college: Four critical years.* San Francisco: Jossey-Bass.

Astin, A. (1997). *What matters in college: Four critical years revisited.* San Francisco: Jossey-Bass.

Blimling, G.S., Whitt, E.J., & Associates. (1999). *Good practice in student affairs.* San Francisco: Jossey-Bass.

Bresciani, M. J., Zelna, C. L., & Anderson, J. A. (2004) *Assessing student learning and development: A handbook for practitioners.* Washington, D.C: National Association of Student Personnel Administrators.

Council for the Advancement of Standards in Higher Education. (2015). *CAS professional standards for higher education* (9th ed.). Washington, DC: Author.

Ciliska, D., DiCenso, A., Melnyk, B. M., & Stetler, C. (2005). Using models and strategies for evidence-based practice. In B. M. Melnyk & E. Fineout-Overholt (Eds.), *Evidence based practice in nursing and healthcare: A guide to best practice* (pp. 185-219). Philadelphia, PA: Lippincott Williams & Wilkins.

Creamer, E.G., Mutcheson, R.B., Sutherland, M., & Meszaros, P.S. (2013). Assessing the extent that the gender and STEM practice-oriented literature is evidence-based. *International Journal of Higher Education, 2*(3), 81–90.

Evidence-based Education. (n.d.). In Wikipedia. Retrieved from https://en.wikipedia.org/wiki/Evidence-based_education.

Gansemer-Topf, A., & Ryder, A. (2017). Competences needed for entry-level student affairs work: Views from mid-level professionals. *College Student Affairs Journal, 35*(1), 40–54.

Hammer, M. (2012). The Intercultural Development Inventory: A new frontier in assessment and development of intercultural competence. In M. Vande Berg, R. M. Paige, & K. H. Lou (Eds.), *Student learning abroad* (pp. 115–136). Sterling, VA: Stylus Publishing.

Lindsey, R. B., Robins, K. N., & Terrell, R. D. (2009) *Cultural proficiency: A manual for school leaders* (3rd ed.). Thousand Oaks, CA: Corwin.

McCormick, A. C., Kinzie, A., & Korkmaz (April, 2011). *Understanding evidence-based improvement in higher education.* Paper presented at the annual meeting of the American Educational Research Association, New Orleans, LA.

National Association of Diversity Officers in Higher Education. (2014). *Standards of professional practice for chief diversity officers.* Retrieved from http://www.nadohe.org/standards-of-professional-practice-for-chief-diversity-officers

National Association of Student Personnel Administrators. (2017). Retrieved from https://www.naspa.org/focus-areas/equity-and-diversity

National Association of Student Personnel Administrators. (2017a). Retrieved from https://www.naspa.org/events/2017scaod

National Association of Student Personnel Administrators & The American College Personnel Association. (2004). *Learning reconsidered: A campus-wide focus on the student experience.* Retrieved from https://www.naspa.org/images/uploads/main/Learning_Reconsidered_Report.pdf

Pascarella, E. T., & Terenzini, P. T. (1991). *How college affects students: Findings and insights from twenty years of research.* San Francisco: Jossey-Bass.

Po, A. L.W. (1998). *Dictionary of evidence-based medicine.* Abingdon, England: Radcliff Medical Press.

Pope, R. L., Reynolds, A. L., & Mueller, J. A. (2004). *Multicultural competence in student affairs.* San Francisco: Jossey-Bass.

Ryder, A. J., & Kimball, E. W. (2015). Assessment as reflexive practice: A grounded model for making evidence-based decisions in student affairs. *Research & Practice in Assessment, 10,* 30–45.

Tervalon, M., & Murray-García, J. (1998). Cultural humility versus cultural competence: A critical distinction in defining physician training outcomes in multicultural education. *Journal of Health Care for the Poor and Underserved, 9*(2), 117–125.

Worthington, R. L. (2012). Advancing scholarship for the diversity imperative in higher education: An editorial. *Journal of Diversity in Higher Education, 5,* 1–12.

Chapter 11

UTILIZATION OF THEORY, RESEARCH, AND ASSESSMENT TO ENHANCE MULTICULTURALISM, DIVERSITY, SOCIAL JUSTICE, AND INCLUSION

Amy French

CASE STUDY

Doctor Carroll has recently been hired as the vice president of student affairs at Statestown University. Statestown University is a predominantly White, mid-sized regional campus in the southeastern part of the United States. The majority of students come to Statestown from a 160-mile radius. Currently the campus serves 20,000 undergraduate students, with 75% residing on campus. In recent years, the state has increased accountability measures and enforced evidence-based funding models. In addition, the university has become embroiled in racial tensions between students, staff, and faculty due to the silence from the administration following a racially charged incident at the annual homecoming rally last year.

Immediately after arriving on campus, Doctor Carroll held an all staff meeting with her division. She commended the staff on the work they do to support the students, encouraged collaboration between departments, and promised increased professional development funding for the division. Next, Doctor Carroll presented a new vision for the division of student affairs at Statestown University. Her ideal division placed student learning at the center, provided services to all students, particularly minoritized students, and focused on the strategic plan initiatives of educating the whole person through curricular and co-curricular activities and creating a welcoming campus climate. She stated, "It is through student learning that we can enact change in our society. We need to know what we are doing well, what we need to improve on, and what we need to change to meet the needs of all of our students." She then provided a worksheet to all in attendance and invited the staff to discuss these questions at their tables for a few minutes. The worksheet contained a list of five questions:

1. How is your department evidence-based?
2. What assessment methods has your office employed over the last five years to assess multiculturalism, diversity, inclusion, and/or social justice?
3. Who have you assessed in your specific functional area? Students? Staff? Campus partners?
4. How can the division utilize instruments to gauge multicultural programming efforts?
5. How are you supporting all students, particularly minoritized students, to be successful?

Doctor Carroll allowed 30 minutes for discussion before bringing the group back together for closing remarks. She assured the division that this was only the beginning of an assessment discussion that the division would continue under her leadership. She acknowledged that each of the questions on the worksheet were complex and would take training, honest reflection, and due diligence. She closed her inaugural address to the division with the following statement:

We at Statestown have to place priority on evidence-based practices in order to meet benchmarks such as increasing retention and graduation rates. We also must support students' psychosocial well-being and their ability to become multiculturally competent citizens. Everything we do within the division of student affairs should connect back to these benchmarks. I look forward to working with all of you to continue promoting students at Statestown University.

Questions to Consider

1. Why do you think Doctor Carroll emphasized assessment in her inaugural address to the division of student affairs?
2. What message is Doctor Carroll sending to the division? Do you think this approach was effective?
3. What external factors may contribute to Doctor Carroll's message?
4. What assumptions does Doctor Carroll make in presenting the worksheet tool?
5. How do you expect the division of student affairs staff to respond to Doctor Carroll's appeal?
6. What professional competency areas does Doctor Carroll address?

INTRODUCTION

Across the United States, we see incidents occurring between campus administrators and students related to diversity, social justice and inclusion. While some incidents are contoured with social justice undertones, some have blistered to a point of unmistakable injustice. This chapter will introduce relevant professional competencies of multiculturalism, diversity, social justice, and inclusion intended to support both graduate students and student affairs educators in identifying various metrics and instruments available to assess multicultural knowledge, skills and awareness. The focus is to encourage professionals in higher education to circumvent a failure of knowledgeability when navigating multicultural, diversity, and inclusion phenomena on their respective campuses. Administrators, student affairs educators, and graduate students must procure data from assessments and delineate between appropriate models.

This case study above, while fictional, is not unfathomable. Doctor Carroll made assumptions regarding assessment that administrators and other campus leaders often make when engaging in a conversation on assessment, particularly multicultural assessment. She assumed that everyone had a working knowledge of assessment, could delineate between assessment and evaluation, and could recognize learning outcomes as measurable indicators of success in the field. She also presumed that all professionals within the division understood the importance of serving minoritized students. This chapter's focus is to ensure that, when prompted, the reader will be able to discuss assessment, identify relevant professional competencies related to multiculturalism, diversity, social justice, and inclusion within the assessment, evaluation and research competency area, and identify appropriate instruments to support multiculturalism and the student affairs profession.

This chapter begins by contextualizing the history of assessment within the student affairs profession. Next, the terms assessment and evaluation will be clarified. A discussion surrounding student learning outcomes will follow. Assessment tools and models specific to inclusivity and social justice will be examined. Lastly, I introduce a dialogical assessment model that I conceptualized based off of Freire's (1970) concept of conscientizacao. This model is intended to assist professionals in understanding the cyclical nature of assessment at the programmatic, divisional, and institutional levels. This conversation will be guided from a multicultural perspective and the professional competencies set forth by the Council for the Advancement Standards (CAS) for Master's Level Student Affairs Professional Preparation Programs. In order to accomplish these goals, it is imperative to begin with the history of student affairs assessment to anchor this discussion.

Historical Context

Assessment has always been a function of the student affairs profession (American Council on Education, 1937). In 1949, the *Student Personnel Point of View* (American Council on Education, 1949) outlined five criteria for evaluating programs: student satisfaction and dissatisfaction with services; faculty satisfaction pertaining to student personnel programs; usage of student services; continued improvement and recognition efforts for staff development and training, and evaluation related to the relationship between student personnel staff and faculty which should be evaluated for quality cooperative efforts. As the profession evolved, student affairs educators and scholars began to focus on student development theory. With this evolution came new assessment methods designed to measure growth and learning over time. In 1979, the Council for the Advancement of Standards in Higher Education (CAS) created guidelines to standardize and assess functional areas within the profession. The profession has examined student characteristics, learning, diversity, needs, and satisfaction since the mid-1980s (Sandeen & Barr, 2006). The mid-90s through the 2000s led to an increased focus on accountability. Today, assessment has become a central focus of many stakeholders, particularly legislators and accrediting agencies.

Since the early 2000s, attention on student learning and ability for students to apply new knowledge in the workforce has been heightened. Bresciani, Zelna and Anderson (2004) contend that institutions are "expected to provide evidence to their internal and external constituencies that the quality of education and the student experience are commensurate with rising costs, with their statements of excellence, and with their desire to retain the competitive edge" (p. 1). Banta and Palomba (2015) highlighted that student affairs educators' ability to assess students' out of classroom learning experience is imperative to the field because assessments often focus on topics such as student development theory, counseling, advising, diversity, assessment, and law to guide curriculum, which offers a broad repository to gauge the student experiences and measure student learning. Collaboration between student affairs educators, faculty, and institutional research offices has grown in importance (Henning & Roberts, 2016) as a response to mounting assessment work.

In an effort to respond to rising expectations in the area of assessment, the American College Personnel Association and National Association of Student Personnel Associates collaborated in 2004 to jointly publish *Learning Reconsidered: A Campuswide Focus on the Student Experience* (Keeling, 2004). This document emphasized the value afforded to student affairs educators, particularly the role those individuals play in working with students in co-curricular areas and defined learning as "a comprehensive, holistic, transformative activity that integrates academic learning and student development, processes that have often been considered separate and even independent of each other" (p. 4). Keeling (2004) supported multi-method approaches to assessment in order to understand the student experiences and encouraged all institutions to "establish routine ways to hear students' voices, consult with them, explore their opinions, and document the nature and quality of their experience as learners" (p. 28).

Moreover, ACPA's (2006) *ASK Standards* identify 13 focus areas for assessment skills and knowledge: assessment design, articulating learning and development outcomes, selection of data collection and management methods, assessment instruments, surveys used for assessment purposes, interviews and focus groups used for assessment purposes, analysis, benchmarking, program review and evaluation, assessment ethics, effective reporting and use of results, politics of assessment, and assessment education. Throughout this document, specific outcomes for each area are offered to assist student affairs educators with developing competence in their functional area. This framework offers a launchpad to improve practice. By 2006, the Council for the Advancement of Standards in Higher Education (CAS standards) designed specific standards for assessment services.

In 2010, ACPA and NASPA jointly published competencies to guide the assessment conversation and provide specific benchmarks in beginning, intermediate, and advanced proficiency levels. Year 2015 brought about revised competency areas through the *Professional Competency Areas for Student Affairs Practitioners* document, which provides additional criteria for practitioners (ACPA-College Student Educators International & NASPA-Student Affairs Administrators in Higher Education, 2015). The assessment, evaluation, and research (AER) competency area in the document offers qualitative and quantitative measures to direct assessment procedures, critique assessment, manage process, and shape political environments.

The Council for the Advancement of Standards in Higher Education (2015) lists assessment as the last of the twelve general guidelines. According to the CAS standards (2015), programs and services must:

- Specify programmatic goals and intended outcomes;
- Identify student learning and development outcomes;
- Employ multiple measures and methods;
- Develop manageable processes for gathering, interpreting, and evaluating data;
- Document progress toward achievement of goals and outcomes;
- Interpret and use assessment results to demonstrate accountability;
- Report aggregated results to respondent groups and stakeholders; and
- Use assessment results to inform planning and decision-making;

These eight action items describe the fundamental components of assessment. Assessment must begin by establishing goals and intended outcomes. Student learning is paramount to the work student affairs educators do daily. These outcomes need to be measured using various methods that ought to be versatile to accommodate the busy student affairs educator in gathering useful and accurate data. Student affairs educators must then interpret the results, report the findings to the appropriate constituency groups, and use the results to make decisions to further support the students. The CAS standards, when conceptualized, form a loop that can perpetuate the assessment process. This loop will be expounded upon later in this chapter but is crucial to explain here in order to frame the discussion.

There has been an influx of multicultural initiatives throughout American higher education such as office development, program initiative creation, and curricular changes but few efforts have relied on assessment to know whether these diversity efforts have made an impact (Harper & Hurtdao, 2007; Krishnamurthi, 2003; Pope 1992; Smith, 2009; Smith & Parker, 2005) on institutions over the last several decades. Given the current social and political climate on college campuses, it is imperative to incorporate measures pertaining to diversity and inclusion throughout student affairs programming. As scholars, practitioners, and students, we must move beyond the concept of meeting minimum expectations, which is often associated with competency benchmarks. We, as a profession, must conceptualize benchmarking as a starting point to the assessment process and delve deeper into assessing multiculturalism on college campuses to meet the needs of all students, faculty, and staff. Assessment should permeate all aspects of the programmatic functions in order to gauge learning, growth, and climate on a college campus.

Assessment and Evaluation

Understanding the history of student affairs assessment provides a point of reference for us as we explore assessment and evaluation; two terms that are often used interchangeably. I contend these terms carry unique distinctions within student affairs and higher education both in concept and in practicality. Upcraft and Schuh (1996) define assessment as "any effort to gather, analyze, and interpret evidence which describes institutional, departmental, divisional, or agency effectiveness" (p. 18) and includes program or initiative effectiveness (Schuh, Biddix, Dean, & Kinzie, 2016). Assessment relies on research methods, but there are specific nuances that distinguish assessment from research. Schuh et al. (2016) provide four noteworthy distinctions between assessment and research: assessments are guided by theory while research tests theory, assessments are time bound, assessments attract public and political interest, and assessments are usually funded from the unit or divisional budget rather than outside entities. Evaluation, in effect, uses assessment data to "determine the match between intended outcomes . . . and actual outcomes" (Suskie, 2009, p. 12). Evaluation "investigates and judges the quality or worth of a program, project, or other entity rather than student learning" (p. 12). Evaluation utilizes the various assessments that have been conducted to guide decisions for the program or functional area.

While assessment has been given more attention over the last decade, we must take steps to incorporate assessment into our daily operations as practitioners and scholars. Pope and LePeau (2011) recognize assessment and evaluation as key in creating multicultural change on campus. For example, assessment can provide insights to a student affairs director whose office has experienced high turnover of professionals of color and evaluation may be used to measure the effects of a multicultural center's programs on a campus climate. Assessment and evaluation, when operationalized effectively, should work in tandem to improve colleges and universities.

It is important to mention here that those conducting an assessment should consciously consider assessment methods and evaluation techniques through a culture-specific lens. Issues of ethnic and cultural diversity are at the vanguard of our society and should be on the forefront for all student affairs educators. There are methods available to guide professionals in this work. Before discussing the specific methods, it is imperative to understand the various dimensions of multicultural assessment. The following section will expound upon competency areas as well as define multicultural competency.

MULTICULTURAL ASSESSMENT

As discussed in the previous section, assessment and evaluation are used to guide decisions on a college campus in an effort to make continued improvements. Multicultural assessment builds on that definition to include a cultural context in which people of differing cultures interact. These interactions in traditional assessment models omitted the influence of identity and culture on the results. The goal of multicultural assessment is to implement systematic inquiry based on empirical strategies that appropriately include the diversity of our students, faculty, and staff to continually enhance colleges and universities in areas of social justice, equity, and inclusion. Multicultural assessments are intended to reveal issues that permeate higher education institutions to guide campus leaders. As Pope, Mueller, and Reynolds (2009) observed about diversity on campus, "there are few areas of university life untouched by these issues" (p. 640). The acknowledgement of this statement will guide the conversation throughout this section. Let us start by discussing some history that has led us to this present conversation.

History of Multicultural Assessment

Assessment and evaluation with minoritized populations has a long history. The glaring exclusion or misrepresentation of minoritized populations is evident throughout history. One well known example that demonstrates research bias is the way IQ tests did not include minority students during instrument standardization. Cultural differences, social class, and language background were left out of the equation when comparing findings, which created flawed reporting.

In order to continue the discussion surrounding multicultural assessment practices, Padilla (2004) identifies three assumptions to guide educational assessment and research. The three assumptions are:

a) the White American is the standard against which other groups should be compared;
b) the instruments used for assessing differences are universally applicable across groups, with perhaps only minimal adjustment for culturally diverse populations;
c) although we need to recognize such sources of potential variance as social class, educational attainment, gender, cultural orientation, and proficiency in English, these are nuisances that can later be discarded. (p. 127)

These assumptions have undergirded assessment, evaluation, and research thus necessitating the development of culturally appropriate methodologies. Minoritized populations have been harmed by not being acknowledged within the data, by being acknowledged through a deficit-oriented narrative within the data, or by being represented with an asterisk at the bottom of a results section (Shotton, Lowe, & Waterman, 2013). New research methods, particularly qualitative methods, have begun to uncover ways to more accurately represent minoritized populations to best articulate their narratives and experiences.

Over the last decade, there has been an influx of multicultural competency guideline development, particularly regarding how to measure effective practice. The dawning of the accountability age of higher education has begot a forced conversation related to meeting standards. Wehlburg (2008) cautions "data have been collected (and filed, piled, and stored) for the benefit of others. But it seems clear that higher education has not done a very good job of using assessment data to improve student learning or the quality of the undergraduate experience" (p. 2). With this heightened emphasis on assessment, professional organizations such as the American College Student Personnel (ACPA), the National Association of Student Personnel Administrators (NASPA), and the American Psychological Association (APA) have responded to the accountability movement by distributing guidelines, holding specific institutes, and offering resources to translate theoretical constructs into working guidelines. These guidelines assist student affairs educators in streamlining, measuring, and focusing inclusive efforts in their functional areas to become more multiculturally competent. Theory, research, and assessment must be the foundation for enhancing our work in student affairs in the areas of multiculturalism, diversity, social justice, and inclusion.

Elements of Multicultural Competence

According to Pope and Reynolds (1997), multicultural competence is "a necessary prerequisite to effective, affirming, and ethical work in student affairs" (p. 270) and is defined as "the awareness, knowledge, and skills needed to work with others who are culturally different from self in meaningful, relevant, and productive ways" (Pope, Reynolds, & Mueller, 2004, p. 14). Pope, Reynolds, and Mueller (2004) encourage a continued conversation surrounding the definition of multicultural education in order to effectively meet the demands of multicultural issues and identify seven core student affairs competencies. These competencies are:

1. Administrative and management
2. Theory and translation
3. Helping and interpersonal
4. Ethical and legal
5. Teaching and training
6. Assessment and evaluation
7. Multicultural awareness, knowledge, and skills

Multicultural awareness, knowledge, and skills entail the "awareness of one's own assumptions, biases and values; an understanding of the worldview of others; information about various cultural groups; and developing appropriate intervention strategies and techniques" (p. 9). Research and assessment "require that professionals have the ability to complete self-studies, program evaluations, and campus assessments, and make meaning of the data collected" (p. 9). Pope et al. (2004) emphasize that multicultural competencies should be imbedded into the other six competency areas: administration and management; theory and translation; helping and interpersonal; ethical and legal; teaching and training; and assessment and evaluation. Numerous student affairs practitioners and scholars have placed increased attention on including multicultural awareness, knowledge, and skills as best practice approaches within the field (King & Howard-Hamilton, 2000; McEwen & Roper, 1994; Pope & Reynolds, 1997; Pope et al., 2004; Pope, Reynolds & Mueller, 2014).

Komives and Woodward (1996) included multicultural issues as central to the development of student affairs educators and included other competency areas such as leadership, teaching and training, advising and counseling, program development and advising, and assessment, evaluation, and research. According to Talbot (1996), "the student affairs profession will need to assume a leadership role in helping institutions bridge the gap between old skills and paradigms and the new tools necessary to effectively meet the needs of changing student populations" (p. 380). This brings us to the necessary discussion surrounding multicultural competence and multicultural assessment.

Relationship Between Multicultural Assessment and Multicultural Competence

The theoretical underpinning of assessing multicultural competency in student affairs stems from counseling psychology. Sue, Bernier, Durran, Feinberg, Pederson, Smith, and Vasques-Nuttall (1982)'s model of multicultural competence laid the groundwork for the definition of multicultural competence we use today. Pope et al. (2004) define multicultural competence as the specific "awareness, knowledge, and skills needed to work with others who are culturally different from self in meaningful, relevant, and productive ways" (p. 13).

Pope et al. (2014) explain that "multicultural awareness involves attitudes, values, biases, and assumptions that we all carry with us, whether we realize it or not, that influence our worldview" and multicultural knowledge is our "intellectual understanding or content knowledge about various cultural groups and specific multicultural constructs" (p. 13). This multicultural knowledge includes our understanding of social justice, privilege, acculturation, oppression, identity, and other constructs that influence our ability to understand those who are different from us. Multicultural skills afford us with the ability and opportunity to incorporate multicultural knowledge and awareness into our daily operations. The starting point for us in the student affairs profession, is to begin asking ourselves how we can best relate with individuals different from us.

Multicultural competence training has become the foundation for students, faculty, and student affairs staff on college campuses across the United

States. Part of this training emphasizes that multicultural competence is not only about understanding others but also about understanding more about people with whom we most closely identify. This means, for example, that if you are a White person, it is important for you to engage with other White people to understand more about the nuances associated with the experiences and realities of all of you. Likewise, you are encouraged to grow in your understanding about individuals with whom you differ.

Multicultural competence focuses on making change on campuses at the individual, group, and organizational level. A multiculturally competent campus brings together knowledge about all of its students, (including identity, background, religion, ability, class, culture, etc.) and transforms that knowledge into standards, policies, and practices that allow various campus entities to work together. These standards, policies, and procedures should be based on assessment methods that are intentionally implemented to support students, staff, and faculty on campus. Multicultural assessment utilizes tools to pinpoint where improvements can be made related to social justice, equity, and inclusion.

In our work as student affairs educators, we must use multiculturally effective intervention strategies. To do so, institutions need to provide appropriate multicultural training to their student affairs educators. Additionally, student affairs educators must incorporate multicultural assessment strategies in order to maintain a metaphorical dashboard to recognize when we should celebrate our successes and when we should identify areas for programmatic, departmental, and institutional improvement. Some tools to help student affairs educators conduct multicultural assessment will be described in the following sections. First, a discussion on campus climate that champions inclusion and diversity within its assessment efforts will guide the discussion in order to emphasize the important role student affairs educators have within this conversation on multicultural assessment.

Championing a Culture of Inclusiveness and Diversity on Assessment

Statestown University shares similarities with college campuses across the United States in terms of demographics, geography, and curriculum. Upon arrival, Doctor Carroll placed multicultural assessment as a top priority for her leadership platform. Doctor Carroll launched into a conversation with her staff and campus partners that presumed prior knowledge surrounding culture and how it could be assessed within the student affairs division. Perhaps a more effective approach could have been to begin a conversation about the importance of a multicultural campus before discussing assessment protocols.

Culture is defined as "collective, mutually shaping patterns of norms, values, practices, beliefs, and assumptions that guide the behavior of individuals and groups in higher education and provide a frame of reference within which to interpret the meaning of events and actions" (Kuh & Whitt, 1988, p. 12). Student affairs educators make decisions routinely based on their own perspectives, which are most likely influenced by their culture and identity. How do we, as campus leaders, make the best decisions to support all our students, particularly minoritized student populations? I contend that one response is to incorporate assessment processes that analyze an institution's cultural properties, reveal how individuals make meaning, and expose the experiences of previously unidentified groups within the college or university. Culture must be assessed in order for administrators to make the best decisions for the institution.

In performing cultural assessments, we must remain acutely aware of the challenges we may encounter. Culture presents challenges because of the unique characteristics that represent beliefs and assumptions formulated by people about individual interactions and their environment. As such, it encompasses layers, subcultures, and nuances unidentifiable from those who are not members of that particular culture. This creates a great challenge for practitioners and scholars when it comes to assessing multiculturalism. This challenge can be overcome by intentional methodological design, purposeful sampling, and a clear understanding of what culture is and how it influences our students, faculty, and staff. Making multicultural assessment a routine practice within your department or on your campus could promote diversity, social justice, and inclusion efforts on campus.

Understanding the campus climate for minoritized students, faculty and staff is crucial in order to adequately promote multiculturalism, social justice, diversity and equity at the institution. Rankin and Reason (2005) define campus climate as "the current attitudes, behaviors, and standards of faculty, staff, administrators, and students concerning the level of respect for individual needs, abilities and potential" (p. 264). Without understanding the perceptions and experiences of the minoritized individuals, it is impossible to change the culture. A campus climate study can provide an avenue to gauge the current racial climate, understand perceptions regarding the inclusiveness of the campus overall, uncover experiences and interactions shaped by social identity, and provide suggestions to make the campus more welcoming and inclusive. These studies provide data to decision makers that are intended to effect change. While institutions maintain a fragmented assessment strategy, policy decisions are often driven by data. Campus climate studies can provide researchers with data that focus on equity and advancing minoritized students.

For example, campus administrators may presume that the campus has work to do in areas of inclusion within specific identity groups on campus.

There could be a general feeling on campus that the campus is less inviting to certain undergraduate students. After conducting the climate study, it is found that Black undergraduate students feel dissatisfaction with the racial climate on the campus. The campus climate study reveals that Black undergraduate students feel safe and welcome in their residence halls, dining halls, and other community spaces but unwelcome in the academic settings such as the library, classroom, and study areas. Campus climate studies are intended to effect institutional change guided by the evaluation of the current climate pertaining to racial diversity (Harper & Hurtado, 2007; Smith, 2009). With this data in hand, the campus could begin to promote targeted initiatives, programs, and trainings for staff and faculty that encourage inclusion of Black students in the academic areas on campus.

ASSESSMENT TOOLS ON MULTICULTURALISM, DIVERSITY AND INCLUSION

Much research in student affairs literature examines methods for designing multicultural interventions (Barr & Strong, 1988; Brown, 1991; Ebbers & Henry, 1990). Appropriate instrumentation selection is vital to conduct assessments of diverse student populations. Misusing methods can be destructive and present misinformation that inevitably could be damaging to the students, staff, and institution. Building trust and establishing rapport on campus are necessary when conducting these types of assessment. Some student populations may welcome the traditional standardized survey instruments, while for others these traditional methods may be undesirable. Methods such as focus groups or individual interviews may be more appropriate in order to collect meaningful data pertinent to a specific population. The use of qualitative methodologies within multicultural assessment allows for researchers to delve deep into the data to uncover nuances associated with intricate aspects of culture, identity, and lived experiences. Quantitative data can also serve an important purpose within assessment and evaluation, but when studying nuances of social identity, culture, and lived experiences, it can be necessary to go beyond the numbers.

Before launching into a description of some assessment tools that measure diversity, culture, and inclusion, it is important to identify some skills that practitioners and scholars must acquire prior to using the tools. Practitioners and scholars must attain skills in active listening, empathic relating, behavioral modeling, and other interpersonal communication skills to assist in collecting information. Pope, Reynolds, & Mueller (2004) identified five necessary aspects for becoming a multiculturally competent researcher based on McEwen & Roper (1994) and Wilkinson & McNeil (1996):

1. Awareness of assumptions that influence the research process
2. Issues in defining the populations of interest
3. Appropriateness of measurement instruments
4. Data collection techniques
5. Alternate research approaches. (p. 102)

Assessment tools to measure multicultural competence (Pope & Mueller, 2000; Mueller & Pope, 2001) have been designed to extrapolate data associated to multicultural competence. Therefore, we need to scrutinize the frameworks that are designed to study multicultural issues on college campuses. Several instruments are described below that relate to multiculturalism and diversity on college campuses. This is not intended to be an exhaustive list of multicultural instrumentation, but instead illustrate some common assessment tools that can be attained and/or adapted to fit your campus or program.

Multicultural Organization Development

The Multicultural Organization Development (MCOD) was developed to help create more multiculturally sensitive organizations (Cross, Katz, Miller, & Seashore, 1994). MCOD theory states that a multicultural organization is healthy because it

> reflects the contributions and interests of diverse cultural and social groups in its mission, operations, and . . . service delivery; acts on a commitment to eradicate social oppression in all forms within the organization; includes the members of diverse cultural and social groups as full participants, especially in decisions that shape the organization; and follows through on broad external social responsibilities, including support of efforts to eliminate all forms of social oppression and to educate others in multicultural perspectives. (Jackson & Hardiman, 1981, p. 1)

Jackson and Hardiman's (1994) process provides the steps to achieve a long-term systemic organizational change that involves identifying a multicultural internal change team, assessing the organization's readiness for organizational change, focusing on senior leadership capacity to lead the multicultural change effort, and establishing a self-renewing process for multicultural systems change. Four steps are proposed by Jackson and Hardiman (1994) regarding this endeavor:

1. Establishing a diverse and thorough MCOD assessment plan.
2. Developing a MCOD intervention plan based on information gathered through the assessment phase.

3. Implementing an MCOD implementation plan that is integrated into all organizational subsystems.
4. Using an evaluation process that assesses the value and effectiveness of the MCOD plan and makes changes as appropriate.

This MCOD's intention is to develop a cycle of continued, far-reaching, and transformational improvements to the campus community. By assessing daily practices, underlying beliefs, and core values, the MCOD promotes the transformation of organizations into just and socially diverse systems (Pope et al., 2004; Greiger, 1996; Greiger & Toliver, 2001; Sue, 1995). Therefore, the MCOD can be a methodological tool to create change. The MCOD does rely heavily on environmental factors to influence the institutional changes to promote diversity and inclusion. Its effectiveness hinges on campus leadership and self-reporting, which could impact its ability to effect change.

Multicultural Change Intervention Matrix (MCIM)

Pope (1992) conceptualized a two-dimensional illustration of the MCOD principles to apply to student affairs and higher education to develop the Multicultural Change Intervention Matrix (MCIM). The first focus of the MCIM is the possible targets of multicultural intervention (individual, group, or institution), and the second explores types of intervention wherein a paradigm shift occurs during second-order change. This model offers a plan that student affairs educators can utilize in order to promote systemic change. Pope (1992) identified three applications of the MCIM for student affairs educators: assessment, strategic planning, and curricular transformation.

While this model offers an avenue to create multicultural awareness, the MCIM faces threats to reliability because it hinges on an individual's participation and openness. Because faculty, staff, and administrators are involved in implementing the MCIM, it is possible that these individuals may report heightened levels of openness and knowledge pertaining to multicultural awareness that are inaccurate. Additionally, the success of this instrument relies on the multicultural training of those who use the MCIM. This leaves the model volatile, particularly if those conducting multicultural efforts on campuses believe the current diversity and inclusion efforts are sufficient.

Diverse Learning Environments Survey

The Diverse Learning Environments (DLE) survey was created by Hurtado and Guillermo-Wann (2013) in an effort to assess campus climate (discrimination, positive and negative cross-racial interaction, sense of belonging, academic validation, etc.), educational practices (curriculum of inclusion, co-curricular diversity activities, support services, etc.), and it offers outcomes such as habits of mind, pluralistic orientation, social action, and civic engagement. This survey is web-based and can be administered to community college students who have completed 24 or more hours of college credit, or can be administered to second- and third-year students at four-year institutions. Institutions have the option to add additional modules catered to their locality. The DLE is designed to be used along with other assessment tools such as the MCIM, MCOD, and focus groups wherein triangulation of data allow for a better gauge of the campus climate on that campus. It is not intended to be used alone, as it may not most accurately represent the nuances associated with multiculturalism, identity, and inclusion on campuses.

Multiple Dimensions of Cultural Competence

The Multiple Dimensions of Cultural Competence (MDCC) instrument was developed by Sue (2001) with a focus on institutions rather than the individual. Both individual and institutional assessment should be considered in order to bring to fruition a more inclusive learning environment for students and a more welcoming environment for faculty and staff. The MDCC is a tool that organizes specific racial/cultural group perspectives, nuanced components of cultural competence, and concentrates on cultural competence. This model provides a framework for understanding the need to develop a social justice orientation and the model encourages that actions are taken by both institutions and individuals.

Multicultural Assessment of Campus Programming (MAC-P)

McClellan, Cogdal, Lease, and Londono-McConnell (1996) established the Multicultural Assessment of Campus Programming (MAC-P) questionnaire to understand how the student, faculty, and staff perceptions pertaining to the university's efforts to address the diverse needs of the student body are met. This was the first instrument to assess these interventions. The MAC-P examines the following:

- How students feel about the university's commitment to diversity;
- How they perceive majority and minority relations on campus; and
- How campus programming efforts increase awareness and understanding of diversity.

The MAC-P is a 42-item instrument that showed reliability over time. To allow for the completion of a factor analysis, 1,328 college students, and 167 college faculty and administrative staff completed a revised MAC-P. From the analysis, six factors emerged: institutional responsiveness, student relations, cultural accessibility, diversity recognition, student's cultural integration, and cultural sensitivity. This questionnaire has potential to continue to support multicultural and diversity efforts on college campuses.

Additional Assessment Approaches

While many assessment tools rely on quantitative measures like data collected from surveys or other traditional research methods, qualitative measures must be part of the equation when gauging multiculturalism, diversity, and social justice issues on college campuses. Holvino (2008) developed a matrix that examines organizational characteristics through a three-phase process (from monocultural to transitional to multicultural) across nine dimensions: mission, structure and roles, policies and procedures, informal systems and culture, people and relationships, leadership, environment, services or products and language use. A questionnaire follows the matrix to allow for dialogue between organization members intended for goal and strategy planning to transition from monocultural to more multicultural.

Lastly, Flash (2010) built the Multicultural Competence in Student Affairs Organizations (MCSAO) instrument. The MCSAO relies on 189 items across eight factors: (1) organizational climate and culture of commitment, encouragement, and support for multicultural competence; (2) peer or colleague influence, behaviors, and expectations for multicultural engagement; (3) clear and coherent multicultural mission; (4) organizational focus on gender identity, expression, and sexual orientation; (5) multiculturally inclusive services; (6) support for and creation of diversity of multicultural programming and events; (7) incorporation of multiculturalism in strategic and formal organizational practice; and (8) multicultural recruitment practices.

Each of the assessment tools discussed above focus on improving diversity and inclusion efforts on colleges and universities. Taking into consideration the changing demographics on college campuses, student affairs educators must be prepared to work in a multicultural environment (Ebbers & Henry, 1990; Pope & Reynolds, 1997). Institutions must understand the diverse student population on campus and understand how to design programs and make policies that resonate with those student populations (Brown, 1991; McEwen & Roper, 1994).

According to McEwen and Roper (1994), student affairs educators should emphasize culturally sensitive research techniques and instrument designs as part of their ethical responsibility. As with any methodological approach, there are limitations to each of these instruments. None of the models provide a perfect model for conducting multicultural assessment, but we must be mindful that this should not stall our efforts to do this work. Hurtado (2009) cautions that "when we do not assess diverse learning environments, assessment instruments of student outcomes simply document the cycle of disparities in educational outcomes (traced back to preparation prior to college) without identifying areas for improving student learning and development" (p. 1). If anything, this should serve as a motivation for continued scholarship within the field of multicultural assessment in order to promote social justice, diversity, and inclusion on college campuses.

DIALOGICAL ASSESSMENT MODEL

As student affairs practitioners, we have a duty to support all of our students and mindfully develop assessment methods designed to include rather than exclude. We should conduct our work alongside our students and with their best interest in mind. We should intentionally evaluate and measure the experiences of our students. Both the CAS standards and the ACPA and NASPA professional competencies help guide us in this assessment work. The CAS standards provide student affairs educators with clear steps to follow when strategizing multicultural assessment. The assessment, evaluation, and research competency area from ACPA and NASPA prescribes quantitative and qualitative methods to use when conducting this type of work. As a Freirean scholar, I conceptualized a dialogical assessment model that I hope will illustrate how scholars and practitioners can utilize theory, research, and assessment to enhance multiculturalism, diversity, social justice, and inclusion on campuses across the country. This model incorporates the professional competencies by placing them on a continuum that is represented with a spiral.

The dialogical assessment model is based on Freire's (1970) concept of conscientizacao, which is when individuals learn "to perceive social, political, and economic contradictions, and to take action against the oppressive elements of reality" (p. 3). This action to overthrow oppressive systems stands to manifest in a variety of forms in an effort to achieve human liberation. Much assessment invariably becomes prescriptive, responds to benchmarking that is set forth by external demands, and perpetuates systemic oppression. Deficit-focused assessment for minoritized populations has saturated assessment and evaluation work over the last few decades. To move away from this type of assessment, it is imperative to understand the dialogical assessment model that I developed. A multicultural campus should allow space to share diverse opinions, must respect various learning styles, and utilize multicultural assessment models that promote diversity, equity, inclusion, and social justice.

Furthermore, Manning and Coleman-Boatwright (1991) encouraged campuses to move beyond individual awareness and education in order to achieve heightened levels of intercultural communication, group awareness and systemic change. This dialogical assessment model places attention on both the tacit and the explicit aspects of multicultural assessment practices and prioritizes dialogue between the student affairs educators, students, faculty, and other campus administrators to prompt systemic change. Good assessment practices start with intentional conversations focused on improvement and extend outward in an effort to wield positive campus change.

The dialogical assessment model shown in Figure 1 attempts to connect Freirean conscientizacao with assessment to promote a paradigmatic shift in the way we think about multicultural assessment. The dialogical assessment model utilizes a spiral to illustrate how assessment on college campuses should be a multi-dimensional process. The practice of assessment work is a process. The spiral demonstrates how each component relies on other components to progress throughout the continuum.

The components described in Figure 1 are not new. In fact, when examined closely, they reflect the CAS Standards for assessment and evaluation. Rather than situating the components in a rigid construct however, the spiral allows for flexibility and nuances associated with assessing multicultural, diversity, and social justice efforts. Pope, Reynolds, and Mueller (2004) suggested that enhancing multicultural awareness, knowledge, and skills for all higher education leaders is critical to create educational environments that embrace diversity. The aspects in this model include: self-reflection, listen, give voice, invite critique, establish outcomes, employ multiple methods, value identities, document progress, gauge intention verses impact, present findings, and make decisions. Below you will find an explanation of the components within the dialogical assessment model and how they relate to the CAS standards and professional competencies to help promote comprehensive multicultural assessment.

Self-Reflection

Self-reflection encourages the student affairs educators to consider their views of the world, explore their ethics, and reflect on their behaviors within the spaces they occupy. Consider why you want to conduct the proposed assessment. Some questions to guide you through the self-reflection process might include:

- What contribution will your role within the multicultural assessment process make to support minoritized student populations on your campus?

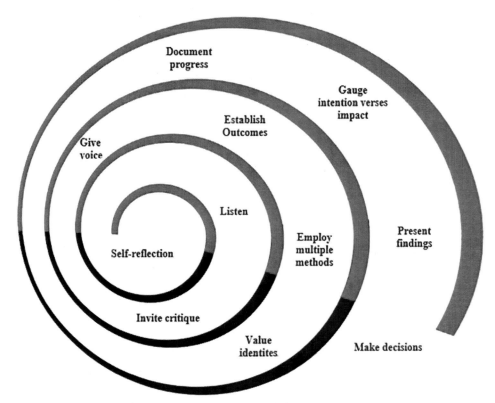

Figure 1. Dialogical Assessment Model. Note: The spiral is representative of a continuous assessment process. While some components of the model will occur in a specific order, they are not organized in a rigid manner. Some components in the model may occur before others, and some components may need to be revisited more frequently.

- What approaches will you infuse into your assessment practices to ensure that you are building trust within the population under study?
- How might your findings support minoritized students and/or create a more inclusive campus environment?
- What hurdles might you encounter while conducting this assessment?
- When considering your positionality on your campus, are there factors that you need to account for in order to successfully execute the assessment?

After reflecting on your role within the process, you will begin to move forward to conduct the assessment. Freire (1970) asserts that self-reflection leads to action. Within this dialogical assessment model, you will advance to the next step of listening after participating in self-assessment in an effort to engage in authentic dialogue to support our students.

Listen

In the dialogical assessment model, listening is an essential element. If conscientizacao is to be achieved, the student affairs educator must listen to the minoritized students, faculty and staff on campus. Listening requires that the receiver attach meaning to the information shared by the students, faculty, and staff. Without attaching meaning to the information provided, the shared information may become meaningless, may allow for misinterpretation, and could undermine the purpose of the multicultural assessment. In practicing good listening, programmatic goals and intended outcomes will be developed. The identification of student learning and development outcomes could also be formed which are identified as steps in the CAS standards.

Invite Critique

One aspect of inviting critique involves remaining conscious of your bias and assumptions related to the particular population or campus phenomena under scrutiny. Invite critique of your methodological approaches with those involved in the assessment. Be mindful that your methods are appropriately and accurately representing the minoritized population. Maintaining an open door to critique may be one way for the practitioner or scholar to establish rapport and trust. This practice of inviting critique is also intended to minimize error and increase reliability.

Give Voice

One way to establish trust within any community is to engage in dialogue and allow minoritized voices to be heard. Give voice to the issues that minoritized students, faculty and staff call to attention. According the CAS standards, student affairs educators are encouraged to use multiple measures and methods when conducting assessment work. The assessment protocol should not exclude or silence anyone. The selection of inclusive assessment methods is critical if the practitioner intends to share the nuanced aspects often associated with minoritized populations.

Another critical aspect assigned to giving voice considers another CAS guideline which relates to moving toward the development of procedures in order to gather, interpret, and evaluate data. This practice within the dialogical assessment model intentionally explores the narratives of the students under study and takes great strides to broaden the scope of the assessment or evaluation in order to increase impact and influence lives. 'Give voice' incorporates the student voices and utilizes various data points in order to support the students.

Establish Outcomes

Set forth clear outcomes that are measurable and relatable to your campus and to the program or student population being assessed. Ensure that student learning is a component of these outcomes along with developmental outcomes. These outcomes should be empowering and compliment the 'give voice' component mentioned above. The goal is to recognize minoritized students and remove systems of oppression that have silenced these individuals. When establishing outcomes using the dialogical assessment model, consider setting outcomes that are developmental, supportive, and intended to enhance the lived experiences of our students.

Employ Multiple Methods

This aspect of the dialogical assessment model mirrors the CAS standards for assessment and evaluation. Identify multi-modal methods to assess culture, multicultural competence, and campus climate on your campus. Utilizing one methodological approach may provide some valuable information, however in order to understand how to conduct multicultural assessment, it is important that practitioners go deeper by using more than one approach. Furthermore, as student affairs educators we must refer back to the purpose of the assessment, consider the outcomes, and then use different methods to conduct the assessment. Employing multiple methods increases reliability and values the dialogical aspects of the model. In order to appropriately 'give voice' to those who are minoritized on our campuses, we must find avenues to appropriately measure, evaluate, and value their experiences.

Value Identities

Another component of the dialogical assessment model is to value the minoritized populations and their identities in addition to the cultures and beliefs they espouse. As student affairs educators we must reject colorblindness and discrimination of any kind, respect the beauty and power found in the uniqueness of culture, identity, and the intersections that permeate within these various identities. In order to appropriately value the identities of those under study, the data need to come from the individuals or groups being assessed. The student affairs practitioner must be intentional in the methodological approach so that the assessment or evaluation responds to humanness, upholds dignity, and values the various identities on our campuses. Devaluing identities will undermine the premise of multicultural assessment and will end in the perpetuation of oppressive systems, which is in direct opposition of the concept of Freire's conscientizacao.

Document Progress

Student affairs educators should take particular care to identify progress toward the goals and/or outcomes. The CAS standards invite student affairs educators to document progress. Because culture is dynamic, documenting progress at various checkpoints throughout the assessment is necessary to ensure that the minoritized populations are accurately represented, to confirm that minoritized voices are heard, and to safeguard against bias.

Additionally, documenting the progress with participants and others involved in the campus community will create transparency. This transparency may assist in establishing and maintaining trust. Outwardly sharing progress offers a way to communicate with all stakeholders and increases the knowledge regarding the types of evaluation, research, and assessment being conducted on campus.

Gauge Intention Versus Impact

While the intention is often positive, the student affairs educator must be cognizant of the potential impacts associated with the assessment results. These impacts could lead to unintended consequences that could do more harm than good for the minoritized students, faculty, or staff. To avoid the unintended consequences by the impacts, we need to consider revisiting the components above such as self-reflection, listen, give voice, invite critique, and value identities in an attempt to mitigate damaging impact. Additionally, the student affairs educator must consider the goals and intended outcomes by paying keen attention to respect of culture, identity, and experience. To do so we must ask ourselves and our assessment team the following questions:

- How do we expect the assessment will impact the students, faculty, and staff on campus?
- What measures can be incorporated into the methodology to mitigate unforeseen damages, should they arise?

The onus of responsibility falls on the student affairs educators when conducting multicultural assessment. We should be cautious when doing assessment work to mitigate possible damage and uphold the values set forth by our professional competencies and CAS standards.

Present Findings

Considering the dialogical assessment model that is hinged on continued conversation between the various stakeholders involved in the assessment, it is critical to present the findings in a transparent and purposeful manner. As student affairs practitioners we must provide the findings to the groups who participated in the study and mindfully engage in dialogue about the findings with students, faculty, and staff. We also must take care to share the findings in an intelligible manner that is culturally relevant and represents the various individuals, groups, and identities of those who participated in the study. Moreover, we must make sure to give voice to the findings that challenge the status quo. When sharing controversial findings, we must be cognizant not to minimize those findings, but rather expose those findings in an appropriate manner. In addition, we must remember that the purpose of good evaluation is to make decisions regarding our students, programs, and campuses. Decision makers on college campuses can use the findings to guide initiatives, policies, and programming.

Make Decisions

The ultimate purpose of assessment is for student affairs educators to use data collected from assessment measures to make decisions and inform planning. By using the evaluation results, student affairs educators can reiterate the results and support why decisions are being made within the program, department, or university. These decisions should be based on the findings, which should consider any anticipated impact on the minoritized student, faculty, and staff populations. This component of the dialogical assessment model should encourage decision making and prompt changes, if warranted. These decisions should not be made in silos or based on isolated findings. These decisions should be grounded in theory, research, and assessment in order to enhance multiculturalism, diversity, social justice, and inclusion on campus.

Continue Revisiting the Dialogical Assessment Model

The projected growth in the diversity of the United States population should not be the catalyst to enact change on college campuses for heterogeneous student populations. It must come from a place of consciousness and intentionality in order to genuinely offer support to the students our institutions serve. According to Pope, Reynolds and Mueller (2014) "as long as only a few experts are responsible for addressing multicultural issues on campus, lasting and consequential multicultural change is unlikely to occur" (p. 6). Following the conclusion of an evaluation, it is imperative to continue the dialogue. The dialogical assessment model cautions against a one-time assessment because it would fail to initiate transformative change. Continued assessment is required, which is why a spiral is used to demonstrate the concept. Revisiting each concept on a routine basis to perform assessment work is required.

CONCLUSION

At the beginning of this chapter, a case study was presented wherein Doctor Carroll, the vice president of student affairs at Statestown University, challenged her staff to focus on assessment and learning outcomes in order to support the students at Statestown. With racial tensions rising, the campus climate at Statestown could be perceived as volatile. Doctor Carroll calls the student affairs educators to participate in assessment and evaluation with specific focus on assessing diversity, multicultural, and social justice programs. While her approach could be criticized as being abrupt, she leaves little room for misinterpretation. Her decisions will be guided by assessment and evaluation. All student affairs educators who report to her must prioritize assessment and evaluation practices that respect and value minoritized student populations.

Doctor Carroll recognizes that as a leader, she must have a clear understanding of the campus programs, services, and initiatives, particularly as they pertain to diversity, social justice, and inclusion. Doctor Carroll challenges all her staff to gather a clear understanding of the measurable outcomes from various programmatic activities. Doctor Carroll seems to understand that satisfaction surveys and attendance do not capture the nuances associated with student learning, much less diversity, inclusion, and social justice efforts.

As Statestown University increasingly grapples with navigating the political landscape and attempts to respond to external accreditors and legislators, Doctor Carroll understands that the division of student affairs plays an integral role in recruitment, retention, and graduation efforts. Assessment of current student affairs programs and initiatives is a first step to responding to these outside stakeholders. Significant attention must be given to the work of diversity, social justice, and inclusion at Statestown University in order to promote a more inclusive campus and support the students at Statestown.

Questions to Consider

1. Reflect on how the dialogical model of assessment can be implemented on your campus.
2. In thinking about assessment and evaluation, how might you incorporate self-reflective practices into the work that you do?
3. What are some ways you can begin to incorporate the dialogical assessment model into your student affairs practice?

4. Within your current role, how might you invite conversations pertaining to inclusive assessment and evaluation practices?
5. What are some necessary assessment and evaluative methods? Explain one in detail and provide an example of how it may be used on a college campus.

REFERENCES

ACPA-College Student Educators International. (2006). *ASK standards: Assessment skills and knowledge content standards for student affairs practitioners and scholars.* Washington, D.C.: Author.

ACPA-College Student Educators International & NASPA-Student Affairs Administrators in Higher Education. (2015). *Professional competency areas for student affairs practitioners.* Washington, D.C.: Author.

American Council on Education. (1937). *The student personnel point of view.* Washington, DC.: Author.

American Council on Education. (1949). *The student personnel point of view* (Rev. ed.). Washington, DC: Author.

Banta, T., & Palomba, C. (2015). *Assessment essentials: Planning, implementing, and improving assessment in higher education* (2nd ed.). San Francisco, CA: Jossey-Bass.

Barr, D. J., & Strong, L. J. (1988). Embracing multiculturalism: The existing contradictions. *NASPA Journal, 26,* 85-90.

Bresciani, M., Zelna, C., & Anderson, J. (2004). *Assessing student development and learning: A handbook for practitioners.* Washington, DC: NASPA-Student Affairs Administrators in Higher Education.

Brown, C. (1991). Increasing minority access to college: Seven efforts for success. *NASPA Journal, 26,* 85-90.

Council for the Advancement of Standards in Higher Education. (2015). *CAS professional standards for higher education* (9th ed.). Washington, DC: Author.

Cross, E. Y., Katz, J. H., Miller, F. A., & Seashore, E. W. (Eds.). (1994). *The promise of diversity: Over 40 voices discuss strategies for eliminating discrimination in organizations.* Boston, MA: McGraw-Hill.

Ebbers, L. H., & Henry, S. L. (1990). Cultural competence: A new challenge to student affairs professionals. *NASPA Journal, 27,* 319-323.

Flash, L. J. (2010). *Multicultural competence in student affairs organizations (MCSAO) questionnaire: Research summary.* Unpublished manuscript.

Freire, P. (1970). *Pedagogy of the oppressed.* New York, NY: Continuum.

Greiger, I. (1996). A multicultural organizational development checklist for student affairs. *Journal of College Student Development, 37,* 561-573.

Greiger, I., & Toliver, S. (2001). Multiculturalism on predominantly White campuses: Multiple roles and functions for the counselor. In J. G. Ponterrotto, J. M. Casas, L. A. Suzuki, & C. M. Alexander (Eds.), *Handbook of multicultural counseling* (2nd ed., pp. 825-848). Thousand Oaks, CA: Sage.

Harper, S. R., & Hurtado, S. (2007). Nine themes in campus racial climates and implications for institutional transformation. *New Directions for Student Services, 120,* 7-22.

Henning, G. W., & Roberts, D. R. (2016). *Student affairs assessment: Theory to practice.* Sterling, VA: Stylus.

Holvino, E. (2008). Developing multicultural organizations: A change model. http://www.chaosmanagement.com/images/stories/pdfs/MCODmodel.pdf

Hurtado, S. (2009). Assessing higher education advancement toward a new vision of society. *Diversity & Democracy, 12*(1), 1-3.

Hurtado, S., & Guillermo-Wann, C. (2013). *Diverse learning environments: Assessing and creating conditions for student success.* Final report to the Ford Foundation. University of California, Los Angeles: Higher Education Research Institute.

Jackson, B. W., & Hardiman, R. (1981). *Organizational stages of multicultural awareness.* Amherst, MA: New Perspectives.

Jackson, B. W., & Hardiman, R. (1994). Multicultural organizational development. In E. Y. Cross, J. J. Katz, F. A. Miller, & E. W. Seashore (Eds.), *The promise of diversity: Over 40 voices discuss strategies for eliminating discrimination in organizations* (pp. 231- 239). Boston: MA: McGraw-Hill.

Keeling, R. (Ed.). (2004). *Learning reconsidered: A campus-wide focus on the student experience.* Washington, DC: ACPA-College Student Educators International and NASPA-Student Affairs Administrators in Higher Education.

King, P. M., & Howard-Hamilton, M. (2000). Becoming a multiculturally competent student affairs professional. In NASPA (Ed.), *Diversity on campus* (pp. 26-28). Washington, DC: NASPA.

Komives, S. R., & Woodard, D. B. (Eds.). (1996). *Student services: A handbook for the profession* (3rd ed.). San Francisco, CA: Jossey-Bass.

Krishnamurthi, M. (2003). Assessing multicultural initiatives in higher education institutions. *Assessment and Evaluation in Higher Education, 28,* 263-277.

Kuh, G. D., & Whitt, E. J. (1988). *The invisible tapestry: Culture in American colleges and universities* (ASHE-ERIC Higher Education Report No. 1). Washington, DC: Association for the Study of Higher Education.

Manning, K., & Coleman-Boatwright, P. (1991). Student affairs initiative toward multicultural university. *Journal of College Student Development, 32,* 367-374.

McClellan, S. A., Cogdal, P. A., Lease, S. J., & Londono-McConnell, A. (1996). Development of the multicultural assessment of campus programming (MAC-P) questionnaire. *Measurement and Evaluation in Counseling and Development, 29*(2), 86-99.

McEwen, M. K., & Roper, L. D. (1994). Incorporating multiculturalism into student affairs preparation programs: Suggestions from the literature. *Journal of College Student Development, 35,* 46-53.

Mueller, J. A., & Pope, R. L. (2001). The relationship between multicultural competence and white racial consciousness among student affairs practitioners. *Journal of College Student Development, 42,* 133-144.

Padilla, A. M. (2004). Quantitative methods in multicultural education research. In J. A. Banks & C. A. M. Banks (Eds.), *Handbook of research on multicultural education* (pp. 127-145). San Francisco, CA: Jossey-Bass.

Pope, R. L. (1992). *An analysis of multiracial change efforts in student affairs* (Doctoral Dissertation, University of Massachusetts Amherst). Retrieved from ProQuest (order # 9305881).

Pope, R. L., & LePeau, L. A. (2011). The influence of institutional context and culture. In J. Arminio, V. Torres & R. L. Pope (Eds.), *Why aren't we there yet? Taking personal responsibility for creating an inclusive campus* (pp. 103-130). Sterling, VA: Stylus.

Pope, R. L., & Mueller, J. A. (2000). Development and initial validation of the Multicultural Competence in Student Affairs—Preliminary 2 scale. *Journal of College Student Development, 41,* 599-608.

Pope, R. L., Mueller, J. A., & Reynolds, A. L. (2009). Looking back and moving forward: Future directions for diversity in student affairs. *Journal of College Student Development, 50,* 640-658.

Pope, R., & Reynolds, A. L. (1997). Student affairs core competencies: Integrating multicultural awareness, knowledge, and skills. *Journal of College Student Development, 38,* 266-277.

Pope, R. Reynolds, A. L., & Mueller, J. (2014). *Creating multicultural change on campus.* San Francisco, CA: Jossey-Bass.

Pope, R., Reynolds, A. L, & Mueller, J. A. (2004). *Multicultural competence in student affairs.* San Francisco, CA: Jossey-Bass.

Rankin, S. R., & Reason, R. D. (2005). Differing perceptions: How students of color and White students perceive campus climate for underrepresented groups. *Journal of College Student Development, 46,* 43-61.

Sandeen, A., & Barr, M. J. (2006). *Critical issues for student affairs: Challenges and opportunities.* San Francisco, CA: Jossey-Bass.

Schuh, J. H., Biddix, J. P., Dean, L. A., & Kinzie, J. (2016). *Assessment in student affairs* (2nd ed.). San Francisco, CA: Jossey-Bass.

Shotton, H. J., Lowe, S. C., & Waterman, S. J. (2013). *Beyond the asterisk: Understanding native students in higher education.* Sterling, VA: Stylus.

Smith, D. G. (2009). *Diversity's promise for higher education: Making it work.* Baltimore, MD: Johns Hopkins University Press.

Smith, D. G., & Parker, S. (2005). Organizational learning: A tool for diversity and institutional effectiveness. *New Directions for Higher Education, 131,* 113-125.

Sue, D. W. (1995). Multicultural organization development: Implications for the counseling profession. In J. G. Ponterrotto, J. M. Casas, L. A. Suzuki, & C. M. Alexander (Eds.), *Handbook of multicultural counseling* (2nd ed., pp. 825-848). Thousand Oaks, CA: Sage.

Sue, D. W. (2001). Multiple dimensional facets of cultural competence. *The Counseling Psychologist, 29,* 790-821.

Sue, D. W., Bernier, J. E., Durran, A., Feinberg, L., Pederson, P., Smith, E. J., & Vasques-Nuttall, E. (1982). Position paper: Cross-cultural counseling competencies. *Counseling Psychologist, 10*(2), 45-52.

Suskie, L. (2009). *Assessing student learning: A common sense guide* (2nd ed.). San Francisco, CA: Jossey-Bass.

Talbot, D. M. (1996). Multiculturalism. In S. R. Komives & D. B. Woodard (Eds.), *Student services: A handbook for the profession* (3rd ed., pp. 380-396). San Francisco: CA: Jossey-Bass.

Upcraft, M., & Schuh, J. (1996). *Assessment in student affairs: A guide for practitioners.* San Francisco, CA: Jossey-Bass.

Wehlburg, C. M. (2008). *Promoting integrated and transformative assessment: A deeper focus on student learning.* San Francisco, CA: Jossey-Bass.

Wilkinson, W. K., & McNeil, K. (1996). *Research for the helping profession.* Cincinnati, OH: Brooks/Cole.

Chapter 12

IMPLEMENTING SOCIAL JUSTICE: FORMING A PROFESSIONAL IDENTITY

Evette L. Allen & Chayla Haynes

CASE STUDY

Josie is the program advisor for the multicultural organization round-table (MORT) and a second-year master's student in the Student Affairs and Higher Education program at Mission State University. As she was packing up to head to her afternoon advanced student development theory course, she received a visitor. John Carlos, a junior at Mission State and Chair of MORT stopped by to chat with her. John was not always the Chair of MORT. He assumed the role, after another student unexpectedly stepped down the semester before. Under John's leadership, the MORT successfully facilitated a self-initiated redesign, coordinated campus-wide cultural heritage programming, and held its inaugural student leader retreat. The Student Activities professional staff were also greatly impressed with John. Josie had begun talking to him about a future career in student affairs and John was excited by the idea. To foster John's growing interest in a career in student affairs, Josie's supervisor encouraged him to apply to NASPA's Undergraduate Fellows Program (NUFP) and agreed to serve as his mentor. So, when John stopped by unexpectedly, Josie thought he was coming by to get more information about the NUFP program.

Instead, John was there for more personal reasons. John shared something with Josie that she did not know after nearly two years of advising MORT. John was undocumented and he had legitimate concerns about his status because of the uncertainty of the Deferred Action for Childhood Arrivals (DACA) program. He shared with Josie that any repeal of DACA can undermine his long-term goal to apply for graduate

259

school and pursue a career in student affairs. Josie did not know what to say, but immediately felt the gravity of the situation. Josie let John know how much she appreciated that he shared that information with her and she would help where she could. As Josie left the office for class, she wondered to herself, "where can I do the most good?" and "how can I best assist this student?"

As we write this chapter, student affairs educators across the United States are contending with a multitude of social justice issues that are affecting the everyday lives of their diverse (and seemingly most vulnerable) students. The state legislation to keep transgender students from using public bathrooms on campus that align with their gender identity, the campus rebellions to fight the pervasive racism and White supremacy at institutions such as the University of Virginia, the U.S. travel ban on refugees from Muslim majority countries, the threats to repeal Affirmative Action and the Deferred Action for Childhood Arrivals (DACA) are just a few of the many turbulent circumstances that are shaping sociopolitical context of higher education and student affairs work today. Accordingly, College Student Educators International (ACPA) and Student Affairs Administrators in Higher Education (NASPA) have argued that student affairs educators with complex understanding of power, privilege and oppression are needed to advance the profession's commitment to social justice and inclusion in higher education. Our chapter aims to support new and future student affairs educators in developing the knowledge, skills, and dispositions needed to employ social justice orientations in practice. In this chapter, we argue that social justice orientation is a critical skill and central to student affairs work and thus, to work in student affairs effectively, a social justice orientation is needed. The chapter begins with a discussion about social justice in student affairs work and the case for student affairs educators with a social justice orientation. Next, we offer recommendations for student affairs educators to consider as they seek to incorporate social justice into everyday practices. Finally, the chapter closes with an application exercise, where readers can use the material presented in this chapter to process the exemplar case above.

SOCIAL JUSTICE AND INCLUSION: AN EVERYDAY PRACTICE

Social Justice and Inclusion is a core competency area of student affairs work and preparation (ACPA & NASPA, 2015). Development in this competency area helps student affairs educators to foster identity affirming and socially just learning environments for students of all backgrounds. While these values are often emphasized as important, they are not always enacted with the same level of importance (Linder, Harris, Allen, & Hubain, 2015). Thus, the purpose of this chapter is to introduce graduate students and future student affairs professionals to information that will assist in developing a professional identity through the lens of social justice, or in other terms, become a student affairs educator equipped to do critical social justice work in the field. The chapter will emphasize the need for social justice to be viewed as an ongoing process (Cuyjet, Howard-Hamilton & Cooper, 2011; Landreman, King, Rasmussen, & Jiang, 2007) rather than a checkmark on a checklist of competencies. To checkmark oneself as socially just is assuming that social justice work is finite, when it is indeed a process and a goal (ACPA & NASPA, 2015; Bell, 2013). For example, Danowitz and Tuitt (2011) reevaluated a higher education program to embed social justice into the fabric of their program, rather than just a one-time course. Such practices affirm that developing a true social justice orientation extends beyond one course or workshop and indeed takes time and intentional effort. This type of social justice orientation should be a part of the identity of student affairs educators wherein they are able to reflect on social justice practices for every aspect of Student Affairs. From new student orientation (Boening, 2005), advising students, to public policy affecting students and planning inclusive programs, student affairs educators should have a keen attention to matters of social justice throughout the field of student affairs and the world. Therefore, the authors offer tools to move student affairs educators, graduate students in student affairs programs and future student affairs educators from a mere appreciation for social justice to social justice praxis. Individuals who read the chapter will be challenged to evaluate how they currently use and incorporate principles of social justice, leaving them with tools to embed social justice into their everyday practices as student affairs educators.

The Case for Social Justice Oriented Student Affairs Educators

For the purposes of this chapter, *student affairs educators* are individuals who are committed to a career of assisting students with gaining critical knowledge and skills about themselves and society. Student affairs educators are key individuals who lead the path in ensuring that students in institutions of higher education are in environments where they feel valued and included. It will be essential that such individuals lead the way to ensure that an increasingly diverse student body has policies and practices that employ equity and align well with changing demographics.

For several decades within student affairs there have been conversations related to the competencies and knowledge needed for aspiring and new student affairs educators (Burkard, Cole, Ott, & Stoflet, 2005). These competencies are used to ensure that aspiring and new student affairs educators meet the demands of the field and are able to effectively work with students from all backgrounds. Over the last decade there have been more comprehensive outlines for such competencies as evidenced in publications such as the ACPA and NASPA (2015) Joint Task Force document. One area in particular, the call for student affairs educators with a social justice orientation, is ever-present as student affairs educators are called to be the backbone of inclusive growth for the field of Student Affairs in years to come. Several authors note social justice and understanding underrepresented populations as essential learning components for student affairs educators (Burkard, Cole, Ott, & Stoflet, 2005; Castellanos, Mayorga, & Salas, 2008; Pope, Reynolds, & Mueller, 2004).

In this vein, it is important to note that the field of student affairs certainly values social justice. However, it is just as important to acknowledge the path to social justice as the field has shifted from attention to diversity to a social justice orientation. The authors acknowledge this shift by highlighting the Social Justice and Inclusion competency as mentioned in the ACPA and NASPA (2015) Joint Task Force document where it is listed that a social justice orientation should be a process and a goal with the goal of full and equal participation of all groups in a society that is mutually shaped to meet their needs. *Social Justice* is defined as "both a process and a goal that includes the knowledge, skills, and dispositions needed to create learning environments that foster equitable participation of all groups and seeks to address issues of oppression, privilege, and power" (ACPA & NASPA, 2015, p. 14). Social justice is not simply raising awareness, but rather actively addressing issues of systemic oppression in ways that lead to more equitable policies and practices (Goodman, 2001; Watt, 2007).

Using the above definition, student affairs educators are needed to lead the way in dismantling systems of oppression for the betterment of individuals, institutions, and ultimately our world, and to lead the critical learning, both within and outside of the classroom, that takes place for students on college campuses. As leaders in the field, social justice educators can call into question practices that are not equitable to all and work with students to develop a critical consciousness wherein they are able to advocate for marginalized students. Students who are educated about diversity and social justice issues are more likely to have a greater moral development (Parker, Barnhardt, Pascarella, & McCowin, 2016), which can extend to empathy and advocacy for others. Thus, as student affairs educators are developing their skills as social justice advocates, they are better able to assist students on the students' social justice journey.

Further, the need for student affairs educators with a social justice orientation is evidenced in reports from students with marginalized identities navigating college campuses. Since students from various marginalized backgrounds report feelings of isolation and hostile campus climates (Howard-Hamilton, Phelps, & Torres, 1998; Linder, Harris, Allen, & Hubain, 2015; Seelman, 2014), it is important that student affairs educators learn the appropriate knowledge, skills, and disposition to create equitable learning environments that challenge power, privilege and oppression (ACPA & NASPA, 2015) and help develop students from all backgrounds. For example, on college campuses, students of color experience racial microaggressions and negative experiences in the classroom resulting in feeling devalued and marginalized (Linder, Harris, Allen, & Hubain, 2015). Related to gender, transgender students report difficulty within housing on college campuses (Seelman, 2014). Specifically, such individuals are at higher risks for being denied access to housing and bathrooms on college campuses. Additionally, genderqueer and transitioning students are navigating college spaces where they are not understood and some student affairs practitioners and educators view their efforts as inappropriate (Marine, 2011). In all examples listed above, social justice educators with the knowledge, skills, and dispositions to advocate on issues of social justice, power, privilege, and oppression are better able to support students.

Understanding the need for student affairs educators to develop a social justice orientation, future and aspiring student affairs educators need the self-awareness, knowledge and skills to develop and maintain a social justice orientation.

HOW TO DEVELOP A SOCIAL JUSTICE ORIENTATION AS A STUDENT AFFAIRS EDUCATOR

Using the definition referenced above, a student affairs educator has *a commitment to a journey of gaining the knowledge, skills, and dispositions needed to create equitable learning environments across multiple identities.* As an individual working or aspiring to work within the field of student affairs, it is essential to possess a social justice orientation.

Developing a social justice competence as a student affairs educator includes awareness, knowledge, skills, and dispositions (ACPA & NASPA, 2015; Castellanos, Gloria, Mayora, & Salas, 2007; Chun & Evans, 2016; Howard-Hamilton, Cuyjet, & Cooper, 2011; Pope, Reynolds, &Mueller, 2004). *Multicultural Awareness* is the attitudes, beliefs, values, and self-awareness needed to serve students from various cultural backgrounds; *Multicultural Knowledge* is the information individuals have about various cultures; and *Multicultural Skills* allow an individual to have the necessary tools for effective communication across cultures (Pope, Reynolds, &Mueller, 2004).

Multicultural Dispositions are the characteristics displayed that show commitment to dismantling power, privilege, and oppression (ACPA & NASPA, 2015).

Therefore, a person working within student affairs should embody the following: (1) a disposition that allows him/her/hir to identify systems of socialization and how those systems affect an individuals' opportunities or lack thereof; (2) an understanding of how individuals maintain systems of power, privilege and oppression; (3) the ability to engage in critical reflection to identify personal biases; (4) an openness to learning opportunities that advance ones understanding of inclusion, oppression, privilege, and power; (5) the ability to translate knowledge of social justice into practice; and (6) the passion to advocate on issues related to social justice (ACPA & NASPA, 2015; Howard-Hamilton, Cuyjet, & Cooper, 2011; Pope, Reynolds, & Mueller, 2004).

An understanding of what it takes to be a student affairs educator precedes the action needed to move toward a journey of commitment. By commitment, we mean a commitment to address power, privilege and oppression in practice. Thus, we argue that to develop as a social justice educator requires that you: (a) know your privileged and marginalized identities, (b) understand socialization to oppression, (c) know your biases, and (d) be able to translate knowledge into practice. Each of these areas speaks to the knowledge, skills, and/or dispositions needed to effectively advocate for social justice as a student affairs educator.

Understand Yourself and Your Privileges

An understanding of self in relation to social justice is a critical first step as a social justice educator. It is important that student affairs educators also acknowledge that they are constantly evolving and their development will take time. The process of learning about oneself is not concrete, and thus must be a continuous journey (Ortiz & Patton, 2012). In this same vein, student affairs educators must recognize that developing their social justice orientation will be a continuous journey made up of intentional daily tasks. For example, when an individual hears a stereotypical comment made by a family member or co-worker, there is a decision to be made to be intentional about addressing the stereotype or to dismiss the stereotype. Such an act may seem small, but could be the reality that the family member or co-worker needs to spotlight ignorance. As student affairs educators learn more about their identities, the ways that they maintain or are complicit in disenfranchising marginalized populations, specific and intentional action must be taken. These daily lessons and intentional action will be how student affairs educators develop their social justice orientation.

Student affairs educators with a social justice orientation are aware of his/her/hir own assumptions, biases, and values and have an understanding of various worldviews and cultures (Pope, Reynolds, & Mueller, 2004). Knowledge of the self goes beyond knowing yourself to also understanding yourself in relation to others (Ortiz & Patton, 2012). This includes a critical interrogation of self as it relates to one's upbringing and socialization messages around that upbringing (Ortiz & Patton, 2012). It is not enough to want the world to be more equitable, there has to be some self-work and action as well. Starting with assessing social identities is a great entryway.

In the words of Harro (2013), "We must begin by making an inventory of our own social identities with relationship to each issue of oppression" (p. 46). Social identities are those identities that have an impact on how individuals are able to strategically move through spaces. Social identities include but are not limited to identities based on race, ethnicity, gender, sexual orientation, religious and spiritual beliefs, and disability status. Social identities affect how individuals move through spaces and issues of opportunity and access. Understanding social identities also calls for understanding identities of privilege and marginalized identities. Thus, a student affairs educator with a social justice orientation is a person who has taken assessment of his/her/hir identities in ways that allow him/her/hir to acknowledge identities of privilege and marginalization. Privileged identities are those where benefits are granted based on an identity and individuals enjoy membership in groups that hold power (Adams, Bell, & Griffin, 1997). "The term *privileged identity* refers to an identity that is historically linked to social or political advantages in this society" (Watt, 2007). By the same token, marginalized groups often have a lack of resources and less people in decision-making positions, resulting in the maintenance of power for privileged groups and oppression for marginalized groups (Adams, Bell, & Griffin, 1997). Individuals with privilege should be aware of their privilege in an effort to use it to dismantle systems of oppression for marginalized groups. For example, an able-bodied student affairs educator who starts a discussion to bring attention to the lack of accessibility in a particular building for persons with disabilities has used privilege to bring awareness to a marginalized group. Bialka, Morro, Brown, and Hannah (2017) conducted a study to examine the social experiences of students with disabilities in an organization created with specific attention to their needs. The organization proved to negate assumptions about persons with disabilities and to create a space of visibility for persons with disabilities. Such an organization is an example of a way to support a marginalized group.

Power is evident in scenarios such as the one mentioned above as it presents the opportunity to share stories and to be heard. Most often, those in power have the ears of the masses and those in power have two decisions to advocate or to stand by and say nothing, remaining complicit in systemic oppression. Student affairs educators with privileged identities often have the platform, the voice, and the audience to make a stance about particular issues, and they should use the platform in productive ways that align with the values of the profession.

Individuals who want to develop their social justice orientation should be aware of the areas in which they hold privileges, and how those privileges affect how they move through life. Student affairs educators should ask themselves critical questions such as:

1. What privileged identities do I hold?
2. What are the ways I have benefitted and currently benefit from those privileged identities?
3. What are ways that I have upheld marginalization by being complicit in those benefits?

For example, with attention to race, student affairs educators with White privilege must ask themselves how race affects their lives as well and the lives of both students and their colleagues of Color. With attention to sexual orientation, individuals with heterosexual privilege must ask themselves how sexual orientation affects opportunities for them to move through spaces that are more difficult for students and their colleagues who are marginalized within that identity group. Moreover, an assessment of self assists privileged student affairs educators with taking responsibility for the marginalized experiences of students and colleagues, and the ways privilege is upheld. To turn a blind eye to a system that inherently contributes to oppression, is to move away from a social justice orientation.

Overall, individuals should be prepared to understand, empathize, and advocate for those who are marginalized in areas where they have privilege. Student affairs educators should also be aware of the negative effects privilege can have on those who hold it as well (Howard-Hamilton & Hinton, 2011). For example, socialization into roles and patterns of behavior, denial of emotions and empathy, limited self-knowledge and a distorted view of self, discrepancy between external perception and internal realities, fears and pain, and diminished mental health (Goodman, 2001; Howard-Hamilton & Hinton, 2011) are a few ways that privilege can affect those in dominant groups. In essence, attention to privileged identities is important for privileged and marginalized groups. Social justice educators should use this reflection on self and self in relation to others to take those daily steps toward developing their social justice orientation.

Understand Socialization to Oppression

Understanding yourself is a first step, but once individuals have knowledge of social identities, individuals must also understand their levels of socialization. *Socialization* can be an unknown effect for marginalized or privileged individuals wherein they succumb to the socially prescribed norms of behavior for their identity group (Lock & Strong, 2010). An individual's social identities affect cultural practices, worldviews, ideas, and values, thus knowledge of one's own culture and understanding about life is critical (Cuyjet & Duncan, 2013). Harro (2013) discusses a revised socialization process that assists individuals in understanding how their multiple identities affect their values, beliefs, and worldview. In sum, the model emphasizes that individuals are born into a world where oppression already exists and whereby those closest to us along with social institutions (i.e. education, religion, government) instill within us who should have power and who should not. Rewards to those who maintain the status quo and the persecution of those that seek to dismantle the norm, reinforce this socialization. The result is either those who remain silent, do nothing and let the cycle continue, or those who recognize the inequity in such a cycle and seek to challenge the system. Below are the pieces of the cycle of socialization explained.

1. The beginning of the cycle, indicated as the first circle in the model, highlights that individuals are born into identities they did not choose, and thus are born into a world that already has established social norms in relation to their identities.
2. The first socialization, indicated by the first arrow in the model, points to the ways close family members help to socialize people by teaching them the roles and rules they must follow. This affects how they view themselves and others, how they interact with others, and how they relate to others. These messages are learned from those closest to us and can send positive or negative messages about individuals, groups, and social justice.
3. Institutional and Cultural Socialization, indicated by the second circle in the model, occurs as individuals come into contact with social institutions such as school, places of workshop, businesses, media, etc. The social norms previously established upon entering the world are now learned and serve as rules for engaging.
4. Enforcements, indicated by the second arrow in the model, emphasizes the pressure to maintain the status quo and how individuals watch those who adhere to the status quo receive rewards while they watch those who do not adhere to the status quo get ridiculed.

5. Results, indicated by the third circle in the model, point to how the cycle of socialization is devastating for all, marginalized and privileged groups. Results could be misperception, dissonance, silence, stress, collusion, anger, guilt, hate, self-hatred, violence, crime, etc.
6. Actions, indicated by the third arrow in the model, concerns the choice to take action and disrupt the cycle or the choice to remain silent and content with the current state of affairs.

Understanding personal socialization assists individuals with advocating for marginalized groups and for understanding the concerns of marginalized groups. For example, people of color are more likely to discern instances of racism on college campuses in comparison to White students (Pfeifer & Schneider, 1974; Strayhorn, 2013), and gender non-conforming individuals are more likely to experience harsh living conditions on college campuses (Seelman, 2014). Social justice educators who have tapped into their socialization should be able to reflect on the ways they were socialized and what they may need to learn in order to continue on their journey of social justice. Additionally, student affairs educators who have reflected on their socialization can acknowledge how socialization has affected their individual and group identities. For example, student affairs educators can specifically reflect on how their view of society, their opinion of what is right or wrong, and their biases toward others are impacted by their identities and how they were socialized related to those identities. Understanding that information helps student affairs educators point to and address specific actions that need to occur to unlearn negative socialization based on their identities. For student affairs educators that have done the work to acknowledge how their higher socioeconomic status might affect their view of working class individuals as lazy, they can then make effort to work in spaces or research information that allow them to learn more accurate information about a population which they know little about. Here are a few questions a social justice educator could ask about his/her/hir socialization:

1. In what ways have I been socialized since birth in relation to social identities in which I have privilege?
2. In what ways have I been socialized since birth in relation to social identities in which I am marginalized?
3. In what ways has my socialization affected my beliefs about myself or others?
4. In what ways has my socialization affected how I relate to or interact with others?

Unchecked socialization contributes to the maintenance of power, privilege and systemic oppression. Students and professionals with marginalized identities should not stand alone to bear the brunt of the work associated with meeting their own needs. Student affairs educators with a social justice orientation are invested in understanding how their identities affect how they have been socialized and thus affect their beliefs and values about life and opportunities for others.

Learn and Regularly Check Biases

Biases are preconceived notions about individuals or groups based on our background and experiences. Our biases contain the stories we make up about people before we get to know them and are based on limited information. Learning about biases is an extension of reflecting on one's socialization experience. As reflection on socialization calls for individuals to understand the ways that their identities and messages about their identities affect how they move through spaces, reflection on biases calls for individuals to pay attention to their biases about individuals and groups. Student affairs educators committed to social justice should reflect on social identities, their experiences, and backgrounds to be truthful with themselves about the biases they hold toward certain people or groups. Biases come up regularly and individuals will need to be prepared to move away from them. For example, are you most comfortable around students who look like you and who share your same identities? Do you have long conversations with students who share your same spiritual or religious beliefs, while spending only five minutes with those who do not? Such bias can result in devaluing experiences or further marginalization of some students, and results in a lost opportunity to develop as a social justice educator. Social identities often reflect norms prescribed by society to the extent that the norms often result in biased decisions and actions by and toward certain social groups.

As a student affairs educator, checking your biases helps you to be honest with yourself about the ways that you treat students and other colleagues based on identities. The truth is, you might not always treat everyone the same and it will be important for you to pay attention to the times when you might be more lenient to certain students, more friendly to certain students, or more comfortable with certain students. As a social justice educator, one should pay attention to his/her/hir actions in everyday situations where he/she/ze is more lenient, more comfortable, or friendlier to certain people or groups, and take action to address those biases. When calling out your biases, you don't just stay in that space, but be prepared to take action to reduce those biases. The result is more equitable opportunities for all students. Questions that current and aspiring student affairs educators can ask themselves about bias are:

1. What are my gut reactions when I interact with people from [INSERT IDENTITY] backgrounds?
2. Around what groups or people am I uncomfortable? Why am I uncomfortable in such situations?
3. Around what groups or people am I comfortable? Why am I comfortable in such situations?

Translate Knowledge into Practice

The Behavioral Model of Multicultural Competence (Howard-Hamilton, Cuyjet, & Cooper, 2011) highlights a cycle of multicultural competence that emphasizes how challenging prejudice is a lifelong process. This is one of the many examples of how a social justice orientation must be a daily practice. Social justice advocacy in practice is apparent in a commitment to self-education, use of inclusive language, cultural learning opportunities, respecting differences, and a plan for dealing with resistance and feelings of defeat.

Self-education is accepting the responsibility for learning about other groups with which one will be working. In practice this may be regularly reading articles about cultures you do not understand, stepping outside of your comfort zone to network with someone from a culture different than your own, or attending an event or lecture about a topic on which you have very little information. The more you learn about other cultures, the more opportunities you have to learn about yourself. Understanding cultural values, practices and history of various groups can also contribute to avoiding cultural appropriation. "Cultural appropriation is the lifting of aspects of one culture or society for use by another culture. Some of the most commonly appropriated facets of foreign cultures include art, music, and fashion" (Ruth, 2016). Thus, student affairs educators who are knowledgeable about other cultures have demonstrated the initiative and respect to see beyond their identities and values in ways that further develop their social justice orientation.

An examination of language is important so that social justice oriented student affairs educators are aware of language that marginalizes students and other professionals. Thus, a social justice educator should critically evaluate language in ways that question how language upholds stereotypes and reinforces norms in society. In practice this may be awareness and examination of language used to describe students. For example, calling an identity group of students "normal" reinforces that those who do not hold that identity are considered not "normal." Those in power set the tone for what is normal (Adams, Bell, & Griffin, 1997), and a student affairs educator who understands power and oppression is able to work to dismantle common narratives about what is accepted as normal. In practice, effective use of language could also be the ability to take criticism regarding use of language. For example, if a student lets a student affairs educator know that using the word ghetto is racist and offensive, the student affairs educator should evaluate his/her/hir contribution to oppression and view the critique as an opportunity to learn. In sum, a student affairs educator would use the criticism to see how his/her/hir language contributes to oppressive systems rather than ignoring the feedback altogether.

Respect of differences is the ability to view someone as different and still be able to work effectively with that person. A student affairs educator should not have to remove someone's difference to be able to work with and for him/her/zir. Emphasizing a tenet of Critical Race Theory (CRT), a colorblind philosophy does not allow individuals to accept the reality that race heavily impacts the lives of People of Color (Delgado & Stefancic, 2012; Dixson & Rousseau, 2005). Long gone is the concept that America is a melting pot (Adams, Bell, & Griffin, 1997). America as a melting pot is the idea that we all mesh together to form one well-tasting pot of soup or other lovely dish. However, the concept promotes the idea of assimilation (Adams, Bell, & Griffin, 1997) and does not allow agency for non-dominant groups. Instead, the concept of embracing social justice should concentrate on the many ways individuals and groups are different and important to the fabric of our institutions.

Using the definition of social justice by Adams, Bell, and Griffin (2007) with a concentration on the psychological and physical impact on individuals, social justice advocacy should include the challenge of discriminatory policies and practices, biased systems, and ignorance and stereotypes. Essentially, student affairs educators should use knowledge of self and others to ensure equitable spaces for all.

As issues emerge based on ignorance and stereotypes, student affairs educators should challenge those stereotypes and ignorance. Allen (2014) researched the ways that Black students are placed into boxes based on stereotypes about how they should act in relation to their race. Black students in the study indicated that they were labeled as "acting White" for how they spoke, how they dressed, and certain hobbies, among other things. In this vein, Black students were placed into boxes because of others' stereotypes and ignorance. Student affairs educators can challenge such stereotypes through awareness and advocacy.

Finally, student affairs educators need a plan for dealing with resistance and feelings of defeat. As student affairs educators gain more understanding of themselves and systems of oppression, their journey may appear daunting. There are a number of different issues in society that need to be addressed such as police brutality, poverty, access to healthcare and access to education, to name a few, and student affairs educators might find themselves asking the questions, "Where can I do the most good?" Start where you are and use the tools listed above to build from there. As an example, refer to the case study at the beginning of this chapter as we walk you through how to use knowledge and skills related to social justice and transfer that knowledge to everyday practice. In the case study above, Josie was introduced to information from John, the president of a student group advised by Josie. The information John shared was that he was undocumented and that any repeal of DACA could undermine his long-term goal to apply for graduate school and pursue a career in student affairs. Josie was left with the questions: "how can I do the most good?" and "how can I best assist this student?"

First, in understanding her privileges, Josie should consider how her identity in this area could affect how she moves forward with helping this student. Is she completely unaware of this situation because she has not had to think about it; was this a situation that she did not think so serious because it did not affect her? Examining privilege is important to advocating for marginalized groups. Second, in understanding the socialization of oppression, Josie should be aware of how she might uphold oppressive practices as it relates to undocumented students and look for ways to challenge the system rather than idly sit by as undocumented students are further marginalized. Third, as Josie checks her biases, she should be honest about and consider the biases she holds about undocumented students. Understanding her biases, she can move forward with her own research to obtain facts about this population so that she can be well informed moving forward. Finally, Josie can translate her knowledge into practice by taking action and being open to learn more about advocating for this group along the way.

CONCLUSION

The sociopolitical context shaping higher education and student affairs work today demands that student affairs educators adopt a social justice orientation. The adoption of a social justice identity helps student affairs educators to see beyond their worldview and consider the oppression of others so that they can contribute to more equitable policies and practices for all. In that regard, the ACPA/NASPA Joint Taskforce established the social justice and inclusion competency to underscore the importance of this developmental area in student affairs work. Social justice and inclusion are centered in student affairs work because of our profession's commitment to creating learning environments that are identity-affirming and socially just. In that respect, it is imperative that the necessary skills, knowledge and dispositions be developed for educators to effectively engage in student affairs work.

We opened the chapter with an exemplar case that we revisit below. Completing this application exercise will help readers evaluate their professional competence in the area of social justice and inclusion. The questions we pose below will help readers process the case presented and apply the material presented in the chapter. Questions that are difficult for readers to answer highlight social justice and inclusion skills, knowledge, and dispositions that are likely underdeveloped.

1. What privilege might Josie hold that inadvertently makes her unconscious to the oppression that students like John Carlos experience? What privilege identities do you hold? How did you become aware of the blind spots you maintained because of your privilege?
2. What system(s) of oppression are contributing to John Carlos' lived experience? Josie is a student affairs educator at a State University in Student Activities. How does your institution and unit meet the needs of undocumented students?
3. What programs can Josie and her supervisor design to promote greater consciousness among students and colleagues about the oppression that undocumented populations experience?
4. How might student affairs educators advocate for undocumented students to demonstrate that oppression operates at the local (i.e., campus/state), national, and global levels?
5. How might understanding that social justice is a process and goal help Josie manage any feelings of helplessness she may be experiencing?

REFERENCES

Adams, M., Bell, L. A., & Griffin, P. (1997). *Teaching for diversity and social justice.* New York: Routledge.

Adams, M., Bell, L. A., & Griffin, P. (2007). *Teaching for diversity and social justice.* New York: Routledge.

Allen, E. L. (2014). Acting White among Black college students: A phenomenological study of social constructions of race. *Electronic Theses and Dissertations.* 962. https://digitalcommons.du.edu/etd/962

American College Personnel Association and National Association of Student Personnel Administrators, Joint Task Force on Professional Standards and Competencies. (2015). Professional competency areas for student affairs educators.

Retrieved from https://www.naspa.org/images/uploads/main/ACPA_NASPA
_Professional_Competencies_FINAL.pdf

Bell, L. A. (2013). Theoretical foundations. In M. Adams, W. J. Blumenfeld, C. Castaneda, H. Hackman, M. Peters, & X. Zuniga (Eds.), *Readings for diversity and social justice* (pp. 21–25). New York: Routledge.

Bialka, C. C., Morro, D. D., Brown, K. B., & Hannah, G. G. (2017). Breaking barriers and building bridges: Understanding how a student organization attends to the social integration of college students with disabilities. *Journal of Postsecondary Education & Disability, 30*(2), 157–172.

Boening, C. H., & Miller, M. T. (2005). New student orientation programs promoting diversity. *The Community College Enterprise, 11*(2), 41–50.

Burkard, A. W., Cole, D. C., Ott, M., & Stoflet, T. (2005). Entry-level competencies of new student affairs professionals: A Delphi study. *NASPA Journal, 42*(3), 283–309.

Castellanos, J., Gloria, A. M., Mayorga, M. M., & Salas, C. (2008). Student affairs professionals' self-report of multicultural competence: Understanding awareness, knowledge, and skills. *NASPA Journal, 44*(4), 643–663.

Chun, E., & Evans, A. (2016). Rethinking cultural competence in higher education: An ecological framework for student development. *ASHE Higher Education Report, 42*(4), 7–162. doi:10.1002/aehe.20102

Cuyjet, M. J., & Duncan, A. D. (2013). The Impact of cultural competence on the moral development of student affairs professionals. *Journal of College and Character, 14*(4), 301–309.

Cuyjet, M. J., Howard-Hamilton, M. F., & Cooper, D. L. (2011). *Multiculturalism on campus: Theory, models, and practices for understanding diversity and creating inclusion.* Sterling, VA: Stylus Publishing, LLC.

Danowitz, M. A., & Tuitt, F. (2011). Enacting inclusivity through engaged pedagogy: A higher education perspective. *Equity & Excellence in Education, 44*(1), 40–56. doi:10.1080/10665684.2011.539474

Delgado, R., & & Stefancic, J. (2012). *Critical race theory: An introduction* (2nd ed.). New York, NY: New York University Press.

Dixson, A. D., & Rousseau, C. K. (2005). And we are still not saved: Critical race theory in education ten years later. *Race, Ethnicity, and Education, 8*(1), 7–27.

Goodman, D. (2001). *Promoting diversity and social justice: Educating people from privileged groups.* Thousand Oaks, California: SAGE Publications, Inc.

Harro, B. (2013). The cycle of socialization. In M. Adams, W. J. Blumenfeld, C. Castaneda, H. Hackman, M. Peters, & X. Zuniga (Eds.), *Readings for diversity and social justice* (pp. 45–52). New York: Routledge.

Howard-Hamilton, M. F., & Hinton, K. G. (2011). Oppression and its effect on college student identity development. In. M. J. Cuyjet, M. F. Hamilton, & D. L. Cooper (Eds.), *Multiculturalism on campus: Theories, models and practices for understanding diversity and creating inclusion* (pp. 22–39). Sterling, Virginia: Stylus Publishing, LLC.

Howard-Hamilton, M. F., Phelps, R. E., & Torres, V. (1998). Meeting the needs of all students and staff members: The challenge of diversity. *New Directions for Student Services, 1998*(82), 49.

Hubain, B. S., Allen, E. L., Harris, J. C., & Linder, C. (2016). Counter-stories as representations of the racialized experiences of students of color in higher education and student affairs graduate preparation programs. *International Journal of Qualitative Studies in Education (QSE), 29*(7), 946–963.

Landreman, L. M., Rasmussen, C. J., King, P. M., & Jiang, C. X. (2007). A phenomenological study of the development of university educators' critical consciousness. *Journal of College Student Development, 48,* 275–295.

Linder, C., Harris, J. C., Allen, E. L., & Hubain, B. (2015). Building inclusive pedagogy: Recommendations from a national study of students of color in higher education and student affairs graduate programs. *Equity & Excellence in Education, 48*(2), 178–194. doi:10.1080/10665684.2014.959270

Lock, A., & Strong, T. (2010). *Social constructionism: Sources and stirrings in theory and practice.* Cambridge, NY: Cambridge University Press.

Marine, S. M. (2011). "Our college is changing": Women's college student affairs administrators and transgender students. *Journal of Homosexuality, 58*(9), 1165–1186.

Ortiz, A. M., & Patton, L. D. (2012). Awareness of self. In J. Arminio, V. Torres, & R. L Pope (Eds.), *Why aren't we there yet? Taking personal responsibility for creating an inclusive campus.* Sterling, VA: Stylus Publishing, LLC.

Parker, E. T., Barnhardt, C. L., Pascarella, E. T., & McCowin, J. A. (2016). The impact of diversity courses on college students' moral development. *Journal of College Student Development, 4,* 395.

Pfeifer Jr., C. M., & Schneider, B. (1974). University climate perceptions by black and white students. *Journal of Applied Psychology, 59*(5), 660–662.

Pope, P. L., Reynolds, A. L., & Mueller, J. A. (2004). *Multicultural competence in student affairs.* San Francisco, CA: Jossey-Bass.

Ruth, M. (2016). Cultural appropriation. *Salem Press Encyclopedia.*

Seelman, K. L. (2014). Transgender individuals' access to college housing and bathrooms: Findings from the national transgender discrimination survey. *Journal of Gay & Lesbian Social Services, 26*(2), 186–206. doi:10.1080/10538720.2014.891091

Strayhorn, T. L. (2013). Measuring race and gender differences in undergraduate students' perceptions of campus climate and intentions to leave college: An analysis in Black and White. *Journal of Student Affairs Research and Practice, 50*(2), 115–132.

Watt, S. K. (2007). Difficult dialogues, privilege and social justice: Uses of the privileged identity exploration (PIE) model in student affairs practice. *College Student Affairs Journal, 26*(2), 114–126.

Chapter 13

THE PROFESSION'S NORM: BECOMING A MULTICULTURALLY COMPETENT STUDENT AFFAIRS EDUCATOR

Paul Porter

Colleges and universities are currently playing host to the most diverse student populations in the nation's history (Debard, 2004; Renn & Reason, 2012). Although this influx brings new values, traditions, and experiences (Howard-Hamilton, 2000, p. 67), it also opens the door for a wide variety of experiences, backgrounds, concerns, obstacles, and expectations. Centuries of unwritten rules and traditions that continue to favor some populations over others, hostile racial campus climates, and the struggle to find a sense of belonging or support negatively affect students of color, women, sexual minorities, and low-income students (Strayhorn, 2012).

These variables, in juxtaposition to a political environment that continues to present numerous difficulties to students who identify as racial minorities, LGBTQ+, undocumented citizens, people of different faith traditions, and low-income levels, amplify the need for student affairs educators and professionals to display proficiencies in areas necessary to engage with and accommodate individuals from diverse backgrounds and identities. Subsequently, they also point to the need for educators in student affairs to re-evaluate their own communication styles and tendencies. The way we engage with people—verbally, nonverbally, and even environmentally—is critical to the collegiate experience of minoritized students. With this in mind, this chapter is written to introduce (or reiterate) the call for student affairs educators to prepare themselves for the influence of cultural diversity on their work, as well as explore the dynamic between multicultural competence and intercultural communication competence and discuss strategies for using intercultural communication competence to advance student affairs practice.

THE CALL FOR MULTICULTURAL COMPETENCE

Creating multicultural campuses has become an aspirational goal for many colleges and universities today. However, moving beyond aspirations to actual concrete steps can be a rather challenging task. When asked, most campus administrators acknowledge this quest for diversity, yet few have the awareness, knowledge, or skills to achieve this laudable goal. (Pope, Reynolds, & Mueller, 2014, p. 1)

The premise behind this observation is simple: higher education's struggle is *not with diversity, but rather with inclusive practices.* Colleges and universities want diversity, yet struggle to recruit, retain, or advance diverse audiences. Often, strategic diversity efforts are surface level reactions in response to moments of crisis and often shelved or forgotten over time (Williams, 2008; Williams, Berger, & McClendon, 2005). Moreover, two dialectical tensions directly affect students from minoritized and underrepresented populations. First is the importance of belonging in juxtaposition to the history of college campuses as spaces of sameness. Second is the mental, physical, and behavioral effects of negative campus climates against the use of rhetoric suggesting that diversity, equity and inclusion are high-level institutional priorities. These tensions highlight the disconnection faced by professionals in higher education and student affairs—it is clear that the concept of diversity and multiculturalism is recognized as important. However, putting action behind virtue is difficult.

Belonging vs. Sameness

When considering the idea of *belonging* and *sameness,* it is important to understand how belonging affects college students. In its simplest form, belonging is synonymous with acceptance. Strayhorn (2012) links the word belonging to terms such as *membership, community, affiliation,* and *support* to explain that in order to belong, one must be (or at least feel) included into a particular group.

Higher education's goal of helping students create a sense of belonging and inclusion dates back to the mid-20th century, when the 1949 *Student Personnel Point of View* (ACE, 1949) recommended that through college experiences, students develop an appreciation of cultural values, develop the ability to adapt to changing social conditions, as well as the motivation to seek and to create desirable social changes. Meanwhile, student affairs educators were charged with the responsibility of creating spaces that nurtured student growth. Among these tasks are creating climates in which students are appropriately oriented to their collegiate environment, find satisfaction in their living facilities, understand and use their emotions, develop ethical and spiritual values, and find a sense of belonging on campus. Regarding the need to feel embraced in the institutional community, the committee asserted, "To a large extent the social adjustment of an individual consists of finding a role in relation to others which will make him feel valued, will contribute to his feeling of self-worth, and will contribute to a feeling of kinship with an increasing number of persons" (ACE, 1949, p. 5). Similarly, in an outline of his Culturally Engaging Campus Environment (CECE) model, Museus (2014) includes sense of belonging as a factor, notes that "sense of belonging is positively associated with success among racially diverse student populations in college" (p. 214).

Additionally, despite Watt's (2007) charge that educators in student affairs raise their critical consciousness and "find ways to have more meaningful discussions about diversity, privilege, and social justice" (p. 114), the field continues to allow college campuses to function as spaces of sameness. Williams (2013) draws a metaphor between the wolf and the cheetah, suggesting that higher education must function with a *wolf pack* mentality in order to develop strategic diversity initiatives. The spirit behind this metaphor is well-intentioned: in order to embrace diversity, all facets of higher education (student affairs educators, faculty, paraprofessional staff, alumni, donors, etc.) must work synergistically. However, I believe that this mentality has worked against the goal of diversity. The psychological concept of in-groups and out-groups applies here. Giles and Giles (2013) define the in-group as "a social category in which you identify strongly" (p. 142). Conversely, out-groups are categories in which one does not identify.

Membership in in-groups does not automatically result in hostility toward out-groups, but can and often does create prejudicial behaviors resulting from preferential treatment toward fellow in-group members (Allport, 1954; Brewer, 1999). If we apply this concept to higher education and student affairs, we are reminded that college campuses are "complex social systems defined by the relationships between the people, bureaucratic procedures, structural arrangements, institutional goals and values, traditions, and larger socio-historical environments" (Hurtado et al., 1998, p. 136). College students feel safety, support, and motivation to perform when they feel a sense of belonging on their campus. When they feel traumatized or isolated, they struggle to matriculate and often leave. The hostility minoritized students feel is not always overt (although an unfortunate collection of instances would indicate otherwise); however, they are palpable enough to relay unwelcoming messages loud and clear.

Rhetoric of Diversity vs. Campus Climate

Higher education has been intentional about working diversity-related themes into its institutional vernacular. Quaye and Harper (2014) note,

"*Diversity, multiculturalism, pluralism, equity* and *equality, inclusiveness,* and *social justice* are among the many buzzwords used to espouse supposed institutional values. Colleges and universities use these terms liberally in mission statements, on websites, and in recruitment materials" (p. 11). The presence of diversity in higher education's vocabulary provides an image of college campuses as beacons of cross-cultural engagement, collaboration, and harmony. Regrettably, the campus climate experienced by minoritized students paints a different picture.

Woodard and Sims (2000) define campus climate as "students' perceptions of their experiences both in and out of the classroom" (p. 540). Solorzano, Ceja, and Yosso (2000) add the racial dimension to their research, defining *campus racial climate* as "the overall racial environment of the college campus" (p. 62). Drawing influence from the work of Hurtado (1992) and Hurtado et al. (1998), Solorzano et al. (2000) employ the following four characteristics to define a positive racial campus climate:

(a) the inclusion of students, faculty, and administrators of color;
(b) a curriculum that reflects the historical and contemporary experiences of people of color;
(c) programs to support the recruitment, retention and graduation of students of color; and
(d) a college/university mission that reinforces the institution's commitment to pluralism.

However, as stated earlier centuries of unwritten rules and traditions driving institutional culture continue to favor one population over another. Candidly, the campus experience for minoritized students is different than that of its majority population counterparts, and research has consistently reinforced the claim that those experiences are generally negative (Ancis, Sedlacek, & Mohr, 2000; Hurtado, Milem, Clayton-Pedersen, & Allen, 1998; Rankin & Reason, 2005; Reid & Radhakrishnan, 2003). The reality of campus environments is especially difficult during the first year of college, largely considered a time in which minoritized students "adjust to an environment that is often foreign, socially exclusive, culturally irresponsive, and wrought with contradictions" (Hawkins & Larabee, 2009, p. 179). College students become less dogmatic and more open-minded in their views toward racial, cultural, and value diversity as they progress from freshman to senior year (Pascarella, Edison, Nora, Hagedorn, & Terenzini, 1996). If accurate, this notion presents challenges for minority students upon arrival to campus. Any congruence between these two findings certainly explains why minority students are more likely to report feelings of isolation, psychological distress, and poor academic performance (Cabrera, Nora, Terenzini, Pascarella, & Hagedorn, 1999), feel a lesser sense of belonging (Johnson, Soldner,

Leonard, Alvarez, Inkelas, Rowan-Kenyon, & Longerbeam, 2007), devote less time to socializing, and choose to live with their parents by their sophomore year (Locks, Hurtado, Bowman, & Oseguera, 2008).

Harper and Hurtado's (2007) study of common themes regarding campus climate revealed a lack of shared cultural space for students, clear instances of racial segregation in common areas such as campus dining halls and Greek life, and minimal discussions of race and racism beyond courses in ethnic studies. These findings align with the previously discussed reality of covertly isolating and unwelcoming messages communicated to individuals perceived as out-group members on campus. Although the delivery of these messages is implicit, the reception is not. Reported instances of racial incidents (Hurtado, 1992), written and oral microaggressions, physical threats, and physical assault (Rankin & Reason, 2005), recurring acts such as staring, awkward and nervous behavior, and mistaking one student of a particular race or ethnicity for another (Swim, Hyers, Cohen, Fitzgerald, & Bylsma, 2003), and feelings of invisibility in the classroom, segregation in study groups, and profiling by campus police (Solorzano, Ceja, & Yosso, 2000) have been synonymous with campus experience for students of color. Alongside historical instances of racism, self-reported anti-LGBTQ sentiments from heterosexual students (Bowen & Bourgeois, 2001), increases of anti-Semitic and anti-Muslim messages (Taylor, 2017) have historically pervaded college campuses nationwide.

Perhaps the most disturbing findings were the assumed satisfaction of minority students regarding campus racial culture and stifled voices of staff. Harper and Hurtado (2007) noted that due to the severe lack of cross-racial interaction, "student leaders who were presumed to have understood the general pulse of the campus were generally unaware of the disparate affective dispositions their racial/ethnic minority peers held toward the institutions" (p. 18). Staff members interviewed as part of the study acknowledged the presence of minority student satisfaction and displeasure on their institutions, yet refused to articulate their observations due to the fear of angering senior level administrations.

There is a clear discord here. On one hand, the desire to use visual and written images to craft a narrative of college campuses as diverse, progressive spaces is considered critical to the success of recruiting diverse students. Moreover, documents like the *Student Personnel Point of View* (ACE, 1949), *Principles of Good Practice for Student Affairs* (ACPA & NASPA, 1997), and *Professional Competency Areas for Student Affairs Practitioners* (NASPA & ACPA, 2010) explicitly encourage student affairs educators to center their focus on changing student demographics. On the other hand, students from racially minoritized populations (Stewart, 2013) and other minoritized groups (Astin & Oseguera, 2004) remain hindered by academic, social, and financial resources. Moreover, minoritized and underrepresented students are often left without a support system to hear their experiences or appropriately to relate to their concerns of campus life.

For higher education to meet the needs of its evolving student population, the profession as a whole must put focus on diversity, equity, and inclusion into its everyday practices. Student affairs is critical to this effort because the foundation of its professional practice "embraces all aspects of a student's development—intellectual, social, emotional, spiritual, physical, academic, vocational, financial and moral" (Pope, Reynolds, & Mueller, 2004, p. 121). It should be noted, however, that no pictures of diverse bodies on institutional signage, scholarship initiatives, committees, case studies, theories, or social media debates will meet this objective. Rather than trying to change minds and attract more and different bodies to campus, we must instead focus inward and work to build culturally competent people, spaces, policies and narratives that can ensure success, increase retention, and recruit through practices that reflect our desire to guarantee that every student, faculty, and staff member feel a sense of belonging. This reality adds to argument that the need for high levels of multicultural competence and showcased ability to cultivate genuine relationships grounded in empathy and trust with diverse student populations is indispensable (Howard-Hamilton et al., 1998; Mueller & Pope, 2001).

MULTICULTURAL COMPETENCE

Multicultural competence derives from research in clinical psychology reaching as far back as the early 1980s (Pope, Reynolds, & Mueller, 2004). In 1989, Cross, Bazron, Dennis, and Isaacs (1989) coined the term *cultural competence* to encourage systemic change regarding the recognition of diversity in the context of health care. Defined as "a set of congruent behaviors, attitudes, and policies that come together in a system, agency, or among professionals and enable that system, agency, or those professionals to work effectively in cross-cultural situations" (p. 13), cultural competence is particularly important, because its focus on systems (encompassing people, policies, structures, behaviors, etc.) provides a frame of reference for understanding and engaging various cultural identities beyond person-to-person interaction.

Multicultural competence has built a considerable following in student affairs literature (Castellanos et al., 2007; Cheng & Zhao, 2006; Mueller & Pope, 2001; Pope et al., 2004; Pope & Mueller, 2000; Pope & Mueller, 2005; Pope & Reynolds, 1997; Watt, Howard-Hamilton, & Fairchild, 2004). As part of the psychological practice, the idea of multicultural competence became salient as practitioners sensed the need to incorporate content applicable to the growing multicultural population (Holcomb-McCoy & Myers, 1999). A direct result of higher education's "prolific demographic explosion of diverse cultural groups" (Flowers & Howard-Hamilton, 2002, p. 119) is a concerted effort to understand the role of multicultural competence in student affairs work and the development of instruments to assess student affairs scholars and educators. As such, instruments including the Multicultural Counseling Inventory (Sodowsky, Taffe, Gutkin, & Wise, 1994), Multicultural Counseling Knowledge and Awareness Scale (Ponterotto, Gretchen, Utsey, Rieger, & Austin, 2002), and the Multicultural Awareness-Knowledge and Skills Survey (D'Andrea, Daniels, & Heck, 1991) surfaced as assessment models.

The Model of Multicultural Competence was designed to examine the manner in which individuals progress from reluctance to engage in discussions about multiculturalism and interact with people from groups outside of their cultures, to an acknowledgement of the multicultural process, as well as provide a behavioral map to gauge the process of students who are initially weary of engaging in a discourse of multiculturalism and diversity. The most well-known multicultural competence instrument in this field, the Multicultural Competence in Student Affairs-Preliminary 2 instrument (MCSA-P2, Pope & Mueller, 2000), is a 34-item, tripartite instrument scored using a 7-point Likert-scale ranging from 1 (*not at all accurate*) to 7 (*very accurate*) for student affairs administrators to gauge their feelings toward the presence and influence of multiculturalism and diversity in student affairs. The MCSA-P2 is a product of revisions made to the original instrument to ensure a balance in cultural representation of the MCSA-P1. Pope and Mueller (2000) noted, "Special care was taken to ensure that all groups involved in the development of the instrument were diverse in membership in terms of race, gender, age, sexual orientation, worldview, and other social identity variables deemed appropriate and important" (p. 600).

Pope and Mueller (2000) designed the MCSA-P2 with the intention of reviewing characteristics of three categories: multicultural awareness, multicultural knowledge, and multicultural skills. "The tripartite model of multicultural competencies is an important heuristic tool for helping individuals develop the necessary awareness, knowledge, and skills to work effectively with individuals who are culturally different from themselves" (Pope & Reynolds, 1997, p. 272). These categories result from Pope and Reynolds' (1997) analysis, which spoke to growing concerns of the lack of services offered to underrepresented student populations that were capable of producing appropriate and meaningful experiences.

The MCSA-P2 is scored using a single, total score. Upon designing the scale, the creators decided to use a one-factor model for the instrument, rather than multi-factor models. Pope and Mueller (2000) noted, "The instrument would more appropriately assess the overarching construct of 'general multicultural competence" (p. 603). The instrument was created under the belief that creating a framework to measure levels of multicultural competencies would serve as a leading context to further research in the field.

Other instruments for assessing multicultural competence of student affairs educators have been discussed in Chapter 11 on "Utilization of Theory, Research, and Assessment to Enhance Multiculturalism, Diversity, Social Justice, and Inclusion."

INTERCULTURAL COMMUNICATION COMPETENCE

Importance of Intercultural Communication Competence in Student Affairs Practice

Human communication is a complex and dynamic process in which individuals engage in a collection of episodes and employ different forms to successfully share and receive verbal, nonverbal, and/or environmental messages. These forms are influenced by the extent to which people perceive each other and anticipate certain interpretations and responses. Pearce (1989) explains that we both craft and hear messages around our perception of others as *native* or *not native*. He notes,

> Usually we assume that others are pretty much like us, and that we know their resources because they are the ones that we have appropriated from our culture. As a result, we treat them 'like a native' of our own culture, expecting them to interpret, evaluate, and respond to the events and objects of the world as we do because they tell the same story. Because they are different persons with their own personalities, we expect them to differ from us, but we expect even those differences to be interpretable by our standards. (p. 93)

The work of student affairs educators is largely contingent upon their ability to effectively host, engage with and understand those they support. This is especially true when considering that we can no longer assume that every individual communicates or responds to communication with the same cultural lens. Part of working in multicultural spaces is recognizing the importance of positive and effective interaction with people who look, think, feel, and live differently than us. Equally significant is the need for attention to the numerous details that are part and parcel with diverse identities, as well as understanding that the way people respond to diversity (especially in higher education) greatly influences the ability of many to be active and thriving participants in their spaces. **This should be our profession's norm.**

The wealth of literature on multicultural competence as a critical component to working in student affairs is worthy of great respect. Nevertheless, the incongruence between belonging and sameness, as well as rhetoric and reality indicate that higher education and student affairs is failing to develop effective practices to help transform their institutions into culturally competent systems.

It appears our profession has been focusing its energies in the wrong place. Multicultural competence has embedded itself into the fabric of student affairs practice. However, a textbook understanding of awareness, knowledge, and skill does not translate into the development of a tangible skill set. As such, the proposal here is that we focus on developing intercultural communication skills as a launchpad to increase multicultural competence. In doing so, we get much closer to addressing our issues with diverse students and settings: our ability to communicate with different cultures.

Intercultural communication competence is defined as "the degree to which you effectively adapt your verbal and nonverbal messages to the appropriate cultural context" (Neuliep, 2017, pp. 425-426). Much like multicultural competence, intercultural communication competence consists of multiple characteristics—the most commonly recognized include knowledge, awareness/attitudes, motivation, and skill. It should be noted that these components are often referred to as starting points. We can interpret this wording as a suggestion that one does not just become competent in intercultural communication. Rather, we must continuously advance our understanding of people, places, events, etc. that are outside of our cultural norms (something to consider when thinking about the frequency of diversity-related content as part of our graduate curriculum professional development). Emphasis on context is particularly important, as contextualizing the characteristics of intercultural communication competence causes us to question and consider if these guidelines are individually or universally applicable (Martin & Nakayama, 2017).

Motivation is the characteristic that distinguishes intercultural communication competence from multicultural competence. Martin and Nakayama (2010) define motivation as "the desire to make a commitment in relationships, to learn about the self and others, and remain flexible" (p. 471). **This is where intercultural communication competence begins.** Including motivation as a characteristic suggests that for individuals to enhance their abilities necessary to engage with people from different cultural backgrounds and not only engage in culturally different spaces, but also create warm and affirming spaces, they must want to do so. According to Schmitz (2012), "If a person has a healthy curiosity that drives him or her toward intercultural encounters in order to learn more about self and others, then there is a foundation from which to build additional competence-relevant attitudes and skills" (p. 416). Motivation as an essential part intercultural communication competence also reflects an understanding that building cultural knowledge entails individuals (especially those in majority populations) spending times in spaces where they are out-group members.

Building Intercultural Communication Competence

A few years ago, I worked at an institution that hosted an annual breakfast in which faculty and staff would volunteer to serve food to students. The event offered traditional American breakfast foods—scrambled eggs, sausage, hash browns, and pancakes—and was served in *assembly line fashion*. Two specific students who stood in line to receive food still resonate with me. First, they were served scrambled eggs and then were given two sausage links. The two students, clearly shocked, looked at each other, and back at the person serving them. At that moment, I got them clean plates and walked them through each of the items. I offered to serve them eggs, clarified that the sausage was made of pork, and offered to serve both hash browns and pancakes. I also asked if there were any other food restrictions I should be aware of. Upon the end of the event, the two students, both of which were practicing Muslims, thanked me for my understanding and care. Since then, the event now labels each food station, and offers turkey, as well as vegan food alternatives when possible.

This story is a reminder that effective work in student affairs must be grounded in the invested interest of all educators and professionals. This collectivist philosophy is referred to as *an agenda of common caring*, in which there is a caring for not just the individuals in a community, but also the systems and procedures that influence the community and those within it (Bouge, 2002). Building intercultural communication competence must start from a place of desire, investment, and care (again, this is why motivation is such an important characteristic). Further, it must also demand a demonstrated mastery of knowledge about different cultures as well as a deep sense of self and other awareness. The word *building* is used here on purpose, as it provides a reminder that intercultural communication competence is not something that people just get; rather, it is a collection of information, reflection, and skill sets gained over time and driven by aspiration to continuously increase and evolve knowledge and awareness.

Student affairs educators play a variety of roles that are central to shaping the culture of college campuses and creating environments that are conducive to student success. Further, it is very important that student affairs scholars, educators and leaders understand: **intercultural communication competence is part-and-parcel with multicultural competence; and multicultural competence is part-and-parcel with student affairs work**.

There is no toolkit or algorithm of behaviors that result in intercultural communication competence; rather, it requires a compilation of (sometimes nebulous and even undefined) variables. That said, from residence life to student conduct, career services to orientation. I offer the following tips for building intercultural communication competence.

Develop Cultural Humility

Awareness involves recognition of how we perceive others as well as how we see others perceiving us. In an attempt to elicit discussion and self-reflection in the field of medicine, Tervalon and Murray-Garcia (1998) coined the term *cultural humility* as a vehicle to address power imbalances that may affect interpersonal communication in the medical context (particularly between medical provider and patient). They note, "cultural humility incorporates a lifelong commitment to self-evaluation and self-critique" (p. 117). Part of developing a sense of cultural humility entails embracing this commitment as well as working to navigate it. Action steps to begin gauging levels of knowledge, attitudes, or behaviors with regard to engaging with diverse populations include seeking answers to our questions through personal conversations, books, and convention presentations. It may also include utilizing assessments like the Implicit Association Test (Greenwald, McGhee, & Schwartz, 1998) and the Multicultural Competence in Student Affairs-Preliminary 2 test (Pope & Mueller, 2000). It is quite appropriate that the word *humility* is used here. Self-awareness cannot be achieved without sincere introspectiveness. In short: people can't lie to themselves. Equally frightening is the reality that with self-awareness comes the revealing of truths that may be harmful to our egos. The concept of the reflected appraisal suggests that one of the variables individuals use to construct their self-perception is how they perceive others perceiving them.

If used honestly, the aforementioned instruments allow us to advance our cultural humility because each instrument (and our score within each item) can help us build a list of areas to focus our attention. The intention should never be to check off each activity, but rather to enhance our knowledge, awareness, motivation, and skill to a point where our scores reflect our growth. The implicit and explicit biases within each of us make this a challenge. As such, a *perfect score* should take years of interaction with a diverse cadre of people, places, and artifacts, reflection of the world around us (that which we create and that which we inherit), as well as learning and unlearning attitudes, beliefs, and values that drive our behaviors. The journey involved with mastering each item is well-aligned with the definition of cultural humility. Equally congruent is our acceptance of the reality that mastery requires compromising and sacrificing any structures of power and privilege from which we benefit.

Engage in and Help Preserve Safe Spaces

Members of particular groups tend to inhabit spaces perceived as safe to their in-groups. This is not to suggest that spaces are segregated; rather that they serve as enclaves in which stereotypes can be challenged and individuals can find support and resources specific to their culture. The most common example of this is the concept of the social or academic counter-spaces, defined as safe enclaves in which minoritized students assemble and feel protected from stressors and injustices experienced in broader contexts.

The use of counter-spaces in education is not uncommon, particularly informal social identity-affirming counter-spaces, which "help participants manage the stress associated with succeeding in a predominantly White learning context" (Carter, 2007, p. 547) and provide minoritized students with "space, outside of the classroom confines, to vent their frustrations and get to know others who shared their experiences of microaggressions and/or overt discrimination" (Solorzano, Ceja, & Yosso, 2000, p. 70). Counter-spaces are safe areas that have been carved out by students, faculty, or even institutional mandate that are open to all members of the campus community, but more often claimed by one group over others. Examples may include the campus multicultural center, department of women and gender studies, or spaces with common areas including the campus student center or academic buildings. Additionally, faculty and staff from minoritized and underrepresented groups also provide counter-space to students as the presence of a familiar face, story, and voice can be considered a safe and comforting option for seeking refuge and re-charging.

Visiting the campus multicultural center, attending culturally-themed events (both academic and social), or building relationships with students, faculty, and staff who identify as members of minoritized and/or marginalized groups are optimum ways to engage in safe spaces. Engaging in these spaces allows for learning about their synergy and dynamic, as well as opportunities to debunk myths, and develop a better understanding of the way in-group members communicate with different people, places, things, and events. Given the importance of counter-spaces, there is a delicate balance that one must navigate. When people (especially those from perceived majority populations) interject themselves into spaces occupied by members of other groups, it can be perceived as intrusive. As such, a cultural broker bridging gaps or providing linking between yourself and another cultural group can help increase knowledge or mediate conflict (Jezewski, 1990). This by itself requires some relationship development and/or maintenance in order to appropriately gain access to out-group spaces. As relationships escalate, self-disclosure increases. This happens gradually as trust between relational partners is built, common ground is discovered, and expectations for interaction become clearer (Wood, 2015).

Understand the Influence of Positionality

It is often easy to mistake multicultural competence as a value system when, in actuality, multicultural competence focuses more on what individuals know of multicultural issues, recognize the impact of perceptions, and develop strategies for effective and appropriate communication. In other words, there is a marked difference between recognizing that racism is wrong, and understanding all the dimensions, feelings, narratives, and implications of both overt and covert racism as well as understanding how one's behavior has been complicit in allowing racism to metastasize.

It has become quite easy to make diversity and social justice the sole responsibility of multicultural/diversity affairs offices, LGBTQ+ centers, women's centers, and international affairs. As a result, student affairs educators have the unfortunate luxury of turning a blind eye to issues faced by minoritized and underrepresented students. At best, educators can claim obliviousness despite good intentions. At worst, they can boldly show aloofness without repercussion. Educators must understand how their positionality has implications on both their social and professional worlds. Takacs (2002) defines positionality as an understanding of "where you stand with respect to power, an essential skill for social change agents" (p. 169). Most obvious is the fact that the way in which individuals fit into structures such as Whiteness, maleness, heterosexuality, and cisgendered identity informs their worldview. However, like the duality of in-groups and out-groups, the presence of majority groups and majority views implies the presence of minority groups and minority views. Understanding and acknowledging the existence of social and structural hegemony and positionality can help people realize how the performance of identities (both majority and minority) affect various relational dynamics, thereafter recognize how these respective dynamics emerge during communication episodes. Both the belonging for people from minoritized and underrepresented populations and the role positionality plays are important in the context of higher education and student affairs. If student affairs operates as holistically as it claims, then any fluctuation of the presence of minoritized and underrepresented students, faculty, and staff (e.g. enrollment and retention trends, on-time matriculation, hiring/departure trends, promotion into leadership positions, etc.) would not only be noticed, but have a direct and noticeable impact on institutions beyond numbers. It was in a very similar spirit that Anthias (2002) posed the questions,

> Are population movements accompanied by cultural and identity shifts? Are minority groups integrated culturally and do they identify with the country of migration or the homeland? To what extent have they been able

to forge a positive identity that retains a sense of roots and yet includes a feeling of belonging to the country of residence? (p. 491)

Positionality may never create empathy, but it should lead to an increased awareness, and behaviors that reflect genuine acknowledgement and concern for how they perceive others and how others perceive them.

Get Trained

Considering the lack of mandated diversity-centered courses in student degree graduate programs (Flowers, 2003; Talbot, 1996), student affairs educators across all levels must be prepared to place greater emphasis on multicultural and intercultural communication competence as a professional requirement and institutionalize a culture where participation in professional development opportunities focuses on diversity, equity, and inclusion is regularly expected and monitored as part of employee performance reviews. In short, opportunities to raise knowledge, awareness and skill must not be *check-box obligations*. Rather, they should be the **profession's norm**.

Professional development opportunities that highlight the realities of topics such as race, gender, class, and orientation in the 21st century United States serve as a necessary vehicle to bring students to a common language, assist them in articulating their positions on such topics (Elenes, 2010), create new knowledge on the realities of marginalized groups (Ukdokodu, 2010), and lead to students successfully adapting to social change and increased intellectual self-concept (DeAngelo, 2001). More immediately, without diversity training, intercultural communication issues extend beyond poor socialization and sink into the fabric of professional practice. Members of hiring committees run the risk of decision-making that is influenced by their own racist, albeit subconscious, tendencies. Obstacles such as adverse racism, institutional politics, and cultural misunderstandings can potentially harm initiatives to diversify a faculty or staff (Kayes, 2006). Further, overemphasis on scholarly backgrounds, experience, and research creates the risk of pigeonholing professionals into some functional areas and out of others (Smith, Turner, Osei-Kofi, & Richards, 2010).

Equally important is the need to determine exactly how far the bottom line of diversity training in student affairs reaches. Flowers (2003) called for student affairs faculty to design formalized diversity plans and develop strategies to not only define diversity but also recognize the multiple identities and content areas that comprise their "diversity integration plan" and "devise a strategy to determine which specific aspect of diversity knowledge may be suitable for a given course" (p. 78). This approach allows for administrators to further their knowledge of diversity beyond racial diversity, and begin acquiring a working knowledge of areas such as Title VII, Title IX, and affirmative action.

Actions like these can be very effective in normalizing the presence of difference on our campuses, and embracing the uncomfortable conversations and even conflicts that emerge. Moreover, as intercultural communication competence becomes a more foundational part of multicultural competence, the manner in which we communicate with our students, and actively work to create environments that are safe and inviting will directly result in the reduction of social, physical and mental burdens, detachment from the campus environment, as well as carry long-lasting emotional implications.

The rapid increase of representational diversity of students in higher education represents a half-century old transformation that must rely on intercultural communication practices and cultural competence to survive. If higher education is to meet its goal of existing as a space that embraces pluralism, then student affairs educators must be prepared to play a significant role in shaping the campus atmosphere, facilitating healthy discourse, and forming the basis for students to live and learn harmoniously with others. This work requires all professionals in the field to possess a keen sense of multicultural competence to act appropriately and empathetically with culturally different people. (Howard-Hamilton et al., 1998; Mueller & Pope, 2001).

At its core, multicultural competence is a by-product of human communication- a skill set predicated on mindfulness and other-orientation. The beauty of student affairs work lies in its selflessness. As educators, we are called to direct all of the energies into inclusive and equitable practices that result in feelings of belongingness and foster student growth. As educators, it is imperative that we never forget that. However, just as important as the work we put into our students is our own professional development and commitment to giving our student our best selves and our professional identity. Building our multicultural competence is a tremendously important step in that direction.

REFERENCES

Allport, G. W. (1954). *The nature of prejudice.* Cambridge, MA: Addison-Wesley.

American College Personnel Association & National Association of Student Personnel Administrators. (1997). *Principles of good practice for student affairs.* Washington, DC: G. Blimling, E. Whitt, M. Baxter Magolda, A. Chickering, J. Cross-Brazzell, J. Dalton, Z. Gamson, G. Kuh, E. Pascarella, L. Reisser, L. Roper, C. Schroeder, P. Oliaro, S. Gordon, L.M. Barsi, S. Salvador, G. Roberts, K. Beeler. Retrieved from http://acpa.nche.edu/pgp/principle.htm

American Council on Education. (1949). *Student personnel point of view.* Washington, DC: E. G. Williamson, W. W. Blaesser, H. D. Bragdon, W. S. Carlson, W. H. Cowley, D. D. Feder, H. G. Fisk, F. H. Kirkpatrick, E. Lloyd-Jones, T. R. McConnell, T. W. Merriam, D. J. Shank. Retrieved from http://www.myacpa .org/pub/documents/1949.pdf

Ancis, J. R., Sedlacek, W. E., & Mohr, J. J. (2000). Student perceptions of campus cultural climate by race. *Journal of Counseling and Development, 77,* 180–185. Retrieved from http://www.counseling.org

Anthias, F. (2002). Where do I belong? Narrating collective identity and translocational positionality. *Ethnicities, 2*(4), 491–514.

Astin, A. W., & Oseguera, L. (2004). The declining" equity" of American higher education. *The Review of Higher Education, 27*(3), 321–341.

Bogue, E. G. (2002). An agenda of common caring: The call for community in higher education. In W. M. McDonald, & Associates (Eds.), *Creating campus community: In search of Ernest Boyer's legacy* (pp. 1–20). San Francisco, CA: Jossey-Bass

Bowen, A. M., & Bourgeois, M. J. (2001). Attitudes toward lesbian, gay, and bisexual college students: The contribution of pluralistic ignorance, dynamic social impact, and contact theories. *Journal of American College Health, 50*(2), 91–96.

Brewer, M. B. (1999). The psychology of prejudice: Ingroup love and outgroup hate? *Journal of Social Issues, 55*(3), 429–444.

Cabrera, A. F., Nora, A., Terenzini, P. T., Pascarella, E., & Hagedorn, L. S. (1999). Campus racial climate and the adjustment of students to college: A comparison between White students and African-American students. *The Journal of Higher Education, 70*(2), 134–160.

Carter, D. J. (2007). Why the Black kids sit together at the stairs: The role of identity-affirming counter-spaces in a predominantly White high school. *The Journal of Negro Education, 76,* 542–554. Retrieved from http://www.jstor.org/stable /40037227

Castellanos, J., Gloria, A. M., Mayorga, M., & Salas, C. (2007). Student affairs professionals' self-report of multicultural competence: Understanding awareness, knowledge, and skills. *NASPA Journal, 44,* 643–663. Retrieved from http://journals .naspa.org/jsarp/vol44/iss4/art2/

Cheng, D. X., & Zhao, C. (2006). Cultivating multicultural competence through active participation: Extracurricular activities and multicultural learning. *NASPA Journal, 43,* 13–38. Retrieved from http://journals.naspa.org/jsarp/vol43/iss4 /art3/

Cross, T., Bazron, B. J., Dennis, K. W., & Isaacs, M. R. (1989). *Toward a culturally competent system of care.* Washington, DC: Georgetown University Child Development Center.

D'Andrea, M., Daniels, J., & Heck, R. (1991). Evaluating the impact of multicultural counseling training. *Journal of Counseling and Development, 70,* 143–150. Retrieved from: http://www.counseling.org/Publications/Journals.aspx

DeAngelo, L. (2001). Students learning, and race-based public policy: A look at diversity curriculum and co-curriculum, presented at the Annual Meeting of the American Research Association, Seattle, WA.

DeBard, R. (2004). Millennials coming to college. *New Directions for Student Services, 2004*(106), 33–45.

Elenes, C. A. (2010). Transformando fronteras: Chicana feminist transformative pedagogies. In S. Harper & S. Hurtado (Eds.), *Racial and ethnic diversity in higher education* (3rd ed., pp. 457–468). New York, NY: Learning Solutions.

Flowers, L. A. (2003). Investigating the representation of African American student affairs administrators: A preliminary study. In J. Jackson & M. Terrell (Eds.), *National Association of Student Affairs Professionals Journal Special Issue: Diversifying student affairs: Engaging, retaining, and advancing African Americans in the profession* (pp. 35–44). Washington, DC: National Association of Student Personnel Administrators.

Flowers, L. A., & Howard-Hamilton, M. F. (2002). A qualitative study of graduate students' perceptions of diversity issues in student affairs preparation programs. *Journal of College Student Development, 43,* 119–123. Retrieved from jcsdonline.org

Giles, H., & Giles, J. (2013). Ingroups and outgroups. In A. Kurylo, *Intercultural Communication: Representation and construction of culture* (pp. 140–162). 55 City Road, London: SAGE Publications, Ltd. doi: 10.4135/9781544304106.n7

Greenwald, A. G., McGhee, D. E., & Schwartz, J. L. (1998). Measuring individual differences in implicit cognition: the implicit association test. *Journal of Personality and Social Psychology, 74*(6), 1464.

Harper, S. R., & Hurtado, S. (2007). Nine themes in campus racial climates and implications for institutional transformation. *New Directions for Student Services, 2007*(120), 7–24.

Hawkins, V. M., & Larabee, H. J. (2009). Engaging racial/ethnic minority students in out-of-class activities on predominantly White campuses. In S. Harper & S. Quale (Eds.), *Student engagement in higher education: Theoretical perspectives and Practical approaches for diverse populations* (pp. 179–188). New York and London: Routledge.

Holcomb-McCoy, C., & Myers, J. E. (1999). Multicultural competence and counselor training: A national survey. *Journal of Counseling and Development, 77,* 294-302. Retrieved from http://www.counseling.org

Howard-Hamilton, M. F. (2000). Programming for multicultural competencies. In D. Liddell & J. Lund (Eds.), *Programming Approaches That Make a Difference: New Directions for Student Services, No. 90* (67–78). San Francisco, CA: Jossey-Bass.

Howard-Hamilton, M. F., Phelps, R. E., & Torres, V. (1998). Meeting the needs of all students and staff members: The challenge of diversity. In D. Liddell & M. Healy (Eds.), *Programming approaches that make a difference: New directions for student services, no. 88* (pp. 49–64). San Francisco, CA: Jossey-Bass.

Hurtado, S. (1992). The campus racial climate: Contexts of conflict. *The Journal of Higher Education, 63*(5), 539–569.

Hurtado, S., Clayton-Pedersen, A. R., Allen, W. R., & Milem, J. F. (1998). Enhancing campus climates for racial/ethnic diversity: Educational policy and practice. *The Review of Higher Education, 21*(3), 279–302.

Jezewski, M. A. (1990). Culture brokering in migrant farmworker health care. *Western Journal of Nursing Research, 12*(4), 497–513.

Johnson, D. R., Soldner, M., Leonard, J. B., Alvarez, P., Inkelas, K. K., Rowan-Kenyon, H. T., & Longerbeam, S. D. (2007). Examining sense of belonging among first-year undergraduates from different racial/ethnic groups. *Journal of College Student Development, 48*(5), 525–542.

Kayes, P. E. (2006). New paradigms for diversifying faculty and staff in higher education: Uncovering cultural biases in the search and hiring process. *Multicultural Education, 14,* 65–69. Retrieved from http://www.caddogap.com

Locks, A. M., Hurtado, S., Bowman, N. A., & Oseguera, L. (2008). Extending notions of campus climate and diversity to students' transition to college. *The Review of Higher Education, 31*(3), 257–285.

Martin, J. N., & Nakayama, T. K. (2010). *Intercultural communication in contexts* (5th ed). New York, NY: McGraw-Hill.

Martin, J. N., & Nakayama, T. K. (2017). *Intercultural communication in contexts* (7th ed.). New York, NY: McGraw-Hill.

Mueller, J. A., & Pope, R. L. (2001). The relationship between multicultural competence and white racial consciousness among student affairs practitioners. *The Journal of College Student Development, 42,* 133–144. Retrieved from http://www2.myacpa.org/publications/jcsd

Museus, S. D. (2014). The culturally engaging campus environments (CECE) model: A new theory of success among racially diverse college student populations. In M. B. Paulsen (Ed.), *Higher education: Handbook of theory and research* (pp. 189–227). Cham, Switzerland: Springer.

National Association of Student Personnel Administrators & American College Personnel Association. (2010). *Professional competency areas for student affairs practitioners.* Washington, DC: National Association of Student Personnel Administrators.

Neuliep, J. W. (2017). *Intercultural communication: A contextual approach.* Thousand Oaks, CA: Sage Publications.

Pascarella, E. T., Edison, M., Nora, A., Hagedorn, L. S., & Terenzini, P. T. (1996). Influences on students' openness to diversity and challenge in the first year of college. *The Journal of Higher Education, 67*(2), 174–195.

Pearce, W. B. (1989). *Communication and the human condition.* Carbondale, IL: Southern Illinois University Press.

Ponterotto, J. G., Gretchen, D., Utsey, S. O., Rieger, B. P., & Austin, R. (2002). A revision of the Multicultural Counseling Awareness Scale. *Journal of Multicultural Counseling and Development, 30,* 153–180. Retrieved from psycnet.apa.org

Pope, R. L., & Mueller, J. A. (2000). Development and initial validation of the Multicultural Competence in Student Affairs-Preliminary 2 scale. *The Journal of College Student Development, 41,* 599–608. Retrieved from http://www2.myacpa.org/publications/jcsd

Pope, R. L., & Mueller, J. A. (2005). Faculty and curriculum: Examining multicultural competence and inclusion. *Journal of College Student Development, 46,* 679–688. Retrieved from http://www2.myacpa.org/publications/jcsd

Pope, R. L., & Reynolds, A. L. (1997). Student affairs core competencies: Integrating multicultural awareness, knowledge, and skills. *Journal of College Student Develop-*

ment, 38(3), 266–277. Retrieved from http://www2.myacpa.org/publications/jcsd

Pope, R. L., Reynolds, A. L., & Mueller, J. A. (2004). *Multicultural competence in student affairs.* San Francisco, CA: Jossey-Bass.

Pope, R. L., Reynolds, A. L., & Mueller, J. A. (2014). *Creating multicultural change on campus.* John Wiley & Sons.

Quaye, S. J., & Harper, S. R. (Eds.). (2014). *Student engagement in higher education: Theoretical perspectives and practical approaches for diverse populations.* New York, NY: Routledge.

Rankin, S., & Reason, R. (2005). Differing perceptions: How students of color and White students perceive campus climate for underrepresented groups. *Journal of College Student Development, 46,* 43-61. Retrieved from http://www2.myacpa.org/publications/jcsd

Reid, L. D., & Radhakrishnan, P. (2003). Race matters: The relation between race and general campus climate. *Cultural Diversity and Ethnic Minority Psychology, 9*(3), 263.

Renn, K. A., & Reason, R. D. (2012). *College students in the United States: Characteristics, experiences, and outcomes.* New York, NY: John Wiley & Sons.

Schmitz, A. (2012). *A primer on communication studies.* Great Britain: Creative Commons.

Smith, D. G., Turner, C. S., Osei-Kofi, N., & Richards, S. (2010). Interrupting the usual: Successful strategies for hiring diverse faculty. In S. Harper & S. Hurtado (Eds.), *Racial and ethnic diversity in higher education* (3rd ed., pp. 361–379). New York, NY: Learning Solutions.

Sodowsky, G. R., Taffe, R. C., Gutkin, T. B., & Wise, S. L. (1994). Development of the Multicultural Counseling Inventory: A self-report measure of multicultural competencies. *Journal of Counseling Psychology, 41*(2), 137.

Solorzano, D., Ceja, M., & Yosso, T. (2000). Critical race theory, racial microaggressions, and campus racial climate: The experiences of African American college students. *Journal of Negro Education, 69*(1/2), 60–73.

Stewart, D. L. (2013). Racially minoritized students at US four-year institutions. *The Journal of Negro Education, 82*(2), 184–197.

Strayhorn, T. L. (2012). *College students' sense of belonging: A key to educational success for all students.* New York, NY: Routledge.

Swim, J. K., Hyers, L. L., Cohen, L. L., Fitzgerald, D. C., & Bylsma, W. H. (2003). African American college students' experiences with everyday racism: Characteristics of and responses to these incidents. *Journal of Black psychology, 29*(1), 38–67.

Takacs, D. (2002). Positionality, epistemology, and social justice in the classroom. *Social Justice, 29*(4 (90), 168–181.

Talbot, D. M. (1996). Master's students' perspectives on their graduate education regarding issues of diversity. *NASPA Journal, 33,* 163–178. Retrieved from http://journals.naspa.org/jsarp/

Taylor, K. (2017, Apr 17). Colleges forced to address rise in anti-muslim, anti-semitic rhetoric on campuses. *Insight into Diversity.* Retrieved from http://www.insight

intodiversity.com/colleges-forced-to-address-rise-in-anti-muslim-anti-semitic
-rhetoric-on-campuses/ http://www.insightintodiversity.com/colleges-forced-to
-address-rise-in-anti-muslim-anti-semitic-rhetoric-on-campuses/

Tervalon, M., & Murray-Garcia, J. (1998). Cultural humility versus cultural competence: A critical distinction in defining physician training outcomes in multicultural education. *Journal of Health Care for The Poor and Underserved, 9*(2), 117–125.

Ukpokodu, O. (2010). How a sustainable campus-wide diversity curriculum fosters
academic success. *Multicultural Education, 10,* 27–36. Retrieved from http://www
.caddogap.com.

Watt, S. K. (2007). Difficult dialogues, privilege and social justice: Uses of the privileged identity exploration (PIE) model in student affairs practice. *College Student
Affairs Journal, 26,* 114–126. Retrieved from http://www.sacsa.org.

Watt, S., Howard-Hamilton, M. F., & Fairchild, E. (2004). An assessment of multicultural competence among residence advisors. *The Journal of College and
University Student Housing, 44,* 32-37. Retrieved from http://www.acuho-i.org
/Resources/JournalofCollegebrUniversityStudentbrHousing/tabid/90/Default
.asp

Williams, D. A. (2008). Beyond the diversity crisis model: Decentralized diversity
planning and implementation. *Planning for Higher Education, 36*(2), 27.

Williams, D. A. (2013). *Strategic diversity leadership: Activating change and transformation
in higher education.* Sterling, VA: Stylus Publishing, LLC.

Williams, D. A., Berger, J. B., & McClendon, S. A. (2005). *Toward a model of inclusive
excellence and change in postsecondary institutions.* Washington, DC: Association of
American Colleges and Universities.

Wood, J. T. (2015). *Interpersonal communication: Everyday encounters.* Toronto: ON:
Nelson Education.

Woodard, V. S., & Sims, J. M. (2000). Programmatic approach to improving campus
climate. *NASPA Journal, 37*(4), 539–552.

INDEX